Vladimir Biti
Post-imperial Literature

Culture & Conflict

Edited by
Isabel Capeloa Gil, Catherine Nesci
and Paulo de Medeiros

Editorial Board
Arjun Appadurai · Claudia Benthien · Elisabeth Bronfen · Joyce Goggin
Bishnupriya Ghosh · Lawrence Grossberg · Andreas Huyssen
Ansgar Nünning · Naomi Segal · Márcio Seligmann-Silva
António Sousa Ribeiro · Roberto Vecchi · Samuel Weber · Liliane Weissberg
Christoph Wulf · Longxi Zhang

Volume 20

Vladimir Biti
Post-imperial Literature

Translatio Imperii in Kafka and Coetzee

DE GRUYTER

ISBN 978-3-11-153973-7
e-ISBN (PDF) 978-3-11-073224-5
e-ISBN (EPUB) 978-3-11-073231-3
ISSN 2194-7104

Library of Congress Control Number: 2021944637

Bibliographic information published by the Deutsche Nationalbibliothek
The Deutsche Nationalbibliothek lists this publication in the Deutsche Nationalbibliografie; detailed bibliographic data are available on the Internet at http://dnb.dnb.de.

© 2024 Walter de Gruyter GmbH, Berlin/Boston
This volume is text- and page-identical with the hardback published in 2022.
Cover image: akg-images/Africa Media Online/George Hallett/africanpictures.net
Typesetting: Integra Software Services Pvt.

www.degruyter.com

Acknowledgments

While working on this book, I have published earlier versions of its chapters 1–3, 5–6 and 10–11 in the following journals and volumes:

Chapter 1 "Post-imperial Europe: The Return of the Indistinct" in Vladimir Biti, Joep Leerssen, and Vivian Liska, eds., *The Idea of Europe: The Clash of Projections*, Leiden and Boston: Brill, 2021, 36–53.

Chapter 2 "Translating the Untranslatable: Walter Benjamin and Homi Bhabha" in *Primerjalna književnost* 42: 3 (2019), 247–266.

Chapter 3 "The Ethical Appeal of the Indifferent: Maurice Blanchot and Michel Foucault" in *Interventions: international journal of postcolonial studies* 23: 3 (2021), 68–78.

Chapter 5 "State of Exception: The Birthplace of Kafka's Narrative Authority" in *Primerjalna književnost* 43: 1 (2020), 115–125.

Chapter 6 "Almost the Same but not Quite: Kafka and His 'Assignees'" in *Word and Text* IX (2019), 161–175.

Chapter 10 "From Lectures to Lessons and Back Again: The Deterritorialization of Transmission in *Elizabeth Costello*" in *Frontiers of Narrative Studies* 7: 1 (2021), 1–23.

Chapter 11 "Deprived of Protection: The Ethico-Politics of Autorship in Ian McEwan's *Atonement*" in *Frontiers of Narrative Studies* 4: 2 (2018), 342–358.

I extend my gratitude to the publishers of these journals and volumes for their permission to use the revised versions of these essays here.

Vladimir Biti, July 2021

Contents

Acknowledgments —— V

Introduction —— 1

Part I: Post-imperial Europe: The Revenge of Peripheries

1 Post-imperial Europe: The Return of the Indistinct —— 29

2 Translating the Untranslatable: Walter Benjamin and Homi Bhabha —— 43

3 The Ethical Appeal of the Indifferent: Maurice Blanchot and Michel Foucault —— 59

Part II: Franz Kafka and the Performance of Sacrifice

4 Unleashed Contingency? The Deterritorialization of Reality in *The Trial* —— 71

5 State of Exception: The Birthplace of Kafka's Narrative Authority —— 100

6 Almost the Same but not Quite: Kafka and His 'Assignees' —— 110

7 Positional Outsiders and the Performance of Sacrifice —— 126

Part III: J. M. Coetzee and the Politics of Deterritorialization

8 The Withheld Self-revelation: The 'Real' and Realities in *Waiting for the Barbarians* —— 145

9 Conscience on the Pillar of Shame: The Grace of the Graceless in *Disgrace* —— 180

10 From Lectures to Lessons and Back Again: The Deterritorialization of Transmission in *Elizabeth Costello* —— 198

Appendix

Deprived of Protection: The Ethico-Politics of Authorship in Ian McEwan's *Atonement* —— 221

References —— 237

Index —— 255

Introduction

Translatio imperii as the generator of post-imperial literature

The curious elective kinship between the South African Nobel laureate John Maxwell Coetzee and the Central European classic author Franz Kafka is well known. This book explores its background in the traumatic constellation of *translatio imperii* that emerged after the dissolution of the East-Central European empires in the aftermath of the First World War and resurfaced after the crumbling of the West European colonial empires subsequent to the Second World War. Induced by the division of empires into well-developed centers and underdeveloped peripheries, the translation in question did not only begin with the turmoils of the twentieth century. Ever since medieval times, European empires have established a political, economic, religious, cultural and/or linguistic gap between their enlightened and benighted regions as the very basis of their identities, requiring *translatio imperii* as their *conditio sine qua non*. The operation consisted of several interconnected aspects, the hierarchy of which varied from one empire and epoch to another. In political and economic terms, an empire's concern was how to safeguard its administrative maintenance and economic profit in its conquered foreign territories; in historical terms, how to transfer its past and present glory in an undamaged condition for posterity; and in religious and cultural terms, how to translate its center's values for the retrograde provinces without affording too much room for their devaluation. In the empires' last decades, during which they were confronted with rebellions from their peripheries that demanded reform to their administrations' outdated techniques, *translatio imperii* turned into the central agenda. In East-Central European empires, this took the shape of a transition from a 'sovereign' to a 'disciplinary' administration of the peripheries, while in West European empires it was a switch from a merciless assimilation to an affirmative regeneration of the colonial constituencies. This restructuring of the endangered imperial common-being became the urgent task of late empires, which resulted in the new identity politics of both Kafka's European and Coetzee's African domiciles. Both writers experienced the troublesome transition to nation-state democracies, be that in the modern European or postmodern African form. Relating these two historically and geopolitically distant forms of *translatio imperii* to one another, this book claims that Kafka, as the writer of the first, prefigures Coetzee, as the writer of the second. In a series of close readings, it investigates in which particular ways the respective reconfiguration of governmental techniques induced the restructuring of power relations between the agencies of their fictions. Kafka and Coetzee responded to the traumatic withdrawal of inherited transcendental guarantees from the world of human commonality by displacing their narrative authority beyond the reach of their readers.

This entailed an elusive and shifting, "translational" configuration of their fictional worlds, which I regard as post-imperial literature's distinctive feature. This literature consistently reintroduces the fundamental power opposition *between* its subjects *into* the identities of each of them. Through such an internal division of the authors' and characters' identities, it translates the *either-or* relation between them into an *as-well-as* one. Being internally redoubled, one identity both develops and refuses responsibility for the other as its mirror image. At the very outset of the European post-imperial age (1919), Mikhail Bakhtin raised the question of art's responsibility for life and vice versa. Although "it is certainly easier [for authors] to create without answering for life, and easier [for characters] to live without any consideration for art", he writes,

> [t]he poet must remember that it is his poetry which bears the guilt for the vulgar prose of life, whereas the man of everyday life ought to know that the fruitlessness of art is due to his willingness to be unexacting and to the unseriousness of the concerns in his life.
>
> (1990: 2)

This new literary politics, as envisaged by him, corresponds to the operations of the rising disciplinary power that started an analogous transformation of subalterns into their own masters and masters into their own subalterns. In fictional works, the characters gradually free themselves of their patronizing authors who, in turn, start to sympathize with them. They even introduce their doppelgangers, a peculiar sort of character with whom they simultaneously identify and disidentify. In his *Author and Hero in Aesthetic Activity* (ca 1920–1923), Bakhtin realizes that the authors that react to their heroes as "someone close to [them], someone [they] apparently know very well", must invest effort to disentangle in their novels the third-person from the first-person perspective. "The artist's struggle to achieve a determinate and stable image of the hero is to a considerable extent a struggle with himself" (1990: 6). The path to the sovereign reference leads through the temptations of self-reference.

Bakhtin's remarks were clearly inspired by Dostoevsky's work, whose involved authorial consciousness was also an enduring source of inspiration for Kafka (Dodd 1992; Conti 2016: 469–472). However, Kafka's authorial consciousness not only dis/identified with much more humble characters than Dostoevsky's, such as remote provincials, stonemasons, cobblers, battle-horses, verminous bugs, apes, dogs, presumptive moles, mice, and even bridges, but granted these creatures the higher status of being his doppelgangers and/or even narrators. The deeper the humiliation, the higher its sublimation. That is to say, his authorial "appetite for alterity" (Silverman 1986: 181) was much more radical, driving him, in the footsteps of his compatriot and contemporary Hugo von Hofmannsthal, to sacrifice his authorial human self "to any creature, to any thing, to any phantom, to any spectral product of a human brain" (Hofmannsthal 1979: 67).[1] As the messenger of a mythic space beyond human history, he did not hesitate to enter a "swampy ground of fluctuating experiences" (Benjamin 2007a: 131), a hybrid area of myth's reentry into history that, in various ways, affected both historical objects and subjects.

Unlike this mythic space that is reigned over by the unpredictable will of gods, history is ruled by goal-directed human actions, but does not allow all humans to act as its subjects. Many among them, such as Hofmannsthal's 'creatures', 'things', 'phantoms', and 'spectral products', are denigrated to helpless objects. However, their banishment from historical progress back into the realm of mythic destiny also disconcerts some dislocated historical subjects who, for one reason or another, feel embarrassed by such discrimination, trying to exempt themselves from it. Attaching themselves to these victims as the mythic past's enforced remnants, they invoke an all-encompassing divine area beyond the reach of imprisoning history. Driven by such a longing for a space outside of human affairs, Kafka waited for his Muse in vain (and in pain) for hours, days and months, as he repeatedly lamented in his letters and diaries. Through such an extraterritorial 'link', he hoped to be able to exempt himself from historical progress's 'distinct' territory into a mythic destiny's 'indistinct' province. His favorite protagonists, positional outsiders who were already inhabiting this province, did not need to pull themselves out of historical territory. They knew the province's grip from their firsthand experience of extraterritoriality, which he, as the detached author, was at pains to transform into his sublime ex-territoriality. Whereas the political processes of *translatio imperii* derogated yesterday's gods to today's creatures, Kafka, in a remedial literary counter-maneuver, gradually elevated these creatures' disempowerment into his authorial power. The deeper the dispossession caused by history proved to be, the higher satisfaction offered the return of destiny that was induced by this dispossession.

Coetzee expands the circle of the author's sympathy for the humiliated positional outsiders even further. The protagonists of his novels, pushed by both history and their societies to the outermost periphery, are themselves outsiders (such as Susan Barton or Michael K), unexpectedly become outsiders (such as the Magistrate or David Lurie), or promote themselves into such outsiders' protectors

---

[1] Here and in the remainder of this book, all translations into English are mine unless otherwise noted.

(such as Mrs. Curren or Elizabeth Costello). Coetzee often translates either protectors into outsiders – as in the case of the Magistrate who begins as the barbarians' protector, gradually turning into his empire's outsider – or outsiders into protectors – as in the case of David Lurie who only becomes the protector of tortured animals after he having been expelled from the scientific community. In Coetzee's fictional works, next to the relationship between humans and creatures or animals for that matter, this protection also encompasses the racial, gender, colonial, political, (quasi)parental, educational, and class relationships, which the writer never tires of reconfiguring. In his quasi-autobiographical works, the protection of the narrated by the narrating self or 'ordinary people' by a prominent writer undergoes the same reconfiguring translation. Responding to the processes of *translatio imperii* that dethrone all inherited authorities, Coetzee thus translates the subjects and objects of all these relationships into one another, often exchanging their initial positions. The parents become children, the masters become servants, the teachers become pupils, and the settlers become indigenous barbarians.

However, the principal relationship of protection, which Coetzee has to grapple with in his daily work, is that between the author and the character. Following his translational disposition, he does not hesitate to translate it from his everyday reality into some of his fictional worlds. Through such a display, he undermines Bakhtin's modernist demand that is put on the author and character to be responsible for each other. Thus, in *Slow Man*, Elizabeth Costello as the writer and Paul Rayment as her character both *accept* and *refuse* responsibility for the other as the mirror image of themselves. She is ready to protect him but selfishly demands of him not "to live without any consideration for art" (Bakhtin 1990: 2) because she as a writer needs a life that fits her high literary standards. He who kindly hosts her in his apartment, selfishly refuses to act as her authorial puppet (Coetzee 2006b: 117) because of his desire to act as the protector of an adopted son (Coetzee 2006b: 44–45; 73). Another case in point is Coetzee's earlier novel *Foe* (1986) in which the eponymous writer selfishly rejects the life story of the female castaway Susan because, in the form as proposed by her, it would betray the readers' and in particular booksellers' expectations (Coetzee 1987: 116–117). Susan, for her part, equally selfishly realizes that her life will remain insubstantial in the eyes of future generations if she consents to drop her *protégé* Robinson from her story (Coetzee 1987: 40; 123). In lieu of dropping him, she is ready to drop her daughter.

By inextricably coupling responsibility with selfishness in the protection of the other, Coetzee gives up Bakhtin's modernist conviction that the self's responsible attitude to the other manages, at the end of the day, to regain control of him or her by establishing his or her "determinate and stable image" (Bakhtin 1990:

6). In the world of today, neither the authors' nor characters' selves can escape intertextual transfers that dispossess them of their authenticity one way or another. This means, among all other things, that the protective relationships from Coetzee's fictions unavoidably redouble those from, say, Plato's, Cervantes's, Defoe's, Dostoevsky's, Conrad's, Hofmannsthal's, Kafka's, or Beckett's works, or the Gospels for that matter. Each attempt to escape such a copied life into the authentic one merely spawns a new substitution.

As in Bhabha's theory of 'cultural translation', translations prove to be all-pervasive and in command of our lives. Captured in the processes of *translatio imperii*, ultimately, Kafka as the 'central' writer and Coetzee as the 'marginal' one also undergo them. Although Kafka belongs to the European 'center', he operates at its Czech and Jewish peripheries, which associate him with other peripheries; and although Coetzee belongs to the South African 'periphery', he operates at its white and English-speaking center, which associates him with other centers. In this way, post-imperial translational literature simultaneously 'joins' and 'disjoins', 'worlds' and 'unworlds' its writers. Kafka and Coetzee attach themselves to one another by detaching themselves from their inherited Central European and South African political, ethnic and cultural surroundings.

Although their reformed imperial and new post-imperial political units resolutely relinquished their imperial pasts, their vampires stubbornly disconcerted their presents. The reformed empires (e.g. the Dual Monarchy and the British Commonwealth) were at pains to delimit their democratic present from their discriminating past but "the theft of the land from the Indians or the rape of slave women comes back in unforeseen form, generations later, to haunt the oppressor" (Coetzee 2007: 48). The post-imperial countries (e.g. Czechoslovakia and the Republic of South Africa), in their turn, denied any connection with past empires, suppressing how their masters were educated in the imperially established provincial schools and thus spontaneously adopted late imperial identity politics. This surreptitious toxic infiltration of the denied into the denier's identity not only impregnates post-imperial countries' technologies of power but also those of literature. They are contagiously entangled, but whereas postcolonial studies tend to reduce the latter to the former, this book's focus is on the literary technologies. Its aim is to disentangle the enshrinement of the political and literary administration of power by departing from literature. It is through its peculiar fictional response to the reshuffling of political common-being that the literature of an age establishes 'elective affiliations' with its distant counterparts. In both its modern inner-European and postmodern outer-European versions, the traumatic constellation of *translatio imperii* offers an appropriate departure point for the investigation of such a transborder literary alliance.

It warrants attention that neither Kafka's Czechoslovakia nor Coetzee's South African Republic were exemplary nation-states but rather, due to their long imperial pasts, were multiethnic, multicultural, and multilingual composites. Feeling underprivileged in them, many of their constituencies acted as enduring factors in their disintegration in the same way as their recent national elites had acted in their former empires. Thus, across the forcefully nationalized post-imperial political space, transborder communities arose as the zones of ethnic, religious, class or cultural solidarity. Operating as the unprocessed residues of national translations, they developed a sort of intranational cosmopolitanism against the official national ideology of their states. Contemporary political theorists (Agamben, Butler, Esposito) interpret such proliferation of the internal "pockets of resistance" to the politically guided unification, in both late empires and their successor states, as the direct outcomes of the "egalitarian discrimination" that is genuine to them. The collateral effect of such a production of homogeneous political units is the would-be humans, the spectral humans, and the non-humans, the 'filthy' remnants of the imperial in the post-imperial political spaces who are prevented from becoming legible in them and thus compelled to forge alliances across them (Agamben 1998: 121; Esposito 2011: 209; Butler 2004: 92).

In his diary entry of 14 January 1920, Kafka remarks that one comes into the world dripping from the filth that one cannot help but inherit from one's ancestors (Kafka 1976: 401). The diarist in Coetzee's *Summertime*, for his part, asks himself:

> Yet where in the world can one hide where one will not feel soiled? [. . .] How to escape the filth: not a new question. An old rat-question that will not let go, that leaves its nasty, suppurating wound. (Coetzee 2012: 287–288)

Although located in new historical epochs and political spaces, Kafka's and Coetzee's positional outsiders operate as the contagious leftovers of the former ones. Since their dislocations are generated by the same *translatio imperii* that pushed their authors to political and social margins, Kafka and Coetzee authorize them to interrogate their presents out of their traumatic zones of indistinction. Kafka was a German-educated and German-speaking secular Jew in Prague, the capital of the Czech province of the Austro-Hungarian Empire, whose Austrian settlers blamed their Jewish co-citizens for having stolen and misused their language. After the Empire's collapse, i.e. toward the end of Kafka's life, Czechs' animosity toward their Jewish co-citizens was on the rise. This is why Kafka never qualified as truly Jewish, German or Czech, forever remaining an outsider to any collective belonging. In addition, apart from feeling like an outsider to his own Jewish family, he found his whole generation catapulted "outside the law, no one knows it and yet everyone treats us accordingly" (Kafka 1976: 24). Guided by this experience of multiple non-belongings, he creates an equivocal authorial authority that both strongly attaches itself to the represented positional outsiders and carefully detaches itself from them into the invisible position of their supervisor. Kafka's authorial politics to his fictional agencies announces the rise of the 'capillary' surveillance of the population that analogously aims at the identification *of* subjects through an identification *with* them.

Coetzee's position within South African society is even more complex. He was born into the white minority which, on behalf of the Dutch and British empires, settled, ruled, and exploited the country from the early seventeenth deep into the twentieth century. But even if Coetzee openly admits that he is their involuntary co-perpetrator, considering that he stems from an ethnically mixed, secular, English-speaking family, he is all but a proper representative of the Afrikaner rulers' religious and linguistic homogeneity. At the same time, because "English in South Africa is what one might call a deeply entrenched foreign language" (Coetzee 1993: 7), he feels as equally a stranger in the English language as Kafka did in German. "Having joined a pool of no recognizable ethnos whose language of exchange is English," he belongs to an expanding transnational community that "has no discernible ethnos" and "in which differences wash away" (Coetzee 1992: 342). Like Kafka who was divided between his Jewish and German-speaking identities, Coetzee felt neither the white Afrikaner minority nor the English language which separated him from it as the places of his belonging. As for his family, again like Kafka, the "he" of his early youth confesses that "he denies and detests his father" (Coetzee 2012: 67), whereas he himself, in an interview, describes his mother as "a supporter, if not of apartheid as a social system, then certainly of the people who ran the country" (Kurtz and Coetzee 2015: 110). Confirming the above-delineated futile desire to escape the filth of one's ancestors, he, on the one hand, systematically detaches himself from belonging to any *ethnos*, religion, country, or language, but, on the other hand, admits that "each of us [. . .] is reluctant to concede that our past is inescapable" (Kurtz and Coetzee 2015: 33). To reiterate, this untiring (mis)translation, simultaneous attachment and detachment, identification and disidentification between the self and other, is post-imperial literature's distinctive feature.

It is precisely this belonging to neither the past nor the present, neither the home nor abroad, neither oneself nor the other – but a longing for both – that spawns both Coetzee's and Kafka's authorial politics. Kafka established an elusive narrative authority that, while closely attached to the debased positions of its doppelgangers, simultaneously and gradually exempted itself from them into a complete non-position. In his works, no subordinate entity proves capable of relinquishing its own identity to the same radical degree as its superior agency, to transform the devaluation inflicted upon it by its superior into such a consistent self-devaluation as Kafka's narrative authority. It is precisely this fine gradation of self-blame, until it reaches an insuperable authorial degree, that Coetzee admires the most in Kafka's work (Coetzee 1992: 204–205). This is because he also makes his narrative authority receive its vocation from the 'other scene', relegated beyond its doppelgangers' restricted horizons. Like Kafka's authority, it introduces itself through various outsiders imbued with worldly identities, while at the same time maintaining the privilege to act as their untiring otherworldly re-framer. Operating out of the invisible areas of that which is excluded, both Kafka's and Coetzee's narrative authorities expose their agencies' exclusionary truths to attrition. However, this book's thesis is that their very authorial politics cannot avoid the translation that they apply to others, which is what ultimately dooms them to exposure.

Translatio imperii as a constellation of literature's un/worlding

As I argued in *Tracing Global Democracy* (2016) and *Attached to Dispossession* (2018), literary works emerge in response to particular traumatic constellations, i.e. political arenas characterized by the reconfigured and recalibrated geopolitical, social, economic, jurisdictional, racial, national, religious, gender, cultural, and/or linguistic asymmetries between their collective and individual agencies.[2] A sudden revolutionary reshuffling of these asymmetries' established hierarchy, followed by their unexpected collision, collusion, and overlapping, induces the expulsion of some of their agencies. Banished into the "zones of indistinction", the excluded domains of legislated political orders (Agamben 1998: 63, 112, 181), their lives loose dignity, profile and articulation. Responding to this inflicted deterritorialization, they forge alliances with distant and dispersed 'kindred souls' in order to deterritorialize, in a joint effort, their respective political territories, disengage their engagements, and reconfigure their configurations.

According to Agamben (2005a: 37–39), it was the French Revolution that induced the first such exceptional constellation in the European political space, and it was Kant who in his aesthetics formulated the first individual response to it. According to the German philosopher, an artistic genius mobilizes through his or her activity a new kind of human commonality by consistently disengaging

---

[2] This section partially draws on my *Attached to Dispossession*.

the automatic application of his or her community's habitual rules. Pulling itself out of the *sensus communis logicus* or "common sense" (*Verstand*) and into the *sensus communis aestheticus* or "public sense" (*Vernunft*) (Kant 2007: 123–125), his or her exemplary work of art demands that its recipients give up their usual determining judgment in favor of a reflective one. In this way, such works develop a "negative capability" (Coetzee 2004a: 200), i.e. "reasoning on reasoning" in their recipients (Kant 2007: 136–137) to move them out of their self-enclosed realities into a common world that searches for its verification in an open-ended dialogue (Kant 2007: 6–7). In short, Kant proposes individual exemption as the technique for creating a freer kind of commonality from the one that follows on from the collectively imposed reality.

Since the time of French Revolution, such artistic and intellectual self-exemption systematically counteracted the juridical states of exception, collecting more and more individuals along the way who, for one reason or another, were coerced into refashioning their identities. Individuality is by definition a state of exemption that cannot be shared with others or translated into regular states. I interpret this inextricable entanglement of the public collective state of exception and the clandestine individual self-exemption from it as a traumatic constellation that consistently nurtures modern literary works. Relegated into the "zones of indistinction", their authors are violently separated from their familiar communities and forced to search for a new, remote one on the world's looming horizon. This explains, among all other alliances, the elective kinship between Coetzee and Kafka (and other European writers) in the political state of exception induced by *translatio imperii*.

Such an opening toward the unknown and inarticulate others would be unimaginable without the previous establishment of commercial and communicational networks, as well as the invention of new technologies for literature's transmission. Communicational, mercantile, monetary, and spiritual mobility foster and accelerate each other. To pick up on just three well-known illustrations, Paul Gilroy emphasized the role of slave shipping in the establishment of Western modernity (Gilroy 1993), Benedict Anderson pointed out that print-capitalism enabled growing numbers of people to relate themselves to others in profoundly new ways (Anderson 1991: 36), and Arjun Appadurai clarified to what extent the rise of mass media increased the influence of imagination in the shaping of global processes (Appadurai 1998: 54). This is how the artistic subjects that feel injured by their countries' state of exception sense the need and get the opportunity to co-create a spatial, temporal, cultural and/or political 'elsewhere'. By compulsively meeting this need and using this opportunity, their literary works enter the process of worlding. This answers Thomas Beebee's fundamental question from his discussion of Nietzsche's skeptical stance to world literature: "[W]hom is world literature consoling, and in what way?" (Beebee 2011: 376) Literature opens itself to distant otherness in order to heal the traumatic experience of the indistinction characteristic of its authors' dispossessed present.

However, contrary to the dominant celebratory renderings of this turn toward the distant others, literary authors do not identify with these inarticulate others without previously appropriating them. No identification *with* the distant others comes into being without a simultaneous identification of these others *as* familiar beings; a sort of self-assertion inheres to any displacement of the self into the other. What Kaja Silverman (1986: 185) calls "idiopathic" and "heteropathic" identifications do not exclude but imply each other. Since the distant and inarticulate others are by definition a threatening spectral appearance, they must first be domesticated. It is only after they lose their unhomely character, that the authors' selves receive their traumatic appeals. Although the authors claim to be victimizing themselves for these others, they in fact, in an operation of "inverse ventriloquism" (Anderson 1991: 198), make these others speak for themselves or their own traumatic constellations. As I will try to show in the following, their passionate attachment to the distant others ultimately "veils a defacement [. . .] of which it is itself the cause" (De Man 1984: 81), i.e. it erases the traces of the particular loss that gave rise to their narratives.

Through such a spontaneous extension of their own unhomeliness onto the others with whom they forge an 'elective kinship', the authors turn their literature's worlding into the homeless and dispossessed individuals' getting-together. Concomitantly, this literature celebrates hybridity, liminality, and in-betweenness (Bhabha 1994: 12–13), the unhomely, the uncanny, the indistinct, the untranslatable, the incommensurable, the unsayable, the inexpressible, and the nonsensical (Apter 2013: 9–11); it becomes a "deowned literature" that "belongs fully to no one" (Apter 2013: 15), or a "comparison literature" that is "written for translation, born-translated" (Walkowitz 2009: 569). As Kafka's and Coetzee's oeuvres exemplarily demonstrate – according to this book's argument – it also contagiously entangles art and life. Neither are novels and stories completely fictional nor are aphorisms, parables, diaries, letters, fragments, notes, essays, lessons, lectures, philosophical dialogues, secular confessions, autobiographies, interviews, and "bio-texts" completely factual. They are irreconcilable but interdependent; because they do not *belong to* they *long for* one another, i.e. they require to be translated into their missing counterparts as I am going to demonstrate in my analyses. What pushes this literature into a persistent translation, is precisely its genuine untranslatability. Acting as the *translatio imperii's* untranslatable residues, post-imperial authors make the translation of such residues into their literature's chief agenda. However, instead of uncritically identifying with this agenda, this book connects it to their particular post-imperial realities.

These realities were extremely diverse, inducing diverse profiles and degrees of their translation into literary worlds. One and the same traumatic constellation does not affect all its collective, let alone individual constituencies in the same way. As regards the collective ones involved in the translation of East-Central European empires – to take an example for the sake of illustration – the Jewish constituencies in the outgoing German, Austro-Hungarian, and Russian Empires were more directly endangered than in the outgoing Ottoman one. Following the same logic of a careful differentiation, although the nationalization of the late German and Austro-Hungarian empires turned many Jews into the targets of hatred, excommunication, and persecution, their victimization acquired a different form in each of them. Consider the situation of the Berlin-born Jew Walter Benjamin in Weimar Germany. Germany's Kaiser Wilhelm II had already undertaken a 'Germanization' of the imperial citizenship, resulting in a deteriorated perception of non-German citizens toward the end of the nineteenth century (Brubaker 1992: 51–52; Wolff 2013: 25–35). However, unlike their Slavic co-citizens, the Jews were still predominantly spared of this politics' consequences. On the eve of the following deterioration, the vast majority of them still renounced Jewish religious and cultural peculiarity by adhering to German constitutional values, German as their mother tongue, and the Enlightenment ideal of a "man without qualities" (Musil 2014). Their assimilation and acculturation had an almost half-century tradition. Despite the gradual rise of antisemitism from the early 1880s onwards, their alignment with Protestantism was firm (Beller 1989: 152–155) and the Zionist idea of a Jewish Palestine had little appeal to them. Since Wilhelm II's aggressive rhetoric of "unmixing" was foremost directed against the Slavs in Eastern borderlands (Thum 2013), Berlin Jews were mostly protected from it prior to the establishment of the Weimar Republic.

Established after the defeat of the German Empire in the First World War and shattered by humiliating territorial losses, the political transformation into a republic, and a large influx of 'homecomers', Weimar Germany engaged a variety of remedial, compensatory, and restorationist political agendas. In order to divert the residents' attention from the impotent state with its damaged institutions, it led a politics of Germandom, assimilating co-nationals in the borderlands and the newly established nation-states. Such a redefinition of the German nation, to include these border and transborder co-nationals, induced the exclusion of non-German co-citizens at home, above all the Jews. This spawned a rise in antisemitism in the Weimar Republic that confronted German Jews with difficult choices. It is small wonder that Benjamin suddenly found himself standing

> in the open air in a landscape in which nothing remained unchanged but the clouds, and in the center, in a force field of destructive currents and explosions, the tiny frail human body. (Benjamin 1979b: 291)

As he was radically bereft of his country's political protection, the world appeared to him as having been emptied of all its recognizable properties.

In the Austrian part of this disaggregating imperial Europe, another assimilated Jew, Hugo von Hofmannsthal, had suddenly been exposed to the rising antisemitism in his country. Hugo's father, a rich and successful trader (until the stock-market crash of 1873) who strongly supported and attentively guided his son's education, abandoned his Jewish origins by marrying a Catholic patrician's daughter. Consequently, Hofmannsthal was a carefully-educated, Catholic, Viennese patrician who barely remembered his Jewish origins (Broch 1974: 73–74), but this was to unavoidably change under the pressure of rising Austrian antisemitism. The Jewish background that persisted in a "dimly unconscious" condition (Broch 1974: 80) – having been powerful, as in the case of Freud, probably precisely because of this vagueness (Beller 1989: 87) – suddenly became conscious by making Hofmannsthal state that "the nature of our age is ambiguity and indeterminacy. It rests only on the slippery [. . .]. A slight chronic dizziness vibrates in it." (Hofmannsthal 1979: 60)

In such exceptional states, which enormously increase their victims' sensibility for the latent, non-materialized possibilities of their present, Hofmannsthal sees his task as being the expression of "that which does not exist anymore, which does not exist yet, which could be, but in the first place that which never happened, the sheer impossible and therefore beyond all real" (1980: 132). As a "measureless conjurer of shadows" (1979: 70), the poet is invited to connect by his "magic" "the past and the present, the animals and the humans, the dream and the thing, the big and the small, the sublime and the trivial" (1979: 68) and, above all, to call the dead back to life. For Hofmannsthal, language is a "huge, fathomlessly profound empire of the dead, which is why we receive from it the highest life" (1980: 132). The poet's sacrificial task is to take the position of an entirely deprived being exposed to enormous denigration and suffering by placing himself at the service of the "suffering of the thousands" (1979: 71).

Whereas the past-oriented Hofmannsthal, like Benjamin, was an eminently urban Jew located at his Empire's very center, Joseph Roth was a remote provincial Jew, a 'frontier man', born in the newly acquired Austro-Hungarian province of Ukraine, just 15 km from the Russian border. This was not only a geopolitical and cultural handicap but also economic and social, as Roth, contrary to Hofmannsthal and Benjamin who grew up in urban, established, and wealthy families, spent a fatherless childhood in a modest provincial family. In his *Radetzky March*, the anxious Viennese perception of the Ukrainian Jews is reflected in Commissioner

Trotta's observation that they wage "an incessant campaign of rapine" against foreign property and belongings (Roth 2002: 167). The Jews themselves, in the novel, have no doubt that the end of the world is approaching (Roth 2002: 243). After Ukraine lost the Emperor's protection, the Jewish dislocation within its godforsaken periphery indeed became disastrous. Ukraine's *provincial* solitude in terms of the Empire drove the Jews into an even more frightening *ethnic* solitude in terms of the province. If a Ukrainian identity was, in its insignificance, regularly confused with other provincial identities, the Jewish identity was, in the Ukrainian defensive reaction against this accumulated denigration, clearly marked, stigmatized, and sentenced to *erasure*. Roth left behind his native province to take up his studies in Vienna but was thereupon again forced to leave to save himself form the rising antisemitism in the Republic of Austria. Ironically enough, he chose the Weimar Republic for his new domicile, finishing his novel in Berlin shortly before the Nazis seized power.

As I tried to spell out in more detail in *Attached to Dispossession*, these three different Jewish dislocations in the same constellation of *translatio imperii* spawned three completely different, individual literary responses. Kafka as a Prague Jew, away from the imperial center and surrounded by Czech antisemitism, generated the fourth. Each of these literary translations of their political realities left behind its own untranslated residue. To trace it down in its specificity, this book attentively differentiates the discussed writers. As an English-speaking half-Afrikaner, Coetzee is a dislocated member of the colonizers' breed like one of his 'elected relatives', the Pole Joseph Conrad. However, the latter was a British citizen far removed from the colonies, whereas Coetzee, as a South African citizen, was at the heart of one of them. Kafka, for his part, did not belong to the breed of colonizers but, on the contrary, to the victims, and his German was a result of the Jewish assimilation into the breed of masters rather than, as with Coetzee's English, of his family's detachment from this breed. Further on, Kafka's father was a tyrant rather than a weakling like Coetzee's, and Kafka's mother did not operate as a link to the broader cosmopolitan world as did Coetzee's. Besides, the Jews of Kafka's, Hofmannsthal's, Benjamin's and Roth's time were exposed to insults and persecutions which, however atypical an Afrikaner Coetzee was, he never experienced. His sympathetic imagination discovered outsiders and 'degenerates' out of a shame of racial persecutors, not that of the persecuted "mangy race" as Kafka, Hofmannsthal, Benjamin and Roth. At the same time, Coetzee feels dislocated among the Afrikaner colonizers in a different way to McEwan, for example, among the British ones. As opposed to Coetzee, English is McEwan's native tongue but he entered it as the son of a Scottish father who, due to the father's military postings to British colonial outposts, spent his early childhood in vivid contact with foreign languages. Contrary to Coetzee, he was born as the citizen of a colonizing empire, but, from the outset, his country's colonial past and present disturbed his British habitus.

As a consequence, these various authors' appropriative translations of their realities into worlds of fiction effectuated different untranslated residues.

Sections and chapters

The book is divided into three thematic sections and an appendix. The first section, "Post-imperial Europe: The Revenge of Peripheries", investigates how the European centers coped with the re-entry into their horizons, firstly, of their silenced European peripheries, starting in the 1920s, and, secondly, of their suppressed colonial ones starting in the 1940s. Previously protected subjects suddenly turned into marginal ones, and the previously marginal into the protected. Exposed to the revenge of the freshly empowered subjects, the disempowered ones, by setting up bridges to their distant and analogously dispossessed 'relatives', subvert the footholds of the European intellectual heritage.

The section opens with the chapter "Post-Imperial Europe: The Return of the Indistinct", which outlines the two interconnected faces of post-imperial Europe, namely the subaltern and the superior one. The subaltern one was revealed through the dissolution of the East-Central European (German, Austro-Hungarian, Ottoman, and Russian) empires in the aftermath of the First World War; the second, superior one came to the fore through the crumbling of the West European (British, French, Dutch, Spanish, Portuguese) empires in the aftermath of the Second World War. In the first case, through the Treaty of Versailles, the Western nation-state powers introduced the principle of national self-determination into the post-imperial East-Central European region. However, this process of 'civilizing' East-Central Europe caused a general sense of disappointment in its newly established states since it only exacerbated the extent to which they lagged behind their Western models. As is testified to by their populations' huge enforced migrations, rather than benefiting from modern European mobility, they were victimized by it. To defend themselves from their new masters, they forged alliances with one another, jointly subverting the civilizing techniques that were applied to them. In this way, in lieu of consolidated nation states, religious, ideological, class and gender transborder communities arose as the unprocessed residues of the undertaken national translations. These hybrid formations were the first manifestation in which Europe's indistinct 'past' reemerged with the effect of ruining its goal-oriented national differentiation.

The second form of the return of its indistinct past was the resurfacing of 'animality' within humankind's progress. After the Second World War, decolonization spawned the homecoming of colonized peripheries into the colonial countries that had, for a longtime, kept them at a distance as the dumping grounds of their systematic cultivation. This 'return of the repressed' blurred the distinction that they had achieved, initiating a sense of commonality with their formerly denigrated co-citizens. Forced to confront its imperial past, West Europe started to expiate it. Many prominent modern philosophers attempted to solve this predicament by re-attaching Europe to its task of rescuing universal humankind, but the difficulty that they faced was that the very agency called upon to rescue it, i.e. universal humankind, increasingly acquired indistinct traits. If Europe failed to accomplish ultimate distinction, either through its translation into its constitutive nations, as undertaken by its East-Central subalterns after the First World War, or common humanity, as undertaken by its Western superiors after the Second World War, this happened because its national and universal faces repeatedly introduced their unprocessed residues into one another. They could not rid themselves of their contaminating interdependence. As a result, no matter who acts as its ultimate carrier – transnational superiors or national subalterns – Europe steadily reaffirms the division between them while it strives to overcome it. Instead of figuring as a solution for the imperiled human common-being, it thus remains an open problem that must always be coped with anew.

The second chapter, "Translating the Untranslatable: Walter Benjamin and Homi Bhabha", focuses on one of this book's central notions, the *translation*, comparing its revolutionary rewriting by Benjamin as the German-Jewish post-imperial thinker and Bhabha as the Indian-American postcolonial theorist. In the composition of this book, the inchoate 'elective kinship' between Benjamin and Bhabha anticipates the elaborate one between Kafka and Coetzee. On the one hand, the political reconfiguration of the German Empire brought the Berlin Jew Benjamin to a similar outsider position as the translation of the Austro-Hungarian Empire brought the Prague Jew Kafka; on the other hand, the British Empire's translation into the Indian nation-state turned Bhabha, a member of the Pars minority, into an outsider in the same way as the same Empire's translation into the South African nation-state isolated the English-speaking half-Afrikaner Coetzee. Benjamin's and Bhabha's new countries did not represent the interests of all their peoples equally but rather selectively and unevenly, which means that in both post-imperial Germany and postcolonial India, the former imperial discrimination of the 'marginal' and 'inappropriate' population was invigorated instead of being abolished (Brubaker 1992: 51–52; Agamben 2005a: 14–16; Loomba 1998: 10–12). Considering this, it is only understandable that both Benjamin and Bhabha abandon the traditional understanding of translation as a reconciliation of differences. Instead, it becomes a process that initiates differences in the same way as life, for instance, incessantly diversifies its creatures. As these differences follow on from translation, rather than preceding it, Benjamin conceives languages, and Bhabha cultures, as hybrid and in-between rather than pure and autonomous entities. It is this characteristic of theirs that renders them untranslatable. Since the untranslatable is the element that offers resistance to the translational mechanisms of victorious history, both Benjamin's and Bhabha's foregrounding of it contains emancipating political implications. A language/culture cannot assimilate into another language/culture without maintaining its internal difference and it cannot liberate itself from another language/culture without having embodied this language's/culture's trace. In the final analysis, Bhabha's idea of "cultural translation desacralizes the [. . .] assumptions of cultural supremacy" (1994: 228) by undoing the asymmetry between languages that for long centuries accompanied the Western practice of translation. In this context, Bhabha's engagement of Benjamin's notion of untranslatability acquires a special significance. It establishes a clandestine 'elective kinship' between the two thinkers who, doomed to cope with the traumatic constellations of their respectively post-imperial and postcolonial age, strove to overturn these ages' political asymmetries. Following this objective, both translated the distinct into indistinct, hybrid, and amalgamate identities. However, making up for the frustrations that were inflicted on them by their post-imperial, respectively postcolonial, states, Benjamin and Bhabha advocated a commonality in the permanent state of exception, disregarding its concomitant perilous effects. It is precisely the suspension of law, which it executes, that makes room for the reemergence of sovereignty in an illegitimate, extra-legal form, characterized by violence.

The third chapter, "The Ethical Appeal of the Indifferent: Maurice Blanchot and Michel Foucault", delves into the effects of decolonization and the Holocaust within the opuses of the two French thinkers who, in the setting of May '68, rethink the modern French Republic's key concept: the *revolution*. Ever since its emergence, it has rested on an ambiguity. While it insisted on the present's intellectual sovereignty over the past, it could not get rid of its pre-modern predecessor, re-evolution, which insisted on the present's genetic dependence on the past. This is how the modern concept of revolution inconspicuously interfered with the pre-modern concept of re-evolution as a cyclical return to origins. This cyclical logic never smoothly absorbs the linear one without simultaneously being displaced by its uncanny residue. In turn, the same uncanny leftover operates in the opposite direction, accompanying the putative liquidation of the cyclical logic by the linear one. This disjunctive conjunction of the present and the past characterizes the relationship between the events of May '68 and the theoretical work that followed it. Rather than being homely and familiar, the post-May thinkers' present was interrupted by the interventions of remnants from the colonial past and the Holocaust. This casts a new light on the ethical appeal of the indifferent in the works of Michel Foucault and Maurice Blanchot. Like Benjamin, who insisted on the untranslatable, Maurice Blanchot addressed the obligation to "recollect that which escapes recollection" and which "transforms our possibilities into impossibilities" (1980: 15, 114). He saw *écriture* as a practice of "always going beyond what it seems to contain and affirming nothing but its own outside" (1993: 259) placed "beyond the reach of the one who says it as much as of the one who hears it" (1993: 212). Yet while disempowering literary authors, *écriture* simultaneously empowers its own authorial capacity, threatening to institute itself as a new powerful transcendental. To avoid this, Blanchot weakens its determining force on the model of Foucault's "flawed transcendentalism" (Blanchot 1987: 71–72) that makes the empirical simultaneously possible and impossible. In his re-description of Foucault, the transcendental is exposed to persistent *désoeuvrement* by its empirical "outside". According to Foucault, Blanchot was attracted, in the dense structure of language, to "an absence that pulls as far away from itself as possible" and "has nothing to offer but the infinite void" (Foucault 1987: 28). He was powerfully seduced by this void, regardless of the price of denial and solitude that he paid for this fascination. But for Blanchot, Foucault was equally ready to completely dissolve his identity, to let his thought pass "through what is called madness," to "withdraw from itself, turn away from a mediating and patient labor [. . .] toward a searching that is distracted and astray [. . .] without result and without works" (Blanchot 1993: 199). Thus, in both works, the resistance to the imposed transcendental turns into a passionate attachment to a new quasi-transcendental that puts all modern selves under equal ethical pressure, disregarding their entirely different political conditions. The effect of this disregard for the political dimension is that the sublime ethical rendering of the indifference spawns harsh ramifications.

The book's second section, "Franz Kafka and the Performance of Sacrifice", investigates Kafka's attachment to the positional outsiders who are sacrificed by the political, social, and juridical reconfiguration of imperial common-being. Their sudden deterritorialization induces, in return, their deterritorializing view of reality, enabling Kafka to lay bare the latter's arbitrariness. However, he eventually exempts himself from these outsiders in the same way as they try but fail to exempt themselves from reality. While their victimhood belongs to fictional reality, his sacrifice belongs to the fictional performance.

The section opens with the chapter "Unleashed Contingency? The Deterritorialization of Reality in *The Trial*" that first takes issue with the influential readings of Kafka's work by Walter Benjamin, Maurice Blanchot, Gilles Deleuze and Félix Guattari, and Giorgio Agamben, who insist on the absolute deterritorialization of his fictional world. Kafka translates the legal and historical space of distinct facts into a world of unlimited possibilities, the sense of which he then places beyond the horizon of his readers. Benjamin states: "Perhaps Kafka, whose every day on earth brought him up against undecipherable behaviors and indistinct announcements, at least in death wished to pay back to his fellow beings with the same currency" (2007a: 124, trans. modified). Blanchot, in his turn, analogously claims that no reality by which Kafka might be measured exists outside of literature. He equally insists on the untranslatability of Kafka's deterritorialized fictional reality into any identifiable terms. Feeling stranded in the reality into which he was thrown, Kafka responded to its unhomeliness by completely exempting his authorial self from its logical parameters. In Deleuze and Guattari's terms, finally, Kafka was deterritorialized by his reality's discriminating order to which he responded by unleashing its suppressed potentialities and thus transforming it into a floating assemblage of indistinct items. In all these influential readings, Kafka's radically deterritorialized fictions establish the upside-down rule of contingency over reality. However, these interpreters disregard how Kafka was terrified by the rise of the arbitrary in his age's execution of law. Due to the modernization of the outgoing empires' legislation, state power turned into an anonymous machine with myriad operators but no identifiable responsible agency, which exposed its subjects to an enduring uncertainty and discontent. Once its ultimate authority became inaccessible, its dispersed operators felt free to apply the law as they pleased, which, as Kafka repeatedly laid bare, seriously threatened their subjects. Although disciplinary power proclaimed itself to be the carrier of emancipation, it eventually established an asymmetry between the law's operators and objects that revivified the sovereign legislation instead of abolishing it. This asymmetry is, among all other relationships in *The Trial*, epitomized in the relationship between the chaplain and Josef K., in which the latter reproaches the former that 'his' law is biased. However, contrary to Agamben who, supporting Benjamin, Blanchot, and Deleuze and Guattari, states that Kafka abolishes the legal system in order to release "bare life's" limitless potentiality beneath its confines, I claim that the author does not unilaterally side with Josef's opinion. Reintroducing the opposition between the law's operator and object into both the chaplain's and Josef K.'s behavior, Kafka makes both of them objects and operators at the same time, which is why neither can be exempted from the abuse of the law. Although Josef K. stubbornly denies his involvement, the author drives him, step by step, to realize it. Considering that the relationship between him and his doppelganger is equally ambiguous – Kafka behaved equally mercilessly to Felice Bauer as Josef does to Fräulein Bürstner (both F. B.) – I argue that, in this way, he relegates the guilt for the abuse to his doppelganger by only accepting the shame for it.

In the fifth chapter, "State of Exception: The Birthplace of Kafka's Narrative Authority", I analyze Kafka's unfinished story "At the Construction of the Great Wall of China" that, from the perspective of an anonymous stonemason, focuses on the unification of the Chinese Empire in the Ancient and Middle Ages. The depicted distilling of a unity out of an empire's enormous diversity is reminiscent of Kafka's Austro-Hungarian Empire that was at the time of writing at pains to overcome its increasing disintegration. However, as in the Chinese case, the envisioned homogenization merely reaffirmed the gap between the center and its peripheries. Governments' insistences on the peripheral collectives' belonging to a particular ethnic group compartmentalized the imperial population, encapsulating them within the confines of their allocated identity. In this way, the subdividing mechanisms of 'capillary supervision' entered the Habsburg political space, paving the way for its transformation along national lines. The power became an anonymous machine with myriad operators, rendering its ultimate agency unverifiable. The story's narrator addresses this disappearance of the supreme authority into the divine sphere, which makes it impenetrable for the common people. Even though they are entitled to know it, it is stranger to them than the "life beyond". In "The Problem of Our Laws", Kafka's narrator states "it is an extremely painful thing to be ruled by laws that one does not know" (1988o: 482). In the parable "An Imperial Message" that, although embedded in "The Great Wall", was autonomously published during Kafka's lifetime, the Emperor indeed introduces 'capillary supervision' by switching from the public, visual demonstration of his will to the assembled princes to its private, oral transmission to anonymous peripheral subjects. Kafka's heroes and narrators are turned into the helpless targets of this fictional law that looms large on the horizon of his time. It relies upon its representatives' contingent performances that pretend to be authorized but cannot prove this due to the "high command's" inaccessibility. Aberrations do not threaten it from outside, but are from the very beginning its constitutive parts. When Josef K. refuses to accept such martial law as the necessary "order of the world" (Kafka 2009: 159), he speaks for all of Kafka's outsiders who tend to dismantle its utter fictionality and randomness. However, they engage the same maneuver of self-exemption, which their executors take advantage of while imposing the law upon them. In response to the executives' silent message that we can formulate as "Examine our law as much you like, it is beyond the location that it has assigned you!", they claim something like "Our extreme dislocation places us beyond the reach of your law!" In this way they turn from riveted subhuman creatures into mobile superhuman observers in possession of sovereign insight. Whenever Kafka's figures and narrators lay claim to this 'state of exception', they act as the appointed and carefully supervised messengers of his withdrawn authorial agency. His narratives are constructed in the piecemeal manner of the Great Wall of China: the fragments of the upcoming redemption as distributed by the "high command's" limitless possibilities. The "high command", in its turn, remains inaccessible.

The sixth chapter, "Almost the Same but not Quite: Kafka and His 'Assignees'", opens with the claim that the transformation of the imperial community into a modern society entails its unprocessed residues, a sort of inner colonies that contest and invert it. They emancipate it from its galloping compartmentalization that imprisons its constituents within their individual cages. In fact, many among Kafka's characters, banished into the darkness of their self-enclosure, discover that which escapes this society's daylight. The way in which its forgotten truth manifests itself to its inhabitants for whom the access to it is forever denied is instantaneous, glaring, and perplexing. In "Before the Law" it is described as a radiance (Kafka 1988f: 23), in *The Trial* as a flashing appearance (Kafka 2009: 164), which is why the man from the country and Josef K. must evoke it like the "you" from "An Imperial Message". However, Kafka's characters also engage some further technologies of exemption from the vicissitudes of history, as epitomized by Robinson Crusoe's *attentive exploration* of the 'heterotopia' allocated to him. As Kafka notes, Robinson's idea was to get to know the terms of his banishment as accurately as possible in order to outmaneuver them (2012: 207). Thus, the man from the country carefully explores the doorkeeper during his yearlong sitting until "he has come to know even the fleas in his fur collar" (1988f: 23); Bucephalus, Alexander the Great's battle horse, transferred into the modern society, turns into a peculiar advocate who scrutinizes the law's books. Whereas Bucephalus is only a protagonist, whom the story's narrator observes from a slight distance, the humble narrators of "The Problem of Our Laws" and of "At the Construction of the Great Wall of China", the learned ape in "A Report to an Academy", and the canine loner in the "Investigations of a Dog" behave as advanced, self-reflective explorers. Guided by their exploratory spirit, all of them undergo the 'vindictive' transformation from almost subhuman instances into agencies which develop superhuman abilities. Eventually, next to these explorers of history's suppressed possibilities, there are characters that subversively mimic prehistory amidst history, such as Odradek from "The Cares of a Family Man" or the parasitic insect from Kafka's "Letter to the Father", which "not only bites but even goes as far to suck blood for the sake of preserving its life" (2008: 85). By dismantling the logic of power that inheres in history's apparently egalitarian law, they enable the prehistorical law of vengeance to outlive its historical 'overcoming'. Unlike these characters who, riveted to their confined places, try to remedy their predicament, Kafka places his author completely 'above the fray', in a 'posthumous shelter' that enables him to deal with the suppressed truth in a more calculated, strategic way. While he entangles them with one another, he takes care to distance himself from their tightly connected histories.

The seventh chapter, "Positional Outsiders and the Performance of Sacrifice", investigates how, after the First World War, a state of exception became the dominant paradigm for population administration in Europe, reducing many distinct identities to bare life. Without having done anything wrong, they were calmly eliminated from their states' citizen rights, bereft of human status, and forced into a subhuman existence. Kafka's authorial commitment to them is well known. By incessantly creating such messengers of prehistorical time, he revealed his own tendency to leap out of the determined course of development as characteristic of human history. Nevertheless, it is necessary to distinguish between two kinds of positional outsiders, the *enforced prehistorical* ones and the *self-appointed ex-historical* ones, precisely because Kafka is at constant pains to melt them into each other by way of their cross-breeding. On the one hand, he systematically entitles animal figures or objects by raising them to the status of his narrators or focalizers. On the other hand, guided by his personal experience of multiple dispossessions, he lets his author unreservedly commit himself to these creatures and objects. Both sides of the author-character relationship thus underlie the same principle: Only after having been forever prevented from physically reaching one another does the possibility for their dreaming identification with the other become wide open. The failure of *belonging* to each other releases the energy of *longing* for each other. Many of Kafka's characters dream of such authorial exemption from their frustrating present, but, cut off from the possibility to reach it, compensatorily oblige their selected trustees to provide it in the future. The author, in his turn, being safely exempted from history, dreams that the characters who suffer amidst its turmoil will forget about his comfortable ex-historical shelter. But, bereft of the possibility to verify this, he turns to the readers, calculatingly attaching them to the characters who face impending death and thus winning their trust. "I am not really striving to be good", writes Kafka, "but very much the contrary", to become "the only sinner who won't be roasted". (1976: 387) Hence, in authoring his works, he engages the same method of subversive mimicry against the reader that the outsiders in his fictions apply against the characters in power. This political contamination of his narrative ethics led his postmodern literary successors like J. M. Coetzee or Ian McEwan to the insight that no representation of victims can avoid repeating victimization. In this retroactive perspective, Kafka's authorial sacrifice for the revival of the prehistorical truth presents itself as a retaliating political operation. However, Kafka was reserved toward the absolute victims' argument that might be rendered in the following way: "As we are bereft of our rights by our societies' power distribution, we cannot bear moral responsibility for our deeds; it is up to the masters to bear it". He preferred to turn his fictions into the overt stages for compromising such calculated sacrifices. Whereas his characters follow their petty sacrificial interests as generated by their restrictive circumstances, he takes recourse in a withheld, postponed, 'disinterested' commonality with his readers. But since this commonality was in its final analysis designed to compensate for his own victimhood, it was not exactly bereft of interest.

The book's third section, "J. M. Coetzee and the Politics of Deterritorialization", focuses on the writer's strong tendency to deprive his self, agencies and settings of any identifiable location in a given reality. Instead of hosting them, reality leaves them stranded through its decomposition, turning their lives upside down. Their *actual* dispossession of a common territory is compensated by their *virtual* deterritorialization of themselves and others that establishes an elevated kind of commonality between them.

The section opens with the chapter "The Withheld Self-revelation: The 'Real' and Realities in *Waiting for the Barbarians*", investigating how Coetzee's authorial self, following Kafka who "guarded himself from being fixed by his fellow humans" (2012: 207), evades all identifiable terms. It chooses a strategy of withheld self-revelation – "I am what I am not" – that only identifies itself through its disidentification. This spectral agency recalls Jacques Lacan's "real" that, being dispossessed by reality, in return operates as the latter's dispossessor. I argue that this dispossessed dispossessor figures as the ultimate legitimizing horizon in Coetzee's narrative strategy. Linking the insignificant subhuman with the all-embracing superhuman, it authorizes both his agencies' and his own exemption from human identities. *Barbarians*' main protagonist, the Magistrate, feels ashamed of his Empire's treatment of the barbarians. Before this turn, he used to be an inconsiderate womanizer who, taking advantage of his position, misused young girls by disregarding their physical aversion to such an old man; besides, he was a hunter who killed animals without concern. Suddenly flooded with shame for such self-asserting male behavior, he starts humiliating himself before a girl's disfigured body, which offers a constant resistance to his curiosity. Yet although he regards his new behavior as benevolent and humane, his sympathizing with the political and social outsiders implies an imperial desire for his self's expansion through their appropriation. Although the girl's silent resistance to his insatiable lust for knowledge already induces his body's rebellion against his consciousness's conquering appetites, the inarticulate "real" only fully overflows his articulate reality after the Empire turns his body, on the model of the barbarian ones, into the surface for its humiliating and mutilating engravings. Those who have not freely elected their subhuman humiliation cannot expect their superhuman elevation. Despite all his systematic efforts, the Magistrate eventually fails in reintegrating the excommunicated "real" into the historical reality. What he instead manages to stage is the capitulation of this reality before the flood of the "real". However, by ruining his attempt at elevating himself through a consistent self-humiliation, the author transforms him into an intermediary of intertextual exchanges with some other narratives' protagonists who were equally reserved towards their empire's intervention against the supposed barbarian peril, such as the stonemason from Kafka's "The Great Wall of China", Traveling Explorer from his "Penal Colony", and Marlow from Joseph Conrad's *The Heart of Darkness*. Through such tacit elevating transfers, both the protagonist-narrator and the setting of *Barbarians* receive a rich compensation for their deterritorialization. They acquire substitute, widely dispersed imagined territories from which Coetzee's narrative authority benefits the most. However, it remains to be seen whether Coetzee, through this adaptation of his works to the widely acclaimed literary masters' patterns, has not *adopted* that which he presents as having himself *adapted* to.

The ninth chapter, "Conscience on the Pillar of Shame: The Grace of the Graceless in *Disgrace*", switches to the setting of post-apartheid South Africa in Coetzee's *Disgrace*. Although the novel provides its characters with more or less clear political, racial, and social determinants, the unstable hierarchy of power relations exposes their positions to revision and dispossession. In a shaky state in the grip of *translatio imperii*, the protection of its citizens can, overnight, turn into repression. Acting as a protected citizen, David Lurie unconcernedly gives rise to his abundant sexual appetites for underprivileged women until the sudden loss of his privileged social status forces him to atone for this. Like the disempowered Magistrate, he discovers his long-suppressed fatherhood, which replaces the proud, serial demonstrations of his white male 'service to Eros' (Coetzee 1999a: 52). In the footsteps of the Magistrate and Kafka's Josef K., the service of his conscience to the "verdict of the universe" (1999a: 195) gradually replaces the former service of his body to Eros. In the same way that Kafka, as the author, endorses Josef K. in this switch from one unconditional service to the other, Coetzee, as the author, pushes Lurie's self-dispossessing agenda as if it were his own. Both authors' self-tormenting conscience is thus promoted to the only all-embracing standpoint of redemption, overwhelmed by shame for the human race that cannot but humiliate some of its representatives. Both act as victims who are deeply ashamed at belonging to the same race as their perpetrators, galvanizing most diverse readers to join their expiating community. But, like Josef K.'s awakened conscience, Lurie's has a long way to go before it reaches the sacrificial readiness of his author's conscience. Even after having replaced his gracious urban mistress with his graceless farm-keeping daughter, he does not give up all his previous vanity and self-righteousness at once but continues to ironize his country's post-apartheid administration, because it surreptitiously resumed the totalitarian regime's summary justice instead of abolishing it. Eventually, it dawned on him that his remedial mission of saving the lost grace of the world acted as a self-appointed "censor" that cleansed his world of those in disgrace. Disgraced and ashamed of his former vulture self, he starts to long for an utterly disgraced "nowhere" and "nobody". If the law did not previously apply to him because he was protected and possessed privileges, now it does not apply for the reverse reason, i.e. because he withdrew himself from its protection. Only after one's self is debased to the degree of an abandoned animal bound for "a hole in the ground" (1999a: 189) can it qualify for an all-embracing point of redemption. In this regard, Lurie acts as the doppelganger of his author's resolute refusal to take any political side. Coetzee's authorial conscience recognizes no other authority but that of an all-embracing Truth, serving as its messenger. Lurie's service to the abandoned animals cannot but be subordinate to it.

The tenth chapter, "From Lectures to Lessons and Back Again: The Deterritorialization of Transmission in *Elizabeth Costello*", departs from the peculiar structure of *Elizabeth Costello* that consists of eight "lessons", which in their turn play host to seven lectures. When a fiction consists of lessons that embed lectures, the latter are delivered simultaneously to the present direct addressees and to absent indirect ones. Both Costello and Coetzee refuse to accept the consensual illusion of their lecture halls by preferring to address a scattered and heterogeneous readership. In Lesson Six, Costello states that "a body of balanced, well-informed modern folk in a clear, well-lit lecture venue" (Coetzee 2004a: 175) has its limits, which a writer who deserves the attribute of being a "realist" must transgress. She sees "realism's" task as translating the consensual community of oral performances as the medium of 'sovereign power' into the dissensual addressees of written transmissions as the medium of capillary surveillance. Coetzee, for his part, sides with Kafka who drew all references to reality into the references to the agencies who make them (1992: 203). This is why their lectures strategically break the realist illusion by drawing attention to their fragile, selfish, unreliable performers who cannot act as unbiased agents of commonality. The best way to provoke dissent is to put emphasis on the consensual reality's discarded 'real', such as violated children, exterminated peoples, or suffering animals. By responding to its call from an ever-new point of view and establishing a migrating point of view, Costello and Coetzee untiringly distance themselves from the artifice of reality that surrounds them. In Costello's view – to which her author remains notoriously reserved – among the many voices of the 'real', those of despised animals enjoy a privilege. Laying bare his suffering before his human attendants, Kafka's ape Red Peter, she says, paid back his offenders and violators by reminding them of their cruelty.

Acting as an ambassador of the violated, she tries to reiterate his vindictive gesture. Like Hugo von Hofmannsthal's Lord Chandos, she is convinced that "every creature is a key to all the others" (Hofmannsthal 2005: 120). At the same time, like the Lord's wife Elizabeth or Hofmannsthal himself, she feels unhomely in a language that has broken its connection with reality, depriving us of certainty as to how and whether at all our performance will be understood by others (Coetzee 2004a: 21). To prevent such a misunderstanding, in the footsteps of Jesus who took the suffering of others upon himself, she tries but fails to develop an all-embracing sympathetic imagination. What prevents her impartiality is her filtering of received calls through 'literary criteria'. An analogous filtering applies Coetzee to her by making her into an intermediary of intertextual transfers, starting from Socrates and Plato, passing through Francis Bacon, Hofmannsthal and Kafka, and ending in his novels *Foe* and *Slow Man*. Challenging his readers with this infinite series of simulacra, Coetzee confronts them with their enduring entrapment within a fake reality. As its transmission into the 'proper reality' has to be postponed, the 'negative capability' of keeping the fake one at bay proves to be the only warrant of this reality's ultimate materialization.

In the appendix, "Deprived of Protection: The Ethico-Politics of Authorship in Ian McEwan's *Atonement*", the British novelist is read as a post-imperial writer. What connects him with Kafka and Coetzee is his strong inclination to give protection to abandoned beings, characteristic of subjects that have themselves been bereft of protection by their family's, society's, or age's authorities. In my interpretation, it was not only McEwan's fatherless post-war childhood and the deeply divided and guilt-ridden constellation of post-imperial Britain but, in the first place, the defenseless condition of the post-imperial world that gave rise to his novels' strong ethical disposition. Children are affected by the loss of parental care in several of them, but I focus on *Atonement*, which dispossesses both the Tallis and the Quincey children of parental devotion. The epitome of a fatherless childhood, however, is that of Robbie, the abandoned, adopted and re-abandoned son who desperately longs for a father to center his life. Precisely as such, he is strongly inclined to take into his protection various helpless dependents, such as Briony and the Quincey brothers or the dismembered children in the chaos of the war. His remorseful attachment is redoubled by Briony who, although a 'born writer', devotes herself to nursing the victims of war. At the end of the day, such readiness for difficult life experiences proves to have only been an instrument for the improvement of her creative abilities – a reversal of Robbie's conviction that "he would be a better doctor for having read literature" (McEwan 2001: 93). In her mature view, life's only task is to aggravate and thus refine the mission of literature. The grown-up Briony trusts that she has become "so worldly now as to be above such nursery-tale ideas as good and evil", launching instead a search for "some lofty, god-like place, from which all people could be judged alike, not pitted against each other, as in some life-long hockey match, but seen noisily jostling together in all their glorious imperfection" (McEwan 2001: 115). In her retroactive view, literary maturement implies rejecting authorial anger toward fellow beings in favor of an endless compassion for them. However, while through her meandering from one point of view to the other she consistently avoided facing the truth, she was in fact repeating her mother who, by keeping herself away from confrontations with her husband (McEwan 2001: 148–149), only strove for her own comfort (McEwan 2001: 71). If the young Briony was predetermined by her mother's evasiveness, the old Briony is captured by her disinterestedness. Besides, her care for the unprotected acts as the doppelganger of McEwan's ethical strategy. Both distance themselves from their deluded literary youth but the author, in shaping his own literary transformation, 'parenthesizes' that of his doppelganger. By dismantling the selfishness of Briony's mentoring, he surreptitiously renders his caretaking superior. He pretends not to be entrapped in her delusions as she is in those of her characters. If Briony's exposed narrative politics turn these doppelgangers into the devices of her atonement, McEwan's hidden politics of authoring turn them into the polygons of his self-healing protection.

Part I: **Post-imperial Europe: The Revenge of Peripheries**

1 Post-imperial Europe: The Return of the Indistinct

> How to escape the filth: not a new question. An old rat-question that will not let go, that leaves its nasty, suppurating wound.
>
> J. M. Coetzee, *Summertime*

Post-Versailles Europe: The compensatory indistinct of subalterns

The dissolution of East-Central European Empires in the aftermath of the First World War, followed by the founding of new nation states as well as the successor states to these empires, induced the region's traumatic post-imperial condition. With the Treaty of Versailles, Western nation-state powers introduced the principle of national self-determination into the reconfigured East-Central European region, which endowed each nation with the political right to establish its own autonomous state. Such national modelling of the religiously, ethnically, culturally, and linguistically hybrid East-Central European states was not a unilateral imposition but a decision enthusiastically embraced by the carriers of their liberation movements who regarded the establishment of new states as a welcome opportunity for their own political affirmation. An ambiguous relationship emerged between the West-European "mentors" and their East-Central European "protégés" through this "joint statism" (Guha 2002: 74) that inconspicuously merged the imperialist interests of Europe's centre with the nationalist interests of its periphery. The protégés highly coveted the respect of their mentors, yet were kept at a distance not only by their own sinister realities but also by their mentors' long entrenched prejudices against them. They were systematically treated as "almost the same but not quite" subjects (Bhabha 1994: 122), destined to an interminable process of perfecting themselves and thus subject to a constant geopolitical and historical lag behind the model. As Dipesh Chakrabarty aptly remarked, imperial centers allocated a pre-modern place "elsewhere" and an outdated "not yet" time to these 'barbarians', which relegated them to an enduring "waiting room of history" (Chakrabarty 2000: 7). Although he primarily addresses Europe's relationship toward its *external* others, his description also perfectly fits Europe's attitude to its *internal* others. Since the age of Enlightenment, both 'axes' constituted Europe's "joint venture" that, being from the outset exposed to a steady reconfiguration, acquired a statist shape with the Treaty of Versailles.

Although the delineated "joint statism" that came into being in the aftermath of the First World War was expected to 'Europeanize' East-Central European states, it ultimately deepened their frustration. It firmly attached their peoples to the vague prospect of their independence, but by imprisoning them in an enduring dependence upon their mentors ultimately impeded the very aim of this attachment. Within a Europe that was determined to unify its constituencies, East-Central European states proliferated enemies and instigated new conflicts by spontaneously transferring on to their "Oriental" European neighbors the stigma of inferiority that their West-European mentors had imputed upon them. Thus, instead of being abolished, Western "Orientalism" experienced an unprecedented expansion (Bakić-Hayden 1995). Far from being eliminated through the unification of all European nation states, 'Christian Europe's' discrimination of 'European Turkey' clandestinely became the basic principle for Europe's reproduction.

In the post-imperial East Central Europe of the 1920s and 1930s, disappointment was commonplace. The imperial *successor states* were involved in revengeful animosities with neighboring states, such as Turkey towards Greece. Furthermore, they were torn by their majority population's hatred of domestic minorities, especially the Jews, but also the Armenians and Greeks in Turkey, or the Slavic minorities in Germany, Hungary, and Austria. In addition, they were bereft of tens of millions of their co-nationals who had remained in what were now foreign nation states, such as Austrians and Germans in Poland, Czechoslovakia, and Yugoslavia, Hungarians in Romania, Czechoslovakia, and Yugoslavia, and Russians in incipient non-Russian nation states. They were also exposed to huge influxes of these stranded external co-nationals, such as Turkey to the Russian and Balkan Muslims, Hungary to the Romanian, Czechoslovak, and Yugoslav Hungarians, or Weimar Germany to the Baltic, Polish, and Czechoslovakian Germans. Besides, the embitterment of the successor states arose from the territorial concessions that they were forced to make. The Ottoman Empire lost Russian, African and Balkan territories, Austria was obliged to 'return' the Sudetenland to Czechoslovakia and Upper Silesia to Poland, while Hungary was coerced into giving up its former territories to Czechoslovakia, Romania, and Yugoslavia. They lost their former glory, like the Austro-Germans who were now "transformed from a *Staatsvolk* of a Great Power into what they perceived as second-class citizens of third-class states" (Brubaker 1996: 124). This humiliation of their external compatriots rigidified the successor states' politics toward their borderlands and gave rise to various compensatory manoeuvres of national self-aggrandizement. Finally, the sensible intellectuals in some of them were plagued by war guilt, foremost those of Austria and

Germany after they had confronted their compatriots' wartime hysteria against external and internal 'traitors'.

By contrast, the *newly established nation states*, plagued as they were by miserable social and economic conditions, poor infrastructures, unemployment, inflation, rigid and immobile social stratification, and corrupt and inefficient administrations in their countries (Berend 1998: 3–47), blamed this desolate state of affairs on long-term exploitations and humiliations inflicted upon them by former empires and foreign powers. The sense of backwardness was overwhelming and endemic, numerous obstacles to modernization fueled bitterness, hatred, and revolt. Being underprivileged in their new states, many of their constituencies, such as the Ukrainians, the Croats, the Slovaks, and especially the Jews perceived themselves as the Versailles Treaty's victims (Kożuchowski 2013: 8–9). The outbursts of frustration with the Treaty's outcome also induced revengeful animosities between the new countries, such as Poland and Czechoslovakia, Romania and Yugoslavia, and Italy and Yugoslavia. It ultimately paved the way for the establishment of populist dictators within them (for example Yugoslavia's King Alexander, Poland's Piłsudski, and Romania's Antonescu). Populism had been on a continual rise in East Central Europe since the turn of the century by systematically introducing in-distinction into the clear West-European distinction between socialist and communist ideologies on the one hand and nationalist, fascist, and anti-Semitic ones on the other. Taking advantage of the communicational, traffic and institutional networks, which had been established in East Central Europe in the last decades of the nineteenth century with the aim of implementing the mobility of modern West European democracies in the region, populists used it for the opposite purpose, i.e. to heal the population's feeling of uprootedness that resulted from such imposed mobility. Mobility, as the basic prerequisite of West European democracies, thus seems to have simultaneously acted as a West European ally and an East-Central European enemy.

If modernity has something to teach us, then it is that "one man's imagined community is another man's political prison" (Appadurai 1998: 32). Not everybody benefited from mobility, the proudly flagged distinctive trait of modern European civilization. As soon as it entered the East-Central European space after the dissolution of empires, it replaced its West European liberating face with a coercive one, initiating huge and hitherto unimaginable migrations of populations. "By 1890 close to 40 percent of all Austro-Hungarians had left their original place of Heimat and migrated to their current homes from another part of the monarchy" (Judson 2016: 334). Almost four million men and women moved overseas, but hundreds of thousands returned within a few years so that, as a result of all these immense dislocations, the populations of imperial cities such as Vienna, Budapest, Prague, and Zagreb enormously increased

(Judson 2016: 335). The former empires' metropoles or core nations faced equally harsh consequences. "The Fall of the Habsburgs automatically turned the 25 percent of the Viennese population born outside the frontiers of the new Austria into foreigners, unless they chose to opt for citizenship" (Hobsbawm 1996: 15). After the breakup of the Soviet Union, twenty-five million Russians who had been colonized in various territories across the Empire from the mid-sixteenth century until the mid-twentieth century (Brubaker 1996: 150) suddenly remained outside the Russian Federation (Brubaker 1996: 6–7). Three million Hungarians were left in Romania, Slovakia, Serbia, and Ukraine, two million Albanians in Serbia, Montenegro, and Macedonia, two million Serbs in Croatia and Bosnia and Herzegovina, and one million Turks in Bulgaria (Brubaker 1996: 56). It goes without saying that such a traumatic reconfiguration of post-imperial Europe's geopolitical circumstances deeply disquieted and disoriented the majority of its population, giving rise to an overwhelming sense of its disorientation and defenselessness.

However, to reiterate the central thesis of the two faces of the modern processes, such disabling dislocations of populations were coupled with some enabling effects. While post-imperial Europe's huge reconfiguration seriously endangered its population's material survival, it simultaneously immensely increased the mobility of its imagination (Appadurai 1998: 6). In the completely reshaped geopolitical space that now loomed large on the horizon, as Arjun Appadurai put it, "[e]ven the meanest and most hopeless of lives, the most brutal and dehumanizing of circumstances, the harshest of lived inequalities" became "open to the play of the imagination" (1998: 54). This means that, however frustrating the enforced deterritorializations of the East-Central European populations were, they were nevertheless accompanied by some emancipating consequences.

To address their *frustrating aspect* first, late empires had already constructed their communicational, traffic, and mercantile networks to improve military control over their peripheral constituencies, to facilitate their economic exploitation, and to avert them from switching to other empires. Next to fostering the import of food and raw materials from these provinces (Barkey 1996: 106), late imperial traffic networks envisaged the subsequent export of the finished products in the opposite direction. Although modernization claimed to be equalizing all its participants, it thus deteriorated the economic imbalance between them still further (Berend 1998: 20–22). As in the case of the Austrian Emperor Joseph II's linguistic standardization that had taken place a century or so earlier, the following message underlay the integration of imperial provinces: Only those that succumb to it are regarded as progressive and modern. Those that remain loyal to their odd traditional habits confine themselves to their self-enclosed localities, excluding themselves from the universal process of civilization. They are stigmatized as backward. This is how modernization put the imperial provinces under pressure for accelerated adaption, which they, although poorly equipped, were forced to come to terms with.

Nonetheless, such subterraneous discrimination paved the way for the *emancipating aspect* of imperial modernization. It involuntarily provided the common background against which the provinces could learn their differences and homogenize themselves (Evans 2006; Cornwall 2006: 174–175). Through traumatic migrations that were induced by this modernization, they got the opportunity to make acquaintances with many other provinces that were hitherto barely known to them. Although the encounters with them were sometimes uncomfortable, discouraging and even terrifying, considering the geopolitical, religious, cultural, and linguistic differences that separated imperial provinces from each other, it enabled provincial communities to strengthen their resistance to the centers' discrimination by forging alliances with those who were equally subjected to it. Melting with them into transborder communities directed against their oppressor and perpetrator, they disregarded their huge differences.

Their resistance adopted the form which Homi Bhabha described as "subversive mimicry" in his ground-breaking analysis of colonial circumstances (Bhabha 1994: 94–132). In terms of Bhabha's analysis, the colonized subject, in his or her reiterated attempts to erase the difference that separates him from the colonizer through the adoption of the latter's distinct achievements, reaffirms this difference by inadvertently distorting them (Bhabha 1994: 122). Although Bhabha applies his concept to the circumstances of European colonies, the population of European imperial provinces subverted modernization in the same way. They unwillingly or willingly turned its identifying techniques, which they were hard pressed to accept, upside down. This re-signification was a spontaneous act of affirmation of their anachronous habits. In this way, the late imperial age opened the door for the post-imperial rise of the indistinct. Let us recall what Nietzsche states in his famous analysis of *ressentiment* in *On the Genealogy of Morals*:

> While all noble morality grows from a triumphant affirmation of itself, slave morality from the outset says no to an "outside," to an "other," to a "non-self"; and *this* no is its creative act. The reversal of the evaluating gaze – this necessary orientation outwards rather than inwards to the self – belongs characteristically to *ressentiment*. In order to exist at all, slave morality from the outset always needs an opposing, outer world; in physiological terms, it needs external stimuli in order to act – its action is fundamentally reaction. (Nietzsche 1996: 22)

To illustrate, the railways that were built to enable the centers' economic expansion gradually turned into the instruments of the periphery's resistance to it (Schenk 2013). Or, provincial elites who were educated in the imperially established provincial schools or in the imperial centers themselves engaged this very knowledge for their opposition to them (Barkey 1996: 110). If the idea of this education was to differentiate imperial *societies*, provincial elites engaged it to homogenize their *communities*. The modern invention of society thus inadvertently became "the condition for the more exact profiling of the concept of community, inasmuch as it could now advance into a collective name for all that which cannot be subsumed in the concept of society" (Rosa et al. 2010: 37–38). However, it was not only the Habsburg Empire's political differentiation that systematically produced its unprocessed residues in the form of ethnic nationalisms that were "forged in the context of Habsburg imperial institutions and in the possibilities these institutions foresaw" (Judson 2016: 452). The Ottoman Empire also raised vipers in its bosom since the wave of commercialization and monetization that contributed to its "modernization and unification [. . .] eventually brought about various nation-based movements intent on separation from the empire" (Keyder 1996: 32).

The delineated operation of subversion by adoption, which was already germane of late imperial peripheries, re-emerged in the new nation states after the breakdown of the empires. However, if in the late imperial peripheries it was carried by the national elites as the subalterns of imperial centers, their carriers became *these same elites*' subalterns in the new nation states. As an outcome, across the post-imperial East Central Europe that had been expected to assimilate into West Europe by differentiating its nation states, transborder communities arose as the zones of "national indifference" (Zahra 2010). Operating as the untranslatable residues of national translations, they developed a sort of intra-active transnationality against the officially imposed cosmopolitanism. Gradually, their proliferation subverted the nation-state platform of Europe's integration. According to Elisabeth Povinelli, such zones are reservoirs of suppressed possibilities that distribute their potentiality into the aggregate that they are (an unacknowledged) part of, setting in motion its disarticulation (Povinelli 2011: 3–4; 11–13). Enmeshing a multiplicity of small worlds into an interactive totality, such transborder communities created an alternative model of worldly mutualism. Their energy of longing for imagined homelands deactivated their sense of belonging to the given nation states. A series of contemporary political theorists such as Giorgio Agamben, Roberto Esposito, and Judith Butler interpret these internal "pockets of resistance" to the imposed unification as the direct outcomes of the "egalitarian discrimination" genuine to modernization's globalization. In their view, the collateral effects of the production of a homogeneous human world are the would-be humans, the spectral humans, and the non-humans who are prevented from becoming legible within the established space of humanity (Agamben 1998: 121; Esposito 2011: 209; Butler 2004: 92).

Indeed, the geopolitically reconfigured East-Central European space became a harsh political prison for many of its constituencies, which is why their sense of belonging to their newly formed nation states was replaced with a sense of longing for that which these states excluded from their constitutions and official memories. New state nationalisms befell and impoverished these constituencies, pinned them to the wall of dominating nations, stripped them of choice, silenced their alternatives, and nullified their complex identity by an imposed demonization of the "other" (Brubaker 1996: 20–21). Since they longed for a different way to cohabit the political spaces that they were affiliated to, the door was wide open for forging alliances with the deprived from abroad who likewise felt "stranded in the present" (Fritzsche 2004). However, while identifying with them across the newly drawn state borders along national, religious, class, gender, ideological, and/or cultural lines, they exposed the nation states to which they were affiliated to disintegration. By knitting together various frustrations into platforms that promised a remedy for them, they managed to mobilize the most heterogeneous victims for their agendas (Hanson 2010: xvi). In this way, amalgamate and explosive transborder communities came into being amidst the post-imperial states' politically established national communities. They turned out to be the most important agents of the rising indistinct in the geopolitically reconfigured East-Central European space after the dissolution of empires.

Before we turn to the response of West-European states to this unexpected 'perversion' of the nation state as the envisaged platform of European unification, it deserves reminding that these states' very establishment was discriminatory and violent.

> Ever since the fifteenth century (and in the case of England much earlier), Western Europe has embarked on a huge homogenization drive with various degrees of success (the Spanish reconquista, England's expulsion of the Jews in the twelfth century, the religious wars in France and Germany), which, in conjunction with the strong dynastic states, had laid the foundations of the future nation-states. (Todorova 1997: 175)

As the French political philosopher Ernest Renan put it in his famous lecture "What Is a Nation?", the essence of a nation is that its individual representatives erase atrocities committed by their compatriots from their memories. "Every French citizen has forgotten St. Bartholomew's Day and the thirteenth-century massacres in the Midi" (Renan 2006: 46). In view of these violent purifications of West-European state bodies, which they were at enduring pains to expel from their official historical records, the East-Central European nation states' harsh exclusionary mechanisms represented for them a painful reminder of their own pasts. Their strong reservations toward such a demonization of others tended to prevent the traumatic return of this obliterated operation of self-establishment.

Postcolonial Europe: The repenting indistinct of superiors

Already with the Enlightenment, West Europe launched the project of a gradual self-exemption from its violent past. One of its chief engineers, Immanuel Kant was at pains to emancipate man from his destructive habits. In the treatise "Idea for a Universal History with a Cosmopolitan Purpose" (1784), he states that if history were delivered to man's naturally inborn base and selfish goals, it would amount to a "senseless course" of devastation, upheavals and the complete exhaustion of human powers (Kant 2006: 42, 47). "For each of them will always misuse his freedom if he does not have anyone above him to apply force to him as the laws should require it" (Kant 2006: 46). Kant's expectation, however, is that the united world society looming large on the horizon of his age will prevent citizens from living such an inappropriate, animally-blind life by subjecting them to the "condition of compulsion" (*Zustand des Zwanges;* Kant 2006: 46, trans. modified) or the pressure of historical necessity. By his natural disposition constructed from "warped wood", man needs mankind "to break his self-will and force him to obey a universally valid will under which everyone can be free" (Kant 2006: 46). If he were not compelled to obey this supreme general agency, he would be destroyed by his essentially selfish and hostile nature, instead of developing the ability to reason that distinguishes him from animals. For Kant, the natural disposition is a wild compulsive force that must be domesticated through a patient self-overcoming of man under the custody of mankind. Modernity puts man under the pressure of such a persistent overcoming of his basically animal nature.

The difficulty that Kant's argument must face, however, is that man's self-willingness, compelled by mankind to discipline itself, *characterizes the very agency expected to discipline him*. The violence that had to be repressed thus returns. The agency called upon to supervise man's long journey to final freedom displays, in Kant's rendering, significantly coercive traits. While it encourages man to disobey his inherited identity, it commands him to obey his universal human duty. It thus repeatedly dooms him to an "animal" bondage. Was not the same universal claim, that is now raised by "reasonable" universal history, raised in the Renaissance by the Christian community that, subjecting people to God's transcendent law, produced ecumenical uniformity and equality out of diversity and differences (Badiou 2003: 109)? Is not Kant, in this manner, surreptitiously reintroducing into the Enlightenment the colonial difference between the "humans" of proper faith and the "animal" infidels that was established by the

Renaissance *orbis universalis christianus* (Mignolo 2000: 725–726)? This is how his imperative for man and collectivities to relentlessly individualize themselves involuntarily reproduces man's violent disposition that it was expected to leave behind. Whoever adopts it necessarily subverts the idea of man as a being emancipated from his blind compulsions.

The project of European modernity as launched by the Enlightenment thus appears, from its very outset, to have been accompanied by a traumatic re-emergence of "animality" within the envisaged "humanity". It involuntarily headed toward the "indistinct" that it hardly strove to leave behind, which again forced it to renew and intensify its efforts at overcoming itself. On the eve of the dissolution of empires through the violent outbreak of their oppressed peripheries, Nietzsche became aware of the equivocal character of the Enlightenment project: "My humanity amounts to a continuous self-overcoming [of its inhumanity]" (Nietzsche 1980: 276). Since inhumanity subversively resurfaces within its "overcomer", its sublimation becomes an interminable task. He still believed that, through such persistent endeavor, the indistinct "animal" hatred toward others transforms into a distinct "human" love for them. In his *On the Genealogy of Morals* (1887), the contagious seed of "a hatred the like of which has never been on earth" miraculously results in "the deepest and most sublime of all kinds of love" (Nietzsche 1996: 20). In paragraphs 354 and 355 of his *Joyful Wisdom* (1882/2010), Nietzsche presents his own persistently self-re-evaluating philosophical technique as the culmination of a long development that began with the "denigrated and humiliated" mob; continued with the actor who had learned to command his instincts with other instincts; then the "artist" like the buffoon, the fool, and the clown; thereupon, the proper artist; until the process was finally crowned with the "genius".

In his essay "The Poet and his Time" (1906/1979), Hugo von Hofmannsthal implicitly endorses Nietzsche's trust in redemption through self-dispossession, transferring it from the long-term axis of humankind onto the short-term axis of human life. Because the poet sees something that the blinded others overlook, he exposes himself to a common misunderstanding and contempt. However, despite such denigration, he must persevere with his sacrificial mission for these contemporaries' ultimate well-being. "Living in the house of time, under the stairs, where everyone must pass him and no one respects him [. . .] an undetected beggar in the place of the dogs [. . .] without a job in this house, without service, without rights, without duty" (Hofmannsthal 1979: 66), only such a self-animalized poet can create a human world bereft of "animal" hatred.

However, the post-imperial age shattered such late imperial trust in the "animalized" human residues as the motors of new humanity. Taught by the devastating mass movements, for example, Robert Musil interprets these denigrated and humiliated agencies in a more equivocal manner. In "A sort of introduction" to his *Man without Qualities*, his narrator states that next to nine identities attributed to "every dweller on earth" by their internally diversified societies, there is a tenth attribute, which is "difficult to describe", "merely an empty, invisible space with reality standing in the middle of it like a little toy brick town, abandoned by the imagination" (Musil 2014: 34). But since this indistinct attribute *absorbs into its emptiness all the remaining identity attributes*, "every dweller on earth" ultimately becomes a "man without qualities", with his or her identity subjected to a persistent negation (Musil 2014: 220). A person who no longer feels at home in an extant community replaces it with a longing for such emptied communities. In such a way, a perilous 'organic' feeling grows at the heart of endangered belonging.

In his essay "Beyond the Pleasure Principle", at the beginning of which he introduces the concept of "oceanic feeling", Freud anticipates Musil's anxieties. In "The Mass Psychology and the Analysis of the Ego", he argues that such blind mass binding to a leader eliminates the achievements of a long cultural development such as individual will, consciousness, self-control, logics, and a sense of reality (Freud 2001: 93). His thesis is that "organic communities" are by no means an overcome phase of human history but rather a permanent disintegrating aftereffect of its development. Resulting from the dispossessed collectivities' and individuals' resurfacing desire for self-dissolution, they regularly re-emerge within the differentiated human society. This is how, for instance, the institutions of the army and the Church come into being (Freud 2001: 88–94). The proliferation of these supposedly surmounted modes of self-identification makes the present spectral and uncanny, saturated with the resonances of its terrifying past (Freud 2005: 232; 1947: 295).

As the confrontation between Nietzsche's and Hofmannsthal's enthusiasms on the one hand and Freud's and Musil's reservations on the other testifies, the re-emergence of the animal within the human is an equivocal phenomenon. Derrida, for example, once noticed how fascinating and fertilizing its disintegrating effects were for interwar European thinkers who felt stranded in their present: "[W]hy is [the uncanny] the best name, the best concept, for something which resists consistency, system, semantic identity? Why is it *the* experience, the most thinking experience in Freud and in Heidegger?" (Derrida 2003: 35) The uncanny also became the carrier of his own idea of Europe because Europe "consists precisely of not closing itself off in its own identity and in advancing itself in an exemplary way towards what it is not" (Derrida 1987a: 12). How is this denial of its devastating effects to be explained in the works of the late imperial and post-imperial West European thinkers?

In fact, from the outbreak of modernity onwards, Western philosophers relegated these perilous effects to the retrograde 'non-Europeans' or 'not-enough-Europeans'. It is for them, they say, that the 'proper Europeans' have to relentlessly expiate their distinction by reintroducing indistinction into it. Speaking of Slavs, for example, Herder already raises the question: "Is it astonishing that, after centuries of subjugation and the deepest embitterment of this nation through its masters and robbers, their soft character has been degraded to the most cunning, terrible slavish inertia" (*Knechtsträgheit*) (Herder 1989: 698)? Their spiritual poverty engages mobility in the physical instead of the intellectual space as progressive peoples do. A century thereafter, in *The Crisis of European Humanity and Philosophy*, Husserl complains that the Roma "incessantly rove around Europe [. . .] while we, if we understand each other correctly, will for example never become Indians (*die dauernd in Europa herumvagabundieren [. . .] während wir, wenn wir uns recht verstehen, uns zum Beispiel nie indianisieren werden*)" (Husserl 1954: 318–319). He attempted to solve the crisis of European humanity by reattaching Europe to its 'genuine' task of rescuing universal humankind by gradually suspending limitation caused by such benighted others.

But there are more recent 'engineers' of this *purely potential* indistinct constituent of Europe that attentively detaches itself from its restricted *physical* materialization. In the conclusion of his book *Europe, or the Infinite Task*, Rodolphe Gasché summarizes this long-lasting elaboration of European singularity as follows:

> From Husserl's discussion of a universal rational science having its roots in the life world, to Heidegger's linkage of an originary world to the history of a people, to Patočka's conception of a community of responsibility predicated on the absolute singularity of its members, to Derrida's claim that the concept or idea of universality as an infinite task emerges in a finite space and time, we have seen that singularity can only identify itself by simultaneously appealing to universality. (Gasché 2009: 343)

Being open "toward transcendence, toward the other, and what is other than Europe" (Gasché 2009: 27), an 'emancipating interiorizer of limited exteriorities'" so to speak, Europe is for Gasché, thanks to such an extreme consideration of others, the most responsible representative of universal humankind (Gasché 2009: 31). It never stops questioning itself. Associating this consistently self-interrogating life with the spiritual rather than geographical Europeans, Gasché confronts every human being irrespective of his or her geographical location with this "infinite task" of self-Europeanization (Gasché 2009: 27).

Although connecting on a different tradition, Julia Kristeva concurs with him by seeing Europe as the carrier of Montesquieu's *ésprit général*, a historically guided "texture of many singularities" (Kristeva 1993: 32–33). In line with Gasché's argument, she states that unlike non-European civilizations inimical to contamination and overlaps with other traditions, Europe from the outset exemplified an exogamous society stipulating alliances outside the bloodline (Kristeva 1991: 45–46). The third prominent thinker, who interprets Europe's sacrificial self-de-identification as the prerequisite of its universal mission, is Zygmunt Bauman. He argues that unlike other cultures that are unaware of being distinct because they are unrelated to the others, European culture "feeds on questioning the order of things – and on questioning the fashion of questioning it" (Bauman 2004: 12). This ultimately turns it into an infinite task of a consistent self-dispossession.

In order to defend Europe from a "dispersal into a myriad of provinces, into a multiplicity of self-enclosed idioms or petty little nationalisms, each one jealous and untranslatable", Jacques Derrida also enthusiastically endorses the sacrifice of any given European identity for an "infinite task" (Derrida 1987a: 39). He expects Europe to exempt itself from any determinate identity into a pure potentiality of the "New International", an eminently anti-organic community:

> It is an untimely link, without status, without title and without name, barely public even if it is not clandestine, without contract, "out of joint", without coordination, without party, without country, without national community [. . .] without co-citizenship, without common belonging to a class. (Derrida 1994b: 85)

Derrida formulates his idea of Europe as "[w]e know in common that we have nothing in common", underlining its relentless energy of self- and other-deactivation (2001: 58). Instituting the "global jurisdiction" (Derrida 1992e: 72) of its all-pervading *nothing* as the "most powerful powerless" (Attridge 2004b: 131), his Europe ultimately uproots all identities grounded in a particular time, space, and culture. Because its dissemination exceeds, transgresses, and elusively surpasses the other, its non-community "does not collect itself, it 'consists' in not collecting itself" (Derrida 1995a: 354). In their "plea for a common foreign policy, beginning at the core of Europe", Habermas and Derrida accordingly assume that, in proceeding thus, Europe substitutes a fully inclusive human community for an agglomeration of territorially entrenched entities (Habermas and Derrida 2003).

In a manner typical of weak messianism, Derrida thus deconstructs all small oppositions in favour of the big one between the Europe of free self-dispossessions and the non-Europe of the enforced ones. The first "human" dispossessions take the upper hand over the second "animal" ones. In line with the empowerment of the powerless as characteristic of Derrida's "neither words nor notions" such as the *différance*, trace, undecidability, *tout autre*, or deconstruction, his Europe deprived of all identities operates as the "law of laws" or the agency of justice. While it is itself safely withdrawn from any deactivation, it relentlessly deactivates all "non-Europeans" (Derrida 1985: 121). Its vague and elusive character that lurks in the indistinct past behind the back of identifiable history promises an equally indistinct future to compensate for the long victimhood of its carriers. Paradoxically reintroducing the East-Central European populist retribution narratives — "We have been naught, we shall be all" — Derrida's weak messianic Europe demonstrates the same *triumphant return of the indistinct*, which absorbs into its emptiness all "petty" distinctions.

However, bereaving the idea of Europe of its geopolitical and historical particularity until it becomes such an indistinct entity, involuntarily uncovers the repentance of its creators for the crimes committed by Europe. For example, the myth of a multiethnic, multicultural and multilingual Central Europe equally sublimed its past atrocities. It acquired prominence after the almost complete extermination of the region's Jews, the deportation of its Germans, and a radical reduction of linguistic and ethnographic heterogeneity in its newly established nation states. Once the myth's traumatic background enters the daylight, it dismantles "Central Europe" as a nostalgic, therapeutic, and falsifying back-projection established to heal its creators' wounds. Does not the same repentance underlie the recent indistinct idea of Europe?

Considering this suppression, it is significant to what degree Derrida's radically indistinct idea of Europe corresponds with Foucault's technique of ethical self-fashioning, which authorizes his indistinct "soul" to engulf into its nothingness all his distinct identity attributes. For Foucault, the modern "soul" is "the effect" of the microphysical "technology of power over the body" that consists of the systematic work of normative differentiation. As the most prominent countersite of the modern self, it is the residue excluded from the modern society's rules of identity formation, which by the disconcerting resurgence of its unruly energy invokes further social regulation (Foucault 1977: 29). In Blanchot's interpretation, this in-different remainder of the social differentiation, which continuously sets a new horizon for the social operations, powerfully attracted Foucault (Blanchot 1993: 199). A "man always on the move", he toyed "with the thought that he might have been, had fate so decided [. . .] nothing or nobody in particular" (*un je ne sais quoi ou un je ne sais qui*; Blanchot 1986: 17). It was in the name of the unfathomable potential of this *je ne sais quoi* that he was ready to let his thought pass "through what is called madness", to "withdraw from itself, turn away from a mediating and patient labor [. . .] towards a searching that is distracted and astray [. . .] without result and without works" (Blanchot 1993: 199). One can hardly imagine a more radical dispossession of the West European self as undertaken in the name of its in-different remainder.

Conclusion

It is time to summarize the delineated developments in the post-imperial East Central Europe after the First World War and the post-colonial West Europe after the Second World War. Whether the distinction of Europe rests on its translation into nations as in the first case or humanity as in the second, its carriers have to cope with the resurrection of their indistinct past. In the outcome, the idea of Europe displays two irreconcilable faces, one of which steadily defaces the other. Despite the fascinating appearance of each of them, the consistent defacement within them undermines their applicability as the remedy for the problem of human common-being. The idea of Europe is the "thing" that we need to explain rather than to explain things *with*. It is never a self-evident toolkit but the site of an uncanny encounter. Instead of promising a harmonious reconciliation, it always implies an uneasy cohabitation with its untranslatable leftovers.

2 Translating the Untranslatable: Walter Benjamin and Homi Bhabha

The rise of the indistinct: Two affiliated post-ages

Since Homi Bhabha introduced the notion of 'cultural translation' in the penultimate chapter of his *Location of Culture* (1994: 303–338), translation no longer implies the overcoming of existing differences between cultures. In his peculiar interpretation, it becomes a process that initiates cultural differences in the same way as life, for instance, incessantly diversifies its creatures. As these differences *follow* from translation, rather than *preceding* it, cultures are conceived as hybrid and in-between rather than pure and autonomous entities. Since the translation as their generator eludes identification, the differences between them are neither absolute nor reducible to a common identity. Exempting the translation from the bifurcations that it continuously generates, Bhabha renders it untranslatable. To underline its promotion to the condition of the im/possibility of all its constituent parts, he replaces *languages* as its *objects* with *cultures* as its *reproducers*. This argumentative move automatically eliminates the key dilemma of traditional translation theory: either the translator assimilates his or her language to that of the source text or makes the target text function as part of an altogether different linguistic setting. By insisting on the resistance that one culture offers both to its assimilation into the other culture and to its complete separation from it, Bhabha disengages binary logics. A culture cannot assimilate into another culture without maintaining its internal difference and it cannot liberate itself from another culture without having embodied this culture's trace. This is why no culture brings the process of translation to a successful closure. Instead, this process cuts through distinct cultural identities by making them essentially indistinct. As a result, Bhabha implies that the post-colonial world turns the colonial world's hierarchy upside down, establishing indistinction as its norm instead of distinction. In its global multinational network, hybridity, liminality, and in-betweenness rule the day.

In addition, such a globalization of translation undermines the 'self-evident' opposition that has dominated reflection on this notion over many centuries of colonialism. By extending the translation from the linguistic to the cultural domain, Bhabha seems to be reminding us that, from the outset, the practice of translation accompanied European colonialism with its habitual asymmetries between the rich and the poor or the civilized and the barbarous cultures. By undoing these asymmetries as the instruments of domination, he is in fact interrogating the colonial power relationship. In his own words, his idea of "cultural translation desacralizes the [. . .] assumptions of cultural supremacy" (1994: 228). The thesis that I want to propose is that, in this context, his engagement of the notion of *untranslatability*, introduced by Walter Benjamin in his 1923 essay *The Task of the Translator*, acquires a special significance. It establishes a clandestine 'elective affiliation' between the two thinkers who, doomed to cope with the traumatic constellations of their respectively post-imperial and postcolonial age, take recourse to the weak messianic strategy that systematically postpones its redemption. The latter has a long tradition in European modernity *strictu senso*, which dates back to early German Romanticists who were equally "stranded in their present", longing to reconnect with their castrated past via its scattered ruins (Fritzsche 2004: 55–131).[1] The redrawing of international borders in the aftermath of the German Empire's breakup (1806) induced an irreparable loss of security. The Romanticist identification of the foreclosed possibilities of the past and their restoration of its neglected itineraries were defensive responses to the disappointments induced by the French Revolutionaries' investment in historical progress. Their triumphant history penetrated deeply into the lives of its many participants with devastating effects.

In the similar atmosphere of an unchained history after the crumbling of an empire, what drives Bhabha to evoke Benjamin's notion of untranslatability? We should remind ourselves that, in the post-imperial constellation, this notion disengaged the ruling conception of *language*, which reflected European *imperial* asymmetries in the same way that the prevailing conception of *culture*, at the post-colonial time that Bhabha intervenes in it, reflected European *colonial* asymmetries. Thus, what might have attracted Bhabha in Benjamin's notion are the emancipating political implications in its background. The untranslatable is the element that offers resistance to the translational mechanisms of victorious history, which promotes Bhabha's turn to Benjamin as an example of how his "insurgent intersubjectivity" (Bhabha 1994: 230) comes into being. However, the notion of the untranslatable only appears at one spot in Benjamin's essay and is difficult to understand without considering his whole argument as being scattered across several essays. The respective point reads that "translations prove to be untranslatable" due to the "all too great fleetingness with which meaning attaches to them" (Benjamin 2004: 82, trans. modified, *allzu großer Flüchtigkeit, mit welcher der Sinn an ihnen haftet*, Benjamin 1977a: 61). It deserves attention that the German term *Flüchtigkeit* is associated with the notion of the *Flüchtling* (escapee or migrant), which significantly takes the center stage

---

[1] In his more extensive genealogy, Agamben (2005b: 88–112) traces weak messianism back to St Paul.

in Bhabha's aforementioned essay. Benjamin seems to be suggesting that meaning remains a subversive migrant in any language that tries to domesticate it. Placed amidst its national identity, it introduces transnational displacement into its place, or indistinction into its distinction. In other words, before an act of its *inter*-lingual translation, any language's meaning undergoes an *intra*-lingual escape, which makes its identity indistinct. Its internal fleetingness offers resistance to all acts of its translation into another linguistic identity, rendering it restrictive.

Insisting on such internal "untranslatability" of national languages, Benjamin might have established a spontaneous association with the untranslatability of the dispersed Jews as the perennial migrants of European cultures into any established national identity. For centuries they were caught "in a constant state of flux" (Benjamin 2004: 78), which destined them to "homelessness" "throughout the world", as Gustav Mahler remarked in the sinister atmosphere of their renewed dispossession (Beller 1989: 207) that, nota bene, also gave birth to Benjamin's essay. At the time, however, the same inherited homelessness endangered the awakened national languages that, in the compartmentalized post-imperial Europe, were fiercely vying for their own political identity. For long centuries, they were likewise deprived of it. Benjamin's notion of untranslatability opposes the idea of their national self-determination as the antidote to this homelessness in the same way that it opposes the rising Zionist idea of Jewish national self-determination. Instead, by *transforming their painful lack of distinct identity into a rare privilege*, he turns their homelessness into an appointment for the revolutionary mission of a universal deterritorialization. Benjamin's contemporary Karl Kraus, before he turned Zionist, equally trusted that the Jews were "fated to dissolve entirely into their surrounding cultures, and nevertheless still to remain a ferment in them" (Kraus 1898: 23). Like him, Benjamin was convinced that the inflicted *internal exteriority* to any host culture forced the Jews "to come to terms with things in a way others, generally, were not [forced]. There was thus in a sense a special role for Jews, one might say a secular version of the chosen people" (Beller 1989: 217). Like the migrant meaning at the heart of national languages, they were invited to permanently revivify their hosts' identities by introducing indistinction into their distinction.

Significantly, speaking of cultural translation, Bhabha renders the impact of Indian migrant families on the British post-colonial surrounding in similar terms of a persistent renewal. Their cultural untranslatability permeates the cultural milieu of their hosts with "hybrid sites of meaning" (Bhabha 1994: 234), which culminates in "an empowering condition of hybridity; an emergence that turns 'return' into re-inscription or re-description; an iteration that is not belated, but ironic and insurgent" (Bhabha 1994: 324). In Bhabha's view, this is "how newness enters the world". In both typically remedial arguments, the humiliating condition of migrants, bereft of distinct identity properties, translates into a life-affirming force. To be sure, neither Benjamin nor Bhabha invented this compensatory argument. Already early German Romanticists, embittered by the dissolution of the German Empire through Napoleon's victorious rise to power, had turned the long-term dispossession of German identity through the supremacy of French culture into a source of national pride. In their significant thesis on the German identity in permanent making, its lack of distinction was transformed into an advantage (Biti 2016: 57–68). This consoling self-glorifying maneuver of turning the lack of an autochthonous national tradition into an advantage in comparison to France or England was almost commonplace in the culturally inferior Germany around 1800 (Herder 1989: 551; Schlegel 1965: 26; Wiedemann 1993: 545ff.; Koch 2002: 234; Albrecht 2005: 308).

Benjamin's notion of the untranslatable and its implications

With the inborn instinct of all deprived agencies, which tend to interlock in order to strengthen their resistance, Benjamin's and Bhabha's arguments establish "affiliative solidarity" (Bhabha 1994: 230) with the Romanticist remedial logics. However, in counter-distinction to Bhabha, who in post-colonial circumstances is preoccupied with the *migration of people*, Benjamin focuses on the *translation of languages* in post-imperial circumstances. In order to understand his idea of untranslatability in the whole range of its implications, we must first take a closer look at the distinction he draws, within a given language, between its intended object (*das Gemeinte*) or particular *referent* and its mode of intention (*die Art des Meinens*) or *structure of reference*. He engages it throughout his argument, consistently applying it to both artworks and languages. In both, the structure of reference, genuine to their respective memory archives, outdoes the referent, which an artist or speaker establishes by his or her particular communicative intention. Benjamin already states in the first paragraph of his essay, in which he addresses the nature of artworks, that, despite the artist's intentions, "no poem is intended for the reader, no picture for the beholder, no symphony for the listener" (2004: 75). The structure of reference genuine to these artworks — or what semiotics has thereupon termed *signification* — goes far beyond the referent or *denotation* intended by their respective producers. Applying this distinction between signification and denotation to languages, Benjamin claims that they converge in the referents of their particular words but diverge in their structures of reference, inasmuch as these by far exceed these referents. The languages cannot control their structures of reference because, firstly, these are "in a constant state of flux" and, secondly, continuously supplement each other (Benjamin 2004: 78). Benjamin's elusive signification thus anticipates Lévi-Strauss's concept of the *floating signifier* (Lévi-Strauss 1987: 63–64), which was recently designated by Giorgio Agamben to have been the "guiding concept in the human sciences of the twentieth century" (2005a: 37).

What makes artworks and languages untranslatable is precisely their elusive signification, even if their transmitters ceaselessly translate it into particular denotations. Nonetheless, each materialized meaning excludes from its horizon a huge surplus of non-materialized ones that envelop this meaning. In Benjamin's view, this envelopment of unemployed meaning possibilities determines the reception of the given meaning behind the back of the intention that established it. As the artworks and languages cannot take into possession that which they translate but remain exposed to its untranslatability, their meaning involuntarily reaffirms this untranslatability by itself becoming "fleeting". However, the level of this fleetingness depends on their ability to activate their originals' "untranslatable element" or unemployed meaning possibilities. As the resolute advocate of the suppressed life options, Benjamin entrusts the translator with the task of such mobilization. If he or she succeeds in fulfilling this task of translating the zone of indistinction beyond the original's distinct meaning horizon, the latter experiences its rebirth or return to life.

Following this line of thinking, Benjamin warns that the translational activity retains its "possibly foremost significance" if it is not focused "exclusively on man" but rescues from oblivion that which men "proved unable to translate" (2004: 76). That is to say, the untranslatable that obliges the translator exceeds the structures of reference of *human* languages. That which they cannot translate is *bare life* (*bloßes Leben*; Benjamin 1980e: 202–203) as a dense network of relations, which operates beyond these languages.[2] This network comes to expression in all of its manifestations in the form of their escaping origin that undermines their distinction and sovereignty. Recently, Agamben resumed it in his political philosophy, rendering bare life (*la nuda vita*) (1998: 4, 9–10, 18, 27–28) as the underground ferment of the revolutionary change of given political formations. Its "zones of indistinction" operate as the reservoirs of "pure potentiality" that precedes and blurs human political divisions. Accordingly, within the constellation of European modernity, "bare life has the peculiar priv-

---

2 This is why Benjamin, for example, in *The Origin of German Tragic Drama*, interprets the German word *Ur-sprung* (which in everyday usage means "origin") etymologically as a "primordial leap" (out-of-control) (1980a: 226).

ilege of being that whose exclusion founds the common being of men" (Agamben 1998: 10; trans. modified, *la città degli uomini*). However, it structures the human world from an 'outside' that adheres to it only "through a disjunction and an anachronism" (Agamben 2010: 11).

Anchored as they are in bare life, modern political formations demonstrate "the topological structure of the state of exception": "*being outside, and yet belonging*" to the juridical state (Agamben 2005a: 35). Concerning this structure, Agamben unhesitatingly draws an analogy with the above addressed excess of signification over denotation: "Just as between language and word, so between the [juridical] norm and its application there is no internal nexus that allows one to be derived immediately from the other" (2005a: 40). Both passages entail "a 'trial' that always involves a plurality of subjects" (2005a: 39–40), remaining controversial and conflict-ridden. This is how Benjamin's notion of the untranslatable establishes an unmistakable link with the political state of exception. Although residing outside its translations, the untranslatable haunts them by inducing their destabilizing, floating, and meandering.

Miming as the medium of indistinction

This consistently inappropriate translation of the untranslatable — or *miming* — as it cannot but eternally postpone its verification, marks the very core of Benjamin's weak messianism. The divine world, because it is forever lost, occupies a constitutively ecstatic position toward the human world. It only belongs to this world through its *exemption* from it in the same way that the sovereign, in the state of exception, belongs to the juridical order only in the peculiar form of his *ecstasy* (Agamben 2005a: 35). As Derrida pertinently rendered it, the weak messianic "negative theology consists in regarding every [human] predicate [. . .] as inadequate to the essence [. . .] of God"; "only a negative [. . .] attribution can claim to approach God". "God's name would fit everything that cannot be [. . .] designated, except in an indirect and negative way" (Derrida 2008: 146). Which particular form does this translation of the untranslatable take in Benjamin's complex understanding of language?

If we now return to the argument of "The Task of the Translator", Benjamin commits the translator to the above-delineated hidden network of relations, or life. To activate it, s/he must establish correspondence between the "involuntary memories" of both the original and target languages.³ By bringing them into such mutually enriching dialogue, s/he rescues the "language of truth" (Benjamin 2004: 80) as their absent origin from its distortion by these two languages (2004: 82). Rescuing it means *miming* its mode of revelation (*Offenbarung*) in these languages' mode of communication (*Mitteilung*). Benjamin thus endows the translation with the "special mission" (2004: 78) of "a transformation and a renewal" of both languages (2004: 77). The more a human tongue mimes the mode of revelation instead of applying the mode of communication, the more space it opens up for its various translations. After Agamben, its successful translation "entails a 'trial' that always involves a plurality of subjects" (2005a: 39–40). In the formulation of Barbara Cassin, "the untranslatable is what one keeps on (not) translating" (Cassin 2014: xiv). In the spirit of weak messianism, the longing of human tongues for the language of truth endlessly postpones its materialization.

Benjamin does not address miming explicitly in "The Task of the Translator", but instead introduces it in two later essays, "The Doctrine of the Similar" and "On the Mimetic Faculty". Therein he opens a genealogy of his "translational" conception of language, stating that the *sensuous* miming of others, which characterized the pre-modern behavior of humans, gradually gave way to the modern ability of perceiving *conceptual* similitudes. Even if the development from the immediate sensual miming of things to the linguistically mediated non-sensual resemblances implies an historical overcoming, Benjamin nevertheless ultimately interprets language as the "most perfect archive" of seemingly deactivated resemblances. Because it stores, confronts and relates one to another, "the essences of things, their most fleeting and refined substances, even aromas", it is for him "the highest implementation of mimetic faculty" (Benjamin 1980b: 209). As one of his most astute recent commentators Samuel Weber rightly noticed, Benjamin insists that the language of communication, despite its efforts to part ways with the language of revelation, nevertheless stays "with that from which it parts" (Weber 2010: 197). The sensuous miming never stops returning into the conceptual representation, the untranslatable repeatedly breaks into its translation.

In Benjamin's understanding, a linguistic sign is never just an abstract bearer of reference without simultaneously being a material bearer of similitude. Its

---

3 Following Bergson, Freud and Proust, Benjamin introduces a distinction between the voluntary and involuntary memory in his essay "On Some Motifs in Baudelaire" (2007b: 158). In his understanding, the official belonging of any agency to its present time and space's agencies is systematically subverted by its suppressed longing for those of distant times and spaces.

longing for the language of truth subverts its belonging to a human tongue.[4] When he describes the sudden manifestation of similitude that swallows up the discrete forms of linguistic signs like a "flame" or a "flash" (*Aufblitzen*; Benjamin 1980b: 213), we cannot resist associating his imagery with Freud's image of the flickering-up (*Aufleuchten*) of involuntary memory traces in human apperceptions. Both "flashes" are bound to "a time-moment [*Zeitmoment*]" that "slips past" (Benjamin 1979: 66). In the alien milieu of communication, these remnants of the language of revelation present themselves "to the eye as fleetingly and transitorily as a constellation of stars" (1979: 66). It is the ethical task of the translator to meet their subterranean longing for redemption by making them join one another in an extraterritorial and extemporal "now-time" (*Jetztzeit*). Benjamin conceptualizes it as an uncanny fusion of divergent historical epochs, the far-removed fragments of which enter curious "elective affinities" and reverberate with one another (1977d: 258).

Repeatedly foregrounding such indistinct composites, Benjamin gradually establishes the untranslatable as the final criterion for its translations. As it announces itself merely "in an indirect and negative way", the more indirect and negative a given manifestation comes to be and the more intense feeling of unhomeliness it induces, the higher the reputation it enjoys in his opinion. In the outcome, Benjamin's concept of the untranslatable amounts to an apology of *floating signifiers*, i.e. expressions that — in his own plastic rendering — envelop their content "like a royal robe with ample folds" the king's body (2004: 79). He estimates their chances for afterlife as much better than the chances of established and distinct agencies. This holds for not only languages and artworks but creatures as well. For example, in his 1934 essay on Kafka, Benjamin presents the writer's peculiar figure of Odradek as at the same time a most bastardly and most mobile "receptacle of the forgotten" (2007a: 132). By his monstrous outlook, Odradek epitomizes the "distorted" "form which things assume in oblivion" (Benjamin 2007a: 133). However, portrayed as being permanently on the move and with an "indeterminate residence", he "stays alternately in the attic, on the staircase, in the corridors, and in the hall". He is so "extraordinarily mobile and uncatchable" that the "family man" is concerned he will, as his family's most shameful representative, finally outlive it (Kafka 1988k: 470).

Among the artworks, Benjamin likewise favors those deprived of an aesthetically distinctive identity, in which the "return of the repressed" induced an

---

[4] In fact, while reference has to be attributed to a human tongue's voluntary memory, which makes it belong to a distinct agency, similitude grows from its involuntary memory, which makes it long for the indistinct ones.

"expressionless" appearance. "This only completes a work, which destroys it into a bundle of pieces, to the fragment of a true world, to the torso of a symbol", he claims (Benjamin 1977c: 181). This uncanny, disaggregate composition of the work of art (*das Bruchstückhafte am Kunstwerk*; Benjamin 1980d: 690) as developed in his analyses of various narratives, finds its further elaboration in his conception of allegory from *The Origin of German Tragic Drama*. In this book, the "torso" of the work of art from the essay on Goethe (Benjamin 1977c: 116) transforms into a "desolate confusion of execution sites" (Benjamin 1980a: 401), by which baroque dramas testify to the misguidances of history. In such a devastated world, the work of art cannot be anything other than a patchwork of remnants, which postpones its completion for an unpredictable future (Benjamin 1980a: 355, 362).

The rule of the state of exception

We can therefore infer that, when Homi Bhabha, in his post-colonial rendering of today's world, favors indistinct terms of hybridity, liminality, and in-betweenness (Bhabha 1994: 12–13), he spontaneously attaches himself to Benjamin's traumatic experience of the post-imperial world, which establishes "the state of exception" as its "rule" (Benjamin 1977d: 254). Since then, the state of exception became "the dominant paradigm of government in contemporary politics" (Agamben 2005a: 2), paving the way for Bhabha's interest in Benjamin. In the aftermath of the First World War, Benjamin sensed that the law exempted itself from the public realm into an impenetrable zone of anomie located beyond human control. His contemporary, Carl Schmitt, defined the state of exception as follows: "[T]he sovereign stands outside of the normally valid juridical order, and yet belongs to it, for it is he who is responsible for deciding whether the constitution can be suspended *in toto*" (1985: 7). In other words, to make the law, his authority does not need to underlie it. We can therefore define the post-imperial state of exception as an "included exclusion" of its sovereign agency, which makes the operation of the law perilously capricious in the eyes of its subjects.

Benjamin composed his essay on Kafka during the Weimar Republic in French exile. In 1925 Carl Schmitt remarked that "no constitution on earth so easily legalized a coup d'état as did the Weimar Constitution" (1995: 25), which explains the Republic's regime of a presidential dictatorship and Hitler's subsequent seizure of power. In Kafka's works, as the Republic's banished citizen Benjamin did not fail to notice, the whimsical holders of power uphold its rules only for themselves in order to freely betray and corrupt them (Benjamin 2007a: 114). Put in these terms, his notion of the untranslatable acquires an eminently political dimension, connoting the uncanny return of the despotic prehistorical law in the democratic world of history. In the shadow of 9/11, Agamben reminded us that "World War One (and the years following it) appear as a laboratory for testing and honing the functional mechanisms and apparatuses of the state of exception" (2005a: 7). All of a sudden, with the breakup of empires, the distinct identities of many people were reduced to bare life. They were calmly eliminated from the historical "facts" of the world without any established guilt on their part.

In this historical context, it deserves attention that the famous first sentence of Wittgenstein's *Tractatus* (1921) "The world is all that is the case" — or, more accurately, what the elusive and changeable constellation of its "facts" states is the case — reflects the same uncanny sense of the utter contingency of world affairs. Wittgenstein's two key hypotheses — "[t]he sense of the world must lie outside the world" (Wittgenstein 2016: 6.41) and "[i]f there is a worth in the world [. . .] it must lie outside it" (6.53) — refuse to accept the "lie" of the so-called facts as the necessary "order of the world", to put this in the vocabulary of Josef K. from Kafka's *Trial* (2009: 159, trans. modified: *Die Lüge wird zur Weltordnung gemacht*; Kafka 1994: 233). Like Kafka's Josef,[5] Wittgenstein instead assumes the existence of an excluded transcendental "order" of which the given worldly "order" is but a distorted manifestation. He reinforces this assumption also through his dictum "Ethics is transcendental" (Wittgenstein 2016: 6.421), which relegates ethics to beyond the boundaries of the politically given world. Through the statement "Ethics and aesthetics are one", parenthesized in the same paragraph, he attributes to art the ethical task of saving this transcendental order of oblivion by exploring innumerable possibilities unimplemented by the "factual" world.

Haunted by the feeling of unhomeliness in such a world imposed by history, Benjamin likewise experiences its political distribution of "facts" as discriminating. It dispossesses some of its inhabitants in favor of others, bereaving them of human rights and forcing them into a subhuman existence. These enforced subalterns become the sources of his ethical commitment. They are, as Benjamin formulates in the essay on Kafka, "neither members of, nor strangers to, any [. . .] groups of figures, but, rather, messengers from one to another" (2007a: 117). The true redemption comes from their "intermediate worlds" as

---

5 On the very eve of his court ordered execution, Josef K. asks himself: "Were there still objections he'd forgotten? Of course there were. Logic may be unshakable, but it cannot hold out against a human being who wants to live" (Kafka 2009: 164). He therefore equally attaches his hopes to the unexplored potentialities of the world as Wittgenstein, Benjamin, and some other prominent contemporaries do.

the containers of that which the historical world has pushed into oblivion. Captured in the swampy ground of fluctuating experiences, the suppressed remnants of the prehistoric time, they break out from the restricted mythic space of an exclusively human history into the wider areas of subhuman creatures beyond the boundaries of the imposed "fate". "Everything forgotten mingles with what has been forgotten of the prehistoric world, forms countless, uncertain, changing compounds, yielding a constant flow of new, strange products" (Benjamin 2007a: 131). Since the condition of oblivion deforms these in-betweens, writes Benjamin, we feel guilty when we confront them in the attics, broom closets, and corridors in the same way as we used to feel "before the court of justice" (Benjamin 2007a: 133). Indeed, before the "court of justice" of the postimperial world, these "zones of indistinction" summon us to redeem their inhabitants (Benjamin 2007a: 134).

In *The Origin of German Tragic Drama*, Benjamin likens such zones to "the room of a magician, a physicist, a nursery, a junk room, and a pantry", which are cluttered, disordered, and contain all manner of things without any recognizable meaning or context (1980a: 363). However, their seemingly amateurish accumulation of fragments, rubbish, and emblems, "without a strict idea of a goal", in fact expects a "wonder" from the "figural center" that it demarcates (Benjamin 1980a: 364). From its peculiar "mixture of old elements", it imagines that a "new whole" will emerge (Benjamin 1980a: 355). Explaining in a letter to Max Brod from November 1917 why his notebooks contain heterogeneous literary fragments without any recognizable ultimate goal, Kafka likewise expresses his "hope that a whole will be made up of these bits, an instance of appeal on whose breasts I will be able to beat when I am in need" (1958: 195). If it is anywhere in the world, then a hope for something new resides in these indistinct mixtures. After all, they are epitomized in Benjamin's own notebooks, which were filled with most diverse quotations. Their main task "consisted in tearing fragments out of their context and arranging them afresh in such a way that they illustrated one another and were able to prove their *raison d'être* in a free-floating state" (Arendt 2007: 47). The U.S.-American anthropologist Elisabeth Povinelli has taken up this weak messianic thread by stating that new forms of life persevere as these zones' moments of "miraculization", which never stop disturbing ruling biopolitical formations (Povinelli 2011: 10).

The equivocation of in-betweens

In his essay "How newness enters the world", addressed in the introduction, Bhabha reiterates the delineated Benjamin's messianic engagement of the "zones of indistinction". However, in postcolonial circumstances, he focuses on the new category of in-betweens, detecting them at the boundary between the colony and metropolis. These are colonial migrants and minorities who, in the Western countries as their new domiciles, lead "borderline existences" (Bhabha 1994: 218) and live "hybrid hyphenations" (1994: 219). Since incommensurable elements make the basis of their cultural identifications — "where difference is neither One nor the Other but something else besides" (1994: 219) — they expose the limits of any claim to cultural difference of the metropolis' residents. Their indistinct, neither-nor spaces re-inscribe with their "innovative energy" (1994: 220) the forgotten past in the metropolis' present, redrawing its boundaries and opening it toward a different future. By dramatizing through "the indeterminacy of [their] diasporic identity" (1994: 225) and their in-between positions "the activity of culture's untranslatability" (1994: 224), they ultimately manage to revise the entire "problem of the global space" (1994: 223). Within its "body of the law", that is to say, they establish "a series of caesurae and divisions", (Agamben 2005a: 35) thus turning the global space into the state of exception. Their borderline negotiations hybridize and saturate it with the contingent and indeterminate (Bhabha 1994: 225).

In the same way that Benjamin analyzed Kafka's works, Bhabha analyzes Salman Rushdie's *Satanic Verses* to illustrate such disjunctive rewriting of the global space from the perspective of its in-betweens. According to Benjamin's reading of Kafka, in Jewish tradition, the representative of the official doctrine is the Halakhah, the collective body of Jewish religious laws that has to be duly transmitted through the Haggadah, its narrative implementation. Yet instead of faithfully reproducing the doctrine, Kafka's scattered Haggadah denounces its "sickness". In lieu of serving it, his parables "unexpectedly raise a mighty paw against it" (Benjamin 2007c: 143–144). Analogously, as Bhabha spells out, Rushdie subverts the Koran and contests its authority by relocating its truths into the world of minor and migrant "enunciatory positions and possibilities". Like Kafka's, his cultural translation is desacralizing and insurgent (Bhabha 1994: 226), stressing the foreign "mode of signification" in the midst of the dominant culture (Bhabha 1994: 227). With its "indeterminate temporality of the in-between", the foreign becomes "the unstable element of linkage" to other in-betweens, i.e. of the negation of the dominant culture through negotiation with the dominated ones (Bhabha 1994: 227). While establishing themselves through the subject positions that articulate alternative practices and values, minor and migrant agencies forge an "insurgent intersubjectivity" and "affiliative solidarity" (Bhabha 1994: 230). Like Benjamin, Bhabha invests his hope in such new commonality that emerges from the linkages between these "unstable elements" across the global space. He accordingly speaks of the "third space" which, negotiating incommensurable differences between the cultures of different epochs and locations "creates a tension peculiar to borderline existences" (Bhabha 1994: 218). Its "non-synchronous temporality" that "expands our sensorium to some new dimensions" significantly recalls Benjamin's "now-time" (*Jetztzeit*) that, with the same effect, establishes affinities between bits and pieces of different times and spaces (Benjamin 1977d: 258).

However, by reading the interlocking operations of Indian migrants as a sort of universal emancipation, Bhabha suppresses how they originate in biased phantasms. All subalterns exempt themselves from the frustrating communities which they *belong to* by forging imagined alliances with spatially and temporally distant others which they *long for*. Yet, such a self-exemption from the historical law of common belonging into an indeterminate prehistorical law that one is longing for, is an equivocal operation. The distant others are by definition inarticulate, which makes them spectrally threatening in the migrants' located perception. Therefore, the migrants first have to 'familiarize' them by attributing them desirable qualities that enable their assimilation into the community-to-come. The consequence of such 'preliminary taming' of the inarticulate others is that a sort of self-assertion inheres to any self-exemption from the rules of the community of belonging. In contrast to Bhabha's perception of the migrants' identifying operation as self-denying, what is actually at stake is an operation of "inverse ventriloquism" (Anderson 1991: 198). It is not the unknown others who speak through the migrants' selves but their unknown selves — which they hide in front of both the others and themselves — who speak through the others whom they identify with. This means that they dispossess the others of their distinct identities with the covert aim of making up for their own analogous dispossession by the community which they politically belong to. Because distinct identities would oblige the distant others to their particular locations, the migrants blur them to make these others fit their desired liberation.

As the migrants' turning of the distant others into the "floating signifiers" of their desire inadvertently repeats the dispossessing operation that turned them into the migrants, it presents itself as a remedial rather than emancipating undertaking. The proliferation of the hybrid, liminal, and indistinct in-betweens, characteristic of both Benjamin's and Bhabha's idea of worlding, makes up for the loss of distinction that was politically inflicted upon this proliferation's carrier group, i.e. the subjects of hyphenated identities. They were deeply frustrated by the *translatio imperii* into the nation-states after the dissolution of the German Empire (1918), respectively the British imperial rule in India (1947). Their new countries did not represent the interests of all their peoples equally but rather selectively and unevenly, which means that in both post-imperial Germany and postcolonial India, the former imperial discrimination of 'marginal' and 'inappropriate' population was invigorated instead of being abolished (Brubaker 1996: 51–52; Agamben 2005a: 14–16; Loomba 1998: 10–12). Such developments spawned both intellectuals' efforts to search for an alternative, "untranslatable" commonality that would overcome both the imperial and post-imperial, colonial and postcolonial discrimination. In the vocabulary of Gilles Deleuze, both equally victimize a "bastard", "inferior", "missing" people that "ceaselessly stirs beneath dominations", doomed to be "always in becoming, always incomplete" (Deleuze 1998: 4). It is in the name of this "always incomplete" people — or "pure potentiality" in the underground of ruling distinctions that it putatively represents[6] — that Benjamin and Bhabha project a community in becoming. In the interpretation of Deleuze and Guattari, "[t]o become is not to attain a form [. . .] but to find the zone of proximity, indiscernability, or indifferentiation where one can no longer be distinguished from a woman, an animal, a molecule" (1986: 1). Allocating the "bastards", along Benjamin's and Bhabha's lines,[7] the ethical task of making indistinguishable all that is distinguished, Deleuze and Guattari conceive them as the forces of emancipation and liberation.

However, fifteen years later, Deleuze cautions that the *fundamental equivocation* of their undertaking might disturb the envisaged emancipation. On the one hand the "bastards" democratically expropriate dominating agencies, but on the other, in introducing through their devastating "delirium" a worldwide "displacement of races and continents", they simultaneously "erect a race" which is "pure and dominant" (Deleuze 1998: 4). "[T]here is always the risk that a diseased state will interrupt the process of becoming [. . .] the constant risk that the delirium of domination will be mixed with a bastard delirium, pushing

---

[6] According to Agamben's famous interpretation (1999b: 243–245), which connects on the previous one proposed by Deleuze (1998: 68–90), the exemplary representative of "pure potentiality" is Herman Melville's figure of Bartleby. Through his notorious hesitation, he engages miming operations to outmaneuver various 'fundamentals' by means of which his political space's appointed guardians eliminate potentiality from it (Agamben 1999b: 249).

[7] Next to the works of Deleuze, Guattari, and Agamben, Benjamin and Bhabha's blurring of distinctions powerfully resonates in the recent work of Emily Apter, who introduced their concept of translation into the vocabulary of comparative literature. Speaking in the name of globalization's victims, she equally privileges literature of exilic consciousness (Apter 1995: 92) or one that emerges from a translation failure, mistranslation, the contresense, the unsayable, the inexpressible, and the non-sensical (Apter 2013: 9–11). She also only authorizes such a translation of life into its manifestations that fosters and proliferates life's interminable labyrinths. Inasmuch as such translation "belongs fully to no one" but life that negates all property, it is for Apter "a model of deowned literature" (2013: 15) or "screwed-up literature" that turns the world of properties upside down (2013: 18). Along with Benjamin, Bhabha, Deleuze, and Agamben, she celebrates literature to the degree to which it exempts itself from the world's distinct presence into its remote and indistinct "outside".

literature toward a larval fascism, the disease against which it fights" (Deleuze 1998: 4). Deleuze's fear concerning the "diseased" state as exemplified in the permanent state of exception echoes the dilemma from the book on Kafka, concerning the final effect of his deterritorializing narrative technique: is it liberating or enslaving, revolutionary or fascist, socialist or capitalist? How to disentangle these two inextricable aspects reliably? The dangers inherent in all-equalizing deterritorializations of identities are exemplified in capitalism, Stalinism, and fascism (Deleuze and Guattari 1986: 57) or, as we might now add, various unleashed populisms from a more recent time. Once the prehistoric forces of amalgamation break into the historic word of distinctions, it is impossible to prevent the overturning of the envisaged emancipation into mastery, which makes their advocacy a risky enterprise.

To summarize, the questions that have to be raised concerning the deterritorialization of distinct identities amount to the following: Does everyone benefit equally from its all-engulfing whirl, i.e. curious tourists and travelling intellectuals parallel to exiles, expatriates and refugees? If the proper human only emerges when it is displaced into the indistinct and inhuman, what about those humans whose obliteration of identity distinctions takes the form of territorial dispossession? What about those who are delivered to an utter deprivation of belonging, confronting the imperative to either leave their proper place or become riveted to the land they have been dispossessed of (Butler 2012: 21–24)? The desire which they have to *belong* is, by such deterritorializations, forced to acknowledge the impossibility of ever truly belonging (Probyn 1996: 8). From this point of view, the longing for a community-to-come is an agent of globalization, which kidnaps the right of belonging to given communities. It creates "at least as much trouble as possibility" and contributes "as much to exploitation and poverty as to wealth creation and economic participation" (Alexander 2012: 159). Its inclusiveness rests on exclusion, its tolerance on the long history of imperialism and colonialism accompanied by atrocities (Brown 2006: 37–38). Making up for the frustrations that were inflicted on them by their post-imperial, respectively postcolonial, states, Benjamin and Bhabha advocate such a commonality in the permanent state of exception, disregarding its concomitant perilous effects. For it does not deactivate but rather reanimate, strengthen, and expand the ill-reputed sovereignty. It is precisely the suspension of law, which it executes, that makes room for its reemergence in an illegitimate, extra-legal form, characterized by violence.

In the permanent state of exception, the sovereignty acquires the grotesque form of the whimsical, unpredictable, and tyrannical operations of its populist executors. Since their actions are no longer subject to review by any higher judicial authority, their managerial power is invigorated (Butler 2004: 61). In the new form of political legitimacy with no built-in structures of accountability, populist sovereigns usurp the right to suspend rights, which makes their relation to law exploitative, instrumental, and arbitrary. The population is managed through a deconstitution or "spectralization" of its humanity, which increases the disposability and "consumability" of the managed "items" (Bales 1999: 25). Ultimately, far from eliminating the compromised sovereignty, the state of exception, through its invention of the *translation of the untranslatable*, inaugurates a potentially disastrous populist technique for its re-legitimation and rejuvenation. Contrary to what Benjamin and Bhabha envisioned, it acts as the agent of the recuperation of that which it claims to be dethroning.

3 The Ethical Appeal of the Indifferent: Maurice Blanchot and Michel Foucault

Ever since its emergence, the modern concept of revolution rests on an ambiguity. While it insists on the present's intellectual sovereignty over the past, it cannot get rid of its pre-modern predecessor, re-evolution, which indicates the present's affective dependence on the past. In her seminal book published on the eve of the '68 protests, Hannah Arendt points out how much the idea of *revolvere*, the turning back of the historical process toward the restoration of a bygone age, inspired both American and French revolutionaries. Both wanted "to revolve back to an 'early period' when they had been in the possession of rights and liberties of which tyranny and conquest had dispossessed them" (Arendt 1990: 45).

Because of this constitutive equivocality of the concept of revolution, the French revolutionaries' erasure of their adherence to the past strikes us, in retrospect, as a defense maneuver. Is their presentation of revolution as a definite departure from past customs and laws not significantly unilateral? In this sense, it is interesting that, according to a radical document from 1793, "[t]here is nothing, absolutely nothing in common between the slave of a tyrant and the inhabitant of a free state; the customs of the latter, his principles, his sentiments, his actions, all must be new" (cited in Hunt 1984: 29). The very insistence with which they create their cult of the new as something "outside all forms and all rules" (Hunt 1984: 27) reflects a profound fear of the old. (Starr 1995: 1) This means that the modern concept of revolution, from the very beginning of its historical trajectory, inconspicuously interferes with the pre-modern concept of re-evolution as a cyclical return to origins. Since it proved unable to discard this older concept, "modern theorists and practitioners of revolution" were condemned "to an obsessively repetitive fascination with revolution *as* repetition" (Starr 1995: 2).

The conservative New Philosophers employed this, as it were, malformation of revolution in their argument that, in Michael Ryan's paraphrase, "whatever alternative is set up in opposition to the Master will be yet another Master" (Ryan 1982: 76). Since humankind cannot avoid the repetition of the same, in their opinion the idea of the historical progress proves to be obsolete. In opposition to these New Philosophers, liberal thinkers noticed that this cyclical logic never smoothly overcomes the linear one without simultaneously being displaced by its uncanny residue. Sigmund Freud defines his concept of the uncanny (*das Unheimliche*, which also means "the unhomely") as the unexpected revival of the surmounted mode of thinking (Freud 2005: 232). But the same uncanny leftover certainly operates in the opposite direction, accompanying the putative liquidation of the cyclical logic by the linear one. Arendt has famously argued that in the key declarations of the French Revolution, the apparently universal human rights were spontaneously identified with the restricted national citizen rights, which left stateless populations and individuals without "the right of bearing rights" (Arendt 1979: 299–300). The poor, women, workers, and elderly were now all included, but at the cost of excluded foreigners. This is how exclusion, in the linear logic of history, smuggled itself back into the inclusion that was determined to relinquish it.

This disjunctive conjunction of the present and the past characterizes the relationship between the events of May '68 and the theoretical work that followed it, known under the label of *l'après-Mai* or post-May. As in all *post*-relationships, historical events and their after-effects turn out to be simultaneously discontinuous and continuous. On the one hand, the trauma associated with the failure of May '68 separated revolutionary practice and theory from one another; on the other hand, the obligation of theory to rescue the traumatized political energies reconnected them. Since the direct political action of eliminating power relations ended in a structural complicity with the antagonist, the theory replaced its directness and immediacy with the long-term subversion, dislocation, and deconstruction of power. For example, Jacques Derrida (1981b: 42, 66) insisted on the displacement of direct repetition through its indistinct leftovers, such as the *pharmakon*, the supplement, or the hymen. Consequently, in the intellectual developments following the May events, the urgent and immediate revolutionary drive that characterized the events of May '68 transformed into a strategic postponement of revolution. What the theory now aimed at was not to abolish the past but to draw attention to its uncanny residues and the way they stubbornly persevered in the present by limiting its sovereignty. Derrida accordingly stated the following: "in a certain way the only thing which interests me is the uncanny" (2003: 33–34). Maurice Blanchot, for his part, addressed the obligation to "recollect that which escapes recollection" and which "transforms our possibilities into impossibilities" (1980: 15, 114). Rather than being homely and familiar, the present of post-May thinkers was interrupted by the interventions of the remnants from the colonial past and the Holocaust, and all the more so the more the theorists avoided addressing these traumas directly.

Defining contemporariness as "*that relationship with time that adheres to it through a disjunction and an anachronism*" (Agamben 2010: 11), Giorgio Agamben in retrospect, perfectly captures these thinkers' experience of their post-revolutionary present:

> The contemporary is he who firmly holds his gaze on his own time so as to perceive not its light but rather its darkness. All eras, for those who experience contemporariness, are obscure. The contemporary is precisely the person who knows how to see this obscurity, who is able to write by dipping his pen in the obscurity of the present. (2010: 13)

As we know from Agamben's reading of Aristotle in "Bartleby or On Contingency," the "obscurity" into which the contemporary "dips his pen" is the present's "pure potentiality" or "zone of indistinction" that precedes all its actual distinctions (Agamben 1999b: 243–245). It is the task of philosophy to relentlessly recall this abyss of possibilities in the underground of the actual world, against theology and its incessant attempts to erase its traces from the present memory (Agamben 1999b: 249). Staying loyal to this weak messianic mission of uncovering the actual world's contingency, Agamben (2009: 75–76) portrays the present as being saturated with the unresolved "signatures" of the past, signatures that are secretive, imperceptible, and immaterial but which nonetheless confront the present with the demand to recognize, read, and thus redeem them.

This passionate attachment of Agamben's philosophy to a sacrificed past helps us to understand how the appeal of the indifferent came into being in the post-May post-traumatic atmosphere. However, since the attribute of indifference refers simultaneously to the detached attitude of sovereigns and the amorphous condition of subordinates, one is both empowered and disempowered by its appeal. To understand how equivocal are its effects upon its agencies, consider the revolutionary concept of indifferent *écriture* as elaborated by Blanchot. In his 1952 book *The Space of Literature*, where he introduces the affiliate concept of *désoeuvrement*, Blanchot (1992: 42–48) describes Stéphane Mallarmé as the first writer to dethrone the sovereign literary author by setting loose the unworking energy of *écriture*. In his 1969 book *The Infinite Conversation*, Blanchot interprets *écriture* as an amorphous and indistinct practice of "always going beyond what it seems to contain and affirming nothing but its own outside" (1993: 259); faceless as it is, it takes place "beyond the reach of the one who says it as much as of the one who hears it" (1993: 212). Epitomizing the *désoeuvrement* located at the "other scene," it operates beyond the reach of any of its users, continuously disempowering their authorial claims. However, as Agamben has argued in *The Time that Remains* (2005b: 88–112), the long messianic tradition inherent in Blanchot's notion of *désoeuvrement* makes the disempowerment of others and the self-empowerment strongly reliant on one another. While disempowering literary authors, *écriture* simultaneously empowers its own authorial capacity.

As such, it threatens to replace the author by serving as a new sovereign transcendental that determines all subordinate agencies. To avoid such malformation of revolution through the redoubling of sovereignty in the subordinate agency that dethroned it, Blanchot makes his transcendental disappear, as it were, before its installment, thereby taking recourse in Michel Foucault's famous designation of man in *The Order of Things* (1971: 387). In his essay on Foucault, Blanchot (1987: 76) presents this quasi-transcendental as the "new manner of being which disappearance is," as the state of continuous dispersal, discontinuation, and redoubling. He insists that Foucault's transcendental principle not only *determines* the empirical agency but also *results* from this agency as its after-effect. In short, in Foucault's work the transcendental principle becomes future anterior. This parenthesizes its a priori character and weakens its determining force, producing "an impure alloy of an historical a priori and a formal a priori" or a "flawed transcendentalism" (Blanchot 1987: 71–72). With modernity, as Blanchot interprets Foucault, *a disempowering empowerment of the two incompatible terms, the transcendental and the empirical*, arises: the one makes the other simultaneously possible and impossible. "Transcendence is brought down, the empirical rises up, the modern era is ushered in." (Blanchot 1993: 255) The sovereign takes a new, subordinate shape by shifting from the political to an ethical agency.

Drawing a number of important consequences from this disabling enablement, Blanchot asks:

> What speaks when the voice speaks? It situates itself nowhere, [. . .] but manifests itself in a space of redoubling, of echo and resonance where it is not someone, but rather this *unknown* space [. . .] that speaks without speaking. (1993: 258)

Specifying the peculiar profile of the voice, he writes that "anterior to beginning, it indicates itself only as anteriority, always in retreat in relation to what is anterior" (Blanchot 1993: 259). In order not to be assimilated into the imperial linguistic order, this simultaneously evasive and invasive leftover retreats into a cry or murmur of a "man in passing": "he cries out in dying; he does not cry out, he is the murmur of this cry" (1993: 262; "il crie mourant; il ne crie pas, il est le murmure du cri" [Blanchot 1969: 392]). This is how Blanchot conceptualizes the reiterative unworking of transcendental writing:

> Writing [. . .] will constitute itself [. . .] as always going beyond what it seems to contain and affirming nothing but its own outside, [. . .] affirming itself [. . .] in relation to its absence, the absence of (a) work, unworking (1993: 259; trans. modified: "l'absence d'oeuvre ou le désoeuvrement" [1969: 388]).

In his re-description of Foucault, the transcendental is exposed to persistent *désoeuvrement* by its empirical "outside," or the "zone of indistinction" that escapes its distinguishing procedures (Agamben 1998: 63, 112, 181). In this way,

3 The Ethical Appeal of the Indifferent: Maurice Blanchot and Michel Foucault — 63

the hitherto traumatized "outside" henceforth occupies the traumatizing position, circumventing and subverting its appropriation by the transcendental.

Blanchot seems to have taken the concept of unworking from the writings of Alexandre Kojève, the crucial intellectual figure in postwar France. Kojève (1952: 396) designated the idle man of *posthistoire* as a *voyou désoeuvré*, a man in the condition of the eternal Sabbath. However, Blanchot refuses to share Kojève's apocalyptic Hegelianism and its postponement of the Sabbath to the end of history, because he feels that it surreptitiously re-introduces theology into philosophy. The theological synthesis that violently captures the totality of history, renouncing the compromising involvement of the philosopher in its course, had to be unworked. To accomplish this, Blanchot uncouples *désoeuvrement* from philosophy and aligns it with Mallarmé's modern, self-subverting idea of literature. "Literature denies the substance of what it represents," reads the definition of literature's "essence" in Blanchot's 1949 book *The Work of Fire*: "This is its law and its truth" (1995d: 310). Literature's permanent unrest becomes the model of unworking: "As soon as something is said, something else needs to be said. Then something different must again be said to resist the tendency of all that has just been said to become definitive [. . .]. There is no rest," writes Blanchot (1995d: 22). He thus promotes the Romantic, ceaselessly self-denying idea of literature as the ethical representative of the politically indifferent subalterns. He gives such literature the messianic task of redeeming the subalterns' zones of indistinction. Through his reading of Herman Melville's Bartleby as the "messiah of de-creation," Agamben (1999b: 274) tacitly reaffirms this mission. His Bartleby descends into the underground of the actual world, in which indifference reigns over difference, to keep alive the memory of all the possibilities that were deprived of actualization.

In his essay on Blanchot, Foucault (1987: 13) likewise sides with his friend's claim that the modern age is commanded by literature, which, more than any other discourse, leads us "to the outside in which the speaking subject disappears." Blanchot's insight is crucial because "the being of language only appears for itself with the disappearance of the subject" (1987: 15). According to Foucault, Blanchot consistently testifies to this void in language as induced by its master's irrevocable exile. He treats both discourses that he regularly uses, the reflexive one and the fictional one, as being outside of themselves by pushing the reflexive discourse to the edge of fiction and the fictional discourse to the edge of reflection. In the same way that Foucault, according to Blanchot, made the formal and historical a priori undecidably confront one another (Blanchot 1987: 71–72), Blanchot, according to Foucault, makes reflection and fiction enter an interminable dialogue. None of the two antagonists can overcome its exilic condition. Moreover, Foucault claims that Blanchot not only displays an emptiness genuine to language (Foucault 1987: 12), but also contests an "entire tradition wider than philosophy," denying that emptiness by filling it always anew with a particular content (1987: 13).

His argument is that Blanchot courageously confronted this powerful tradition because he was desperately attracted, in the dense structure of language, to "an absence that pulls as far away from itself as possible" and "has nothing to offer but the infinite void" (Foucault 1987: 28). This attraction to the disregarded indifferent makes Blanchot negligent of the politically established differential order: "To be susceptible to attraction a person must be negligent," writes Foucault (1987: 28). This negligence is nonetheless extremely dangerous because the inarticulate outside, through its endless withdrawal, gradually removes the human subject from his or her articulation (Foucault 1987: 34), making his or her past, kin, and whole life non-existent (1987: 28). In Emmanuel Lévinas's terms, the inarticulate outside tears the human subject out of his or her abode. In his view, this (preconscious, pre-linguistic, pre-present, pre-representative, pre-signifying) locus of alterity "prohibits me with the original language of its defenseless eyes" (Levinas 1996: 12). Because I cannot take cognizance of an instance haunting and obsessing me in such a traumatizing way, I definitely lose the Other as a comfortable, confirming mirror of my identity. Instead, the relationship with Him "puts me into question, empties me of myself" (Levinas 1986: 350).

As if hinting at the Levinasian retreating, ab-solving, ambiguous face, Foucault describes this spectral outside as "a gaze condemned to death," averting and returning "to the shadow the instant one looks at it" (Foucault 1987: 28, 41). As soon as its withdrawal from the field of vision occurs, however, its underground voice becomes discernible (Foucault 1987: 47). As Lévinas writes: "To see a face is already to hear 'You shall not kill'" (1990: 8); or: "The manifestation of the face is already discourse." (Levinas 1969: 66) Reading Blanchot in such a distinctively Levinasian key (without ever mentioning Lévinas), Foucault asks: "Is not this voice – which 'sings blankly' and offers little to be heard – the voice of the Sirens, whose seductiveness resides in the void they open, in the fascinating immobility seizing all who listen?" (1987: 45) For Foucault, Blanchot was powerfully seduced by this lethal void, regardless of the price of denial and solitude he paid for this fascination (Blanchot 1993: 201). This price is yet another reason for Foucault to interpret Blanchot's "thought from outside" as an *ethical resistance to the politically dominant linguistic order*, resistance in the name of its disregarded outside.

In his reading of Foucault, Blanchot, for his part, stresses the irresistible "appeal of *indifference*" to being subjected to further differentiation (1993: 199). Indifference continuously sets the new horizon for the operations of differentiation. Its "flawed transcendentalism" is on the permanent quasi-empirical move.

> Preventing the sick from dying in the street, the poor from becoming criminals, the debauched from perverting the pious is not at all reprehensible, but is a sign of progress, the point of departure for changes that 'responsible authorities' would approve of.
> (Blanchot 1987: 65–66)

The ethical task undertaken by Foucault is to let the disregarded, which is located "outside everything visible and everything invisible" (Blanchot 1993: 256), re-enter the articulated order. Foucault's "redoubling" makes a messianic *promise never to be fulfilled but nonetheless forwarded through the postponement*. He is aware that his search for the truth is irrevocably enmeshed in "the myriad configurations of power" (Blanchot 1987: 68) that pervert his imperatives. This is why he used to "proceed to the very limit" of a given discourse and then, starting the same route again, "turned toward other horizons" (Blanchot 1987: 69). A "man always on the move," he toyed "with the thought that he might have been, had fate so decided, a statesman (a political advisor) as well as a writer [. . .] or a pure philosopher" (Blanchot 1987: 68) or, as the original – but not the translation – continues, "an unqualified worker, that is, nothing or nobody in particular" ("ou un travailleur sans qualification, donc un je ne sais quoi ou un je ne sais qui" [Blanchot 1986: 17]).

At this point, returning to the initial ambiguity of the concept of revolution and its inextricable intermingling of disempowerment and empowerment, one is well advised to recall Lacan's psychoanalysis. In Lacanian terms, Blanchot's and Foucault's *je ne sais quoi* ("nothing particular" and at once "something unfathomable") takes the appearance of the "real," the zone of indistinction of the symbolic order (Lacan 1988: 97), which "resists symbolization" (Lacan 1987: 66) or "subsists outside of symbolization" (Lacan 2006: 324). While being dispossessed by the symbolic distinctions and placed below the threshold of their operations, the real at the same time operates as their supreme dispossessor, which in its turn degrades them into a mere "grimace" of the real (Lacan 1991: 17). As if captured by this fundamental equivocality of his concept, Lacan, in his early work, interprets the real as a realm beyond appearances or imagination (2006: 68–69); in his late work, however, the real figures as *the decisive, most powerful instance in the constitution of the human subject*. In this light, Foucault's radical ethical readiness to completely dissolve his identity, to let his thought pass "through what is called madness," to "withdraw from itself, turn away from a mediating and patient labor [. . .] toward a searching that is distracted and astray [. . .] without result and without works" (Blanchot 1993: 199), presents itself as surreptitious self-empowerment. This insistent self-*désoeuvrement* repeats the analogous gesture of Blanchot's unworking of his own self, based as it was on the same fascination with the annihilating outside. Gradually and imperceptibly, in both works, the resistance to the imposed transcendental condition turns into a passionate attachment to a new transcendental that puts all modern selves under equal pressure, disregarding their entirely different political conditions. This is the final consequence of the sublime ethical rendering of the indifference as it completely ignores its dispossessing and denigrating political dimension.

What is forgotten here is that to be indifferent toward all political identities is miles away from being banished into the political condition of indifference (or 'bare life' deprived of human attributes): the first, ethical self-exemption from all identities implies the unlimited mobility of the self, while the second, politically enforced condition of, for example, 'boat people' or *sans-papiers* condemns people to deprivation and immobility. As Elisabeth Povinelli (2011: 11) writes: "[A] gap seems to open between those who reflect on and evaluate ethical substance and those who *are* this ethical substance." Or, again, as Zygmunt Bauman puts it:

> The first travel at will, get much fun from their travel [. . .], are [. . .] welcomed with smiles and open arms [. . .]. The second travel surreptitiously, often illegally, sometimes paying more for the crowded steerage of a stinking unseaworthy boat than others pay for business-class gilded luxuries – and are frowned upon [. . .] arrested and promptly deported, when they arrive. (1998: 89)

To be sure, Blanchot and Foucault are not the only post-May intellectuals who follow the ethical imperative of self-*désoeuvrement* by disregarding this imperative's traumatic political prerogative. Gilles Deleuze and Félix Guattari, defining deterritorialization as a dislocation of a located agency (1983: 322; 1986: 86), also address its two principal faces: the actual one, represented by enforced movements, evacuations, and deportations, and the virtual one, represented by the liberation of an agency's slumbering creative potential (Deleuze and Guattari 1987: 55–56). Since actual deterritorializations regularly aim at the reterritorialization of the population in question, Deleuze and Guattari see them as being oppressive and restricted, whereas in their view the virtual ones, insofar as they aim at a permanent emancipation of an agency, operate as the proper carriers of democracy. In a word, the deterritorialization that was set in motion by European modernity is good when it liberates, as in the case of individual agencies, but bad when it coerces, as in the case of dislocated populations.

However, if anything, modernity teaches that, in Arjun Appadurai's words, "one man's imagined community is another man's political prison" (Appadurai 1998: 32). As soon as the deterritorialization of identities entered the East-Central European space after the dissolution of empires, it replaced its West European virtual and liberating face with an actual and coercive one, initiating hitherto unimaginable migrations of populations: "By 1890 close to 40 percent of all Austro-Hungarians had left their original place of *Heimat* and migrated to their current homes from another part of the monarchy." (Judson 2016: 334) Almost four million men and women moved overseas, but hundreds of thousands returned within a few years. "The Fall of the Habsburgs automatically turned the 25 percent of the Viennese population born outside the frontiers of the new Austria into foreigners." (Hobsbawm 1996: 15) After the breakup of the Soviet Union, twenty-five million Russians who had been colonized in various territories across the Empire from the mid-sixteenth century to the mid-twentieth century (Brubaker 1996: 150) suddenly remained outside the Russian Federation (Brubaker 1996: 6–7). It goes without saying that such a traumatic reconfiguration of post-imperial Europe's geopolitical circumstances dispossessed the majority of its population of its distinct identities, making it politically "disposable."

Therefore, whoever raises the free mobility of indifferent individual identities to a transcendental principle, disregards the enforced mobility of the politically indifferent masses as the hidden empirical prerogative of this principle and the subterraneous basis of its legitimacy. Indeed, does the individual ethical self-denial not surreptitiously aim at the redemption of the politically dispossessed collectivities by inadvertently reproducing their collective empowerment-through-disempowerment, i.e. the turning of their utter dispossession into the source of their self-aggrandizement? It is in this way that the dispossessed Jews became the guardians of human universality,[1] whereas the proletarians took their utter dispossession as the warrant for their future rise to power: "We have been naught, we shall be all." Such a triumphant empowerment of the ethical indifferent that absorbs into its emptiness all seemingly petty political differences – as in the case of Derrida's *différance*, undecidability, or deconstruction – involuntarily blends the elite individuals' refined way of thinking with the deprived collectives' populist logic. The ethical silently acquires political contours.

These are some of the uneasy consequences of the post-May thought as they present themselves to its descendants. Yet stranded as they were in their post-May political circumstances, both Blanchot and Foucault failed to address them. For this reason, at a distance of some fifty years, the political background of their ethical fascination with the indifferent requires our attention and consideration. Instead of being seduced into reproducing this fascination, we ought to scrutinize it by drawing careful political limits on its compensatory rule.

---

[1] For example, Gustav Mahler treats the Jewish triple bereavement of homeland (Beller 1989: 207) as the epitome of human emancipation, and Kraus (1898: 23) gives the same meaning to the Jewish complete dissolution into surrounding cultures. Liska (2017: 127–136) critically reviews a series of more recent attempts to promote Jewish rootlessness to the blueprint of a limitlessly inclusive human identity.

Part II: Franz Kafka and the Performance of Sacrifice

4 Unleashed Contingency? The Deterritorialization of Reality in *The Trial*

Deterritorializing the logical space of the world

Ludwig Wittgenstein's *Tractatus Logico-Philosophicus*, which was composed during the First World War, bears the clear mark of its birthplace already in its famous first sentence: "The world is all that is the case." As the philosopher spells out, the world amounts to the totality of "facts, not things", yet one whose "sense" and "worth" "lie outside it" (2016: 6.41, 6.53). It follows that the criterion by which legal or historical 'facts' are selected out of all 'things' is out of the reach of world's residents. This new state of world's affairs – that none of its residents can learn which ultimate authority stands behind its "facts" (2016: 2, 2.01) – is the setting which, almost simultaneously with Wittgenstein's philosophical treatise, engenders Franz Kafka's novel *The Trial*. To recall one of its crucial scenes, the chaplain objects to Josef K.'s truth-oriented interrogation of the parable that was presented to him by pointing out that "one doesn't have to take everything as the truth, one just has to accept it as necessary" (Kafka 2009: 159). In other words, all members of a given community, irrespective of their attitude to its legal and historical facts, necessarily belong to the territory of reality that is determined by these facts. However, Josef K. as their victim replies to the chaplain, who as the court official (Kafka 2009: 160) represents them, that taking them as necessary means accepting "that the world is founded on untruth" (Kafka 2009: 159). The German original is much more direct, „Die Lüge wird zur Weltordnung gemacht", i.e., in this way "the lie is made the order of the world", which implies that 'facts' are discriminatory and deceitful. Instead of the egalitarian truth, biased power rules the world, opening amidst of it the imparity between its completely deterritorialized representatives and strictly territorialized victims. When Wittgenstein observes that, next to the truth of the world, its "ethics is transcendental" as well (2016: 6.421), Josef K.'s interrogation of the world's morality acquires legitimacy. Yet the chaplain does not deny the disputable profile of facts. People's opinions on them will always diverge, he says, but this will not change their executive power in the slightest. Does this remark not resonate in Kafka's diary entry of 21 October 1921: "All is imaginary (*Phantasie*) [. . .] but the closest reality (*nächste Wahrheit*) is only that you are beating your head against the wall of a windowless and doorless cell" (1976: 395; trans. modified)? The chaplain concludes: "What is written is unchanging, and opinions are often just an expression of despair at that." (Kafka 2009: 157) Thus, in his view, that which is written lies outside the legal and historical territory of reality, which it sets up for those who belong to it. Despite their disagreement, they must accept the place it allocates them within the delimited territory. This reproduces almost verbatim Wittgenstein's claim that we can interpret the world as we wish but this will not change its facts (2016: 6.373).

However, there is another, less visible Wittgenstein within the same book, one that anticipates the upcoming author of *Philosophical Investigations*. According to him, facts only acquire their necessary character within respective truth-conditions (2016: 4.41).[1] Once displaced outside them, they become contingent and arbitrary. At the very beginning of *Tractatus* (2016: 1.12) he reminds us that the "totality" of facts banishes "whatever is not the case" from the realm of legal and historical distinction. Whereas the chaplain in his capacity of the court official understandably stands for this logical 'totality', the philosopher toward the end of his book appoints both literature and philosophy with the task of exploring the area that is banished from it. Concerning literature, he claims that "Ethics and aesthetics are one" (2016: 6.421), which implies that its vocation is basically ethical. As regards philosophy, he claims that stating the facts in the manner of natural sciences "has nothing to do with philosophy" (2016: 6.53) and that all his propositions, which hitherto referred exclusively to the "logical space of the world" (as delineated in 1.13) were senseless and must be thrown away. They only served as the ladder for reaching the sense-giving area that lies beyond the space of facts (2016: 6.54). Unlike the facts, this sense cannot be *said* but only *shown* – a distinction which Wittgenstein thereupon, in a letter to Bertrand Russell, hardly accidentally addressed as his *Tractatus's* "main point" and the "cardinal problem of philosophy" (Stern 1996: 69–70). It is therefore in these terms that *Tractatus*'s final proposition "Whereof one cannot speak, thereof one must be silent" (2016: 7) ought to be understood. To be silent about something means to engage the language of *showing* instead of *saying*.

---

[1] "Truth-conditions" reads in the German original *Wahrheitsbedingungen*, which is a more ambiguous term. *Wahrheit* does not only mean "truth" but also "reality" (as in Goethe's *Wahrheit und Dichtung* for example). Therefore, when Josef K. states "Man muss nicht alles für wahr halten, man muss es nur für notwendig halten", the English translation of this sentence, accompanied by commentaries in terms of speech act theory, could read: "One does not have to take everything as the truth (in the "constative" sense of matching the state of affairs in the *world*), one just has to accept is as necessary (in the "performative" sense of establishing a binding *reality*)". From all *things* in the limitless world, *Wahrheitsbedingungen* single out the *facts* that oblige the "residents" of a particular reality. Rendered in these terms, Josef K. advocates world, the chaplain reality as the horizon of human orientation.

When Maurice Blanchot remarks that Kafka's language "wished only for silence" (Blanchot 1995a: 81), he unknowingly subscribes to Wittgenstein's thesis.[2] Some thirty five years later, in a very brief allusion to it for the initiated, he states that "in order to keep silent, one must talk" (Blanchot 1983: 92, *pour se taire, il faut parler*). But already in 1947, he is clear about what kind of language he means by silence. If Kafka's novels contain a "truth outside of literature" (Blanchot 1995b: 2), this truth belongs to "the silence of the absence" of all statements, an outside that, "invisible, unknown, and [. . .] inaccessible" (Blanchot 1997: 251), can be reached only by means of fiction. Thus, while Wittgenstein in the *logical* paragraphs of his *Tractatus Logico-Philosophicus* underpins the chaplain's official rendering of the world, in its *philosophical* paragraphs he shares the banished perspective of Josef K. who, on the very eve of his execution, remarks: "Logic may be unshakable, but it cannot hold out against a human being who wants to live." (Kafka 2009: 164) Beings that are put under the heavy pressure of logical facts try to exempt themselves from the territory of reality as delimited by them into the deterritorialized area of life that reveals this territory's arbitrariness. It is the exploration of this limitless, spectral, and indistinct area, which Wittgenstein envisions for philosophy and literature, and with which Blanchot associates his idea of literature, in particular Kafka's. In outlining and developing this line of argument, both spontaneously attach to Josef K.'s deterritorializing perspective against the chaplain's territorial point of view. Does Kafka indeed endorse Josef K. in his dispute with the chaplain?

A good decade ahead of Blanchot, Walter Benjamin also claimed that Kafka's literature deterritorializes the territory of reality. According to him, "Kafka's entire work constitutes a code of gestures" that are pulled out of their "common situations" and put on the stage of "the World Theater which opens up toward heaven" (Benjamin 2007a: 120). "Like El Greco, Kafka tears open the sky behind every gesture; but as with El Greco [. . .] the gesture remains the decisive thing, the center of the event." (2007a: 121) The ultimate 'stage' that hosts this gesture, although indicated behind the more discernible ones, escapes evidence. Divesting "the human gesture of its traditional supports" (2007a: 122), Kafka thus translates it from the legal and historical space of distinct facts into a broader, "impenetrable" and "incalculable" area (2007a: 123) that pushes "ordinary men" to the "limits of understanding" (2007a: 124). As he deprives his world of all former guarantees, such as divine providence or historical fate, his

---

[2] According to Matar, Blanchot does not seem to have read Wittgenstein before the 1960s, i.e. before the French translation of *Tractatus* appeared (1961). The only direct references to him in Blanchot's work stem from 1969 *Infinite Conversation* (1993: 332–339) and 1980 *The Writing of the Disaster* (1995e: 132).

readers have to find their way through his parables "circumspectly, cautiously, and suspiciously" (2007a: 124; trans. modified; *mit Umsicht, mit Behutsamkeit, mit Mißtrauen*). Yet, however attentively the readers explore their ramifications, they cannot exit into the reality 'itself', as for Kafka *reality itself amounts to parable*. After he dissolved the world's transcendental guarantees, he doomed its residents to an interminable search for its sense. Benjamin concludes: "Perhaps Kafka, whose every day on earth brought him up against undecipherable behaviors and indistinct announcements, at least in death wished to pay back to his fellow beings with the same currency" (2007a: 124, trans. modified; *vor unenträtselbare Verhaltungweisen und undeutliche Verlautbarungen gestellt hat, im Tode wenigstens seiner Mitwelt mit gleicher Münze heimzuzahlen*).

In this proposition that bears the weight of the essay's key insight, two points deserve closer elaboration. The first is "at least in death", which refers to Benjamin's interpretation of Kafka's aphorism "On parables" several pages earlier. In this perplexing staged dialogue, to an anonymous collective subject ("we") who sorely complains that the parables of sages are inapplicable in the predicaments of everyday life, one man replies: "Why such reluctance? If you only followed the parables you yourselves would become parables and with that rid of all your daily cares." (Kafka 1988i: 506) To clarify this enigmatic reply, Benjamin engages a Chinese legend, according to which a famous painter disappeared in his masterpiece by waving farewell to his assembled friends who admired it. After the author's dissolution in his testamentary painting, they will have to search for him through its endless labyrinths. Benjamin concludes that Kafka, carefully following the undecipherable parables of a world that was suddenly bereft of its ultimate authority, vanished like the Chinese painter in the labyrinths of his work and thus transformed himself into an interminable parable. Dispersing his authorship into the inextricable meanders of writing, he paid back to his fellow beings for having confronted him, during his lifetime, with "undecipherable behaviors and indistinct announcements".

In his first reading of Kafka from 1947, Blanchot in fact corroborated Benjamin's rendering of writer's radical self-deterritorialization, most probably without knowing it.[3] The key thesis of his "Reading Kafka" is that no reality by which literature might be measured exists outside literature. If there is reality, then in the form of a 'silent' outside which only literature can show. To reduce literature to prior reality means to deny this surplus released by it. To write means to yield oneself to this excess, which introduces an unbridgeable gap

---

3 "Benjamin does not appear to be among the names that possess great importance for Blanchot" and he does not mention him until the late 1960s. (Liska and Conen 2014: 229).

between the writer and his or her 'literary I'; the literary I continuously negates the writer, disengaging his or her life experience. This is the meaning of Blanchot's characteristically paradoxical statement: "Kafka's entire work is in search of an affirmation that it wants to gain by negation" (1995b: 7). Whoever directly affirms the writer's life experience forgets about its deterritorialization through the act of writing, which culminates in silence. "Reading Kafka" strongly opposes critics who pull Kafka out of this silence into whatever actual "truth" and invests serious effort to "return to silence a work that wished only for silence" (1995a: 81). According to *The Space of Literature* several years later, returning Kafka to silence means returning his personality to an "infinite dispersal" (1992: 33) through which it "became no one" (1992: 28), "a faceless third person" (1992: 30), an entity which, in the final rendering of *The Infinite Conversation*, is mobile, fragmented, and persistently missing (1993: 384, n. 2).

This is how Benjamin and Blanchot conceptualize the "death of the author" in Kafka's work much ahead of Barthes's famous essay (Barthes 1977): as the radical deterritorialization of the author's real parameters. The second point of interest in the above quoted Benjamin's proposition is his addressing of Kafka's "indistinct currency", which also vaguely anticipates Blanchot's neutral, faceless and disperse rendering of Kafka's *écriture* (again ahead of Barthes's concept of *écriture*; see Banfield 1985 and 1991). Kafka's "currency" is "indistinct" (*undeutlich*) because generated by an "impenetrable" and "incalculable" area (Benjamin 2007a: 123) that pushes "ordinary men" to the "limits of understanding" (Benjamin 2007a: 124). To elucidate Benjamin's thesis, we have to connect it with his 1923 essay "The Task of the Translator" in which he paradoxically claims that "no poem is intended for the reader, no picture for the beholder, no symphony for the listener" (2004: 75). The artworks exceed all their particular recipients because their signification (*die Art des Meinens*) – which, being continuously supplemented by other artworks, is "in a constant state of flux" (Benjamin 2004: 78) – goes far beyond any of their imaginable denotations (*das Gemeinte*). Benjamin's *elusive signification* as applied to Kafka's spatially and temporally deterritorialized fictions, once again, anticipates Blanchot's thesis of the constitutive gap between the "series of narrated events" and that which presents itself as its "true reading", i.e. the theme (Blanchot 1995b: 4). In fact, Blanchot insists on the untranslatability of Kafka's deterritorialized 'signifier' into any territorial 'signified' in the same way as Benjamin did. To reiterate, both identify Kafka in Josef K.'s 'emancipating' deterritorializing terms as opposed to the chaplain's 'oppressive' territorial ones. Only two years after Blanchot's "Reading Kafka", Claude Lévi-Strauss introduced the concept of the floating signifier (1987: 63–64) that thereupon became "the guiding concept in the human sciences of the twentieth century" (Agamben 2005a: 37). In particular in the century's second half, the idea of emancipation through deterritorialization caught a strong wind in its sails. The *world* bid farewell to *reality,* the globalization entered its triumphant age. Kafka was given the role of its literary announcer.

The equivocality of deterritorialization

Let us now, preliminary, sum up the presented Wittgenstein's, Benjamin's and Blanchot's project of deterritorializing reality as applied to Kafka. Being himself deterritorialized by the new order of the world at the outset of the twentieth century, Kafka as one of its outsiders deprived its apparent 'facts' of their geopolitical, legal and historical validity, turning them in his fictions into the 'floating signifiers' of this world's banished sense. Feeling stranded in the reality into which he was thrown, he responded to its unhomeliness by radically 'deterritorializing' his authorial self, i.e. exempting it from its real parameters. The corollary of this was the deterritorialization of all his settings and agencies, which were unmoored from their geopolitical and historical identities. Through such *virtual* deterritorialization he tried to emancipate, along with himself, all agencies who were banished from reality by *actual* deterritorializations.

Since the authors of the concept of deterritorialization, Gilles Deleuze and Félix Guattari, examine both its actual and virtual side, it offers an apt departure point for the interrogation of the relation between the two. However cautiously and subtly Wittgenstein, Benjamin, and Blanchot deal with this relation, in the final analysis they make the reality's *actual* deterritorializations of its residents responsible for these residents' *virtual* deterritorialization of their reality. Their thesis is that, first of all, the reality's 'logical order' deterritorializes constituencies that do not fit its legal, political, and historical territory. Opposing such actual deterritorializations that protect the reality's territory, in the second step, the banished subjects' virtual deterritorializations pave the way for an open-ended and all-embracing mode of commonality. To establish it, they revivify the world's contingency, which its modernization has done everything to suppress, obliterate, or foreclose, but which still subsist as its slumbering potential.

This tacit opposition between the actual and virtual deterritorializations fully accords with Deleuze and Guattari's distinction between the *relative* and *absolute* deterritorialization, whereby the first takes place in the official, visible space of reality and the second in the subterraneous, invisible area of the world. (Deleuze and Guattari 1987: 55–56) Whereas relative deterritorializations, induced by the process of modernization and the concomitant expansion of capitalism, evacuate populations from one territory to another with the ultimate aim of their reterritorialization, the absolute deterritorialization, set in motion by philosophy, art, music and literature, unleashes the suppressed transformative potential as immanent to all territorialized agencies. The absolute deterritorialization merely emancipates the subversive power of "becoming" (*devenir*) (Deleuze and Guattari 1983: 322; Deleuze and Guattari 1986: 86), which Deleuze and Guattari conceive as "the immanence of immanence" at the heart of all real phenomena (Deleuze 2005: 27). In other words, philosophy, art, music, and literature only place themselves at the service of this "life of pure immanence, neutral, beyond good and evil" (Deleuze 2005: 29) without projecting anything into it in their turn. This life is taken to be their fundamental premise rather than retroactive effect.

Concerning literature Deleuze was, like Benjamin and Blanchot, fascinated by its ability to reactivate the world's castrated possibilities by disintegrating all real agencies and scattering their parts in the elusive labyrinths of anonymous writing. His and Guattari's 1975 study on Kafka was clearly inspired by Blanchot's Kafka-readings. Even in the publications after it, Deleuze continuously refers to Blanchot's depersonalization of literary language (Deleuze 1986: 17, 50, 69–70, 93, 104, 127) and his concept of the neuter as the guiding force of literature-as-writing (Deleuze 1998: 13). If Benjamin authorized the literature's deterritorialization of reality by the inaccessible "world theatre" and Blanchot by reality's "silent outside", Deleuze verifies it by the pure immanence of "*a* life" that underlies all its phenomena.

In his last published paper, he describes this unruly foundation of everything in the following way:

> This indefinite life does not itself have moments, close as they may be one to another, but only between-times, between-moments; it doesn't just come about or come after but offers the immensity of an empty time where one sees the event yet to come and already happened, in the absolute of an immediate consciousness. (Deleuze 2005: 29)

He takes this amorphous "immediate consciousness" (*le vécu*) as generated by "the immensity of an empty time", to precede the constitution of the subject and object or any identity whatsoever that occupies the fulfilled historical time. In fact, its indeterminability already lies at the root of Deleuze's almost three decades earlier resolute substitution of identity for difference and difference for an incessant differentiation:

> Every object, every thing must see its own identity swallowed up in difference, each being no more than a difference between differences. Difference must be shown differing.
> (Deleuze 1994: 56)

If identity *must* be swallowed up in difference, and difference *must* be dissolved in differentiation, it follows that Deleuze from the very beginning puts on philosophers (and concomitantly artists and writers) the *imperative* to serve the engulfing whirl of immanence. He thus counters the *territorial political* imperative as placed on the residents of reality with the aim to respect its facts and agencies, by the *deterritorializing ethical* imperative to deactivate these facts and agencies for the benefit of their suppressed possibilities. In Benjamin's and Blanchot's footsteps, Deleuze counters the chaplain's reality-oriented by supporting Joseph K.'s world-opening point of view.

However, the problem that he has to face in this inversion of the transcendence of reality into the immanence of a life (*une vie*; Deleuze 2005) is that his 'immanence', next to disintegrating transcendent agencies, unavoidably establishes them as well. Its flow is not only deterritorializing but also territorializing, which is why the difference *between* immanence and transcendence returns as the difference *within* the immanence itself. Giorgio Agamben did not let this pass unnoticed, pointing out that Deleuze derives immanence not so much from *manere* (to remain [within the same]) but from *manare* (to flow out or to spring forth [into something else]). (Agamben 1999a: 223) Indeed, he and Guattari do not deny that immanence "disgorges the transcendent everywhere" (Deleuze and Guattari 1994: 47). However, they proclaim to "*want to think transcendence within the immanent, and it is from immanence that the breach is expected*" (1994: 47, italics in the original). It follows that, next to performing *absolute* deterritorialization, immanence also mobilizes *relative* ones, which each new transcendent agency engages against its rivals. This ceaseless reintroduction of transcendence into immanence is unavoidable because immanence is uncertain, indeterminate and frightening, which requires its 'territorialization' into "Some Thing" (Deleuze 2005: 27). The same holds for *autrui* – neither feminine nor masculine, neither singular nor plural – that by its amorphousness challenges the philosopher from 'the other shore' (Deleuze 2005: 17). One of their 'territorializations' into the real phenomena thereby acquires the normative status against which others become deviant.

Deleuze renders this perpetual normative work of immanence in terms of the actualization of the virtual:

> What we call virtual is not something that lacks reality but something that is engaged in a process of actualization following the plane that gives it its particular reality. The immanent event is actualized in a state of things and of the lived that make it happen. The plane of immanence is itself actualized in an object and a subject to which it attributes itself. (2005: 31)

To be sure, such 'territorializations' of "a life" that entails real phenomena, instead of articulating its source's inarticulation as intended, always partially reproduce it. Therefore an in-between outcome, which Deleuze and Guattari locate in the neighborhood zone (*zone de voisinage*) between the empty and historical time (1994: 19). Being "disgorged" by the empty time of immanence, these "between-times (*entre-temps*), between-moments (*entre-moments*)" (Deleuze 2005: 29) never manage to become the determining moments of historical time. They willy-nilly remain related to indeterminate immanence in the same manner – though not necessarily to the same degree – that "a smile, a gesture" of a child (Deleuze 2005: 30), or the animal stumbling, stuttering, stammering, screaming, and moaning (Deleuze and Guattari 1994: 55) adhere to amorphous "immediate consciousness" that generates them.

Even if all 'territorializations' in one or another way bear the mark of their deterritorialized source, the degree of their closeness to it substantially varies. For example, Deleuze and Guattari take children and animals to be its epitomes because their strictly territorialized 'minor' status sentences them to indeterminate consciousness. Their masters, i.e. adults and humans, rivet children and animals to the margins of human reality in the same way that other 'majorities' marginalize their 'minorities' such as whites the coloured, males the females, or rational individuals the irrational collective minds. (Deleuze and Guattari 1987: 293) Now, spontaneously following the (in)famous revolutionary model "We have been naught, we shall be all", Deleuze and Guattari turn all these victims of reality's relative deterritorializations, who are pushed into their indistinct non-territories, into the epitomes of a life's absolute deterritorialization. In this way, testifying to Deleuze's "need for a political subject that would be real" (Citton 2009: 130), as Jacques Rancière aptly noticed, the new "hero of the story" of deterritorialization (2004: 154) dethrones the old hero of the story of territorialization. In our terms, Josef K. replaces the chaplain. But Deleuze's ontological prioritizing of the first hero over the second testifies to his promotion of immanence to the former status of transcendence. Far from being immanent to reality's phenomena, a life is in fact the retroactive retaliating project of the territorially confined minorities. Rather than being all-embracing and neutral, it is generated by their harsh political reality. This is why their deterritorialization culminates in reterritorialization, the operating mode of the majority.

Kafka as the redeemer of the deterritorialized?

Such contamination of Deleuze's allegedly neutral immanence requires the re-examination of Benjamin's and Blanchot's readings of Kafka as well. Both claim that Kafka, through his exemption of the ultimate narrative authority from the reach of his readers, points to the withdrawal of the world's sense from the horizon of its residents. Through such operation, the argument goes, Kafka's fictions turn the reality of their readers, like a glove, inside out. If the readers, in their search for its disappeared sense, experience it by moving from its *inside outwards* – from its logic to contingency – now they are driven to experience it from its *outside inwards*, i.e. from the perspective of those who are forced to live contingency, which dissolves the logic of reality.

In following this thread, Benjamin says, Kafka deterritorializes "common situations" (Benjamin 2007a: 120) by displacing them onto the stage of the "World Theater" (2007a: 121). To elucidate the latter concept, we have to recall the baroque *theatrum mundi* from Benjamin's 1928 *The Origin of German Tragic Drama*, where it is portrayed as pulling its actors out of their frustrating historical present into an extraterritorial and extemporal area of the intertwined past, present, and future. In his 1940 "Theses on the Philosophy of History" Benjamin will label this peculiar area "the now-time" (*Jetztzeit*) (1969: 264). It de-historicizes the world's residents by taking possession of their involuntary memory archive in which "an immemorial [. . .] prehistory murmurs" (1980e: 640), and connects them in such a way into a "mystic communion" (1980e: 639) with unknown actors from distant times and spaces. Anticipating the deterritorializing effects of Deleuze's "absolute immanence", Benjamin's *theatrum mundi* thus annihilates the reality residents' identity markers such as the "I", "reflexive consciousness", or "face", which anchor them in their historical presents (Benjamin 1974: 40, 81, 218). Due to such unmooring of their identities, Kafka's agencies become "expressionless" (*ausdruckslos*; 1974: 181), "undefinable" (1980c: 639), and "unapproachable" (*unnahbar*; 1980c: 647). Through such consistent disidentification they drive closer to the "oceanic commonality" of the now-time, which invites its participants into its free and limitless 'elective affiliations'. Announcing Deleuze's "absolute immanence", Benjamin's *theatrum mundi* displays the profile of the Absent God whose elusive non-time and non-space only come into being through the negation of all identity attributes. The more deterritorialized one is, the more contingent attributes he or she epitomizes and the less accessible to the spatial and temporal territorialization he or she becomes. In a word, establishing a hierarchy of his agencies according to the degree of their contingency, Benjamin's Kafka willy-nilly *reterritorializes* the world, reestablishes the binding force of its new reality.

Blanchot for his part claims that Kafka's fictional language, "by its continuously active negation", prevents itself "from receiving a determined meaning" (Blanchot 1995d: 79). It "always surpasses every truth and every meaning, and it presents us with this very surpassing", which means that "it implies an absolute absence, a counterworld" (1995d: 79). In a passage that is strangely omitted from the English translation of "The Language of Fiction", Blanchot speaks of Kafka's imaginary "inversion of the real world in its entirety", which the everyday life, due to its fragmentation, rarely permits us to experience (1949: 84). By opening our insight into "the existence of non-existence" (1949: 84) Kafka –

being himself "spurned by history" to "the edge of the world" and "the end of time" (1995a: 339, 338) – takes advantage of his extraterritoriality to put at stake "the world as a whole" (1995a: 316). Clarifying the "void" onto which he opens through his consistent unworking (*désoeuvrement*) of the reality of his readers, Blanchot states:

> It is not beyond the world, but neither is it the world itself: it is the presence of things before the *world* exists, their perseverance after the world has disappeared, the stubbornness of what remains when everything vanishes and the dumbfoundedness of what appears when nothing exists. (1995a: 317)

This dissolution of the reality's presence into the spectral 'before-after' departs from the same premise as Benjamin's displacement of its settings and agencies to the stage of *theatrum mundi* or, for that matter, Deleuze's absolute deterritorialization of them. All these operations are taken to merely revivify an extraterritorial and extemporal area that lies in wait in the reality's 'memory archive', occasionally resurfacing in some traumatic circumstances. This limitless area surreptitiously but persistently erodes the reality of persons, names, and identities, resisting this reality's attempts to mediate, appropriate, and assimilate it. Throughout his work, Blanchot consistently derives literature from this silent erosion, alternatively rendered as negation, writing, unworking, the neuter, or disaster. However, in the above argument from "Literature and the Right to Death" he draws on Emmanuel Levinas's analysis of the insomniac condition of *il y a*. Elaborating on this peculiar existential mood (Levinas 1987: 65–67), the French philosopher pointed out the possibility of the sudden vanishing of stable and solid things, which our experience of existence relies on, into nothingness. Once our existence, in such traumatic circumstances, is forced to unmoor itself from things, we suddenly face bare being that turns our reality upside down.

According to Blanchot, Kafka transfers his readers to the position of those whose reality was in such a way turned into its blank negative and thus enables them to experience the horror of the *il y a*. Yet linking the readers with outsiders does not mean establishing a community out of the two of them because the readers as the subjects of existence cannot assimilate into their space the characters as the objects of non-existence. In fact, in this connection the latter take the upper hand. Blanchot insists that the disastrous erasure of existence as experienced by outsiders excludes the *Aufhebung* of history (Blanchot 1995e: 40), or "puts a stop to every arrival" of Messiah (1995e: 1) in order to prevent history from successfully uniting its past, present, and future. He accordingly obliges literature to "evoke the annihilation into which everything always sinks", to "keep watch" over its "measureless absence" (1995e: 84) that cannot but be betrayed through its translation into history. Fully aware of this interminable ethical task, he says, Kafka's literature never stops contesting all its statements. "As soon as something is said, something else needs to be said. Then something different must again be said to resist the tendency of all that has just been said to become definitive." (1995d: 22) Thus, Blanchot makes out of modern literature the ethical re-signifier of the disastrous political *désoeuvrement* that, persistently laying in wait, in certain limit-experiences suddenly reduces existence to bare life. He uncouples this *désoeuvrement* from Hegel's teleological philosophy that, in Kojève's apocalyptic reading, prophesizes Messiah's arrival at the end of history, and aligns it with the weak messianic ethics of Kafka's literature that is – as he reads it – engendered by the perspective of deterritorialized outsiders.

To return in the conclusion of this section to Deleuze and Guattari's Kafka for the sake of summary: I have already indicated that Blanchot's reading of Kafka and the modern literature in general was one of the inspiring sources of his readings of literature. Small wonder, then, that Blanchot's turning of Kafka's narratives into the ethical re-signifier of the subterraneous *désoeuvrement* that, in the politically ruled everyday life, "transforms our possibilities into impossibilities" (Blanchot 1980: 114) and thus silently multiplies outsiders, lies at the very core of Deleuze and Guattari's reading of Kafka as the representative of 'minor literature'. In their understanding, minor literatures and languages deterritorialize the major ones from the position of their *internal outsiders*, which in Kafka's case means of a Prague Jew writing in German. Taking advantage of this position of internal outsider that connected him with the structurally similar 'minors' both among his characters and readers, Kafka undertook his deactivation of hierarchies as imposed on them by their 'majors'. He thus blurred the distinction between the representing and represented subjects – the author and narrator, the narrator and characters – by drawing them into the indeterminate polyphony of "collective assemblages of enunciation", an anonymous machine of language that refuses to be pinned down to any recognizable subject of utterance. By pushing his subjects beneath the legal and historical threshold of individual identification (Deleuze and Guattari 1986: 17–18), he unleashed the suppressed creativity of 'creatures' who are sentenced to live such indistinction on daily basis. Deleuze speaks in this connection of the "bastard people, inferior, dominated, always in becoming, always incomplete" (Deleuze 1998: 4). This "missing people" that "ceaselessly stirs beneath dominations" (Deleuze 1998: 4) has no other way to identify itself than through such subversive literature (Deleuze and Guattari 1986: 16; Deleuze 1998: 4). However, for this "bastard race" that is the invisible carrier of emancipating becoming, to "become is not to attain a form [. . .] but to find the zone of proximity, indiscernability, or indifferentiation where one can no longer be distinguished from a woman, an animal, a molecule" (Deleuze 1998: 1). Putting his narrative technique at the service of the missing people's becoming, Kafka deterritorializes the distinct identities of his agencies by multiplying their "thresholds of indiscernability" (Deleuze and Guattari 1994: 19) with other agencies' identities and thus making out of them all a floating assemblage of indistinct items.

Disentangling Kafka from Josef K., the denier of his involvement with the law

In the delineated influential readings, Kafka's radically deterritorialized fictions establish the topsy-turvy rule of contingency over reality. To take issue with this very influential but misleading thesis, let us start with the remark that Kafka, as the practicing attorney at law, was all but the enthusiastic supporter of an overall obliteration of distinctions and boundaries. On the contrary, he was terrified by the rise of the arbitrary that introduced the "twilight of legal illegality" (Coetzee 1992: 363) into his time's execution of law. Due to the modernization of the outgoing empires' legislation, state power turned into an anonymous machine with myriad operators but no identifiable responsible agency, which exposed its subjects to an enduring uncertainty and discontent. Once its ultimate authority became inaccessible, its dispersed operators felt free to apply law as they pleased which, as Kafka repeatedly laid bare, seriously threatened their subjects.[4] In fact, the very structure of the reconfigured legislation enabled its operators' whimsical executions. As Foucault has shown some half of a century later, the new 'egalitarian' disciplinary power that replaced its 'despotic' sovereign predecessor surreptitiously reintroduced the latter's power asymmetry through its fundamental relationship between the panoptic law that comprehends all its individual subjects and the subjects themselves whose comprehension it escapes (Foucault 1977: 202). Due to that, although disciplinary power proclaimed to be the carrier of emancipation, it got "the precise role of introducing insuperable asymmetries"

---

4 It should be reminded that Kafka was attorney at law at the Workers' Accident Insurance Corporation and represented Czech workers seeking compensation from their Austrian employers for their injuries at work. Next to being structurally inferior and submissive by default, they lacked both the knowledge of the Austrian law and the language to present their claim, which confronted them with an exhausting process of endless delay and made them an easy prey for the law's operators. Kafka's work at the Corporation deeply affected his fictions not only concerning their topics (Litowicz 2002: 110) but also juristic style of thought and terminology (Müller-Seidel 1986: 16–17; Ziolkowski 1997: 226).

(Foucault 1977: 222) and establishing "the inequality of the different 'partners'" "in relation to the common regulation" (Foucault 1977: 223). As witnessed by many of his works – *The Trial* most prominent among them – Kafka not only detected this insuperable asymmetry between the law's operators and objects, but also carefully investigated its corollaries in the new political regulation of human commonality.

Returning from this perspective to the aforementioned scene from *The Trial*, Josef K. objects to the chaplain that 'his' law is biased, i.e. relying on the power relationship instead of just, i.e. relying on the truth that is equally valid for everybody. This reproach is astonishing considering that the new disciplinary administration of population claimed primacy over the old sovereign administration precisely on the basis of its egalitarian character. Whereas a sovereign ruler unilaterally imposes his or her law upon those whom it concerns, disciplinary law is generated by the democratic agreement of its subjects. However, Josef K. realizes that such supposedly consensual law is randomly applied by each of its 'capillary' appointed operators, which ultimately makes its arbitrary. Yet although each of these applications is voluntary, they strike their operators, who are confined by their 'reality-conditions' (Wittgenstein 2016: 4.41, trans. modified; *Wahrheitsbedingungen*) as necessary, i.e. logically derived from the law itself. Kafka addresses this capillary appointment of responsibilities for the constitution of late imperial community, among his other fictions, in "At the Construction of the Great Wall of China", an unfinished interlaced parable that, on its both interconnected levels, indirectly tackles the transition from sovereign to the disciplinary administration of an empire.

In its frame narrative, a withdrawn and anonymous High Command allocates the building of the Great Wall's scattered fragments to the mutually remote Chinese collectivities that are envisaged to join the big imperial nation through the acceptance and fulfillment of their respective tasks. Nevertheless, the command's project remains as distant and strange to them as "the life beyond" (Kafka 1988l: 274; trans. modified; *das Leben jenseits*). In the embedded parable, while passing away, the Emperor addresses the "miserable subject" in the uttermost imperial province by ignoring all "the great princes of the Empire" who had assembled to witness the spectacle of his death. He thus switches from the *public visual* demonstration of his will to the assembled princes as characteristic of sovereign power, to its *private oral*, i.e. capillary transmission to anonymous peripheral subjects as characteristic of disciplinary power. Nonetheless, the narrator argues, the emperor's replacing of the amorphous crowd by a "collection of separated individuals" (Foucault 1977: 201) fails to establish a big imperial community because the privately entrusted law loses its binding force and becomes elusive. Internally processed by the addressees who are separated from one another by their geographical, historical, political, social, cultural and linguistic barriers, it dissolves into an "imaginary norm" (Slaughter 2007: 215) that is wholly dependent on various groups' and individuals' applications in mutually incommensurable circumstances.

Considering this, Josef K. might be right when he senses that the supposedly egalitarian disciplinary legislation, instead of surpassing the despotic sovereign legislation, ghostly revivifies it. Contingency reenters its logical profile not only in its far remote and retrograde peripheries as in the case of "In the Penal Colony", which narrates of an appointed German criminologist's visit to a French colony to find out for his Emperor if it makes sense establishing a similar external dumping ground also for the German 'dregs of society'. (Müller-Seidel 1986: 80–81) Contrary to the mainland's disciplinary legislation, these deterritorialized zones of the imperial territory still applied the summary justice of public executions. However, Kafka composed "In the Penal Colony" in the break of his writing on *The Trial* (1914), in which he investigates another mode of the deterritorialization of the egalitarian by martial law. Taking place at the very heart of empire, this hideous deterritorialization distorts egalitarian law by degrading its constituencies, as it were, to the status of deprived deportees in the colonies.

In the very first sentence, Josef K. is astounded to have been arrested without having done anything "evil" (*Böses*) since he "lived in a country of rights, which was completely at peace (*lebte in einem Rechtsstaat, überall herrschte Friede*), the laws had not been suspended – who, then, had the audacity to descend on him in the privacy of his own home?" (2009: 7; trans. modified). Following English jurisdictional tradition that is focused on crime rather than the criminal, Mike Mitchell mistranslates Kafka's Austrian-German term *Böses*, in the first sentence, rendering it as "wrong" instead of "evil", and thus misses the elusive moral foundation of the Austrian legislation of the time. In his comparison of the German code, that was much closer to the Anglo-American tradition, and the Austrian code at the beginning of the twentieth century, Theodore Ziolkowski remarks:

> Unlike the German code, which began with a definition of crimes and misdemeanors according to the severity of their punishment – that is, purely external and rational criteria – the Austrian code begins with a paragraph defining crime according to an inner criterion: "evil intent" (*böser Vorsatz*). In other words, we are plunged directly into a moral universe that is absent in the German code: "For a crime [to occur], evil intent is required" ("Zu einem Verbrechen wird böser Vorsatz erfordert"). (1997: 236)

Since this law is focusing on the criminal's supposed intent rather than the committed crime, one of the guards who arrived to arrest Josef replies to the reproach of the accused, he is innocent, that his "officialdom" (*Behörde*) "does not seek out guilt in the population but, as it says in the law, is attracted by guilt" (Kafka 2009: 8–9, trans. modified). This again provokes Josef K.'s ironic remark, he is not acquainted with this law, most probably because it "only exists inside your heads" (2009: 9). Indeed, the addressed attraction, being by definition triggered by 'bodily' intuition, can hardly be regarded as having an objectively verifiable rational basis, and how can someone be found guilty on the basis of judge's affects and impressions?

From Josef K.'s perspective, this is precisely the key problem of the law that is applied to him, that it only exists inside the heads of its executives, putting him at their random disposal. When the guard replies to Josef K.'s remark about the chimeric law in his head with "You will soon see how real it is" (2009: 9, trans. modified; *Sie werden bald sehen, wie wahr es alles ist*), Josef's remark "inside your heads" acquires the contours of the aforementioned Wittgenstein's reality-conditions (Wittgenstein 2016: 4.41, trans. modified; *Wahrheitsbedingungen*). They indeed associate the force of the *real* with the limited parameters. As opposed to these limitations, in order for a proposition to be judged *true*, the state of affairs it refers to has to be compared with all possible states of affairs in the *world* (Wittgenstein 2016: 2). Only if it matches the totality of possible states of affairs, it will be judged true, but this totality – the world's final law – is never available, which means that the external term of comparison is irrevocably absent (Schuman 2012: 159–160). It follows that the world is destined to the limited reality-conditions that expose our lives to their operators' arbitrary decisions. Does this mean that, in order to liberate it from such limitations, the reality-conditions have to be dismantled as lie and discarded? Does Kafka endorse Josef K.'s anger against the law's whimsical and unjust operators who determine his reality?

In a recent essay that testifies to the shift in the new Kafka-research from metaphysical and theological to the political and legal terms, Maximilian Bergengruen (2016) argues that "Before the Law" – the title of the parable that the chaplain presents to Josef K. and that only was published in Kafka's lifetime – has to be understood in strictly spatial terms as "standing before the judge" as the law's representative. This casts new light on the basic principle of the Austrian law of the time "All citizens are equal before the law" (*Vor dem Gesetz sind alle Staatsbürger gleich*) as it puts the judge as the law's appointed operator *above* the rest of citizens. There is a clear power asymmetry between the two: The judge is the subject, they are the objects of the law. As if revivifying empires in which emperors, considered to be 'God's envoys', determined the law by their very verdicts, law in the state of exception of Kafka's time only takes shape through its operators' decisions. Nobody knows how it looks like before they stage it by their performance.

In order to understand what enables such resurgence of the imperial principle 'might makes right' in the midst of egalitarian modernity, we have to recall that the German title *Der Proceß* (unlike its English mistranslation *The Trial*) refers to the secret inquisitorial process *(Vernehmung)* as carried out by the examining magistrate *(Untersuchungsrichter)* rather then the public accusatory trial as conducted by the judge in the courtroom. In the Austrian legal system, the state attorney *(Staatsanwalt)* notifies the examining magistrate that there is reason to suspect an individual of a particular crime. Considering the appointed magistrate's extensive authority, Josef K. is practically delivered to his and his assistants' self-willingness. Astounded by this undercover side of his country's public legislation, he complains to one of its lowest operators, the student, "I am not very well acquainted with your legal system" (Kafka 2009: 46) and, after getting a bit more acquainted with it, reveals to his confused uncle that "it's not a case that's being tried in the normal court" (Kafka 2009: 67). In such 'abnormal' cases, as he learns from his lawyer Huld, not only the accused and his defence are cut off from the essential information, what the indictment precisely consists of (Kafka 2009: 81–82), but also the court officials themselves:

> Proceedings in court were in general also kept secret from the lower officials, so that they could hardly ever follow the further progress of any case they were dealing with in its entirety; that meant that the court business turned up on their desk, often without their knowing where it came from, and went on its way without their knowing where it went.
> (Kafka 2009: 84)

As Ziolkowski notices, none of the chief operators of this parallel paralegal system in the novel – such as Huld, Leni, Block, Titorelli, or the chaplain – has ever read its law but only knows it by hearsay. Cut off from the source, they are turned into its humble 'relays' like the stonemasons in "At the Construction of the Great Wall of China", who are confined to a particular part of the wall that they are appointed to build and are thus unable to understand its whole. In fact, as the law only exists in its confusing fictional preambles (*einleitende Schriften*), nobody knows its concrete wording. It has to be invented by its operators, who, each in his or her own terms, thus turns it into a *fictio legis* (Bergengruen 2016: 432–434).

However, sticking to the same political and legal terms of Kafka's time, Günther Teubner in his article "The Legal System before Its Law" (*Das Recht vor seinem Gesetz*; Teubner 2012) shifts attention – and trauma – from the disciplinary law's outsiders to its operators.[5] After all, one should not forget that Josef

---

5 Alison Lewis translates the article's German title as "The Law before its law" but I prefer this translation.

K., as a high-rank bank official, occupies *both* positions. Teubner reminds us that Kafka portrays his characters not simply as outsiders, but also constitutive parts of various institutions with their absurd internal laws. After all, Kafka himself was an insurance clerk (Teubner 2012: 177), moreover vice-secretary in his corporation (Ziolkowski 1997: 226). This complicates not only Bergengruen's representation of the disciplinary law as the polygon of power asymmetry but also Benjamin's, Blanchot's, and Deleuze and Guattari's siding with its alleged outsiders in Kafka's work. Since all Kafka's agencies are situated both outside and inside the law, with one leg in life and the other in the legal system, they are figuring as both its operators and outsiders. Despite their striving to deterritorialize themselves, neither Josef K. nor "the man from the country" succeed in relegating the responsibility for the territory of law to its appointed guardians.

> "The man from the country" – this is no longer only a human being as a party in proceedings, but the entire complex process of the application of the Law, a process which is played out before the door, directly on the threshold that separates life from the law.
> (Teubner 2012: 179)

If nobody is ultimately outside the law, then nobody is allowed to deny his or her responsibility for it. To underline this, Teubner renders the passage from the law to life, arguing in terms of Niklas Luhmann's systems theory, as the unavoidable betray of the first by the second. No application can truthfully reproduce "a law that is *in force* but does not *signify*" (*Geltung ohne Bedeutung*) (Agamben 1998: 51). As "there is no internal nexus that allows [application] to be derived immediately from the [law]" (Agamben 2005a: 40), this passage from the system's interior to its exterior entails "a 'trial' that involves a plurality of subjects" (Agamben 2005a: 39–40). Does the trial to which this novel puts its protagonist then pertain to his permanent failure to make right decisions? Teubner indeed claims that the legal system, failing to apply its guiding difference (*Leitdifferenz*) "right/wrong" without at the same time betraying it, turns this difference always anew toward itself by putting itself on perpetual trial. He designates this self-blaming of the legal system's operators for "constantly producing anew not only right, but also wrong (*Unrecht*)" as their "original sin" (Teubner 2012: 180).

After Luhmann, none of the social systems into which modernity differentiates its administration of society – such as politics, law, economy, religion, or science – can assess its law (or "reality-conditions") comprehensively, which puts their applications of it at the risk of identifying their "lies" with "the order of the world". Max Weber's rendering of modern social systems as the "casings of the bondage to the future" (*Gehäuse der Hörigkeit der Zukunft*) justifies Josef K.'s rage because of their encapsulation into their deceitful realities. Teubner reminds us that Kafka himself frequently challenged their goal-directed universes, devoted to the sheer self-maintenance of their empty laws (Teubner 2012: 181). Nevertheless, he disagrees with both Agamben's reading of "Before the Law" in *Homo Sacer* (Agamben 1998: 49–62) and his reading of *The Trial* in the chapter "K." of his *Nudities* (Teubner 2012: 191–199; 183–184). According to the first, Kafka abolishes the legal system's unbearable "being in force without significance" (Agamben 1998: 51) in order to release "bare life's" limitless potentiality beneath its confines. According to the second, the man from the country resists the same deceit of the law that drives Josef K. into the self-slander. He owes this success to his distrust of this deceit's operator, which instructs the distant 'kindred souls': Keep suspicious of all operators of reality-conditions! (Agamben 2010: 27–28) Inspired by the same revolutionary drive as Benjamin's, Blanchot's, and Deleuze and Guattari's readings of Kafka, Agamben interprets the writer as summoning his distant 'kindred souls' to deterritorialize their realities.

Whereas these thinkers unanimously identify Kafka's authorial strategy with Josef K.'s deterritorialization of his reality, Jacques Derrida interprets it as keeping aloof from the enraged hero. Teubner takes up his claim that Kafka acts as an involved operator rather than the exculpated outsider:

> While Agamben's negativity calls for the abolition of law, Kafka's paradox is a provocation to "insatiably", in ever renewed attempts, propagate distinctions which are intended to get closer to the law "in thoughtful obedience". (Teubner 2012: 186)

If, as Derrida stresses in his alternative reading of Kafka's parable ("Before the Law"), justice might be arising precisely through the operator's failure to apply the law in a right way, then operators must keep pursuing their "original sin" by relentlessly turning their law against themselves. In Teubner's interpretation, Kafka's authorial strategy consists in precisely this perpetual self-blaming of an operator who feels ashamed for his belonging to a restricted *reality*, longing to get rid of it by joining the *world's contingency*.

If Agamben made the self-slanderer a dupe of the law, Teubner promotes him to the consistent exposer – and simultaneously reproducer – of its blind spot. Although he points to Derrida as the source of his inspiration, in doing so he in fact leans on Niklas Luhmann's systems theory. Its fundamental insight is that, since the outbreak of modernity and its differentiation of society, it became impossible to observe things outside of instituted systemic terms (Luhmann 1986b: 50). The individuals who find themselves restricted by these terms of the observation of world phenomena develop the so-called second-order observation in order to pull themselves out of them. Following the self-propelling principle "I am what I am not" (Luhmann 1989: 244), implying "I am different from the identity that others have forced me into", their identity-building becomes "an unfinished and interminable process, an inherent activity of striving and becoming" (Luhmann 1989: 215, trans. mine). In Luhmann's interpretation, the inventor of this individual identity-in-making that is attached to the world "horizon postponed with every operation without ever becoming available" (Luhmann 1995: 151), is modern art, best represented in the novel (Luhmann 1990b: 40). We owe to its consistent 'self-slander' the dismantling of self-enclosed realities and the concomitant unleashing of contingency in the form of an "explosion of the world's unity" (Luhmann 1995: 138, trans. mine).

Following this thread, Teubner celebrates it in the conclusion of his article, stating that only modern literature as epitomized in Kafka's work is capable of an unremitting self-creation. Luhmann thus leads his reading of Kafka's self-slandering authorial strategy back to Benjamin's, Blanchot's and Deleuze and Guattari's Romanticist celebration of literature as *the* modern agent of emancipation. Pointing to the abundant world of latency beyond the realities established by other social systems, the autopoietic literary system ceaselessly reminds these systems of the contingency of what they take to be real (Luhmann 1995: 142–145). This is how its second-order observation establishes superiority over their first-order observations, reclaiming "its right to objectivity" (Luhmann 1990a: 40). Luhmann dubs the ambition that sets it in motion as "the attitude of knowing better" (*besserwisserische Einstellung*) because it can affirm its superior knowledge only through the derogation of the knowledge of the first-order observers who are thereby "relegated to the status of the harmless and naive" (Luhmann 1990b: 46). Their blindness must be denounced, corrected and supplemented whenever it hinders the advancement of humanity in the direction of contingency.

Siding with literature against philosophy, Luhmann thus unhesitatingly leans his theory on the Romanticist inversion of Hegel's historical closure. If Hegel's history pushes humanity in the deadly embrace of Absolute Spirit, Luhmann's evolution pushes society toward the perilous contingency of human affairs. Its supposedly growing inclusive potential (*Anschlussfähigkeit*) amounts to a parallel increase of its readiness to exclude all constituencies who do not meet its elitist requirements. Concerning his pattern of social evolution, Luhmann (1997: 609–615) must finally admit that its progression reproduces, even reinforces the 'overcome' phases instead of resolving them. "The final outcome of the heightening of the inclusion requirements is exclusion." (Luhmann 1986a: 649–650) As with Benjamin, Blanchot, and Deleuze and Guattari, contingency proves to be no less discriminatory than necessity.

This is why Teubner's proposal to treat Kafka's author as the law's self-slandering operator rather than its outsider who is blindly slandering others, i.e. Josef K., does not succeed in exempting the author from his protagonist. The praise of Kafka's superior self-authoring equally misses the target as does its derogation to that of his protagonist. Both the protagonist and his author, striving to surpass the discrimination of humans by the necessity of their reality, inadvertently introduce the discrimination by the contingency of their world. Rather than parting ways, reality and world ultimately intertwine. Considering this unintended overlap, it seems that the outsider and operator are at pains to get rid of one another precisely because they feel to be contaminated by their counterpart from *within*. The outsider (Josef K.) tries to detach himself from the operator (the chaplain) by slandering the latter for the abuse of law. The operator (Kafka) tries to detach himself from the outsider (Josef K.) by slandering himself for being the operator, which is an insight that is denied to the blinded outsider and that therefore proves the operator's superiority. Yet the point is that these two kinds of (in Kafka's vocabulary) "man's original sin" – the slander of others and oneself – are not separate, which they are willing to prove by their deterritorialization of the counterpart's reality but intertwined, which they are trying to hush up.

The conjoining disjuncture of "original sins"

In his frequently discussed aphorism 82 from the 'he' series, dated 15 February 1920 (Kafka 1980: 218; Kafka 2012: 206), Kafka redefines man's "original sin" as a relentless claim for the status of victim, for victims are always innocent and so need not answer for their actions. Those who are deemed responsible are their oppressors, more accurately those whom they blame for acting as their oppressors. When Kafka typically paradoxically claims that man's "original sin" consists in blaming others for having committed the "original sin" on him or her, he obviously finds this blame of others 'sinful', which derogates it to the status of slander. Does he, among others, hint at Josef K. here? Indeed, the slander – in a significantly reversed perspective, i.e. practiced against Josef K. – crops up in the novel's very first sentence as focalized through the protagonist's self-justification: "Someone must have slandered Josef K., for one morning, without having done anything evil, he was arrested" (Kafka 2009: 7; trans. modified). Explaining to himself the arrest warrant against him by someone's 'slander', Josef K. is in fact himself practicing slander. Without any evidence, he transfers the responsibility for the abuse of law to its operators by exempting himself completely out of it. But if the disciplinary law is both all-encompassing and inaccessible – which is its very definition – how can any of the 'relays' involved in its transmission, cut off from the law's totality as all of them are, claim another 'relay's' abuse of it? To render this in Foucault's terms, are all relays of the disciplinary law not carefully separated from one another into a "sequestered and observed solitude", an "invisibility" for one another that is the very "guarantee of order" (Foucault 1977: 200–201)? Apparently, Josef K. refuses to realize that his own 'reality-conditions' are equally self-enclosing and blinding as theirs, which means that he is turning his reality into "the order of the world" no less than they are theirs.

His attachment to the goal-oriented universe of a senior bank executive with only thirty years,[6] is indeed so complete that he readily sacrifices to his professional career the emotional and moral obligations to his family members, female partners, landlady and tenants from the lodging house, colleagues from the bank, and clients. The 'guiding difference' of this universe – *usable/unusable* for his rising up the corporate ladder – is the only law he really considers. Steering his relations with others in accordance with it, he recklessly neglects his half-blind, ailing mother (Kafka 2009: 177; 184–186), avoids his seventeen-year-old niece (2009: 65–66), treats his landlady Frau Grubach aggressively and impolitely (2009: 19–20) just because she has borrowed a large sum of money from him (2009: 25), expects women from lower social ranks to unconditionally serve his hypertrophied sexuality, such as the dancer in the wine-bar Elsa (2009: 21, 77, 177–178) or the typist Fräulein Bürstner despite her obvious aversion to his offers (2009: 22–26), or to help him with his case in exchange for sexual pleasures, such as Leni (2009: 76–78) or the usher's wife (2009: 40–45). Finally, he demonstrates domination and arrogance toward the subordinate officials at the bank (2009: 16, 62, 186) and neglects his year-long clients (2009: 91–94).

Thus, when the guard Franz replies to Josef K. that he behaves "worse than a child" in trying to transfer his guilt to the officialdom (*Behörde*) that, for its part, "does not seek out guilt in the population but [. . .] is attracted by guilt" (2009: 8–9), he seems to be right both with regard to Josef K. and officialdom. First, Josef K. indeed childishly sticks to his refusal of guilt despite many advices to the contrary, such as those of Leni, the usher's wife, the lawyer Huld, or the chaplain. Rejecting them, he stubbornly conducts his "trial against the court" (Politzer 1962: 163–217). Second, Josef K.'s guilt, which the officialdom is attracted by is indeed not legal, as he has not done anything wrong (crime or offense), but moral, as he has done many evil things in terms of his everyday routine, i.e. continuously sinned against his conscience. Considering that he

---

[6] It is worth reminding that in 1913, at exactly the same age of life, Kafka became vice-secretary at his Insurance Corporation. He started to write on *The Trial* a year thereafter.

obstinately refuses to admit this, he is not so much the victim of the officialdom's legal repression as he repeatedly imputes, but of the repression of his own conscience, which he denies. Like Dostoevsky's Raskolnikov, Josef K. thinks that the moral law does not apply to him who lives for 'higher' goals (Conti 2016: 478). Both are so blinded by the "guiding differences" of their self-sufficient universes that they do not realize how damaging they are for their fellow beings. As regards Josef K., the paradigmatic "washed-up clerk" in the age of missing transcendental guarantees, he subordinates everything to his bank universe:

> He has no home life to speak of, no life outside the bank, alienation so complete it escapes his notice. [. . .] He perceives the court in the same terms as the bank, but his analytical powers, so highly valued at the bank, translate into moral obtuseness in the sphere of interpersonal relations. (Conti 2016: 480)

Nevertheless, among his predominantly selfish, exploitative and misogynous relations with women (Robertson 2009: xv), the one with Fräulein Bürstner deserves to be singled out considering that it was planned "to give the novel its overarching coherence" (Robertson 2009: xii). As is well known, the novel emerged in the immediate aftermath of the termination of Kafka's engagement with Felice Bauer, a catastrophe for which Kafka blamed himself because of his treacherous parallel correspondence with Felice's friend Grete Bloch. Elias Canetti designated the scandal as Kafka's "second trial", hideously underlying the one presented in his novel and finding its dramatic expression in the posthumously published extensive volume of his "Letters to Felice" (Canetti 1969: 7). In the manuscript of his novel, Kafka often refers to Fräulein Bürstner by the abbreviation F. B., as he does to Felice Bauer in his correspondence and diaries. When he, in the diary entry of 23 July 1914, compares his confrontation with Felice, her sister Erna, and Grete in a Berliner hotel with the "tribunal" (1976: 293), "the connection between the autobiographic moments and the judiciary becomes fully apparent" (Müller-Seidl 1986: 21).[7] Canetti, who in his 1969 book *The Other Trial* provides a detailed and convincing evidence of it, spells out:

---

[7] In the diary entry of 27 January 1922 (1976: 406–407), Kafka complains that the staff of the hotel where he had booked his room, has registered his name as "Josef K." although he sent them his "legibly written" name twice already. Nevertheless, he is not sure whether "shall I enlighten them, or shall I let them enlighten me". How entangled are Kafka's autobiographic moments with Josef K. testifies his diary entry of 29 July 1914 (two weeks before he started to work on *The Trial*), in which he describes Josef K., "the son of a rich merchant", "after a violent quarrel with his father – his father had reproached him his dissipated life and demanded that he put an immediate stop to it" (1976: 297). No need to remind of Kafka's *Letter to the Father* (Kafka 2008). Obviously, no sharp line separates Kafka from his doppelganger. This equally holds for the

> Felice herself brought up the charges, which were hard and spiteful. It is not clear from the scant evidence whether and to what extent Grete Bloch intervened directly. But she was there and Kafka found her to be the right judge. He didn't say a word, he didn't defend himself, and the engagement went to pieces as he wished. (1969: 66)

Bad conscience with regard to Felice haunted Kafka much after the nasty episode. In a diary entry of 21 September 1917 he notices:

> F. was here, travelled thirty hours to see me; I should have prevented her. As I see it, she is suffering the utmost misery and the guilt is essentially mine [. . .] taken all together, she is an innocent person condemned to extreme torture; I am guilty of the wrong for which she is being tortured, and am in addition the torture instrument. (1976: 385, trans. modified)

It would be certainly misleading to reduce Josef K.'s 'trial' to Kafka's troublesome relationship with Felice Bauer not only because Josef K. blames himself for his inappropriate attitude to Fräulein Bürstner by far not so consciously and severely as Kafka blames himself for his cruelty to Felice. Nevertheless, it deserves attention that while Josef K. approaches all his "women helpers" (2009: 77), i.e. Fräulein Bürstner, the usher's wife, and Leni, in the same promiscuous terms that he approaches the bar dancer Elsa, he fiercely protests against Frau Grubach's attempt to attribute promiscuity to Fräulein Bürstner. If someone is to be blamed for moral "impurity", he says, then he himself is first in line, certainly before Fräulein Bürstner (2009: 21).

Is this to be interpreted as Josef K.'s remorse for his impolite hint at Fräulein Bürstner's habit of returning home late that "can go too far", or maybe he just fears Frau Grubach will report this to Fräulein Bürstner (2009: 21)? Difficult to say. In the aforementioned essay "K.", Agamben claims that Josef K. is a consistent self-slanderer (2010: 10–11). To illustrate this astonishing thesis, he points to his conversation with Fräulein Bürstner (Kafka 2009: 21) in which K. proposes her to "falsely accuse him" (Agamben 2010: 11) of the sexual assault on her. But the attribute "falsely" misses the point here. First, K.'s proposal is made during his action of seduction, which is why he refuses to go away – as she demands of him in order to save her reputation – firmly determined to bring his action, whatever the price, to its successful end. Second, by suggesting her to report him to Frau Grubach for having "burst in" on her (Kafka 2009: 22) "and I guarantee I can get Frau Grubach not only to support it in public, but to really believe it herself" (2009: 22), he is selfishly manipulating her because he knows very well that

---

author's relationship with his other doppelgangers such as Georg Bendemann from "The Judgment", of whom Kafka remarks that Georg contains as many letters as Franz, Bende as many as Kafka, and the vowel e in Bende appears on the same spots as the vowel a in Kafka (Kafka 1964: 296).

Frau Grubach suspects Fräulein Bürstner of promiscuity anyway. That Fräulein Bürstner – whom K., as his "insulting offers" (2009: 23) lay bare, considers an easy prey – is being manipulated, testifies the scene immediately thereafter, in which he

> kissed her on the lips and then all over her face, like a thirsty animal furiously lapping at the water of the spring it has found at last. Finally he kissed her on the neck, over the windpipe, and left his lips there for a long time. (2009: 23, trans. modified; *Gurgel*)

Therefore, Josef K., who approaches Fräulein Bürstner as an ill-reputed lady who gladly underlies 'brushing' (or 'scrubbing'), as her German name suggests in colloquial linguistic usage, is far from unjustifiably slandering himself as Agamben claims. He operates in a calculating manner because he knows he is dealing with "a little typist, who would not keep up her resistance to him for long" (2009: 172). However, after the fact, there are some suppressed signs of his remorse. They are looming on the horizon in the fragment "B.'s Friend", which reports of his repeated attempts to meet "Fräulein Bürstner alone, when she went to the office" and of his letters of apology to her (2009: 167), but in particular in the final chapter, in which Fräulein Bürstner or someone very similar to her, pops up whereas two men are bringing Josef to the execution site (2009: 162). Significantly, he "immediately became aware of the futility of his resistance" (2009: 162), as if her spectral resurrection at the very end of his life clarified to him why he is going to be executed. This intuition of his is corroborated when one of his "half-mute, uncomprehending" (2009: 163) escorts places his hands exactly on K.'s "windpipe" (2009: 165; trans. modified; *Gurgel*), i.e. the same bodily part where K., in the above addressed scene with Fräulein Bürstner, "left his lips for a long time". As the mythic place where Eros and Thanatos meet and part, the windpipe also intrigued Kafka elsewhere.[8] The great avengers used to hit this bodily spot, such as Odysseus whose arrow pierced Antinous exactly there, or various literary vampires who buried their teeth there. Is Fräulein Bürstner one of such resurfacing vampires who operates the executor's knife as her "torture instrument" (Kafka 1976: 385)? Is her apparition

---

8 See, for example, the diary entry of 16 September 1915: "Between throat and chin would seem to be the most rewarding place to stab. Lift the chin and stick the knife into the tensed muscles. But this spot is probably rewarding only in one's imagination. You expect to see a magnificent gush of blood and a network of sinews and little bones, like you find in the leg of a roast turkey." (1976: 342) That Kafka's surmise about the "magnificent gush of blood" is correct, corroborates the slaying of the suitors in *Odyssey*. When Odysseus's arrow hits Antinous's windpipe, and the main Penelope's suitor who is sitting at the table falls backwards to the floor, the splash of his blood reaches the food on the table.

thereby retaliating, at the courtroom of Josef K.'s conscience, all the above enlisted victims of his moral obtuseness? If so, Josef K. only becomes self-slanderer toward the very end of his life – like the man from the country who notices the radiance from the law when it is too late for him to benefit from it – and definitely not because "he knows perfectly well he is innocent", as Agamben argues (2010: 12). On the contrary, at this moment he starts to regret the self-exempting strategy of his life, his enduring preoccupation with "how he could break out of the trial, how he could circumvent it, how he could live outside the trial" (Kafka 2009: 153). Although guilty of others, he systematically deterritorialized his guilt by relegating it to their 'territory'. Through such irresponsible behavior, he became the epitome of the original sin in Kafka's redefinition.

In a recent article, Christopher Conti associated his obstinate refusal of guilt with that of other Kafka's protagonists, such as Gregor Samsa, Georg Bendemann, Hunter Gracchus, and the man from the country. (Conti 2016: 485–86) "The man from the country is not duped by unseen sovereign powers, but by his misrecognising his situation as outside the law." (Conti 2016: 486–87) Countering Agamben's revolutionary political reading of the man from the country as presented in *Homo Sacer* – analogous to his reading of Josef K. in *Nudities* – Conti interprets Kafka's characters as 'sinners' who deny their involvement with the law but must ultimately pay the price for this denial. Both Josef K. and the man from the country are punished because they wanted to exempt themselves from the territory of the chaplain's respectively doorkeeper's reality into the deterritorialized area of outsiders. This peculiar area, according to Agamben's, Benjamin's, Blanchot's, and Deleuze and Guattari's readings of Kafka, both precedes and surpasses the territories of all realities by opening them up toward the deterritorialized contingency of the world. However, if Kafka's characters are sinners who transfer the responsibility for the established realities to their operators because they find themselves banished from them, are then Kafka's interpreters who identify themselves with these characters not repeating their sin? Are they not also doomed to pay the price for the denial of their involvement with established realities?

However, unlike Kafka's influential interpreters, Josef K. seems to have understood his involvement. In the same way in which he progresses from an outsider to the operator of the law who turns the slander toward himself, his author seems to be moving in the opposite direction, i.e. from a self-slandering operator to the outsider who denies his responsibility. As regards the start of his trajectory, it is from the very first sentence that the author – via his doppelganger Josef K., whose ruthlessness he exposes – blames himself for the sins that he has committed against his fellow beings. At this moment, Josef K.'s exposure is unnoticeable as the author reveals the inappropriateness of his blaming of others only discretely and gradually. His "ill-judged reactions, self-deceptions, and faulty reasonings" have to be collected attentively and patiently (Robertson 2009: xxiv). In fact, the author transfers his own sins to his doppelganger in the same way as Josef K. transfers them, for example, to "women helpers", i.e. Fräulein Bürstner, the usher's wife, and Leni (2009: 77), whom he blames of abundant sexual desire that is in fact his own (Robertson 2009: xv). Ultimately, all excessive promiscuity that surrounds him, such as that of the examining magistrate (2009: 49), the judges who hideously enjoy soft pornography (2009: 42), or Titorelli who adores young girls, might also be understood as the unconscious projection of his own. Yet whereas Josef K. transfers his sins and guilt to various others, the author transfers them to a character who is of same age, with an analogous position in his firm, the same exploitative attitude to women and close relatives – which means that the author discretely slanders Josef K. precisely as the doppelganger of himself.

In this sense, we can speak of an indirect or covert authorial self-slandering. It is not Josef K. who slanders himself as Agamben claims. The author slanders himself via his 'deterritorialized' protagonist in the subtle form of "subversive mimicry", which Kafka engaged in his other fictions as well. Like one of his favorite writers Dostoevsky – as Bakhtin has knowingly demonstrated – he used to disintegrate himself into the scattered quasi-representatives by consecutively adopting their mutually interrogating points of view, shifting from one to another in order to finally lay bare their blind spots and misapprehensions (Müller-Seidel 1986: 94–95; 104–105). Both in *The Penal Colony* and *The Trial*, written in 1914 – even if to a lesser degree than in the later *Castle* (1922) – the characters' points of view clash with and refute one another but the author identifies with none of them, leaving such self-entrapment instead to his readers.[9] He is on the contrary oriented toward transgressing the encapsulation of his quasi-representatives in their petty realities. They operate as sheer relays in an immensely "large organization at work" with its impenetrable hierarchy of clerks (Kafka 2009: 37) and grotesque office premises such as attics, ateliers, laundries, pantries, rented rooms, bedrooms, lumber-rooms, small pulpits, and labyrinthine ruins in slum quarters. Concerning this compartmentalization of the modern world, Kafka once remarked that "every person carries a room in itself" (1986c: 41), entrusting to Gustave Janouch:

> Everyone lives behind a grid that they carry around with them. That's why so much is written about animals now. One returns to the animal. It is much easier than human

---

9 The first scholar who insisted on the detachment of the narrator's point of view from those of characters in Kafka's novels was Kundszus 1964 and 1970. He thereby opposed Friedrich Beißner's influential thesis of Kafka's "monoperspectival narration" (Beißner 1952).

> existence. [. . .] one is afraid of freedom and responsibility. That is why it is better to suffocate behind the self-made bars. (Janouch 1968: 43–44)

To prevent this suffocation in the self-inflicted bondage, he opens the windows of his characters' 'casings' to one another by letting their perspectives clash with one another in the horizon of the reader. The horizons of the characters themselves often prove to be insusceptible to other perspectives. Thus, Josef K., who obstinately measures strange court happenings with the meter of his familiar professional universe (2009: 90), gets the supervisor's advice to refocus his thinking (2009: 13), Leni urges him to give up his intransigence (2009: 77), Dr Huld to accept the court such as it is (2009: 85; 136), Titorelli instructs him through legends (2009: 114), and the chaplain cautions him not to follow women advises (2009: 152). But even though the cramped, obscure, and stifling court premises starkly oppose the brightly lit modern setting of his technologically equipped office (2009: 19), he disregards this discrepancy, displaying blindness that ultimately makes the chaplain shout at him: "Can't you see even two steps in front of you?" (2009: 152) Yet although the author patiently meanders through the locations and opinions that oppose those of Josef K. as well as those of his own, he himself waives the right to his own location and opinion. Claiming it would entail the territorialization of his horizon that – belonging to an absolute outsider who is bereft of his own reality – on the contrary vindictively takes advantage of its absolute deterritorialization. Deprived of his own location, an outsider cannot bear responsibility for being thrown out of reality, a condition which apparently justifies him to blame the reality's operators.[10]

Thus, while Kafka's author starts with clandestinely slandering himself for the strictly goal-oriented reality of his doppelganger Josef K., he ends in slandering Josef K. as this reality's chief operator. Pulling himself out of it as an outsider who feels *shame* for its grubby consequences, the author refuses to accept *guilt* for it because he has not acted as its agent. "Shame concerns one's identity and is linked to pride or honour; guilt concerns one's actions, what one says and does, and is linked to responsibility." (Conti 2016: 475) In a gesture of the strong denial of his responsibility, the author shifts it to Josef K. But as his strong denial reveals his equally strong sense of guilt (Robinson 2012: 8–9), it appears that the author unwittingly moves from the "impossibility of identifying" with Josef K. to the "impossibility of disidentifying" with him (Bewes 2011: 6). Denying guilt, he ends in slandering his doppelganger and thus repeats the same 'original sin' with

---

10 In a letter to Max Brod from the beginning of April 1918, Kafka remarks: "The earth that shook off the moon holds itself steadier ever since." "But [being forever lost for this world] we artists have moved to the moon." (1976: 240–41).

which Josef K. opens his trajectory. Neither manages to emancipate himself from his selfish reality, but instead to substitute the 'original sin' of slandering others for the 'original sin' of slandering oneself, or vice versa. The deterritorialization of their realities does not reach the contingent world that it is aiming at, but instead another reality that it is at pains to oppose. Although both territorial reality and deterritorialized world claim originality for their 'sins', their surreptitious interdependence prevents them from achieving it.

5 State of Exception: The Birthplace of Kafka's Narrative Authority

Barely a year after the death of Emperor Franz Joseph, Franz Kafka worked on "At the Construction of the Great Wall of China".[1] From the perspective of an anonymous stonemason, this story seems to be reporting on the Qin dynasty's unification of the Chinese Empire out of seven warring states, which took place during the Ancient Ages when the construction of the wall began, but at the same time on the Ming dynasty's liberation of China from the Mongols that took place during the Middle Ages when that construction ended. In Kafka's literary transformation of historical reality, these two very remote epochs are compressed into the span of a human life. Following his propensity for analogy-building, he disregards historical differences both within China and between it and Europe. The huge geopolitical and historical dislocation of the transfiguring empire – transposed from East Central Europe at the outset of the 20th century to ancient and medieval China – engenders a kind of parable, his favorite literary genre. Parables are, by definition, narrated by slaves or underdogs.[2] To underline the insignificance of its narrator, the parable's first part merges him into a "we" of manual laborers, doomed to observe the construction from the confined point of view of its "most miserable" subjects (*jämmerlichste Untertanen*, Kafka 1994: 75, trans. modified).[3] In fact, the stonemason submits his report after the Great Wall of China had already been completed, thus benefiting from a retroactive insight. During the construction, he and his companions were confined to a particular part of the wall that they were appointed to build and were thus bereft of the general view that was reserved for experts and supervisors.

---

[1] Willa and Edwin Muir translate "Beim Bau der chinesischen Mauer" as "The Great Wall of China," thus bereaving the title of the concepts "at" and "construction" that are, as I will show, extremely important.
[2] Hegel compares them to fables (1975: 391), the subordinate narrators of which do not dare to transmit their "doctrines openly but can only make them understood hidden [. . .] In the slave, prose begins, and so this entire genre is prosaic" (1975: 387).
[3] Next to this parable, the narrative perspective that switches between the "we" and "I" characterizes some of Kafka's other narratives as well, such as "The Refusal" or "Josephine the Singer." In the German critical edition of 1994, which is my departure point, the concluding part of "At the Construction" is narrated from the "I" perspective. In the American edition of *The Collected Stories* (1971), this part is published separately under the title "The News of the Building of the Wall: A Fragment" (Kafka 1988n).

According to the official proclamation, the wall was erected to protect China from an invasion by northern tribes but, fragmentary as it was, it could not really offer protection from those who, due to their nomadic mobility, better understood its flaws than the workers themselves. Nevertheless, the narrator realizes, the system of piecemeal building was deliberately chosen, carefully prepared, and superbly carried out by "the high command" (Kafka 1988l: 271). What this supreme agency was aiming for was a unity of the Empire distilled out of its enormous diversity:

> Groups of people with banners and streamers waving were on all the roads; never before had they seen how great and rich and beautiful and worthy of love their country was. Every fellow countryman was a brother for whom one was building a wall of protection, and who would return lifelong thanks for it with all he had and did. Unity! Unity! Shoulder to shoulder, a ring of brothers, a current of blood no longer confined within the narrow circulation of one body, but sweetly rolling and yet ever returning throughout the endless leagues of China. (Kafka 1988l: 269)

Thus, ultimately, it was neither the Huns nor the Emperor's decree that triggered the wall-building, but the high command's conviction in the necessity of uniting diversity. The narrator pays considerable attention to this political background of the seemingly illogical system of piecemeal construction. He claims that a far-reaching recalibration of the imperial common-being was envisaged through the central assignment of various groups' respective tasks. This is "one of the crucial problems in the whole building of the wall" that he "cannot go deeply enough into" (Kafka 1988l: 270). His scholarly focus and discourse remind us that the mask of a humble stonemason, in accordance with the genre's ventriloquist rule, is in fact worn by an interested and attentive explorer.

For readers during Kafka's time, an analogy with the Dual Monarchy's political reconfiguration after the defeat at Königgrätz in 1866 was undoubtedly at play. In the last decades of the nineteenth century, the frustrated Empire not only reoriented its agenda toward the Slavic population of eastern and southeastern Europe but also translated it from conquering and assimilating into civilizing and affirming terms. No longer denied, the inferior others were now acknowledged in their particularity. Accordingly, the aim of cosmopolitan projects like the Vienna World's Fair (1873) or the encyclopedia *Die österreichisch-ungarische Monarchie in Wort und Bild* (1885–1907) was to establish the monarchy's *unity-in-diversity* (Judson 2016: 317–328). However, as in the Chinese case, the envisioned homogenization merely reaffirmed the gap between the center and its peripheries. Since the Slavs were taken as still living in the mythic phase of human history, they were expected to help the Germans, as the carriers of historical progress, rejuvenate themselves.

Through the centrally governed project of unity-in-diversity, the domination of German culture over its peripheral Slavic constituencies was thus maintained. The expansion of the traffic and communicational infrastructures, as well as the administrative and educational networks, into the Slavic regions strengthened the interaction between governmental institutions and these peripheral collectivities but came at the price of loosening connections between themselves. Governments' insistences on their belonging to a particular ethnic group (Anderson 1991: 162–185; Stourzh 1994: 81) compartmentalized the imperial population, encapsulating its collectivities into their allocated identity confines. This is how the subdividing mechanisms of 'capillary supervision' entered the Habsburg political space, paving the way for its transformation along national lines (Judson 2016: 317–328; Cohen 2013).

Analyzing this restructuring of imperial common-being in his *Discipline and Punish*, Foucault draws an analogy with Jeremy Bentham's penitentiary *Panopticon*:

> Each individual, in his place, is securely confined to a cell from which he is seen from the front by the supervisor; but the side wall prevents him from coming into contact with his companions. He is seen, but he does not see; he is the object of information, never a subject in communication. The arrangement of his room, opposite the central tower, imposes on him an axial visibility; but the divisions of the ring, those separated cells, imply a lateral invisibility. And this invisibility is a guarantee of order. [. . .] The crowd [. . .] is abolished and replaced by a collection of separated individualities. From the point of view of the guardian, it is replaced by a multiplicity that can be numbered and supervised; from the point of view of the inmates, by a sequestered and observed solitude. (1977: 200–201)

Since in the center "one sees everything without ever be seen" and in the peripheries "one is totally seen, without ever seeing" (Foucault 1977: 202), control over the population is accomplished without the public manifestations of power that were characteristic of the previous age of sovereignty. Now the power throws off its corporeality, becoming an anonymous machine with myriad operators, rendering its ultimate agency unverifiable. Its multiplied relays reproduce the power relation by themselves, without any identifiable external force.

By pointing out that "no one whom I have asked knew then or knows now [where] the office [of the high command] was and who sat there" (Kafka 1988l: 271), Kafka's narrator addresses precisely this withdrawal of the ultimate authority from historical evidence. The high command was not a hastily summoned body of mandarins but "has existed from all eternity, and the decision to build the wall likewise" (Kafka 1988l: 273). As the current leaders "traced their plans", through the window of their office "the reflected splendors of divine worlds fell" on their hands (Kafka 1988l: 271). This vanishing of the supreme authority into the divine sphere renders it impenetrable for the common people. Around it, the "fog of confusion" (Kafka 1988l: 274) grows. Even though the common people are entitled to know it, it is stranger to them than the "life beyond" (*das jenseitige Leben*).⁴ Its obscurity exposes them to an enduring uncertainty and discontent.

Kafka was deeply concerned about the consequences of the delineated exception of the law from the realm of those governed by it. Cautioned by the same developments, his contemporary Carl Schmitt notices that, in the recent state of exception, the law only belongs to the juridical order by occupying a constitutively *external* position within it (Schmitt 1985: 7; Agamben 2005a: 2, 35). In "The Problem of Our Laws", Kafka's narrator states "it is an extremely painful thing to be ruled by laws that one does not know" (1988o: 482). When he further remarks that "the laws were made to the advantage of the nobles" who stand above them (Kafka 1988o: 482), he again anticipates Foucault's insight that disciplinary power, praised for its egalitarianism, in fact establishes "the inequality of the different 'partners'" "in relation to the common regulation" (Foucault 1977: 223). Having "the precise role of introducing insuperable asymmetries" (1977: 222), it reaffirms the basic power relation between the law that comprehends all its subjects and those whose comprehension it escapes. Taking the shape of an appearance 'from beyond', it remains an enduring mystery (Kafka 1988o: 482) whose dictum has to be detected by each subject individually, with all the risk of invention that this implies. Since in the disciplinary society, "between the [juridical] norm and its application there is no internal nexus that allows one to be derived immediately from the other" (Agamben 2005a: 40), Agamben interprets this derivation as controversial and conflict-ridden, involving a "plurality of subjects" (2005a: 39–40). As if illustrating Agamben's insight into the modern law's dissensual pluralization much in advance, Kafka concludes "The Problem of Our Laws" by presenting a conflict of its interpretations bereft of resolution.

The further the law reaches on its way to the periphery, the less trust it evokes in its addressees. Instead of feeling protected, they feel victimized by it. In "The Refusal" (Kafka 1988p), a report from a remote, imperial "little town" in the middle of nowhere, the local narrator (again a wolf in sheep's clothing) offers the portrait of a "chief tax-collector", the imperial administration's representative in this godforsaken province. He is an "old man" who "commands the town" although he never "produced a document entitling him to his position; very likely he does not possess such a thing. Maybe he really is chief tax-collector" (1988p: 296).

---

4 Muirs translate "life beyond" as "the next world" (Kafka 1988l: 278).

> But is that all? Does this entitle him to rule over all the other departments in the administration as well? True, his office is very important for the government, but for the citizens it is hardly the most important. One is almost under the impression that the people here say: "Now that you've taken all we possess, please take us as well." (1988p: 296–297)

If we now return to "The Great Wall", when the stonemason first learned of the Emperor's decision to build the wall – thirty years after it was publicly announced – he was a small boy accompanying his father on a walk along the river (Kafka 1994: 79). Approaching his father, an unknown boatman whispered the message in his ear, meeting his deepest mistrust. Like many of Kafka's unfinished works that went unpublished during his lifetime, the parable is interrupted here. Its only published fragment, focusing on the failed transfer of law to the peripheries, is the embedded parable "An Imperial Message". In a manner illustrated in his aphorism "On parables", Kafka lures his reader into taking this embedded parable as a key for the parable which hosts it. In fact, the transfer of trust between parables, like the transfer of law from the Emperor to his subjects, cannot but fail by requiring further transfers to make up for the failure.

Significantly, "An Imperial Message" opens with the same act of entrusting a humble peripheral subject that closes "The Great Wall of China", albeit now from the Emperor's perspective instead of that of his remote addressee. Passing away, the Emperor addresses precisely this "miserable subject, the insignificant shadow" in the uttermost imperial province by ignoring all "the great princes of the Empire" who had assembled to witness the spectacle of his death (Kafka 1988l: 275, trans. modified). In lieu of approaching the attending nobility, in accordance with the centuries-long tradition of public spectacles, he entrusts his last will to the messenger whom he commanded "to kneel down by the bed, and whispered the message to him; so much store did he lay on it that he ordered the messenger to whisper it back into his ear again" (Kafka 1988l: 275). Thus, obviously concerned with the rising mistrust of his peripheral subjects that threatens the maintenance of the empire,[5] he switches from the *public visual* demonstration of his will to the assembled princes to its *private oral* transmission to anonymous peripheral subjects. Choosing a method of its delivery right into the ear of his messenger, whom he expects to dispatch its exact rendering door to door, the Emperor introduces the new "capillary supervision" of all his subjects. Nonetheless, the narrator argues, his replacing of the amorphous crowd by a "collection of separated individuals" (Foucault 1977: 201)

---

[5] The last sentence of the "News of the Building of the Wall" reads: "For it seems that infidel tribes, among them demons, often assemble before the imperial palace and shoot their black arrows at the Emperor" (Kafka 1988n: 281).

5 State of Exception: The Birthplace of Kafka's Narrative Authority — 105

fails to consolidate the endangered imperial common-being because the privately entrusted law loses transparency and becomes elusive. Internally processed by myriad addressees, it dissolves into an "imaginary norm" (Slaughter 2007: 215) or *fictio legis* that is wholly dependent on the interpretation of the individuals who apply it and therefore completely arbitrary.

Kafka's heroes and narrators are turned into the helpless targets of this fictional law that looms large on the horizon of his time. In *The Trial*, for example, its operators prove to be extremely whimsical. In fact, this title, which associates a public dispute in the courtroom, mistranslates the German *Der Proceß* that refers to a preliminary and, by definition, secret process of examination (Ziolkowski 1997: 226). Rather than the written law, it relies upon its representatives' contingent performances that pretend to be authorized but cannot prove this due to the "high command's" inaccessibility. Such circumstances make legislation tantamount to its random execution (Friedman 2000; Bergengruen 2016). It is telling that the guards appointed to arrest Josef K. carry the names of the Austrian and German emperors of the time: Franz and Willem. Delivered to the self-willingness of such petty sovereigns, he is relegated to a "zone of indistinction" deprived of legal rights. While in the simultaneously composed story "In the Penal Colony", Kafka openly confronts the European allegedly liberal and egalitarian legal system with the summary justice of its penal colony, in this novel the legal system is invisibly perverted by the summary justice *from within*. Aberrations do not threaten it from outside, but are from the very beginning its constitutive parts. Kafka knew both from his private and professional experience what he was speaking about. As Foucault spelled out half a century later, within one and the same modern juridical frame, the capillary mechanisms of counter-law disqualify and invalidate the egalitarian law by turning it into a discriminatory inquisitorial machine (1977: 222–227).

Doomed to this frame's devastating effects, Kafka's subjects experience it out of its lawless "heterotopias" proliferating across its expanding network. Thus, epitomizing the Austro-Hungarian juridical system of the time, entirely focused on "inventing the criminal" (Wetzell 2000), the magistrates examine Josef K.'s presumed criminal *motivation* rather than any verifiable *crime*. When he refuses to accept such martial law as the necessary "order of the world" (Kafka 2009: 159), he speaks for all outsiders who, like the narrators of "The Great Wall of China" and "The Problem of Our Laws", tend to dismantle its utter fictionality and randomness. Paradoxically, to turn their passive location of the targeted "objects of information" into the active position of the targeting "subjects in communication" (Foucault 1977: 200), they engage the same maneuver of self-exemption, which their executors take advantage of while imposing the law upon them. While the executors exempt themselves from the law which they apply to others, the outsiders exempt themselves from its undertaken application. Whereas the executives are at pains to exactly locate the law's *subjects,* the outsiders invest their efforts to limit the locating capacity of its *executives.* In response to the executives' silent message that we can formulate as "Examine our law as much you like, it is beyond the location that it has assigned you!", they claim something like "Our extreme dislocation places us beyond the reach of your law!". Kafka himself was such an outsider who "guarded himself from being fixed by his fellow humans" (Kafka 2012: 207).

To limit the power of the executives who are in charge of them, Kafka's appointed outsiders, as it were, adhere to Wittgenstein's dictum: "Distrust of grammar is the first requisite for philosophizing" (Wittgenstein 2016: 106).[6] Rather than obeying this legal "grammar" that turns them into its outsiders, they attach their imagination to its *suppressed possibilities,* as if following Lucy's advice from J. M. Coetzee's *Disgrace*: "When all else fails, philosophize" (Coetzee 1999a: 60).[7] In this manner they transform their restricted location, i.e. reality, into a much more mobile room for maneuver, i.e. world. Here is how Kafka himself describes the powerful connection of his diffuse 'I', which is typically addressed in the third person, to the world of inexhaustible possibilities: "He lives with wits scattered (*in Zerstreuung*). His elements, a free-living gang, fly about the world. And it is only because his room belongs to the world that he can sometimes see them in the distance." (2012: 202) Since many possibilities exist in all human beings, which they can impossibly be aware of, even "a scoundrel can become an honest man, a man happy in his honesty" (Kafka 1976: 414). Therefore, Kafka claims that "the intellectual revolutions that declare everything which has gone before to be null and void are right, for as yet nothing has happened" (Kafka 2012: 188).This elucidates Josef K.'s insight on the very eve of his execution that reality's logic is in fact a semblance: "Were there objections that had been forgotten? There must have been some. The logic is irrefutable, but it cannot resist someone who wants to live" (Kafka 2009: 164).

---

[6] "Distrust of grammar" or, in Kafka's rendering, "the power to say no", are interpreted by both Wittgenstein and Kafka as life-affirming forces. "The power to say no, this most natural expression of the continuously changing, renewing, dying, reviving, human fighting-organism, is something we always have, but not the courage; all the same while to live is to say no, it follows that to say no is to say yes." (Kafka 2012: 208).

[7] In his diary entry of 17 January 1920, Kafka states that for the activities "filled with life" such as calm reflection, judgment, and scrutiny "no space at all is needed"; "even where there is not the smallest crack, they are able to interpenetrate one another and live on in their thousands upon thousands" (Kafka 2012: 203–204). Amidst of a given reality's legal restrictions, they affirm the limitless abundance of the world.

The suppressed possibilities of the reigning "grammar" figure as the source of authorization not only for Kafka and his protagonists, but also for his narrators who make even more extensive use of them. Thus, at the beginning of "An Imperial Message", the narrator operates as a humble relay of its historical transmittance ear to ear, a technique introduced by the Emperor, via his messenger, many centuries ago. However, if the parable was transmitted to him in this oral manner – as testified by "it is said" at its very beginning – from now on it acquires written form that enables it to summon its unknown and distant trustee, the reader. By 'interpellating' him or her through the immediate "you alone",[8] the narrator heightens the efficiency of the emperor's formerly indirect address. What in the imperial oral form was mediated through the messenger becomes in the modern written form an irresistible *summoning*. Activating the potential of the new medium that bridges both spatial and temporal distances much easier, the initially insignificant narrator of "An Imperial Message" suddenly acquires "imperial" abilities. He is now the one who manages the emperor as his character instead of the other way around. As a result, while the report of the narrator of "The Great Wall of China" encompasses an immense amount of time from the first announcement to the eventual completion of its construction, his own report covers "thousands of years" of the message's failed transmission. Both narrators turn from riveted subhuman creatures into the mobile superhuman observers in possession of sovereign insight.

To uncover the ultimate agency of such a subterranean entitlement of theirs, we have to recall Kafka's diary entry of 28 September 1917:

> I strive to know the whole human and animal community, to recognize their basic predilections, desires, moral ideals, to reduce these to simple rules and as quickly as possible trim my behavior to these rules in order that I may find favor in the whole world's eyes [. . .] To sum up, then, my sole concern is the human tribunal, which I wish to deceive, moreover, though without practicing any actual deception. (1976: 387)

Instead, he practices an imaginary self-exemption from the restricted historical world of humans into the inexhaustible potentiality of life (or world). In the diary entry of 24 January 1922 he notices: "It is strange how make-believe, if engaged in systematically enough, can change into reality" (Kafka 1976: 405). This is because

---

8 The term 'interpellation' alludes here, of course, to Althusser's famous street scene in which the presumed police call of "Hey, you there!" reaches one's ear without this addressee being able to visualize the caller (Althusser 1971: 111–114).

> life's splendour forever lies in wait about each one of us in all its fullness, but veiled from view, deep down, invisible. [. . .] If you *summon* it by right word, by its right name, it will come. This is the essence of magic, which does not create but *summons*.
>
> (Kafka 1976: 393, italics mine)

Therefore, whenever Kafka's characters and narrators lay claim to this 'state of exception', they act as the appointed and carefully supervised messengers of his withdrawn authorial agency. Foreshadowing his great admirer J. M. Coetzee, an inhabitant of another post-imperial state of exception, Kafka's authorial agency operates as the *chief* "secretary of the invisible".[9] His narratives are constructed in the piecemeal manner of the Great Wall of China: the fragments of the upcoming redemption (of life's splendour, *die Herrlichkeit des Lebens*) as distributed by the "high command's" limitless possibilities. The "high command", in its turn, remains invisible and inaccessible.

In a letter to Max Brod from November 1917 Kafka expressed his hope that, in a time yet-to-come, "a whole will be made up of these bits" to serve (their readers) as "an instance of appeal" (1958: 195). Up to then, as announced by the title "At the Construction", the work of scattered construction must persevere. Like the presumptive mole from "The Burrow" (the original German title reads, literally, "The Construction"),[10] Kafka's author is persistently *at the construction*, involved in an enterprise-in-making. In the state of exception which makes anything possible, the ongoing destruction, or contamination, of the political common-being does not permit its aesthetic completion. As Coetzee points out in his reading of Kafka's last narrative, nothing can protect its law from the intrusion of a counter-law that perverts it (1992: 228). To recall Foucault's thesis, within one and the same modern juridical frame, the capillary mechanisms of counter-law disqualify and invalidate the egalitarian law by turning it into a discriminatory inquisitorial machine (1977: 222–227). Under such continuously exceptional circumstances, Kafka's narrative authority takes the shape of an elusive "imaginary norm" whose application is in the hands of its addressees,

---

9 The phrase is borrowed from Coetzee's heroine Elizabeth Costello, who herself borrows it from Czesław Miłosz. According to her explanation, she is only one of "the many secretaries over the ages" (Coetzee 2004a: 199). As one of his interpreters (Marais 2009) puts it, Coetzee himself receives his authorial vocation from an invisible otherness, which is why he also acts as "the secretary of the invisible."

10 Muirs translate the German title "Der Bau" as "The Burrow," repeatedly sacrificing the key concept of construction.

with all the risk of subversive invention that this implies. His technique of authoring exposes his readers to the same fictional law that he as the author was exposed to by the whimsical lawgivers of his time. It is up to them to explore its limitless possibilities as he himself has done, via his numerous doppelgangers, with the inaccessible law that he was dependent upon.

6 Almost the Same but not Quite: Kafka and His 'Assignees'

Evoking the truth lost in translation

The end of Kafka's parable "An Imperial Message" reassigns to its reader the position of a 'you', whom its beginning evokes as "the individual, the miserable subject, the insignificant shadow fled in the remotest distance before the imperial sun" (1988c: 24, trans. modified). Although the attributes of this introductory 'you' are also maintained for the concluding one by linking them to one another, upon closer inspection they nonetheless part ways. Since the latter 'you' dreams the emperor's behest to herself or himself, as the narrator specifies, only "when the evening arrives" (1988c: 24, trans. modified), the emperor's sun, a symbol of his power, no longer shines for him or her as it had done for the introductory 'you'. The arrival of the evening implies that the emperor's centralized rule has expired, giving way to the new, impenetrable and impervious administration of the polis. Its center, having replaced the imperial palace, is now presented as the "residence city" that is "cluttered with its own dregs" (1988c: 24, trans. modified).

What took place over the course of these "thousands of years" (1988c: 24) during which the emperor's messenger carried out his entrusted mission can be described in terms of *translatio imperii*. The citizens — the 'dregs' of imperial time — who were at the beginning located beyond the palace's "outermost gate" and figured for long centuries as the unruly objects of emperor's rule, were now themselves turned into rulers, producing their own dregs. Yet whereas, in imperial times, the dregs were located outside the walls of the emperor's palace, they were now placed at the very heart of the city as the new political configuration's highest achievement. The imperial community underwent transformation into a modern society by carefully differentiating its "crowds" and "multitudes" from one another through the establishment of "palaces", "habitations", "chambers", "stairs", "courts", and "gates", (1988c: 24) but it simultaneously produced a series of unprocessed residues, blurring the divisions that had been introduced. As Foucault put it, in the final outcome, these "heterotopias" used to "contest and invert" the system that tried to lock them in as sorts of "inner colonies" (1971: 18). In their apocryphal operations, they "desiccate speech, stop words in their tracks, contest the very possibility of grammar at its source" (Foucault 1971: 18).

Thus what the arrival of the evening's 'moon grammar' ultimately amounts to is this subterranean redrawing of 'daylight' boundaries. Understood this way, the same 'evening' that distills modern society out of the imperial community simultaneously emancipates it from its galloping compartmentalization that imprisons its constituents within their individual cages. Kafka never tired of pointing out how much modern society animalizes its inhabitants:

> One returns to the animal. This is much easier than human existence. [. . .] [O]ne is afraid of freedom and responsibility. That is why one prefers to stifle behind the self-tinkered bars. (Janouch 1968: 44)

If everyone is encapsulated in his or her own truth, the road to the common truth cannot be but blocked: "Truth is indivisible, so it cannot know itself; whoever wants to know it cannot but be Lie itself" (Kafka 2012: 196). Although modern individuals chose for themselves the role of the truth's couriers, they in fact act as its distorters, who hunt each other through the world, calling out to each other their 'messages' that are bereft of their true meaning (Kafka 2012: 192). The only way out of such self-enclosure of individuals into their private rooms is to take advantage of the windows – "openings through which one flows forth into the world" (Kafka 1976: 416) – particularly when the evening arrives. It is precisely such an emancipation that is undertaken by the 'you' at the end of "An Imperial Message". Only a gaze from the window into the 'empire of darkness' makes it possible for the forgotten truth to suddenly re-appeal the observer. After all, it is not the truth itself that matters so much as the endurance of its appeal. As Benjamin noted in one of his letters, Kafka "sacrificed truth for the sake of clinging to transmissibility" (Benjamin 1966: 763).

This orientation of his explains why the 'you' is by no means an isolated instance in his work. Many among his characters, banished into the evening of their 'heterotopias', discover that which escapes the society's daylight. Consider for example the man from the country in "Before the Law" whose eyesight, after having sat for many years before the law,

> begins to fail, and he does not know whether the world is really darker or whether his eyes are only deceiving him. Yet in his darkness he is now aware of a radiance that streams inextinguishably from the gateway of the Law. Now he has not very long to live. (Kafka 1988f: 23)

So it is only when the evening (of one's life) arrives, and when one's return into the daylight's law becomes impossible, that one becomes aware of the whole splendor of the truth. It reveals itself to individuals only when it is too late for them to apply it themselves, in the case of the man from the country because he leaves behind his earthly life, and in the case of the 'you' at the window because the emperor's message got forever stuck on its way. "Nobody could fight his way" through the cluttered residence city, the parable reads, "and especially not with a message from a dead man" (Kafka 1988c: 24, trans. modified). At the end of the day, the emperor's messenger behaves as modern individuals in Kafka's aphorism, frantically transmitting the truth that is emptied of any meaning (2012: 192).

Under such circumstances, one can never be certain whether that which reveals itself is indeed the truth, or just a phantasy of it as induced by a longing for it. The way it manifests itself to those for whom the access to it is forever denied is instantaneous, glaring, and perplexing. In his conversations and diary notes, as we will come to see, Kafka imagines it in a very similar way as Benjamin, for whom the forgotten truth manifests itself "fleetingly and transitorily" (Benjamin 1979: 66) like a "flame" or a "flash" (*Aufblitzen*; 1980b: 213). It is worth noting that Freud as well, for his part, associated the resurfacing of suppressed memory traces with the flickering-up (*Aufleuchten*). (Freud 1975: 368) We find the same rendering of the lost truth in Kafka's fictions. Next to the aforementioned radiance of the truth (of the law) in "Before the Law", there is its flashing appearance in *The Trial*, as experienced by Josef K. from the spot of his execution surrounded by darkness:

> Like a flash of light, the two casements of a window parted and a human figure, faint and thin from the distance and height, lent far out in one swift movement then stretched its arms out even farther. Who was it? A friend? A kind person? Someone who felt for him? Someone who wanted to help? Was it just one? Or all of them? Was help still possible? Were there still objections he'd forgotten? Of course there were. Logic may be unshakeable, but it cannot hold out against a human being who wants to live. (2009: 164)

Yet although the truth is as elusive as a flash, neither the 'you' at the end of "An Imperial Message" nor the man from the country, or Josef K. for that matter, give up its evoking. It is true that Josef K., while laid on the ground, catches sight of someone else on the window, whereas the 'you' himself or herself takes advantage of the window panorama, but, ultimately, their evocation of the lost truth emancipates them both from the pressure of their 'historical fate'. It is for the sake of this emancipation that they cling to it. Josef K., for his part, refused to perform what his guards presumably considered to be his duty — plunging their knife into his own body — but "instead he turned his neck, that was still free, and looked around" (2009: 164) as if searching for the lost truth of his life. As for the 'you', whom the emperor's message was envisaged to be hammered into by the "magnificent beating of [his messengers'] fists on [his or her] door" — he or she, after the failure of the imperial mission, evokes it through dreaming in order to rescue it from oblivion. Through such attachment to prehistory, both of them point to the limits of historical law.

Calculation vs. exposure

The dreaming evocation of the lost truth thus proves to be an important means for the survival of those whom history has overnight turned into its outsiders. It releases possibilities, which history tends to suppress in order not to avert its participants from its course. Like his 'assigned' outsiders, Kafka as the author also engaged dreaming to "disclose reality behind which the idea [of reality] lingers" (Janouch 1968: 56). However, unlike them who acted under the pressure of their 'historical fate', he strategically considered that for those who confront this disclosed reality in their life, its flame is "horrible", and for those who face it in fiction, it is "shocking" (Janouch 1968: 56). To avoid this shock for his readers, he prefers to present it indirectly, through the terrified face of his characters who suddenly meet its shine (Kafka 2012: 194). In accordance with this, he once confided to Max Brod that all convincing passages of his works:

> always deal with the fact that someone is dying, that it is hard for him to do so, that it seems unjust to him, or at least harsh, and the reader is moved by this, or at least he should be. But for me, who believe that I shall be able to lie contentedly on my deathbed, such scenes are secretly a game; indeed, in the death enacted I rejoice in my own death, hence calculatingly exploit the attention that the reader concentrates on death, have a much clearer understanding of it than he, of whom I suppose that he will loudly lament on his deathbed, and for these reasons my lament is as perfect as can be, nor does it suddenly break off, as is likely to be the case with a real lament, but dies beautifully and purely away. (Kafka 1976: 321)

Kafka's authoring thus calculatingly flies around the truth's unbearable light in order "to find a spot in the dark void where the ray of [its] light [. . .] can be powerfully captured" (Kafka 1986b: 104). This strategy enables "a higher type of observation" provided "with its own laws of motion", which is "more incalculable", "more joyful", "more ascendant" in 'its course' than the one that his figures can afford (Kafka 1976: 407). Placed on "another planet", his authoring, at least "in happy moments", enjoys "the freedom of movement completely lacking to me here" (Kafka 1976: 409), i.e. among the fellow beings. As he remarked in a letter to Brod in April 1918, in the compartmentalized world bereft of a unifying truth, art has lost its earthly place anyway. This drove artists to move to the moon, which the earth has shaken off in order to solidify itself, but which they precisely therefore choose as their new homeland (Kafka 1958: 240–241).

The moon is obviously a much more comfortable shelter for the activity of evocation than the window, the stool next to the Law's door, or the spot of execution for that matter. The 'you', the man from the country, and Josef K. are almost immobilized, riveted to their confined places. By evoking the lost truth, they try to remedy their predicament. But despite their efforts, the latter never stops embarrassing them. Faced with execution, Josef K. behaves pitifully: "Then he folded up the clothes carefully, like things that are going to be used again, if not in the immediate future" (Kafka 2009: 164). Toward the end of his life, the man from the country also behaves childishly, begging the fleas 'to help him and to change the doorkeeper's mind' (Kafka 1988f: 23). Compared to this 'touching' behavior by his 'departing' characters, Kafka places his author completely 'above the fray', enabling him to open impartial and sovereign vistas on his fellow beings. While they are still exposed, his 'posthumous shelter' gives him the opportunity for an adequate payback to those who humiliated him while he was alive:

> He reveals himself in his true nature only after his death, only when he is alone. Being dead is for the individual what Saturday evening is for chimney-sweeps: they wash their bodies clean of soot. Then it becomes visible whether his contemporaries have harmed him more than he has harmed his contemporaries. In the latter case, he was a great man.
> (Kafka 2012: 208)

The triumph of the prehistorical law of revenge on those who have wronged you is thus safeguarded. Whereas the author achieves an almost ahistorical, inhuman independence, his characters, enmeshed in history, remain all too humanly restricted:

> A human being, even if he is infallible, sees in the other only that part for which the strength of his sight, and the nature of his sight, is adequate. But like everyone, only to an extreme, he is obsessed with restricting himself to the limits set by the strength of his fellow man's sight.
> (Kafka 2012: 207)

Exploring and mimicking: Limited vs. limitless

Although the 'you', the man from the country, and Josef K. do make an effort to exempt themselves from such dependence on the law of history by evoking its lost truth, it turns out that their exposures to it set unbridgeable limits upon their exemptions. However, Kafka's characters also engage some further technologies of exemption from the vicissitudes of history, as epitomized by Robinson's *attentive exploration* of the 'heterotopia' that his fellow men have relegated him to. Recall that the man from the country, who decided to wait before the Law's door instead of entering through it, carefully explores the doorkeeper during his yearlong sitting until 'he has come to know even the fleas in his fur collar' (Kafka 1988f: 23). As Kafka notes in the diary entry of 18 February 1920, Robinson's idea was to get to know the terms of his banishment as accurately as possible in order to outmaneuver them. (2012: 207) Like the 'you', the man from the country, and Josef K., he operates as the suppressed remnant of prehistoric time amidst the world of historical progress, which Benjamin rightly takes to be Kafka's favorite kind of characters (Benjamin 2007a: 131). Attached to the 'flame' of this time that shines in the darkness of their 'heterotopias', the explorers have a more active attitude to their 'historical fate' than the evokers, although the depth of their exploration depends upon the narrative position that the author assigns them.

They figure either as protagonists or narrators, animal or humble. To the first category belongs, for instance, Bucephalus, Alexander the Great's battle horse, whom the narrator of "The New Advocate" presents as the remnant of remote empires in the modern labyrinthine world that does not leave space for their historic undertakings or heroic deeds. In this world, nobody really knows the law that he or she ought to follow and, besides, there is no leader who epitomizes it. Faced with such uneasy circumstances, Bucephalus turns into a peculiar advocate who, instead of practicing this imaginary law, scrutinizes its books. As an envoy of the lost truth, he is better equipped to uncover the restrictions of the new one. Whereas Bucephalus is only a protagonist, from whom the story's narrator is slightly distanced, the explorer in "The Problem of Our Laws" is its humble narrator who takes a slightly ironical distance from the explorations that have been undertaken by his group of people:

> Some of us among the people have attentively scrutinized the doings of the nobility since the earliest times and possess records made by our forefathers – records which we have conscientiously continued – and claim to recognize amid the countless number of facts certain main tendencies which permit of this or that historical formulation; but when in accordance with these scrupulously tested and logically ordered conclusions we seek to adjust ourselves somewhat for the present or the future, everything becomes uncertain, and our work seems only an intellectual game, for perhaps these laws that we are trying to unravel do not exist at all. (Kafka 1988o: 482)

This self-reflective explorer, who explores the explorations themselves, reappears among others as the humble stonemason in "At the Construction of the Great Wall of China", the learned ape in "A Report to an Academy", or the dog-loner in the "Investigations of a Dog". Guided by their exploratory spirit, all of them undergo the same 'vindictive' transformation from almost subhuman instances into the agencies who, as it were, develop superhuman abilities.

The narrator of the "Investigations of a Dog" parts ways with other dogs because he cannot familiarize himself with their "many distinctions of class, of kind, of occupation" (Kafka 1988h: 312) that widely separate them from one another and engage them "in strange vocations that are often incomprehensible even to our canine neighbors". Under such compartmentalized circumstances, he sticks to the "communal impulse" (Kafka 1988h: 312) that got lost in the canine prehistory. Being thus "stranded in the present" (Fritzsche 2004), like many of Kafka's other characters, he lives "solitary and withdrawn", as "a somewhat cold, reserved, shy, and calculating" dog, "with nothing to occupy me save my hopeless but, as far as I am concerned, indispensable little investigations" (Kafka 1988h: 311). His investigations make him skeptical of the so-called historical progress.

> It is as if one were to praise someone because with the years he grows older, and in consequence comes nearer and nearer to death with increasing speed. [. . .] I can only see decline everywhere, in saying which, however, I do not mean that earlier generations were essentially better than ours, but only younger; that was their great advantage, their memory was not so overburdened as ours today, it was easier to get them to speak out, and even if nobody actually succeeded in doing that, the possibility of it was greater, and it is indeed this greater sense of possibility that moves us so deeply when we listen to those old and strangely simple stories. (Kafka 1988h: 330–331)

In the background of historical necessity, the narrator's investigations uncover the contingency of prehistory when "the edifice of dogdom was still loosely put together, the true Word could still have intervened, planning or replanning the structure, changing it at will, transforming it into its opposite" (Kafka 1988h: 331). As a different investigator from the institutional ones of today — the one devoted to the lost truth of the past — he prizes this "freedom higher than everything else. Freedom! Certainly such freedom as is possible today is a wretched business. But nevertheless freedom, nevertheless a possession" (Kafka 1988h: 346).

The dog's unshakeable 'sense of potentiality'[1] finds its corroboration in Josef K.'s repeated catching sight of possibilities that were discarded, or at least neglected, by so-called historical progress. Acting as Benjamin's "chronic" who lets "nothing that ever happened" go unnoticed (Benjamin 1977d: 252), he scrutinizes apparently insignificant scenes, such as the exterior and environment of the building in which his first hearing takes place (Kafka 2009: 29), a horrible suburban scene that has no visible connection with his case (Kafka 2009: 100), and the three 'shining' scenes while the guards are taking him to the execution site: first, in an illuminated window, two small children in a playpen (Kafka 2009: 161), then "[t]he water, glittering and quivering in the moonlight", and

---

[1] This concept (*Möglichkeitssinn*) is connected with the hero of Robert Musil's novel *The Man without Qualities* (first volume 1930) who develops "primal resistance of the heart" to the "hardened world" into which one was "involuntarily put" (Musil 2014: 130). "You cannot find anywhere a sufficient reason that everything came as it had come; it also could have turned out differently" (Musil 2014: 131).

finally how "[e]verything was bathed in moonlight, with the naturalness and calm no other light possesses" (Kafka 2009: 163). Again and again, the 'moon grammar' fascinates Kafka's assignees but since they still share their fellow beings' daylight, they are prevented to indulge in it to the same extent as the author who enjoys the complete seclusion of a "dead man" (Kafka 1965: 412).

Next to exploring prehistory's possibilities, there are characters who *spontaneously mimic* it amidst history. To illustrate this further technology of exempting oneself from history, in his essay on Kafka, Benjamin introduces the peculiar figure of Odradek as a most bastardly and, at the same time, a most mobile "receptacle of the forgotten" (Benjamin 2007a: 132). By his monstrous outlook, Odradek epitomizes the "distorted" "form which things assume in oblivion" (Benjamin 2007a: 133). However, portrayed as being permanently on the move and with an "indeterminate residence", he "stays alternately in the attic, on the staircase, in the corridors, and in the hall". He is so 'extraordinarily nimble and can never be laid hold of' that the 'family father' is concerned he will, as his family's most shameful representative, finally outlive it (Kafka 1988k: 469–470). What makes these outsiders endure, is that history has turned them into its shame, which, paradoxically, makes them feel shame for history, i.e. take on the role of its denouncers.

This turnover of history's culprits into its denouncers is corroborated by the final sentences of *The Trial*, in which Josef K. is ashamed for being treated "like a dog" by his executors. "It seemed as if his shame would live on after him" (Kafka 2009: 165). According to the "Letter to the Father", it is the same shame that Kafka-son feels for Kafka-father who never stops humiliating him and his friends by applying various animal attributes to them (Kafka 2008: 27). Whereas the father used to stigmatize them as vermin who ought to be 'euthanized', the son pays him back by adopting the role of a parasite that "not only bites but even goes as far to suck blood for the sake of preserving its life" (Kafka 2008: 85). The euthanizing thus changes not only direction but also its carrier. Instead of readily acknowledging an agency that punishes, degrades, and wounds them, the 'misfits' take subterranean revenge upon it. By dismantling the logics of power that inheres in history's apparently egalitarian law, they enable the prehistorical law of vengeance to outlive its historical 'overcoming'. The operation that carries out this turnover has all the characteristics of 'subversive mimicry' as analyzed by Homi Bhabha in postcolonial circumstances (Bhabha 1994: 94–132). But whereas Kafka makes his characters perform it visibly for the readers, his author reserves for himself an invisible, 'parasitic' manner of its performance. In his diary entry of 28 September 1917, he depicts his revengeful narrative strategy as the exposure of the moral weaknesses of other people in such a way that humankind does not notice this insidious public operation of its sending to hell, but accepts it with universal approval and love for the sinner who sent it to hell (Kafka 1976: 387).

Entrusting: Direct and indirect

Although prominent among Kafka's subaltern characters, evocation, exploration, and subversive mimicry are not the only techniques by which they undermine the idea of historical progress. There are other "receptacles of the forgotten" in his work, whose manner of paying back to the representatives of history is less surreptitious. Consider the officer from "The Penal Colony" who fanatically adheres to his former commandant's execution rituals, which historical progress has since surpassed and which his new commandant therefore forbade. This brings him into a position similar to that of the 'you', the man from the country, and Josef K., all of whom are committed to a past to which they are deprived access, although his room for maneuver is more promising than theirs. While they, unable to materialize their commitment in their present circumstances, find their refuge in the reconfigured past, the officer, surrounded on his island by the same deafness for the legacy of the past, has the traveling explorer available, to redeem his endangered mission.[2] This opportunity somewhat empowers his position in comparison to theirs. By *entrusting* the traveling explorer, he behaves like the emperor from "An Imperial Message", who tries to save his endangered empire by entrusting its mission to the messenger. In the same way as the emperor checks if the messenger has properly understood his message, the officer repeatedly checks if the explorer has properly deciphered the message that he wants to entrust him with (Kafka 1988g: 173; 186). However, as with the emperor's message, in the new world nobody really cares for it,[3] the explorer proves repeatedly unable to discern it, (Kafka 1988g: 173–74, 186) which forces

---

[2] In W. and E. Muir's translation, this character is introduced simply as "explorer" although the German word *Forschungsreisende* unmistakably points out the traveling (i.e. limited) character of his exploration, which is very important for my argument. This is why I consistently translate the German word as "traveling explorer".

[3] At the very beginning of the story the narrator says that the disinterested explorer "accepted merely out of politeness the Commandant's invitation to witness the execution". "Nor did the colony itself betray much interest in this execution." (Kafka 1988g: 165) "[T]here was no one present". The soldier who attended the execution out of duty, "let his head hang, and was paying no attention to anything" (Kafka 1988g: 167). In short, only the officer was really interested in it.

the officer to "yell in the explorer's ear [. . .] with the full force of his lungs" (Kafka 1988g: 174).

It is this repeated shouting (Kafka 1988g: 184) that discloses his powerlessness in comparison with the emperor who *whispers* his message into the messenger's ear. Whereas the emperor is superior to the messenger and all others, the officer is inferior to both the new commander and the traveling explorer. He is forced to convince the traveling explorer to change the inimical attitude of the new commander toward the legacy of the past. He presses into him, with a "strong insistence" and "clenched fists", the task of helping him against the acting commandant (Kafka 1988g: 182). The explorer's calculated reservations drive him further into seizing his trustee by both arms, gazing into his face, and shouting loudly (Kafka 1988g: 184). In this way, a powerless submission to the former commandant turns into a powerful aggression toward the traveling explorer who declines to share it and, after this aggression fails to achieve its envisaged effect, into aggression against the aggressor himself. Once the traveling explorer refused to carry out his plan, the officer sets the condemned man free, takes his place, and lets the torturing apparatus execute him himself. This abrupt substitution reinvigorates his constant pending between the powerless inferiority and powerful superiority. Through his commitment to the forgotten past, he already acted as a doppelganger of the inferior 'you', and through his entrusting of the traveling explorer as the doppelganger of the superior emperor. *Almost the same but not quite* like each of them, he contagiously couples their inferiority and superiority with one another. At the end he undertakes a more radical immersion into inferiority in order to get the superior fame of the commandant whom he is attached to, and whom his 'nameless adherents' have secretly buried in the teahouse, in expectation of his triumphant revival (Kafka 1988g: 192).

But the officer's self-sacrificial replacement of the condemned man contains even further potential for the contagious entanglement of opposites. It is worth remembering that the condemned man, whose place the officer takes, was a 'doggish submissive' servant who suddenly assaulted his superior.[4] Thus he has undergone the same transformation from complete subordination into a will for

---

[4] Focalized through the traveling explorer's perspective, the narrator confides to the reader that "the condemned man looked so like a submissive dog that one might have thought he could be left to run free on the surrounding hills and would only need to be whistled for when the execution was due to begin" (Kafka 1988g: 165). After the captain has lashed him with his riding whip across the face because he fell asleep on duty, the servant "caught hold of his master's legs, shook him, and cried: 'Throw that whip away or I'll eat you alive'" (Kafka 1988g: 171). It is for this offence that he was sentenced.

power as did the officer. In his seminal study of the story, Walter Müller-Seidel describes the officer's verbal attack on the traveling explorer as an attempt at domination by speech (*Herrschaft durch Rede*), comparing it to the behavior of Kafka's father, which, as described in his "Letter to the Father", consisted of "insults, threats, irony, spiteful laughter, and [. . .] self-pity" (Kafka 2008: 33). In the same way as the father's violence destroyed the son's capacities to reply (Kafka 2008: 31), the officer's violence silences those of the traveling explorer, who barely gets a word in. Their aggressive speech engraves itself on the docile bodies of their interlocutors in a similar way to the torturing machine, bereaving their victims of the chance to defend themselves against their operations (Müller-Seidel 1986: 123–124). Thus, invisibly, through his firm commitment to 'prehistory', the officer acts as the doppelganger of Kafka-son, and through the violent way in which he demonstrates this commitment, as the doppelganger of Kafka-father. *Almost the same but not quite* like the son or the father for that matter, which means the one as obstructively enabled by the other. The substitution for the condemned man intensifies this mutual obstructive enabling of opposites because, on the one hand, one cannot prove one's commitment to the past in a more submissive way than through one's sacrifice for it and, on the other, one cannot entrust the other to carry on one's imperiled mission in a more aggressive way than this.

The sketched contagious entanglement of opposites makes the very core of Kafka's narrative construction. Among all other things, it explains why, although the narrator exposes the officer's past-oriented fanaticism as violent, he hesitates to channel his sympathies toward the traveling explorer as the representative of historical progress. Unlike the above delineated inferior and confined explorers, this one is superior and mobile. The narrator portrays him as an indifferent visitor who arrives in the colony as the deputy of the so-called progressive part of the world, which establishes such colonies as the dumping grounds for the 'retrograde' elements of their societies. The story was inspired by the book *My Trip to the Penal Colonies* (Meine Reise nach den Strafkolonien, 1912) by the German criminologist Robert Heindl, who was appointed by his Empire to visit other empires' colonies and to investigate the possibility of establishing a German penal colony along a similar model. (Müller-Seidel 1986: 80) This is why the narrator presents him as thinking of himself in the following way:

> He was neither a member of the penal colony nor a citizen of the state to which it belonged. [. . .] [H]e traveled only as an observer, with no intention at all of altering other people's methods of administering justice. (Kafka 1988g: 176)

Even if the officer's "explanation of the judicial procedure had not satisfied him" (Kafka 1988g: 171) because he "was fundamentally honorable and unafraid" (1988g: 184), the traveling explorer had to "remind himself that this was in any case a penal colony where extraordinary measures were needed and that military discipline must be enforced to the last" (Kafka 1988g: 171). Not only is the narrator but also the officer well aware of the traveling explorer's hesitation to intervene into the retrograde administration of a colony as he undoubtedly would do if he would notice its manifestations in his own country. Consider the officer's slightly ironical comment implying that, although they are both serving their countries, contrary to the officer's confinement on this godforsaken island, the explorer is freely traveling throughout the world, which enabled him to develop a more tolerant view of it.

> [Y]ou have seen and learned to appreciate the peculiarities of many peoples, and so you would not be likely to take a strong line against our proceedings, as you might do in your own country. (Kafka 1988g: 180)

As regards the 'tolerance' of the traveling explorer's worldview, both the officer and the explorer know that colonies were established precisely to make space for brutalities, which were forbidden in the public spheres of developed countries. Since the explorer perceives the condemned man as a "stupid-looking, wide-mouthed creature with bewildered hair and face" (Kafka 1988g: 165), he obviously does not think that the highest achievements of human civilization were envisaged for such "poor, humble creatures" (Kafka 1988g: 191). Therefore, when the soldier and the condemned man consider jumping into the boat that takes the explorer off the island, he lifts "a heavy knotted rope from the floor boards" and "threatens them with it" to keep them from attempting such (Kafka 1988g: 192). This gesture manifests his conviction, characteristic of the panicking power-keepers in the outgoing European empires that such 'degenerate creatures' have to be kept in colonies to prevent them from poisoning the 'healthy organisms' of advanced societies. Not only did Kafka's father support this eugenic policy but also many notable scientists of the time, such as the Austrian criminologist Hans Groß, who even encouraged the hospitalization of his hyper-sensible son Otto on this very basis (Müller-Seidel 1986: 67). If society cannot eradicate or transport its 'misfits' far away, read his opinion, it should at least isolate them in domestic asylums. Kafka, who was similarly discriminated by his own father, not only shared the destiny of this 'weak' generation of intellectuals and artists but actively co-created its resilient consciousness (Müller-Seidel 1986: 70–71). Thus, if the officer on the one hand redoubles the power keepers' violence, the traveling explorer on the other copies the power keepers' discrimination. Instead of an *either-or* between them, the reader is confronted with *neither-nor*. As both are contaminated by their opposites, he or she cannot identify with any of them.

The traveling explorer's relationship to the officer has equally contagious effects for both. As his tolerance for diverse habits is gradually dismantled as the intolerance for 'degenerate creatures', he repeats the officer's perversion. But opposed to the calculated cynicism of his worldview — he has limited empathy for the officer[5] but none for the condemned man[6] — the officer readily accepts torture and death for his commitment. Along with his commitment to the past, this readiness parallels that of Kafka himself, who made himself famous for his highly elaborated self-punishing imagery that induced feelings of liberation and happiness (Müller-Seidel 1986: 18–19). In Kafka's horrifying imagination,[7] setting oneself free is always associated with one's exposure to torture. Thus, in his 'Letter to the Father', he remarks that his liberation from the father reminded him of a worm that, "its tail pinned down to the ground, tearing loose from the front and wriggling away to the side" (2008: 62). Also, he once wrote to Milena:

> Yes, torture is very important to me, I am concerned with nothing but being-tortured and torturing! Why? [. . .] The stupidity that lies in it [. . .] I once expressed in this way: 'The animal escapes the whip of the Lord, whipping itself to become the Lord, and does not know that this is only a phantasy, created by a new knot in the Lord's whip belt.'
> (Kafka 1983: 29)

---

5 He "admires the officer" (Kafka 1988g: 167), entrusting to him "I shall never in any circumstances betray your confidence" and "your sincere conviction has touched me, even though it cannot influence my judgment" (Kafka 1988g: 184).

6 Next to explorer's perceiving the condemned man as an ugly creature and "submissive dog" (Kafka 1988g: 165), there is his conviction that "the condemned man was a complete stranger, not a fellow countryman or even at all sympathetic to him" (Kafka 1988g: 176).

7 For example, in the diary entry of 4 May 1913 he reports of the resurfacing "image of a pork butcher's broad knife that quickly and with mechanical regularity chops into me from the side and cuts off very thin slices which fly off almost like shavings because of the speed of the work" (Kafka 1976: 221). In the diary entry of 21 July 1913 we read: "To be pulled in through the ground-floor window of a house by a rope tied around one's neck and to be yanked up, bloody and ragged, through all the ceilings, furniture, walls, and attics, without consideration, as if by a person who is paying no attention, until the empty nose, dropping the last fragments of me when it breaks through the roof tiles, is seen on the roof" (Kafka 1976: 224). And the entry of 16 September 1915 reads: "Between throat and chin would seem to be the most rewarding spot to stab. Lift the chin and stick the knife into the tensed muscles. But this spot is probably rewarding only in one's imagination. You expect there to see a magnificent gush of blood and a network of sinews and little bones like you find in the legs of roast turkeys" (Kafka 1976: 342).

Yet, as Canetti (1969: 117) aptly remarks, self-torturers are so passionately attached to their defeats because they seek salvation in them. The overlap of Kafka's tortured body with that of the officer, who willingly takes the prisoner's place on the lethal bed of the apparatus, becomes stunning in the diary entry of 3 August 1917, in which he describes his phantasy:

> Once more I screamed at the top of my voice into the world. Then they shoved a gag into my mouth, handcuffed my hands and feet and blindfolded me. I was rolled back and forth a number of times, I was set upright and knocked down again, this too several times, they jerked at my legs so that I jumped with pain, they let me lie quietly for a moment, but then, taking me by surprise, stabbed deep into me with something sharp, here and there, at random, wherever their mood drove them. (Kafka 1976: 376; trans. modified)

If the officer's punishing treatment of himself mirrors that of his author, then the author has sneaked into his skin in the same hideous way in which the officer, in his imaginary scenarios, sneaks into the skin of the explorer and the Commandant. He boldly speculates what the one and the other have thought and done, or would think or do under given circumstances, drawing repercussions for his actions against them from these conjectures. (Kafka 1988g: 180–184) By assimilating their optics to direct it against them, he practices 'subversive mimicry'. After it fails to achieve the desired effect, he engages their presumed degradation of him *against him himself*, ultimately eliminating this 'incorrigible remnant of prehistory' from history. If Bhabha for his part analyzed 'subversive mimicry', this inverse operation of self-degradation through the point of view of the others was analyzed by his predecessors, William Du Bois and Frantz Fanon. Du Bois writes of "double-consciousness, the sense of always looking at one's self through the eyes of the others, of measuring one's soul by the tape of a world that always looks on in amused contempt and pity" (Du Bois 1990: 8). Fanon points out its pathogenic consequences, turning the failed self into an abject object of constant obsession, self-reproach and punishment (Fanon 1967: 210–217).

The officer engages 'subversive mimicry' in the direct transference of his trust on the traveling explorer but, after its manipulation fails, he switches to an 'interpellation' of unknown descendants (Althusser 1971) as characteristic of all self-victimizing, i.e. "agentless" acts.[8] The distant progeny is expected to show respect for the legacy of the sacrificed and to be attached to it across historical ruptures and lines of difference, in the same way as the 'you' had been

---

8 According to J. M. Coetzee (1992: 144), an "agentless" act blurs its ultimate agent by making his or her unknown predecessors resonate in his or her voice.

attached to the imperial legacy in the age of its complete oblivion. But unlike the emperor who possessed powerful means for the worldwide distribution of his legacy, the officer's legacy remains dependent upon the only 'assignee' who can transmit it further, the traveling explorer, who for his part mercilessly exposes it as fanatic and perilous. Therefore, whenever Kafka's 'assignees' entrust their victimhood to the others, they manifest their dependency on these others' reaction. They are simply too close to these others to undertake an independent action of their entrusting. Recall how the chaplain responds to Josef K. when asked to come down from the pulpit: "I had to speak to you from a distance at first, otherwise I let myself be too easily influenced and forget my official duty" (Kafka 2009: 153). Distance is the basic prerequisite for the execution of power.

Kafka understands this all too well in his diary entry of 21 August 1913, in which he remarks that he extremely rarely talks even to his closest family members because "I have not the slightest thing to talk to them about" and because "everything that is not literature [i.e. does not address an unknown other] bores me and I hate it" (Kafka 1976: 231). In the diary entry of 24 January 1915 he notes that "[t]he difficulties [. . .] I have in speaking to other people arise from the fact that my thinking [. . .] is entirely nebulous [. . .]. No one will want to lie in clouds of mist with me [. . .]; when two people come together it dissolves of itself and is nothing." (Kafka 1976: 329) Accordingly, he confides to Felice: "Writing is the only form of expression that suits me", as it addresses someone distant who belongs to another world.

> He feels more deserted with second person than when alone. If he is together with someone, this second person reaches out for him and he is helplessly delivered into his hand. If he is alone, all mankind reaches out for him – but the innumerable outstretched arms become entangled with one another and no one reaches to him. (Kafka 1976: 420–421)

Concomitantly, his fictional 'assignees' who directly and straightforwardly commit their trustees are *almost the same but not quite* like the author, which now no longer means contagiously *entangled with* but irrevocably *inferior to* him. While he entangled them with one another, their author took care to disentangle himself from their inextricably intertwined histories. Getting out of history into the remedial prehistory, reminiscent of the secret strategy that he applied to his father: "My writing [. . .] was a deliberately long drawn-out parting from you, yet although you instigated it, I was able to choose its eventual direction" (Kafka 2008: 63). This appears to have been Kafka's habitual way of paying back his former fellow beings for sending him into irrevocable exile, and thus of enabling the vindictive law of prehistory to deactivate the 'egalitarian' law of history. He silently kept loyal to his favorite Charles Dickens whom he, significantly, nevertheless dismantled in the following way: "There is heartlessness behind his sentimentally overflowing style" (Kafka 1976: 388). There is an equal heartlessness behind Kafka's compassion with his assignees. This is how his authorial politics clandestinely resumed their selfish mode of operation that it was at pains to keep at bay.

7 Positional Outsiders and the Performance of Sacrifice

Kafka's narrative authority: Commitment to subhuman creatures

The geopolitically reconfigured post-imperial East Central Europe became a harsh political prison for many of its constituencies, which is why their sense of belonging to their newly formed nation-states was replaced with a sense of longing for that which these states excluded from their constitutions and official memories. New state nationalisms befell and impoverished these constituencies, pinned them to the wall of dominating nations, stripped them of choice, silenced their alternatives, and nullified their complex identity with an imposed demonization of the "other" (Brubaker 1996: 20–21). Since they longed for a different way to cohabit the political spaces to which they were affiliated, they forged alliances with "spectral humans" elsewhere who also felt "stranded in the present" (Fritzsche 2004). This was now suddenly possible because, while post-imperial Europe's modernization seriously endangered some of its constituencies' material survival, it simultaneously immensely increased the mobility of their imagination (Appadurai 1998: 6). Thanks to the substantially improved institutional, traffic and communicational networks, "[e]ven the meanest and most hopeless of lives, the most brutal and dehumanizing of circumstances, the harshest of lived inequalities" became "open to the play of the imagination" (Appadurai 1998: 54). Unexpectedly, these positional outsiders got the opportunity to connect to outsiders from other shores who had hitherto been barely known to them, paving the way for alternative, imaginary kinds of human togetherness, resilient to those that were imposed. However, deprived of resources and thus prevented from materializing themselves in given political circumstances, they were projected as commonalities yet-to-come.

Those who felt "stranded in the present" of post-imperial European states engaged fiction as one of the media for establishing their alternative commonalities. Unlike mass media, myths or discursive prose that, by their very nature, address collective audiences, fiction introduces indistinct patterns of affiliation, which through their non-appropriative identification disregard differences among the affiliates. By attending to "the connective tissues and membranes, that animate each case even while enabling the discovery of shared motivations and shared tropes" (Hirsch 2012: 206), its authors try to escape their historically and politically established identities. Following their "appetite for alterity" (Silverman 1986: 181), they leave behind their inherited selves and cultural norms in order to align themselves with those who have compulsively lost their "human" face.

Such authorial self-displacement into the radical otherness of positional outsiders adopted a peculiar form in the works of Franz Kafka, who consistently dispossessed his narrative authority of established "human" attributes. It is worth recalling that his contemporary Hugo von Hofmannsthal, whom Kafka greatly admired (Wanberg 2016; Gray 2005: 127; Blanchot 1992: 183), described the writer as

> living in the house of time, under the stairs, where everyone must pass him and no one respects him [. . .] an undetected beggar in the place of the dogs [. . .] without a job in this house, without service, without rights, without duty.   (Hofmannsthal 1979: 66)

In the state of exception that ruled the European political space of his time by making its "givens" dizzy, ambiguous and indeterminate (1979: 60), Hofmannsthal sees myriad readers feverishly searching for "the enchantment of the poetry" (1979: 62), which is in his opinion only capable of ordering the chaos of the contemporary world (1979: 78). In order to rescue them, he entrusts the poet with the mission of sacrificing his human self by creating "every second, with each pulse, under a pressure as if an ocean lays above him, lit by no lamp, not even a mine lamp, surrounded by mocking, confusing voices" (Hofmannsthal 1979: 75). Hofmannsthal expects him to act as "a spider, spinning the yarn from his own body, to carry him over the abyss of existence" (1979: 75).

Kafka is the epitome of Hofmannsthal's author who, in the house of his time, withdraws into the disregarded place of the dogs by accepting responsibility for *all* inhabitants of the house, and in particular its outsiders:

> Each of them is an open wound on his soul. [. . .] he suffers from all them, and by suffering from them, he enjoys them [. . .] he suffers by sensing them so intense [. . .] as if they were human. [. . .] He can leave nothing out. He must not close his eyes to any creature, to any thing, to any phantom, to any spectral product of a human brain.
> (Hofmannsthal 1979: 67)

As the true inheritor of this legacy, Kafka's authorial agency makes itself highly attentive to and respectful of the outsiders that inhabit its fictional 'houses'. His work teems with creatures that neither completely belong to humankind nor to the animal world. Consider the peculiar figure of Odradek from "The Cares of a Family Man" who, as Benjamin remarks, epitomizes the "distorted" "form which things assume in oblivion" (2007a: 133). Nevertheless, the narrator allocates to this subhuman creature some superhuman traits, thus making his inferiority superior to his surroundings. Portrayed as being permanently on the move and with an "indeterminate residence", he "stays alternately in the attic, on the staircase, in the corridors, and in the hall". He is so "extraordinarily nimble and can never be laid hold of" that the "family father" is concerned he will, as his family's most shameful representative, finally outlive it (Kafka 1988k: 469–470). Another case in point is Red Peter, the narrator of "A Report to an Academy", an ape who was forced by his hunters to learn human language but through whose words an ape-like voice still reverberates. Deleuze and Guattari argue that his coughing forms a refrain that turns his "syntax into a cry" (1986: 13, 26). This cry has the force of an apostrophe, which human language lacks. Developing out of the material body rather than human personality, it deeply disturbs the humans who mistakenly assumed to have put it behind them. Red Peter is thus another positional outsider from one of the innumerable "zones of indistinction", simultaneously inferior and superior to his human surroundings.

In his seminal essay on Kafka, Benjamin pointed out the writer's enduring fascination with such figures that are "neither members of, nor strangers to, any [. . .] groups of figures, but, rather, messengers from one to another" (2007a: 117). Inhabiting "intermediate worlds", they break out from the restricted mythic space of distinct human history into the unlimited indistinct areas of prehistorical times. This "swampy ground of fluctuating experiences", as Benjamin puts it, "forms countless, uncertain, changing compounds, yielding a constant flow of new, strange products" (2007a: 131). By incessantly creating such messengers of prehistorical time, Kafka cannot but reveal his own tendency to leap out of the determined course of development as characteristic of human history. Indeed, in his diary entry of 24 January 1922 he notes:

> I want to change my place in the world entirely, which actually means that I want to go to another planet; it would be enough if I could exist alongside myself, it would even be enough if I could consider the spot on which I stand as some other spot. (Kafka 1976: 405)

This is precisely what happens in the so-called "he" series of his 1920 diaries in which he, standing on "some other spot", speaks of himself in the third person. By creating such "higher type of observation" (Kafka 1976: 407), he leaps out of the continuity of his self by opening a gap between its acting and observing parts: the second part now becoming *exterior* to the first, yet without ceasing to be its *constituent*. This "internal exterior" only belongs to the world of human action through its exemption from it. In the same way, the divine world, forever lost to human beings, only belongs to their world through its absence from it, or the sovereign, in the political state of exemption, only participates in its juridical order through his *ecstasy* (i.e. ex-stasis; Agamben 2005a: 35). What we testify to in all these cases is "the topological structure of the state of exception": "*being outside, and yet belonging*" (2005a: 35). However, unlike his characters that, condemned to the prehistorical "zones of indistinction", live the vulnerable extraterritoriality of subhuman creatures, Kafka pulls his author out, as we will come to see, into the ex-historical and exterritorial 'state of exception' of superhuman agencies.

The enforced prehistorical and the self-appointed ex-historical outsiders: Cross-breeding

This means that we have to distinguish between two kinds of positional outsiders, the *enforced prehistorical* ones and the *self-appointed ex-historical* ones, although Kafka is at constant pains to melt one into another by way of their cross-breeding. The moral extraterritoriality of the first that exposes them to others, and the political ex-territoriality of the second that imposes them upon others, paradoxically support each other. On the one hand, Kafka systematically entitles animal figures or objects by raising them to the status of narrators or focalizers. Besides the humanized ape Red Peter, the cases in point are the verminous bug Gregor Samsa from "The Metamorphosis", the mouse from "Josephine the Singer", the presumptive mole from "The Burrow", the dog from the "Investigations of a Dog", and the bridge from "The Bridge". Kafka also entitles human outsiders by transforming them into interrogators: consider the stonemason from "The Great Wall of China", the cobbler from "An Old Manuscript", the provincials from "The Refusal" and "The Problem of Our Laws", the hungry "Bucket Rider", the businessman from "The Married Couple", the unexpected prisoner from "The Knock at the Manor Gate", the man from the country in "Before the Law", and the land surveyor in *The Castle*. As unexpected victims of certain political, legal, or economic configurations of forces, all of them are "positional outsiders".[1]

On the other hand, Kafka lets his author, as the self-appointed outsider, unreservedly commit himself to the characters as the enforced outsiders, as if searching for the ethical justification for his political exemption from their world. It has been noted that Kafka's passionate attachment to enforced outsiders grew out of his personal experience of multiple dispossession. (Litowitz 2002: 104) He was a German-speaking secular Jew in the Czech capital Prague who, as such, was accepted neither by the Jews nor Germans nor Czechs; besides, he was an outsider to his family that was dominated by his father's despotic rule;

---

[1] Douglas Litowicz proposes "situational outsiders", defining them as "outsiders by virtue of their situation" (2002: 105), but I prefer the attribute "positional" considering these outsiders' structural banishment into the political and social indistinction. As a result, "Kafka depicts outsiders who never win their battle for justice, instead remaining forever confused, paranoid, ignorant, submissive, alienated, and self-defeating" (Litowitz 2002: 105).

also, he was an attorney at the Workers' Insurance Corporation who fought for injured Czech workers, themselves outsiders in the face of Austrian law; and, after the First World War, his generation fell outside of the law too. In a diary entry of 19 July 1910, he remarks:

> [U]ntil now we had our noses stuck into the tide of the times, now we step back, former swimmers, present walkers, and are lost. We are outside the law, no one knows it and yet everyone treats us accordingly. (Kafka 1976: 24)

Ultimately, considering that the Austrians in Prague, who administered the city, blamed their Jewish co-citizens for having stolen and misused their language, Kafka likewise became a stranger to his German mother tongue. Terrified by this series of dispossessions, he withdrew into a corner of existence, reduced to bare life. "What have I in common with Jews? I have hardly anything in common with myself and should stand very quietly in a corner, content that I can breathe." (1976: 252) Under the turbulent circumstances of *translatio imperii*, it appears, no group-belonging offered protection from the sudden deprivation.

This experience of constant threat and crisis of public space accounts for Kafka's relinquishment of human attributes, relationships, and connections. He and humans parted ways, replacing mutual belonging with a powerful longing for one another from both his and his fellow beings' side:

> Without forebears, without marriage, without heirs, with a fierce longing for forebears, marriage and heirs. They all of them stretch out their hands to me: forebears, marriage and heirs, but too far away for me. (Kafka 1976: 402)

> If he is together with someone, this second person reaches out for him and he is helplessly delivered into his hand. If he is alone, all mankind reaches out for him – but the innumerable outstretched arms become entangled with one another and no one reaches to him. (Kafka 1976: 420–421)

> I am away from home and must write home always again, even if all my home had long ago swum into eternity. All my writing is nothing but the banner of Robinson on the highest point of the island. (Kafka 1965: 392)

Kafka transferred this unrealizable longing for fellow beings from his life's reality into the relationships between the author and characters in his fictions. Both relationships, those in his life's reality as well as those in his fictions, are thus ruled by the same principle: Only after both sides are forever prevented from physically reaching one another does the possibility for their dreaming identification with the other become wide open. The failure of *belonging* to one another releases the energy of *longing* for one another. Consider the "You" at the end of "An Imperial Message" who sits at the window, when the evening arrives that separates him or her from the daylight reality, and dreams to himself or herself about the will of the dead man. Many of Kafka's characters dream to themselves of such authorial exemption from their frustrating present by attaching themselves to a lost past, but, cut off from the possibility to reach such exemption, compensatorily summon their selected trustees to provide it in the future. This is how their subhuman prehistorical condition strives to transform itself into a superhuman ex-historical one. Scenes of such entrusting appeal are abundant in Kafka's fiction: In "The Penal Colony" the officer twice screams in the traveling explorer's ear (Kafka 1988g: 174, 184), in "An Imperial Message" the emperor whispers in the ear of his messenger, demanding that the messenger whispers it back into his ear (Kafka 1988c: 24), in "A Hunger Artist" the protagonist speaks "with his lips pursed, as if for a kiss, right into the overseer's ear" (Kafka 1988b: 309), in "Before the Law" the man from the country poses his last question right into the ear of the doorkeeper (Kafka 1988f: 23), in "A Country Doctor" the ill boy whispers "Let me die" into the doctor's ear (Kafka 1988a: 251), in "The Great Wall of China" an unknown boatman whispers his imperial message into the ear of the narrator's father (Kafka 1988n: 280).

Now consider the opposite perspective of the author. Being safely exempted from history, he dreams that the characters who suffer amidst its turmoil will forget about his comfortable ex-historical shelter. But, bereft of the possibility to approach them directly and check whether they really did so, he turns to the reader, seeking to seduce the latter into ignoring his privilege in the same smooth way. As the characters are in another world, the reader is the only available trustee. However, as he or she nevertheless belongs to a different life history than the author, he or she cannot but be distrustful of the author's manipulative act of entrustment. As Kafka spells out (1976: 321), to win the reader's trust under such unfavorable conditions, he calculatingly attaches him or her to a character who faces an impending death. As the lamenting reader concentrates on the dying character, s/he embraces the author's insidious self-exemption from human death with approval and love. The author thus wins favor in the reader's eyes by apparently *adopting* the latter's basic predilections, desires, and moral ideals, while he is in fact *subverting* them, i.e. outfoxing the reader.

The political 'selection of mercies': Kafka read through his descendants

Hence in authoring his works, Kafka engages the same method of subversive mimicry against the reader that the outsiders in his fictions apply against the characters in power. If we recall Bhabha's analysis of this technology of (de-) identification as the main *political instrument* of postcolonial selves (Bhabha 1994: 94–132), we will not be astonished to find Kafka's postcolonial admirer J. M. Coetzee stating about his own technique of authoring:

> [T]he last thing I want to do is to *defiantly* embrace the ethical as against the political. [. . .] [I]f I speak from the [. . .] negative pole, it is because I am drawn or pushed there by force, even a violence, operating over the whole of the discursive field that at this moment (April 1990) we inhabit, you and I. (1992: 200)

After all, Coetzee was born into the white minority which, on behalf of two European empires, the Dutch and British, settled, ruled and exploited South Africa from the early seventeenth century deep into the twentieth century by dispossessing, discriminating, and mistreating its native population. The deep entanglement of the whites in imperial violence is the main issue of his first novel *Dusklands* (1974), with regard to whose 'Vietnam' part he remarks:

> I would regard it as morally questionable to write something like the second part of *Dusklands* – a *fiction*, note – from a position that is not historically complicit.
> (Coetzee 1992: 343)

The same holds for Kafka whose post-imperial discursive field was equally deeply divided, which is why his authorial gesture of protecting positional outsiders could not avoid complicity with their executors. There is no representation of victims that, in its turn, does not repeat victimization. Induced by the consciousness-raising of the Holocaust in the aftermath of 1968 – as laid out in chapter three – this disenchantment of all sacrificial missions urges us to read Kafka's work anew. It is in following this thread that, for example, Derrida remarked: "You have to betray [i.e. the world you belong to] in order to be truthful [i.e. to the world 'elsewhere']" (Derrida 2003: 11). "There are ethics precisely because there is this contradiction . . . [. . .] I have to respond to two injunctions, different and incompatible. That's where responsibility starts" (Derrida 2003: 32–33).

In this ambiguous context, it is worth noting that the British postmodern writer Ian McEwan, one of the prominent inheritors of Kafka's ethical sensibility in the last decades of the twentieth century, lets the chief protagonist of his novel *Saturday*, Henry Perowne, present the following train of thought:

> This is the growing complication of the modern condition, the expanding circle of moral sympathy. Not only distant people are our brothers and sisters, but foxes too, and laboratory mice, and now the fish. Perowne goes on catching and eating them, and though he'd

never drop a live lobster into boiling water, he's prepared to order one in a restaurant. The trick, as always, the key to human success and domination, is to be selective in your mercies. (2005: 127)[2]

As these are reflections of literary characters, we are of course not expected to take them at their word. They are operating within the whole network of opinions that relate to, oppose, contradict, and/or parenthesize one another. Nonetheless, in a world of unleashed competition for the truth, it is hard to see which authorial strategy ought to avoid such elimination of the 'dregs of society' for the benefit of its ultimate 'truth'. As if anticipating these insights of his post-imperial descendants in the aftermath of the Holocaust, Kafka remarks:

> Every moral standard – however opinions may differ on it – will seem too high. You will see that you are nothing but a rat's nest of miserable dissimulations. The most trifling of your acts will not be untainted by these dissimulations. (1976: 330)

In the given permanent state of exception, ethics cannot figure as the last measure of human affairs.

> [L]ife, because of its sheer power to convince has no room in it for right and wrong. As in the despairing hour of death you cannot meditate on right and wrong, so you cannot in the despairing course of life. It is enough that the arrows fit exactly in the wounds that they have made. (Kafka 1976: 402; trans. modified)

This is how Kafka sees the writer's task in the modern accelerated world of history: To make his or her remedial arrows fit exactly in the prehistorical wounds that he or she has cut open in the representative body of historical progress. Only through such a painful elimination of historical oblivion can the lost "life's splendor" be restored that "lies in wait about each one of us in all its fullness, but veiled from view, deep down, invisible, far off" (Kafka 1976: 393). Kafka's authorial politics consist in ethically sacrificing himself and others for the revival of this prehistorical "splendor".

---

[2] Considering the abovementioned euthanization of people like insects in Kafka's life and fictions, the "selection of mercies" as proposed by one of the protagonists of McEwan's *Black Dogs*, Bernard Tremaine, is even more interesting: "Most people, I told her, instinctively disliked the insect world and entomologists were the ones to take notice of it, study its ways and life-cycles and generally care about it. Naming insects, classifying them into groups and sub-groups was an important part of all that. If you learned to name a part of the world, you learned to love it. Killing a few insects was irrelevant against this larger fact" (McEwan 1992: 32).

The point of view of the wronged: A refusal of responsibility?

But considering that what is splendor for history's losers is by no means splendor for its winners, his author's ethical gesture ultimately presents itself as a retaliating political operation. This background "ulterior motive" compromises its foregrounded ethical profile. In fact, in his frequently discussed aphorism from the 'he' series, dated 15 February 1920,[3] Kafka defines man's "original sin" as a relentless claim for the status of victim, for victims are always innocent and so need not answer for their actions (2012: 206). Does this 'sin' pertain to his own writing? As Benjamin aptly noted, this refusal of responsibility "applies to the sons more than to anyone else" (2007a: 123), at least from the point of view of their fathers. The sons, in their turn, experience their fatherly authorities as "lying on top of them like giant parasites. They not only prey upon their strength, but gnaw away at the sons' right to exist" (Benjamin 2007a: 123). The result of this clash of perspectives is a never-ending process of mutual blaming, an uneasy cohabitation of 'executors' and 'victims' that disquiets the world of humans, preventing them from establishing an impartial perspective "above the fray".

As if being drawn into this vicious circle that leaves nobody's truth uninvolved, some prominent moral thinkers of the so-called late modernity spontaneously identified with the point of view of the wronged, which was so close to Kafka. Their argument might be succinctly rendered as follows: "As we are bereft of our rights by our societies' power distribution, we cannot bear moral responsibility for our deeds; it is up to the masters to bear it". Next to Friedrich Nietzsche and Walter Benjamin who, following this logic, attach themselves to the subalterns' dispossession, consider for example their intellectual descendant Theodor Adorno who, opposing Kant's universal ethics, formulates in his *Minima Moralia*: "Wrong life cannot be lived rightly" (Adorno 1978: 39). That is to say – echoing Kafka's "despairing course of life" from the aforementioned quotation – one cannot expect moral behavior of subalterns whose life is irreparably damaged by their societies' power distribution. These societies' allegedly universal ethos, ignoring their inhuman conditions, exerts violent pressure on their 'deviant' members' customs to obey it. "It is this violence and evil that brings these customs into conflict with morality," spells out Adorno, "and not the decline of morals" for which the dominant morality blames the subalterns

---

[3] The aphorism reads: "Original sin, the old injustice committed by man, consists in the complaint unceasingly made by man that he has been the victim of an injustice, the victim of original sin". For the two most famous discussions, see Benjamin 2007a: 123–27 and Agamben 2010: 21–25.

(Adorno 2001: 17). Deprived both of the prerequisites to appropriate this morality and to resist it, they turn its violence, through self-blaming, self-humiliation and self-tormenting, upon themselves. Published in 1951, *Minima Moralia* develops its ethics out of the damaged life of social outsiders within Europe. Only a year thereafter, Frantz Fanon, in his *Black Skin, White Masks* (French original 1952), investigates the pathogenic consequences of the ruling morality's pressure on the 'weak subjects' of European colonies who, due to this pressure become the abject objects of constant self-torment (Fanon 1967: 210–217).

As testified to by a series of his protagonists such as Gregor Samsa, Georg Bendemann, or the hunter Gracchus, Kafka associated the outsiders' delineated self-victimizing attitude with the weak sons, i.e. "anxious, hesitant, restless persons" like he himself (2008: 7). They never stop complaining that they are victims of their fathers' merciless violence: "you would simply trample me underfoot until nothing of me remained" (Kafka 2008: 21). Not only Kafka's "Letter to the Father" but also his many diary entries and letters demonstrate how much he is inclined to identify himself in these sacrificial filial terms as induced by the constant paternal oppression not only within his own family but also the whole disaggregating imperial society around him.[4] Yet in contradistinction to such pitying and compassionate self-perception that dominate his non-fiction works, he carefully kept himself aloof from the position of victim when shaping his fictional narrative authority, preferring to render it in ambiguous, almost indistinct terms.

The vicissitudes of the filial perspective: The perversion of sacrifice

It deserves attention that such equivocal authoring, especially of his fictional works, is in accord with the retroactive intertwinement of the initially opposed paternal and filial capacities as elaborated in Freud's roughly contemporary cultural-anthropological essays from *Totem and Taboo* (1914) onwards. In the last of these, *Moses and Monotheism* (1939), Freud remarks that while the Jewish religion grew out of paternal authority, Christianity responded to it from a weak filial perspective. Yet however humble the latter presents itself to be, it is guided by the "ulterior motive" of taking over the position of authority:

---

4 On the sufferings of Kafka's 'weak' generation of intellectuals and artists as caused by their authoritative fathers' generation, see Müller-Seidel 1986: 70–71.

> The old God the Father withdrew behind Christ, Christ, the Son, came in his place, just as every son had longed for in those prehistoric times. (Freud 2003: 536)

Kafka anticipates Freud's thesis of the retroactive "inscription of the Jews" into "the history of the Christians" (Caruth 1996: 18) in his diary entry of 28 September 1917, pointing out that the ultimate idea of the literary performer of self-sacrifice is to "deceive" "the human tribunal", albeit in a subterraneous way, "without practicing any actual deception" (Kafka 1976: 387). He manipulates others, so to say, through his very literary performance due to whose surreptitious and deferred effects his filial sacrifice gradually adopts a paternal authority. In fact, according to Kafka's argument, fictional sacrifices take place on two parallel stages. While on the visible stage of represented events an outsider character performs a sacrifice to the others upon which s/he is immediately dependent, on the invisible stage of representation, simultaneously, the author directs his or her sacrificial performance to the distant anonymous addressees. It is this mediated addressing that, through its mobilizing after-effects, retroactively establishes the author as the background 'director' of all relationships between his or her characters. In distinction to Freud who focuses on this clandestine empowerment of the disempowered in *religious* sacrificial narratives, Kafka turns the *fictional* ones into its epitome.

Unlike religious narratives, they openly display their positional outsiders' efforts to benefit from their sacrificial performance for the present others. However, this uncovering of their envisioned empowerment is undertaken with the intention of covering another, authorial one. At the same time as the authors expose the perversion of their characters' sacrificial performances, they 'impartially' disperse themselves into the partiality of each of them, winning the sympathy of their readers for *this* detached sacrifice *of theirs*. When Kafka turns his fictions into the overt stages for compromising his various characters' sacrifices, he in fact targets the covert approval of his 'unselfish' self-othering by his readers. Whereas characters follow their petty interest as generated by their restrictive circumstances, he forges the 'disinterested' commonality of ultimate victims with his readers. In fact, as it is designed to compensate for his own victimhood, it is all but disinterested. On the contrary, it camouflages the benefit which the author draws from its establishment.

Although Kafka consistently performed sacrifices in his diaries[5] and letters,[6] he regarded these non-fiction genres as mere preparatory phases for the fictional ones which enable such camouflage. The entrapment of characters within their interdependence on the level of represented action conceals the simultaneous emancipation from this interdependence by the author's action of representation. While the characters cannot but reiterate their interdependence by involuntarily mirroring one another in their actions, the author exempts himself or herself from them by evenly distributing the aspects of his or her own identity into the oppositions among them. His or her sneaking into their conflicting roles, transforming them into the constituents of one and the same 'scenario', silently deactivates the differences between them. That is to say, while the inhabitants of the visible level of represented action relentlessly reiterate these imparities, on the invisible level of the action of representation the author ameliorates them and melts them down. They act as the ferocious public activists of historical differentiation, he as the detached secret representative of prehistory that, as an 'empire' allegedly bereft of differences, he is at pains to redeem.

Let us now, for the sake of illustration, reread the story "In the Penal Colony" in these terms. It introduces the character of the officer who, by force of allocated circumstances, performs sacrifice at the same time in the opposite capacities, i.e. the executor's and the victim's. In the first voluntary capacity, he wholeheartedly attaches himself to the public rituals of brutal execution that are, however, due to the progressing replacement of the 'sovereign' with the 'disciplinary' political regimes across the globe (Foucault 1977), doomed to elimination even in the far remote colonies.[7] It is not only that their inhabitants, as the narrator remarks, no longer care for such cruel spectacles (Kafka 1988g:

---

5 See, for instance, the diary entry of 4 July 1916 in which he performs in the first person: "I awoke to find myself imprisoned in a fenced enclosure which allowed no room for more than a step in either direction" (Kafka 1976: 363). Or the one of 13 January 1920 in which he performs in the third person: "A prison he could have come to terms with. To end as a prisoner, that would be a goal for a life" (Kafka 2012: 202). And finally the one of 21 October 1921 in which he performs in the second person: "All is imaginary [. . .] but the closest reality (*nächste Wahrheit*) is only that you are beating your head against the wall of a windowless and doorless cell" (Kafka 1976: 395; trans. modified).
6 See, for example, the following performance of the writer's sacrifice in a letter to Felice: "I need seclusion for my writing, not 'like a settler,' that would not be enough, but like a dead man. Writing in this sense is a deeper sleep, i.e. death, and just as you cannot and will not pull a dead person out of his grave, so you will not pull me off the desk at night" (Kafka 1965: 412).
7 Kafka carefully avoids locating his fictions, but the reader nevertheless learns that the colony is somewhere in the tropics (Kafka 1988g: 166), where the officer speaks French (167). The story was inspired by the book *My Trip to the Penal Colonies* (Meine Reise nach den Strafkolonien,

165) but the new commandant plans to abolish them completely (Kafka 1988g: 178). Such developments as necessitated both by the external historical and the internal story's plot, transform the officer as the executor into the victim of the new political constellation. In this restricted, involuntary capacity he must take recourse in the opposite, i.e. private performance of sacrifice by transposing himself into the viewpoints of his recent superiors – the new commandant and traveling explorer – in order to outsmart them and materialize his agenda. He therefore guesses their responses, anticipates their reactions, and forges small 'would-be scenarios' (Kafka 1988g: 180–184), engaging the subaltern strategy of the so-called subversive mimicry.

Although Homi Bhabha applied this concept to the performance of colonized selves, the range of subalterns who 'stage' their selves in their everyday communication with others exceeds just colonial circumstances. Each political regime forces its outsiders to simulating and amalgamating techniques of survival. One of the cases in point is the Underground Man from Dostoevsky's *Notes from the Underground*, which, considering Dostoevsky's influence on Kafka (Dodd 1992), must have left its imprints on his shaping of the officer.[8] Mikhail Bakhtin describes Dostoevsky's protagonist-narrator as an enflamed ideologue whose suddenly stranded position (he is a former civil servant) – very much like that of Kafka's officer – induces his embittered polemics with his society and the world (Bakhtin 1984: 236). Being in his indistinction both extremely dependent on and extremely hostile to the politically and socially distinct others (Bakhtin 1984: 230), he invents a special kind of subversive mimicry, which Bakhtin dubs the "word with a loophole":

1912) by the German criminologist Robert Heindl, who, among other colonies, describes the French penal island of New Caledonia, located about 20.000 km from Metropolitan France (Müller-Seidel 1986: 82–84). As it functioned as the dumping ground for the 'degenerate' elements of French society, the explorer understands that it, in contradistinction to the democratic administration of European population, requires "extraordinary measures" and "military discipline" (Kafka 1988g: 171). This is fully in line with the views that Heindl expresses in his own book (Müller-Seidel 1986: 84). Yet, as the reform of the European empires' legislation was at that time more or less accomplished, it was underway in their colonies as well.

8 Dostoevsky was himself banished to a Siberian penal colony, whose brutal martial law and summary justice he painstakingly describes in *Notes from a Dead House* (1862). This experience was so decisive for his life that Kafka notes in his diary entry of 15 March 1914: "The students wanted to carry Dostoevsky's chains behind his coffin" (1976: 265–66). Although Russian Empire possessed no colonies, it had established Sakhalin as its penal island in 1875. Next to Dostoevsky's interest in such political zones of indistinction, as materialized also in his *Notes from the Underground* (1864), Kafka was also inspired by his critique of the Western modernization of the Russian judicial system (1865), as expressed in the first place in *The Brothers Karamazov* (1880). See Conti 2016: 469.

> A loophole is the retention for oneself of the possibility for altering the ultimate, final meaning of one's own words. If a word retains such a loophole this must inevitably be reflected in its structure [. . .] it is only the penultimate word and places after itself only a conditional, not a final, period. (Bakhtin 1984: 233)

Yet Kafka's officer, who – in the footsteps of Dostoevsky's Underground Man – engages in his conditional speech a "thousand reservations, concessions, loopholes" (Bakhtin 1984: 196) to pave the way for a "sincere refutation" (Bakhtin 1984: 233) of his claims, ultimately fails to get it from the traveling explorer (Kafka 1988g: 184) who thus turns into his potential executor.

Such development of their relationship that deepens the officer's humiliating position enforces the new reshaping of his performance, leading him from a 'filial' subversive mimicry back to a 'paternal' violence. In this reactivated capacity, he first "yell[s] in the explorer's ear [. . .] with the full force of his lungs" (Kafka 1988g: 174), thereafter presses into him, with a 'strong insistence' and 'clenched fists', the task of helping him against the acting commandant (Kafka 1988g: 182), and finally seizes his trustee by both arms, gazes into his face, and shouts loudly (Kafka 1988g: 184). In this way, his submissive plea transforms into verbal aggression. Walter Müller-Seidel compares his verbal and gestural attack on the explorer to the behavior of Kafka's father toward his son as described in "Letter to the Father", which equally consisted of scolding, threatening, irony, evil laughter, and self-bemoaning. In the same way as the father's violence destroyed the son's capacities to reply, the officer's violence silences those of the traveling explorer, who barely gets a word in (Müller-Seidel 1986: 123–124). Paradoxically, while this turnaround of the officer's behavior restores his capacity as the *executor*, it inadvertently merges him with the *victim*, i.e. a prisoner who had likewise replaced the doggish submission to his superior with an angry canine assault against him (Kafka 1988g: 171). The officer's unwitting redoubling of his counterpart's behavior casts a light of the latter's helplessness upon him.

After he definitely fails to convince the traveling explorer, due to his undesired contamination with his counterpart's helplessness, the officer suddenly reinvigorates his victimhood by setting the condemned man free, taking his place, and letting the torture device execute him himself (Kafka 1988g: 185). Far from being a miracle, this substitution merely radicalizes the constant reinforcement of opposites in the officer's behavior. As it galvanizes the "nameless adherents" (Kafka 1988g: 192) to sanctify his figure in their memory, this ultimate self-sacrifice clandestinely targets an ultimate self-empowerment. It draws its inspiration from the adored old commandant whose political sacrifice had likewise attracted dock laborers to surreptitiously work in honor of his fame. But the force of altered circumstances repeatedly ruins the officer's design to walk in the footsteps of his great idol. Since the native addressees of his sacrificial performance, the soldier and the condemned man, do not understand "a word of French" (Kafka 1988g: 167) and are used to being instructed in their "native tongue" (Kafka 1988g: 185), they cannot possibly comprehend what is going on and remain baffled. The only difference between these two underdogs – who most of the time unconcernedly communicate with one another and grotesquely amuse one another despite their substantially different positions – is that the soldier is fully indifferent to the developments that he is obliged to attend whereas the condemned man invests a continuous effort to understand his situation and is definitely "the more animated of the two" (Kafka 1988g: 189). As if contaminated by his torturer's vivid curiosity, he is never tired of launching diverse hypotheses of others' actions, such as at the moment the officer releases him:

> Was it true? Was it only a caprice of the officer's, that might change again? Had the foreign explorer begged him off? What was it? One could read these questions on his face.
> (Kafka 1988g: 185)

But linguistically and culturally disqualified as he is, he completely misinterprets the officer's action, attributing it to the explorer's decision and thus making it miss the target as envisioned by the officer:

> What had happened to him was now going to happen to the officer. Perhaps even to the very end. Apparently the foreign explorer had given the order for it. So this was revenge. Although he himself had not suffered to the end, he was to be revenged to the end. A broad, silent grin now appeared on his face and stayed there all the rest of the time.
> (Kafka 1988g: 188)

Thus the reason why the officer's sacrificial performances repeatedly fail to materialize their agenda is not merely the contaminating inscription of his antagonists' behavior into their outcome but also the contaminating inscription of his own behavior into that of his antagonists. Redoubling the officer's intellectual mobility, the condemned man not only frees himself from his radical immobility but also takes distance from his torturer and disobeys and ignores the traveling explorer's orders (Kafka 1988g: 189–190). The same resilience is displayed by the traveling explorer who despite the officer's praising of his tolerant worldview (1988g: 180), in fact mirrors the officer's contempt for natives by rendering them as "poor, humble creatures" (Kafka 1988g: 191), "stupid-looking, wide-mouthed" "submissive dogs" (Kafka 1988g: 165) who "ridiculously" believe in the future resurrection of their old commandant (Kafka 1988g: 192). As opposed to the native prisoner who "was a complete stranger, not a fellow countryman or even at all sympathetic to him" (Kafka 1988g: 176), the traveling explorer shows some empathy (Kafka 1988g: 184), supportiveness (Kafka 1988g: 190), and even admiration for the officer (Kafka 1988g: 167). Yet as the latter shares the natives' blind faith in their old commandant, he ultimately dismisses them both, especially after he recognizes the absence of the proclaimed ultimate redemption on the officer's dead face (Kafka 1988g: 190–191) and thus confirms the absurdity of his fanaticism.

If the opposed characters thus unwittingly 'intoxicate' each other's performances, making them miss their targets, this is because they unknowingly mirror the author's equivocal relationship to them that persistently fluctuates between victimhood and execution. What disconcerts Kafka's narrative authority from the very beginning to the end might be translated into Italo Calvino's much later question: "How much of the 'I' who shapes the characters is in fact an 'I' who has been shaped by the characters?" (Calvino 1986: 113) Calvino speaks of the "layers of subjectivity and feigning that we can discern underneath the author's name, and the various 'I's that go to make up the 'I' who is writing." (Calvino 1986: 111). In this sense, the officer's and the condemned man's adoption of the others' points of view in order to outmaneuver them are mere replicas of the story's superior point of view that meanders between the characters' perspectives, countering one focalization through the other but without identifying with any of their optics. The superior point of view exempts itself from their blinded bias because they either filially sacrifice their present to the past (as does the backward officer) or paternally their past to the present (as does the enlightened traveling explorer) without grasping (contrary to the author) the contamination of theirs with their counterpart's point of view.

So even if the author, as the victim of his characters, sacrifices his own view to assimilate theirs, he nevertheless, as their executor, exempts himself from their partiality and outsmarts it. Through this clandestine exemption, Kafka's narrative authority perverts the filial attitude as genuine of the officer who does not hesitate to sacrifice himself for the other into the paternal attitude as genuine of the traveling explorer who does not hesitate to sacrifice others for himself. Precisely *through this perversion*, it meets and articulates the longing of its addressees for the 'elevate commonality' of the humans who are defaced by their historical and political domiciles and eager to get rid of their humiliating belonging to them. In order to establish this commonality's historical and political in-difference and to shape it as an allegedly all-embracing meeting place for all earthly creatures, it invites and encourages its adherents to equally sacrifice their historically and politically particular identities. Yet how can this commonality be all-embracing if it is founded on the sacrifice of the fellow beings' distinct identities? This merciless sacrifice dismantles the establishment of its shaper's authority as its selfish background intention.

Thus, the institution of Kafka's narrative authority requires the double sacrifice of others, i.e. both characters and readers, for the benefit of its indiscriminate 'truth'. The readers who unreservedly adhere to this truth enable the substitution of its shaper's filial position for a paternal position. Those on the contrary who disclose its unwilling contamination with the appetite to patronize others, as we have tried to do here, help this authority emancipate itself from its compensatory fantasies. What initiates them is not a desire for the universally valid truth but their shaper's denied wound. However, although such emancipation might be a better method of treating both Kafka's and his readers' suppressed wound than the passionate attachment to the fantasies which it generates, we should remind ourselves that Kafka's narrative authority emancipated itself from the fantasies of its fictional representatives in exactly the same way.

Part III: **J. M. Coetzee and the Politics of Deterritorialization**

8 The Withheld Self-revelation: The 'Real' and Realities in *Waiting for the Barbarians*

"I am what I am not": Sneaking out of historical identification

In Coetzee's quasi-autobiographical recounting the experiences of his youth, in which his narrator presents his former self in the third person, he somewhat ironically sneaks into this hero's consciousness:

> Destiny would not come to him in South Africa, he told himself; she would come (come like a bride!) only in London or Paris or perhaps Vienna, because only in the great cities of Europe does destiny reside. (Coetzee 2012: 281)

By rendering his self in the "fictional" third person, Coetzee takes recourse in Kafka's favored model of an indirect self-presentation. The German-Jewish writer was knowingly reserved toward the direct confessional discourse's truth claims, including those of letter-writing. Addressing Max Brod on 25 October 1923, he apologizes for having "strategically" postponed his answer out of fear of the treacherous words that make letters betray their intended destinations. Only fictional literature that withholds itself of any such destination can justifiably have pretense to truthfulness. It only aims at the truth by negating its betrayals – a circumventing strategy that Kafka significantly calls his "life vocation" (Kafka 1958: 453). As he put it in aphorism 80 in his "Reflections on sin, suffering, hope, and the true way", it is impossible to know the truth in any other form but a lie (Kafka 2012: 196), which is why one always must say no to it: "to say no is to say yes" (Kafka 2012: 208). In aphorism 26, he claims that the truth exists as a goal, but the only way to it is hesitation (Kafka 2012: 192). In his diaries, he describes his notorious reluctance and insecurity as a "hesitation before birth" (Kafka 1976: 405). If we recall that Socrates considered himself a midwife who merely assists in giving birth to the truth, and that the truth can never "be found inside the head of an individual person" but only in-between many people (Bakhtin 1984: 110), we will better understand Kafka's "My life is hesitation before birth" (1976: 405). Accepting one's birth means consenting to one's delusive reality; postponing it means beating one delusion by means of the other.

Following the same weak messianic life vocation of an interminable longing for the withheld truth – rather than belonging to any of its available 'destinations' – Coetzee equally detaches himself from the genre of autobiography. On account of its blindness "to the existence of the pact" with the readers (Coetzee 1984: 1, 5), it overlooks that its representing self cannot but betray the represented one. The same pertains to the genre of secular confession, which proves helpless "before the desire to construct its own truth" (Coetzee 1992: 179). To avoid such unintended infidelity, Coetzee's representing self practices an "exculpatory ambiguity" (Robinson 2011: 9) by "simultaneously baring himself [through an identification with his represented self] and hiding himself [through the simultaneous disidentification with him]" (Attridge 2004a: 157, n. 23). In the fragment quoted above, such a withheld self-revelation is even redoubled because the young computer expert who left London to take up a new job in Aldermaston *himself* ironically recalls his previous obsession from his South African time, which sadly failed to confirm itself. By detaching himself from his youthful delusions about a 'true life', he anticipates the narrator's self-exemption from him. "For nearly two years he waited and suffered in London," he now remarks, "and destiny stayed away" (Coetzee 2012: 281). But his recent retreat into the countryside, the narrator suggests, also entraps him into a new delusion because "[w]hether destiny pays visits to the countryside is not certain, even if it is the English countryside, and even if it is barely an hour by train from Waterloo" (Coetzee 2012: 281). Mockingly commenting on his hero's convictions from the distance of some forty years, the narrator indicates that destiny, significantly rendered in the feminine gender, ignores subjects who helplessly wait for it by blessing only those who resolutely take it into their own hands.

But again, as soon as some subjects do so, divine destiny transforms into human history. Such 'modernization' of the law of human life draws a new demarcation line between the center and periphery. The center becomes the master that resolutely makes history and the periphery a subaltern that is helplessly delivered to its destiny. As testified by the London Waterloo station, which hardly by accident pops up in the narrator's retroactive intervention, only nations that make their history are entitled to commemorate its outstanding events. This inference's corollary is that the closer one dwells to such 'blessed' sites of collective memory, the bigger one's prospects to shape history, which obviously gives an advantage to the English countryside over the South African province.

However, if this holds for common people's collective mentality, it does not for a future artist who strives for individuality. The delineated principle "I am what I am not" once again revises the established demarcation between destiny and history. As a writer-in-making, the hero does not long for *historical* destiny as the majority of people do, but for the *divine* one beyond the reach of history. This destiny's visit cannot be extorted by 'proper' residences such as London or a well-positioned English countryside. Instead, wherever one happens to be, it is just discretely invoked by making oneself ready for its arrival. Accordingly, the hero acts as the proponent of the sublime concept of art that relies on the Muse's 'fatal touch' – therefore the feminine gender of his destiny.[1] Like true love, he believes, true art must be set in motion by a gentle signal from 'outside' (2012: 282). It is this divine grace that exempts the artist, by completely deterritorializing his works, from the reign of historical laws. Through such an extraterritorial 'link', artists and their works are catapulted out of history's distinct territory into destiny's indistinct province. When Coetzee, in 2011, compiled an omnibus edition of *Boyhood* (1997), *Youth* (2002), and *Summertime* (2009), he titled it *Scenes from Provincial Life*. In my reading, "provincial life", next to artist's *allocated* geopolitical and cultural province, points to his *elected* artistic one as well, which through its sublime link with the all-embracing divine destiny pulls him out of his historical allocation.

This promotion of the province into an instrument of elevation returns it into the center of history. If the province resides not only far away from the center but also at its very core, then human history does not succeed in banishing divine destiny from its territory. This relic of the past instead manages, via its artistic representatives, to loosen the grip of historical laws. Whereas human history gradually parenthesized its divine predecessor, destiny responded to its envisioned replacement by establishing its clandestine counter-politics. Considering that "empires come into existence", by definition, "only as a result of the extension of core control over some potential periphery" (Motyl 1996: 23) – or the affirmation of the power relationship that inheres to them – one would expect that the translation of the regime of destiny into that of history spawns the loss of such control, or the abolition of imperial centers' power. But instead of being defeated and antiquated, empires appear to have survived at their successors' cores. This has driven researchers to the conclusion that destiny and history, centers and peripheries, empires and nation-states, operate as one another's unintentional (re)producers. "As intimately intertwined subjects, they developed

---

[1] In this regard, *Youth*'s hero recalls Kafka who repeatedly complained in his letters and diaries that he used to wait for inspiration in vain (and in pain) for hours, days and months. Thus, one 'Kafka' – Coetzee's narrator who stubbornly withholds himself to his geopolitical province, and the other 'Kafka' – Coetzee's hero who passionately adheres to his artistic province – expose one another's delusions. As a result of this "I (Kafka) am what I (Kafka) am not", no 'Kafka' is left to the reader to rely on – and concomitantly no 'Coetzee'. In his letter to Grete Bloch of 18 November 1913, Kafka described the kernel of his terrible insecurity in the following way: "[A]lmost every word that I write [. . .] I would thereupon like to withdraw or, even better, to erase" (1965: 477). Coetzee is equally reserved toward 'historically' definite statements inasmuch as they pretend to have left behind the subversive operations of destiny.

in dialogue with each other, rather than as binary opposites" (Judson 2016: 9–10). This is what the *translatio imperii* eventually amounts to: the disquieting revival of the 'excommunicated'. As *Youth*'s hero puts it, the logic of *either-or* is "a human invention, not a part of the fabric of being" (Coetzee 2012: 277), i.e. the province of the *as-well-as* logic of history's residues.

However, those who are banished out of historical visibility continue their existence merely as broken, double voices. Their representatives are either the superhuman Absent God who announces to the humans their destiny "in an indirect and negative way" (Derrida 2008: 46), or subhuman creatures who out of their amorphous "prose of the world" (Hegel 1975: 193–194) "can only make [their messages be] understood [as] hidden" (Hegel 1975: 391). These two closely intertwined forms of dispossession – the superhuman dispossession *of* the humans and the subhuman dispossession *by* them (Butler 2013: 1–5) – repeatedly confront the humans with a spectral amphibious agency, which their history never stops displacing into the province. Jacques Lacan invented the term "real" to designate this strange *dispossessed dispossessor* that "resists symbolization" (Lacan 1987: 66) or "subsists outside of symbolization" (Lacan 2006: 324), i.e. eludes human reality as established by symbolic distinctions. While being dispossessed and placed below the threshold of reality's operations, the "real" at the same time operates as its supreme dispossessor that degrades its appearances to the status of mere "grimaces" (Lacan 1991: 148). In Lacan's late work, this dispossessed dispossessor figures as the decisive instance in the constitution of the human subject, a province that never stops emptying out its core territory. It remains decisive in the constitution of Coetzee's fictional agencies as well:

> Always, when he tried to explain himself to himself, there remained a gap, a hole, a darkness before which his understanding baulked, into which it was useless to pour words. The words were eaten up, the gap remained. His was always a story with a hole in it: a wrong story, always wrong. (Coetzee 2004b: 110)

Attached to self-othering: Elevation through humiliation

I argue that this dispossessed dispossessor – the "real" – operates as the ultimate legitimizing horizon of Coetzee's narrative strategy. Linking the insignificant subhuman with the all-embracing superhuman, it authorizes both his agencies' and his own exemption from human identities. To escape them, both the author and his agencies shrink and evaporate on the model of Kafka and his agencies who adhere to the same guideline that "the closer one attaches oneself to the subhuman, the nearer one gets to the superhuman".[2] Significantly melting these opposite provinces into one another, the figure of the 'wise fool' connects Coetzee's with Kafka's and Dostoevsky's works (Northover 2012: 42). In fact, after the interwar constellation of *translatio imperii* suddenly dispossessed many writers of belonging, the elevation through humiliation became the distinctive identity technology of not only post-imperial literature's characters but also authors.[3] As one of the first philosophers who sympathetically reflected on such enforced "people without homeland (*Heimatlose*)", Nietzsche stated in his *Joyful Wisdom's* § 377 that their identity formation entirely depends on their "possessors". After the public political space bereaves them of their own form of identification, these dispossessed adapt themselves to the humiliating idea that their 'possessors' have of them. Yet Nietzsche argues that, precisely through such a radical self-othering, they in their turn manage to dispossess their possessors' key values. He famously claims:

> While all noble morality grows from a triumphant affirmation of itself, slave morality from the outset says no to an "outside," to an "other," to a "non-self"; and *this* no is its creative act. (Nietzsche 1996: 22)

In this context, it is worth of remembering Kafka's aforementioned guideline that "to say no is to say yes" (Kafka 2012: 208). According to Foucault's interpretation of Nietzsche's argument, the subalterns create new values by inscribing the

---

[2] Canetti (1969: 141–142) reminds of Kafka's letter to Felice in which he interprets her dream of lying on the ground among the animals as her salvation from the upright stature of humans, which bestows them their power over the animals. It is only by lying on the "subhuman" ground that humans can take notice of the "superhuman" sky as strewn with stars. Canetti argues further: "Since he hated violence, but also did not trust himself to have the strength that is necessary to fight it, he widened the distance between the stronger and himself by becoming smaller and smaller with regard to the strong. Through this shrinking he gained a double benefit: he disappeared from the threat by becoming too small for it, and he freed himself from all reprehensible means of violence; the little animals he liked to transform into were harmless" (Canetti 1969: 142–143). But Canetti fails to notice that Kafka empowered himself through such self-disempowering just as Coetzee does by resuming his compulsive strategy, as we will come to see. Kafka's warning from the letter to Oskar Pollak of 6 September 1903 (Kafka 1958: 17) – "Respect the mole and its kind but don't make it your saint" – points to his reluctant attachment to the subhumans that likewise holds for Coetzee. If they persistently switch from one subhuman to the other, this is because none of subhuman realities is good enough to accommodate the superhuman that only acknowledges the "real" as its residence.

[3] All of the European writers from the early twentieth century with whom Coetzee engages in *Inner Workings* "experienced as young or middle-aged men the upheavals of the First World War, many living through, or into, the Second World War as well" and underwent "the trials of exile, dispossession, and sometimes personal violence" (Attridge 2008: xi).

ruling ones into their dishonored bodies, which are exposed on a daily basis to disease, malformation, and mutilation (Foucault 1984: 82–83). In an interview given to Jacques Rancière, he described the subalterns' invisible operations as an uncanny, indistinct element that haunts the relations among the distinct agencies in a given society (Foucault 2001). Two decades thereafter, Rancière founded his political philosophy on this undifferentiated mass of 'leftovers' deprived of positive identity qualities (Rancière 1999: 8). They figure as the "part of those who have no part" (1999: 11) in the partition of a given community's political space but nevertheless manage to disconcert it. Via Foucault, Rancière, and Arendt, Nietzsche's deprived mob gradually became the legitimate subjects of philosophy and, in the first place, postcolonial theory.[4]

As regards post-imperial writers, while responding like Nietzsche's subalterns to the dispossession imposed upon them, they resume these subalterns' self-creation through self-othering – but on a subtle individual basis. Unlike their collective predecessors, each of them acts out of an invisible, different, and specific trauma with the aim to articulate and affirm it as such in the first place. Consider for example the situation of Walter Benjamin in Weimar Germany. Established after the defeat of German Empire in the First World War and shattered by humiliating territorial losses, the political transformation into a republic, and a large influx of 'homecomers', Weimar Germany engaged a variety of remedial, compensatory, and restorationist political agendas. In order to divert the residents' attention from the impotent state with its damaged institutions, it led a politics of Germandom, assimilating co-nationals in the borderlands and the newly established nation-states. Such a redefinition of the German nation, to include these border and transborder co-nationals, induced in its turn the exclusion of non-German co-citizens at home, above all the Jews. This spawned the rise of antisemitism in the Weimar Republic that confronted German Jews with uneasy choices. It is small wonder that Benjamin suddenly found himself standing

> in the open air in a landscape in which nothing remained unchanged but the clouds, and in the center, in a force field of destructive currents and explosions, the tiny frail human body.
> (Benjamin 1977b: 291)

---

[4] As early as 1903, William Du Bois writes of "double-consciousness, the sense of always looking at one's self through the eyes of the others, of measuring one's soul by the tape of a world that always looks on in amused contempt and pity" (Du Bois 1990: 8). Fifty years thereafter, the founding father of postcolonial theory, Frantz Fanon, offered in his *Black Skin, White Masks* (1967: 210–217) a well-developed analysis of the slave's self-torment after adopting the master's punishing relationship to him. Forty years thereafter, Bhabha focused on the postcolonial selves' subversion of the colonizers' selves through their adoption (Bhabha 1994: 94–132).

The world was completely deterritorialized for some individuals who inhabited it, and they were thus radically bereft of its territorial protection.

In the Austrian part of disaggregating imperial Europe, another assimilated Jew who had suddenly been exposed to the rising antisemitism in his country, Hugo von Hofmannsthal, stated that "the nature of our age is ambiguity and indeterminacy. It rests only on the slippery [. . .]. A slight chronic dizziness vibrates in it" (1979: 60). In such exceptional states, which enormously increase their victims' sensibility for the latent, non-materialized possibilities of their present, Hofmannsthal sees his task to be the expression of "that which does not exist anymore, which does not exist yet, which could be, but in the first place that which never happened, the sheer impossible and therefore beyond all real" (1980: 132). As a "measureless conjurer of shadows" (Hofmannsthal 1979: 70), the poet is invited to connect by his "magic" "the past and the present, the animals and the humans, the dream and the thing, the big and the small, the sublime and the trivial" (Hofmannsthal 1979: 68) and, above all, to call the dead back into life. For Hofmannsthal, language is a "huge, fathomlessly profound empire of the dead, which is why we receive from it the highest life" (1980: 132). The poet's sacrificial task is to take the position of an entirely deprived being exposed to enormous denigration and suffering by placing himself at the service of the "suffering of the thousands" (Hofmannsthal 1979: 71). Hofmannsthal therefore portrays his poet as a martyr-redeemer who is expected

> to create every second, with each pulse, under a pressure as if an ocean lays above him, lit by no lamp, not even a mine lamp, surrounded by mocking, confusing voices [. . .] to create as spider, spinning the yearn from his own body, to carry him over the abyss of existence. (1979: 75)

The dispossessed dispossessor: Franz Kafka

Kafka, for his part, was a German-educated and German-speaking secular Jew in Prague, the capital of the Austro-Hungarian Empire's Bohemian province. His sense of his own Jewishness was, to say the least, controversial. In the diary entry of 8 January 1914, for example, he states:

> What have I in common with Jews? I have hardly anything in common with myself and should stand very quietly in a corner, content that I can breathe. (Kafka 1976: 252)

One of the reasons for his weakened love for his Jewish mother was that he regularly addressed her in German, "Mutter", which made her "not only comic but strange". After the Jewish family's linguistic dispossession, "only the memories of the ghetto [. . .] still preserve" it, "for the word 'Vater' too is far from meaning the Jewish father" (Kafka 1976: 88). In the same way though that Kafka, as a native speaker of German, felt alienated from his Jewish parents, his inherited Jewish cultural background defamiliarized his usage of German. Coetzee once pointed out that what engages him in Kafka's literature "is an intensity, a pressure of writing that [. . .] pushes at the limits of language, and specifically of German" (Coetzee 1992: 198).

However, the Czech Austrians, who administered the country, experienced this from another side. At a time of rising antisemitism, they became inimical of the Czech Jews precisely because they had 'stolen' and 'misused' their language. After the Empire's breakup, the Czechs also turned against the Jews as the Austrian Emperors' centuries-long favorites who had financed their luxurious appetites. In a letter to Milena from mid-November 1920, Kafka sums up all these perilous developments:

> I've been spending all afternoons on the streets, wallowing in anti-Semitic hate. 'Prašivé plenemo' ["Mangy race"] I have now even heard people calling the Jews. Isn't it a matter of course that you leave where you are so hated? (Kafka 1983: 288)[5]

But where to find refuge if he was an outsider even to his Jewish family that was dominated by his father's despotic rule? Everywhere, due to the European Jews' growing "pursuit of profit", migration from the country to the cities, "two-child system", "mixed marriages", and "conversion" (Kafka 1976: 177), they faced their ethnic, cultural and religious disaggregation and decline. The period of their rise and glory was over.

This explains why Kafka qualified neither as truly Jewish nor truly German, let alone Czech, remaining an outsider to all three cultures. His passionate attachment to the various structural victims of *translatio imperii* – provincials, countrymen, stigmatized 'monsters', circus artists, outcasts, settlers, assistants, messengers, bricklayers, cobblers, animals – grew out of his own multiple dispossessions. After having finished the study of law and absolved his doctorate in jurisprudence, he worked over fifteen years as an attorney for the newly established state insurance agency, representing injured Czech workers. Imperial administration sentenced them to a political, economic and linguistic subordination (since the courts

---

5 Stölzl (1975: 75) quotes an appeal published in the Prague Jewish journal *Selbstwehr* two years ahead of Kafka's letter, i.e. already on 16 August 1918: "Conditions in Prague have become unbearable. For us the fact remains that we are so closely circled by hatred that we cannot go any way without encountering this repulsive expression of national spite".

required a decent command of German language). Thus, although they were Czechs, i.e. representatives of the majority population in Prague, their outsider status arose from their precarious position within the Austrian legal system. Such positional outsiders, the protagonists of Kafka's fictions, testify to how in the post-imperial state of exception ultimately no group offered its members a safe and enduring protection against the threat of falling *outside* of the law. Under the extremely unstable circumstances of the turn-of-the-century Empire, anyone and everyone could become such an outsider. This experience of constant threat and crisis of public space – worsened by war, processes of national homogenization, and a permanent state of exception – account for the extreme vulnerability and exposure of his characters, who suddenly find themselves banished from the protection that legally belongs to the inhabitants of historically established territories.

The self-dispossessing dispossessor: J. M. Coetzee

As for Coetzee, his position within the South African society was even more complex, which means that it cannot be interpreted as an exclusively one of an outsider. He was born into the white minority which, on behalf of the two European empires, the Dutch and British ones, settled, ruled and exploited the country from the early seventeenth century and deep into the twentieth century, by dispossessing, discriminating, and mistreating its native population. Coetzee never stops expressing his shame for the harm which his white ancestors and contemporaries have done and keep doing to his country's majority population. Their stigma of colonial criminals is in his view fully justified and he does not feel he can exempt himself from it (Coetzee 1992: 243). After all, the deep entanglement of the whites in the imperial violence is the main issue of his first novel *Dusklands*, published in 1974. With regard to its division into two parts, of which the second one deals with the American involvement in the Vietnam War, he remarks:

> I would regard it as morally questionable to write something like the second part of *Dusklands* – a *fiction*, note – from a position that is not historically complicit.
> (Coetzee 1992: 343)

So rather than being an outsider and victim, Coetzee admits his complicity with wrongdoers. However, one has to consider that the South African white minority is not homogeneous but rather a diverse and conflict-ridden entity as regards its linguistic, religious, and cultural habits. This explains a permanent tension between the Afrikaners and much later British settlers, an animosity invigorated by their historical memories (in the first place of the two Boer wars). As soon as we consider this division of the South African white minority, Coetzee the co-perpetrator suddenly turns into Coetzee an outsider: although an Afrikaner, i.e. the inheritor of Dutch settlers who survived on the foreign soil thanks to their religious and linguistic homogeneity, he belongs both to a *secular* and *English speaking* family. He in fact does not regard himself a proper Afrikaner because he speaks English:

> I am one of many people in this country who have become detached from their ethnic roots [. . .] and have joined a pool of no recognizable ethnos whose language of exchange is English. [. . .] And, as the pool has no discernible *ethnos*, so one day I hope it will have no predominant color, as more "people of color" drift into it. A pool, I would hope then, in which differences wash away. (Coetzee 1992: 342)

Already at the age of twelve, in the rural Worcester into which his family escaped from the enraged Afrikaner nationalism in Cape Town, he felt alien and marginalized within his native community. His parents were stigmatized as traitors to the people, when in reality they were just disinterested in religious and national fanaticism. For this reason they sent their Protestant child to a Catholic school in Cape Town that was also attended by the Greek and Jewish children. From the outset, so to say, his English language destined him for a much broader and diverse community than the one he had been born into. Yet, at the same time, it isolated him within that latter, narrower and homogeneous Afrikaner community. This is how he became an outsider among the wrongdoers.

In addition, like Kafka, he never felt completely at home in this language, i.e. he did not experience it as his mother tongue. In a letter from 11 May 2009, he entrusts to Paul Auster that he has been reading Jacques Derrida's little book *Monolingualism of the Other* (1996) in which Derrida claims that "although he was monolingual in French [. . .] French is/was not his mother tongue. When I read this it struck me that he could have been writing about me and my relation to English" (Auster and Coetzee 2014: 65).

> So when Derrida writes that, though he loves French language and is a stickler for correct French, it does not belong to him, is not "his," I am reminded of my own experience of English, particularly in childhood. [. . .] I thought of the English language as the property of the English, people who lived in England but who had also sent out members of their tribe to live in and, for a while, rule over South Africa. The English made up the rules of English as they whimsically chose [. . .] people like myself followed at a distance and behaved as instructed. [. . .] Wandering into language is always a trespass. And how much worse if you are good enough at English to hear in every phrase that falls from your pen echoes of earlier usages, reminders of who owned the phrase before you!
> (Auster and Coetzee 2014: 66–67)

This is why Coetzee, in Kafka's footsteps, felt neither the white Afrikaner minority nor the language that separated him from it as his places of belonging. On top of that, his relationship to his family members was as equally controversial as Kafka's. On the one hand, his father's family did not belong to the Afrikaner mainstream because of his grandfather's fierce British patriotism (Coetzee 2012: 108) and his father's sympathies for the Union Party, which was defeated in 1948 elections by the Afrikaner National Party. This ruined his father's business career, driving him to alcoholism (Coetzee 2012: 128ff.). In the following years, the new government nationalized the school classes, separating the proper Afrikaner classes from the second-rate 'foreign' ones, i.e. those which Coetzee's parents had chosen for their son.

His mother's family hailed from German-Polish Pomerania and, due to its imported and hyphenated identity, was somewhat unsocialized, wild, and eccentric, which is why it was never really accepted by his father's Afrikaner family. Yet, for the same reason, his mother's family was very sympathetic of its eccentric relative John, his mother's favorite son (Coetzee 2012: 32–33, 66). The mother's origins oriented him toward the modern Europe as the world literature's and culture's avatar and epitome, but at the same time he could not forget European crimes committed on the African soil against the native population. And however disrespectful he was of his father's Afrikaner background, he could not identify with his European mother either. Already as a teenager he felt entrapped in her unconditional love, or as he puts it "this cage in which he rushes back and forth, back and forth, like a poor bewildered baboon" (Coetzee 2012: 104). As a young writer settled in London he remarks:

> What does she hope to achieve by her letters, this obstinate, graceless woman? [. . .] She should concentrate her love on his brother and forget him. [. . .] Then he, the new-forgotten one, will be free to make his own life. (Coetzee 2012: 227)

As a man of age, Coetzee goes even further by stating that his mother was

> a supporter, if not of apartheid as a social system, then certainly of the people who ran the country. [. . .] In the case of people like my mother one can certainly speak of regressions [. . .] that took place as she fluctuated between being her own self and being a white South African. (Kurtz and Coetzee 2015: 110)

The politics of non-belonging: Blaming oneself in lieu of others

From his youth, having declined his belonging to his family, the ruling white minority, and the English language community, Coetzee obstinately tried to exempt himself from their exclusionary logic. As regards the Afrikaners:

> As far back as he can remember, Afrikaners have trampled on people because, they claim, they were once trampled upon. Well, let the wheel turn, let force be replied to with greater force. He is glad to be out of it. (Coetzee 2012: 228)

The delineated vicious circle of adopting the other's violent behavior by simultaneously blaming the other for it, is how the translation of empire into the nation-state operated in South Africa. It completely bereft people of historical memory. They forgot that they have suffered under the same violence that they are today inflicting upon others, their alleged enemies. In his conversation with Arabella Kurtz, Coetzee accordingly states:

> The *raison d'être* of the gang, I would suggest, is to have enemy-victims who can be attacked in the name of defending the gang. A gang without enemies is inconceivable. (Kurtz and Coetzee 2015: 145)

Precisely so as to stop such blind blaming of others for one's own behavior, all the time he carefully avoided taking on the position of an accuser, preferring instead to turn the psychical or physical violence against others on himself. That is how his questioning of others worked from the outset, i.e. since the time he was a boy. In his *Boyhood*, this boy is presented in the third person:

> At first it may wander here and there; but in the end, unfailingly, it turns and gathers itself and points a finger at himself. Always it is he who sets the train of thinking in motion; always it is the thinking that slips out of his control and returns to accuse him. (Coetzee 2012: 51)

So, while all others, involved in political battles, blame one another, he, in a Jesus-like gesture of turning their violence on himself and exempting himself from their enflamed politics, readily accepts their disgrace as his own:

> If Jesus had stooped to play politics he might have become a key man in Roman Judaea, a big operator. It was because he was indifferent to politics, and made his indifference clear, that he was liquidated. (Coetzee 2012: 294)

The extent to which Coetzee sympathizes with Jesus's consistent and radical self-othering, is testified to by his following reflection:

> Violence, as soon as I sense its presence within me, becomes introverted as violence against myself: I cannot project it outward [. . .] cannot but think: if all of us imagined violence as violence against ourselves, perhaps we would have peace. [. . .] Or, to explain myself in another way: I understand the Crucifixion as a refusal and an introversion of retributive violence, a refusal so deliberate, so conscious, and so powerful that it overwhelms any reinterpretation, Freudian, Marxian, or whatever, that we can give it to.
> (Coetzee 1992: 337–338)

In Coetzee's case, the introversion of retributive violence takes the form of a consistent self-exemption from belonging to all kinds of human communities, which could provide him with their territorial protection. Consider, for example, how Coetzee's senior doppelganger from the *Diary of a Bad Year*, Señor C, recalls his lifelong detachment from the mass street festivities:

> Scenes of mass celebration give me a glimpse of what I have missed out on in life, what I excluded myself from by being a kind of creature I am; the joy of belonging to (belonging in) a mass, of being swept along on currents of mass feeling. What a realization for someone to come to who was born in Africa, where the mass is the norm and the solitary the aberration!
> (Coetzee 2007: 170)

Turning the usual "African" order of things upside down, he chose the traumatic aberration of solitude in order to take advantage of its otherworldliness, which in its turn remains unknown and inaccessible to the people in the street. The same self-exemption that Señor C applied to the masses in the street throughout his life, Coetzee's narrative authority practices in its attitude to its characters and readers. It systematically declines their territorial protection, preferring instead a Jesus-like exterritoriality, exposure, and vulnerability. It receives its vocation from an 'elsewhere' residing far beyond all restricted horizons. Although it introduces itself merely through various doppelgangers and their territories, it persistently withdraws from them into the non-position of their excluded enabling domain. It humiliates itself by turning itself into an unprotected leftover of their identities, or a subhuman 'floating signifier' – in order to finally elevate itself into an all-embracing agency of their protection, or a superhuman 'floating signifier'.

Revoking the historical expropriation: Redeeming the imperiled translation zones

The elevation through humiliation of Coetzee's narrative authority departs from the doppelgangers themselves who are, as a rule, humiliated by their communities. In Hegelian terms, they are removed from the 'iron march' of history into the contingency and whimsicality of everyday 'historicity' (Hegel 1975: 245).

Those who are immersed in it are bereft of clear consciousness and therefore cannot participate in history (Hegel 1982: 12). Opposing this discriminating attitude, Kafka searched for his 'heroes' in somber urban, labyrinthine suburban or deserted countryside spaces, whereas Coetzee reveals them in godforsaken, vague, and indistinct settings. The task of the "non-historical" peoples' literatures, according to Ranajit Guha, is precisely to revoke this historical expropriation of both their past and present not only against the foreign colonizers but also domestic elites who embrace the colonizers' historical pattern (Guha 2002: 49). As if following this mission of rescuing the devalued 'historicity', Coetzee takes not only insignificant, helpless and vanishing creatures into his authorial protection (Marais 2009: xiv), but also spaces, which official historical memory has marginalized, alienated and/or abandoned. After the empty ominous locations of both of his early novels, *Dusklands* (1974) and *In the Heart of the Country* (1978), his third novel *Waiting for the Barbarians* (1981) introduces an unspecified frontier of an unknown empire. As the zones of an empire's dis/junction with foreign languages, cultures, and customs, the borderlands represent a huge challenge for all imperial administrations. They usually regard these in-between zones of mixed belonging and hybrid loyalties as a pernicious threat to their empires' welfare. If anywhere, it is precisely in these indistinct, murky, and amorphous translation zones that their identities have to be confirmed, maintained, and, if necessary, violently defended from their potential gravediggers.

During the crises of empires that accelerate the processes of their disidentification, the violence against the borderlands' 'foreigners', 'savages', and 'degenerates' was often publicly advocated and supported. For example, in the second half of the nineteenth century, German nationalists perceived their Eastern provinces (the so-called *Ostmarken*) as endangered by the "foamy splashes of an approaching large Slavic wave" (Thum 2013: 52), which in turn triggered Wilhelm II's radical 'defensive' measures. Some decades thereafter, "[t]hroughout interwar East Central Europe, fears of 'internal enemies' and 'fifth columns,' fears of losing control over the fringes of the state territory, and fears of proving unable to unify the national society led to the policy of forced ethnic homogenization" (Thum 2013: 55).[6] But the then contemporary literature, such as Joseph Roth's interwar *The Radetzky March*, has simultaneously and ironically refracted this officially underpinned derogation of borderlands. Its narrator renders Ukraine, the Dual Monarchy's utmost periphery, as a "swamp"

---

[6] For a perception of imperial borderlands as populated by backward and underdeveloped noble savages, see Promitzer 2003.

that swallows the lives of uninitiated settlers, soldiers and officers (Roth 2002: 141), while the natives circulate across it as "living ghosts" "jammed in" between "West and East" (Roth 2002: 139), struggling to get to grips with its indeterminacy. Ukraine as the civilized world's godforsaken margin (this is what the original Russian etymology of *Ukraine* in fact denotes), with its streets without names and houses without numbers, and with its frogs incessantly chirruping (Roth 2002: 141, 222), resolutely resists all of the democratic changes that are characteristic of the center (Roth 2002: 184).

However, as regards the anxiety of the 'savages' that disconcerted the outgoing empires' population, Kafka's short piece "An Old Manuscript" deserves special attention. It is narrated by a humble cobbler whose report, like the bricklayer's in "At the Construction of the Great Wall of China", switches from first-person singular to the first-person plural perspective. As a typical representative of the mob prejudices, he presents the nomad soldiers as degenerate foreign intruders who have shamelessly taken possession of the square in front of the Emperor's palace, where his workshop is located.

> This peaceful square, which was always kept so scrupulously clean, they have made literally into a stable. We do try every now and then to run out of our shops and clear away at least the worst of the filth, but this happens less and less often, for the labor is in vain and brings us besides into danger of falling under the hoofs of the wild horses or of being crippled with lashes from the whips. (Kafka 1988d: 455)

It is impossible to communicate with these barbarians who only speak their ridiculous "jackdaw" language[7] and "make grimaces" all the time. On top of stealing whatever they please from people, they stage their horrible carnivorous dismemberment ceremonies:

> Not long ago the butcher thought he might at least spare himself the trouble of slaughtering, and so one morning he brought along a live ox. But he will never dare to do that again. I lay for a whole hour flat on the floor at the back of my workshop with my head

---

[7] From the natives' point of view, barbarians by definition speak inarticulate animal languages (*bar-bar*) but it is noteworthy that Kafka refers specifically to jackdaws (*Dohlen*), which translates in Czech as his surname and means the same. Have the Czech natives once designated the Jewish settlers as 'jackdaws' because of their 'barbarous' language and is Kafka's surname a relic of this stigma? Whatever the case, in the process of *translatio imperii*, the attribute of 'barbarian' unpredictably shifts from one target to another, as one empire's barbarians sooner or later become another empire's carriers. Consider for example the competition between the Roman Empire's successors, the Islamic, Byzantine and Carolingian Empires, over their forebear's legacy, in which they labeled one another as barbarians. For the 'barbarians' drawn into the process of *translatio imperii* after the dissolution of Roman Empire, see Ausenda 1995.

muffled in all the clothes and rugs and pillows I had simply to keep from hearing the bellowing of that ox, which the nomads were leaping on from all sides, tearing morsels out of its living flesh with their teeth. (Kafka 1988d: 456)

The Emperor and his officials do not care to stop this disgraceful torment in front of the imperial palace and instead leave their humble subjects to cope with it, "but we are not equal to such a task; nor have we ever claimed to be capable of it. This is a misunderstanding of some kind; and it will make us perish" (Kafka 1988d: 456, trans. modified; *wir gehen daran zugrunde*).

Coetzee's *Barbarians* opens with a similar misunderstanding between an Empire's center and its periphery concerning the barbarous threat to its welfare, but displaces the latter from the center to the borderlands. This reverses the division of roles from "An Old Manuscript": Whereas provincials remain indifferent to the alleged peril, the government undertakes violent preventive measures against it. By doing so, it instinctively follows Hegel's famous advice to the governments to launch war to stop the disintegration of their states through the rise of their subjects' selfishness (Hegel 2011: 473, § 455). In "An Old Manuscript", it is the Emperor's and his officials' delineated disinterest in common affairs that epitomizes this reckless striving for self-existence (*Fürsichsein*), which terrifies the cobbler's mob mentality. Nothing but disintegration can take place in empires in which the barbarians push "right into the capital, although it is a long way from the frontier" (Kafka 1988d: 455), and the same also happens in "At the Construction of the Great Wall of China" where "infidel tribes [. . .] assemble before the imperial palace and shoot their black arrows at the Emperor" (Kafka 1988n: 281). Hegel accordingly warned against Kant's proposed ideal of a perpetual peace:

> Just as the movement of the ocean prevents the corruption which would be the result of perpetual calm, so by war people escape the corruption which would be occasioned by a continuous or eternal peace. (Hegel 1896: 331)

In Kafka's time, the corruption in question acquired the advanced form of a war by everyone against everyone, indicating that the imperial predestined "harmony of spheres" transformed into the post-imperial tyranny of one self-enclosed sphere against the other:

> I was defenseless against the figure across me, she sat quietly at the table and looked at the tabletop. I went around her in circles and felt strangled by her. A third walked around me and felt strangled by me. A fourth walked around the third and felt strangled by him. And so it continued up to the movements of the stars and beyond. Everything feels the grip on the neck. (Kafka 1953: 312)

Disquieted by the disintegration of society into its groups' and individuals' encapsulated realities, Kafka directed his attention to its perilous fragmentation into such "casings of the bondage to the future" (Max Weber; *Gehäuse der Hörigkeit der Zukunft*) and revealed their hidden warring against one another.

In *Barbarians*, on the contrary, Coetzee deals with the *center*'s encapsulation into its delusions by examining its 'hysteric' emergency measures and the ways they effectuate the frontier as their stage. Distracting attention from its own corruption, the central administration blames the 'alienated' and 'indifferent' borderlands for it, trying to reappropriate their territories which were disappropriated by barbarian influences, influxes, and intrusions.

The deterritorializing deterritorialized: The borderland in *Barbarians*

By its very nature, the borderland degenerates core imperial values but the main figure in Coetzee's novel that, according to the alerts sent to the center, bears responsibility for their deterritorialization is the Magistrate, an imperial official who was appointed with quite the opposite task of protecting and consolidating the Empire's territory. But this happened while he was still a young man (Coetzee 1982b: 5) and in the meantime he developed an interest in the natives, adopted some of their habits and got accustomed to the 'wilderness' of their domicile. This deterritorialization of his civil manners by the barbarous ones has reminded some critics of the character of Kurtz in Joseph Conrad's *Heart of Darkness* (Samolsky 2011: 66, Micali 2017: 13–16), who was likewise sent far away from the imperial center into "the heart of the country", presumably Belgian Congo, to be exposed there to a similar 'barbarization'. However, the conclusion that both novels lead to the insight that the only real barbarians are the colonizers, might prove to be "all too easy" (Micali 2017: 15) considering that Coetzee's *Barbarians* refracts Conrad's central perspective through Kafka's peripheral one. Besides, even though Coetzee's novel, due to some undeniable South African references,[8] was often read as an allegory of the South African "twilight of legal illegality" in the 1970s (Coetzee 1992: 363), its godforsaken borderland is all but predominantly African. There are no races in the novel and

---

8 For example, the details of Steven Biko's death (the leader of black resistance who died in police detention on 12 September 1977), as recounted in Colonel Snyman's inquest evidence, are replicated almost directly in Joll's official report to the Magistrate (Wittenberg and Highman 2015: 107).

there was no 'Third Bureau' in South Africa but in tsarist Russia.[9] Further on, according to the report of a South African censor, "the locality is obscure; some oasis in an arid region north of the equator, where winters are icy. It is nowhere Southern African, nor is there any white populace" (Quoted in Wittenberg and Highman 2015: 110).

Indeed, whereas Coetzee set both *Dusklands* and *In the Heart of the Country* in landscapes with which he was intimately familiar, in *Waiting* he envisioned, i.e. constructed an unknown landscape (1992: 142). Being patched together from various travelers' accounts, the novel's 'map' belongs less to the physical than an imaginary geography. "I just put together a variety of locales and left a lot of things vague with a very definite intention that it shouldn't be pinned down to some specific place" (Coetzee in Penner 1986: 35). To avoid the harsh state censorship,[10] he displaced the novel's setting from Cape Town and Robben Island (Mandela's prison), which were envisioned for its first version, to Lop Nor lake next to the Mongolian border in northwest China (Wittenberg and Highman 2015: 112). Certainly, Coetzee's geopolitically abstract rendering of citizens' confrontation with the barbarians, which "could as well be Russian and Kirghiz, or Han and Mongol, or Turk and Arab, or Arab and Berber" (Coetzee in Begam 1992: 33), is not simply the outcome of his political discretion. More substantially, it is his above delineated relentless commitment to explore how the "real's" circulation empties out all realities. No single reality matches its spectrality, which therefore has to be traced down in the space in-between these realities. The more overlapping realities, the more deterritorialized this 'province' in which the "real" is expected to reside becomes.

This is why, more than Conrad's technique of deterritorialization, Coetzee's radical dislocation associates Kafka's one, which was guided by the same commitment. Thus, in his "At the Construction of the Great Wall of China", the Austro-Hungarian Empire, striving to stop its threatening fragmentation at the outset of the twentieth century, transfigures into the ancient Chinese Empire in the process of its unification out of seven warring states. Kafka undertakes another and similarly extreme dislocation in his "Memoirs of the Kalda railway" (1976: 303–313), inspired by his uncle Löwy's memories of the Congo railway construction (Alt 2005: 28) that, interestingly enough, pops up in Conrad's

---

9 Coetzee sets the hero of his *The Master of Petersburg* (Coetzee 1994) in the late years of tsarist Russia, which means that in this "Russian" novel he also focuses on the turning point in a country's history.
10 Wittenberg and Highman (2015: 108) quote Coetzee's letter to Peter Lampack from 1 September 1985: "[W]hile I live here, and while the present regime lasts, I have to distance myself from a 'South African' *Barbarians*."

novella. Although Kafka's adventurous uncle, often addressed in his diaries, understandably recalled tropical temperatures, the story reports of a railway construction in the icy Russian steppes.

Next to such climatic and cultural turnover of its setting, *Barbarians* also associates with Kafka's "At the Construction" through the official deployment of the barbarian threat as the means for the vanishing empire's reanimation and consolidation. Foggy and vague, the idea of the barbarians appears in both narratives "as a blank slip onto which the Empire engraves itself; that is, the Empire gives itself form by writing" on them (Valdez Moses 1993: 120).

> [T]he ghost of barbarian enemies is [. . .] the necessary fulfillment of the Empire's ghost; it is only thanks to the opposition to an external threat that the innumerable people scattered across the vast Chinese territory (in which, as we are told, even the language of neighboring countries sounds strange and shocking) can acquire the sense of belonging to a common civilization. (Micali 2017: 12, trans. mine)

The Tarim basin, in which Coetzee sets his novel's action, has long been contested by various sides. The name of the province which it belongs to, Xinjiang ("new frontier"), dates from the nineteenth century, when the area, formerly known as East Turkestan, officially became part of the Qing Empire after conquest in the mid-eighteenth century. The explorations of Sven Hedin in this area, as presented in his *Central Asia and Tibet: towards the holy city of Lassa* (1903) and later works, which served as the novel's most important documentary sources, have been founded by Chang-Kai-check in the 1930s with the aim of securing the area's subjugation within a larger China. Hedin himself "adhered to the idea of a Great China [. . .] and shared the Chinese view that Tibetans and the Mongols were uncivilized barbarians" (Johansson 2012: 68). He meticulously evokes the former empire of Lou-lan that disappeared through the barbarian invasion and the loss of water, and Coetzee places his novel in the frantic time just before its demise. However, the depicted hysteria of a prerevolutionary period, strongly reminiscent of the panicking South African apartheid (Attwell 2014: 206), is far from being over. "In the wake of 9/11, the Chinese government has sought to portray attacks in Xinjiang as part of a co-ordinated global al-Quaeda jihad [. . .] and their own repressive treatment of Uyghurs as part of 'counterterrorism'" (Wittenberg and Highman 2015: 123). The same holds for today's South African Manichean landscape, still captured in the process of *translatio imperii*.

> Between black and white there is a gulf fixed. Deeper than pity, deeper than honourable dealings, deeper even than goodwill, lies an awareness on both sides that people like Paul and himself, with their pianos and violins, are here on this earth of South Africa, on the shakiest of pretexts. (Coetzee 2012: 157)

Overlapping realities and their reemerging leftover

This is not to say that Coetzee's novel reserves martial law merely for the South African, Russian (via the Third Bureau), and Chinese historical realities. On the contrary, some critics were tempted to interpret *Barbarians* as an anticipation of the state of exception's world-wide expansion. Following Derrida's reading of the apartheid as a metonymic rather than exceptional historical phenomenon (1994b: xiv), Wittenberg and Highman for example argue that

> today, the novel has more bite and urgency precisely for its blurring of referentiality; through it we can recognize contemporary practices and link them, their dynamics and rhetoric, with apartheid, now roundly reviled. (2015: 124)

Coetzee himself seems to be underpinning this interpretation when he, albeit indirectly, extends the state of exception to his new domicile Australia, still affected by its former colonizers', i.e. British and American *translatio imperii*. His senior doppelganger from the *Diary of a Bad Year*, Señor C, quotes his own remarks about pending security legislation in South Africa of 1970s that were made in 2006 during his invited reading in the National Library in Canberra:

> The security police could come in and out and blindfold and handcuff you without explaining why, and take you away to an unspecified site and do what they wanted to you. [. . .] All of this, and much more, in apartheid South Africa, was done in the name of a struggle against terror. I used to think that the people who created these laws that effectively suspended the rule of law were moral barbarians. Now I know they were just pioneers, ahead of their time. (Coetzee 2007: 171)

To appropriately understand this statement, one ought to know that Australia, by suspending "a range of civil liberties indefinitely into the future" (Coetzee 2007: 19), at the time unreservedly joined the American and British war on terror. As for the Americans, following the same logic of "extraordinary times", which demand "extraordinary measures" (Coetzee 2007: 43), George W. Bush declared himself to be above the law: "he cannot commit a crime, since he is the one who makes the laws defining crimes" (Coetzee 2007: 49). As a result, in America at the beginning of the twenty first century,

> on the basis of denunciations from informers ('sources') people simply vanish or are vanished from society, and publicizing their disappearance qualifies as a crime in its own right. (Coetzee 2007: 43)

Nevertheless, one should be wary to interpret *Barbarians*, as Wittenberg and Highman do, as an exemplary instance of "futurity", a term that Amir Eshel uses to designate "literature's ability to raise, via engagement with the past, political and ethical dilemmas crucial for the human future" (Eshel 2012: 4–5). Letting the past culminate in the future means making a history out of them and this is quite the opposite of that which Coetzee demands of the novel, i.e. to be "a rival to history" (1988a: 5). Like Kafka, he systematically refuses to treat such interruptions as events pre-calculated by history. As Kafka spells out in aphorism 20 from his "Reflections", making the past states of exception *anticipate* the future ones means forgetting that they are in fact *retroactively* inscribed into the past:

> Leopards break into the temple and drink all the sacrificial vessels dry; it keeps happening; in the end, it can be calculated in advance and is incorporated into the ritual.
> (2012: 190)

Accordingly, Russel Samolsky (2011: 64–65) argues that, even though Señor C claims that "his" *Barbarians'* torture chamber anticipates the horrors of Abu Ghraib (Coetzee 2007: 171), Coetzee himself in "In the Torture Chamber" interpreted such imaginary diversification of inflicted sufferings as an unreflected collaboration with the torturers (Coetzee 1992: 363). In the writer's dialogic world as reigned by the "real", different perspectives do not complete but rather subvert one another. Its law is discontinuity, not continuity as that of Dostoevsky's world according to Bakhtin. Coetzee does not add different historical realities – South African, Chinese, Russian, Australian, American – to each other in order to finally derive their common truth. This would resume the imperial power's operation, which violently presses the Empire's truth into all subjects until they obey it (Samolsky 2011: 73–74). Abhorring such tyrannical leveling down of all historical realities, Coetzee instead tends to uncover the denied "real" of one from the other's point of view. As no reality can take the "real" into its full possession, the operation steadily goes on by joining one reality after another to the "real's" 'floating signifier'.

To foster the rise of this signifier, Coetzee refracts *Barbarians'* already overlapping historical realities through the fictional ones, such as that of Conrad's godforsaken Belgian Congo, Kafka's ancient China from "The Great Wall" or his French Caledonia from "Penal Colony". Through the reference to the latter that serves as the pretext for *Barbarians*, although "Penal Colony's" action is historically prefigured by that of *Barbarians*, the delineated entanglement of 'backshadowing' and 'foreshadowing' acquires an additional push. It was only toward the end of the nineteenth century that the New Caledonia colony became the dumping ground for the 'dregs' of the French Empire that engaged summary justice in deporting them to it, for example the Parisian Communards (1871). These deportations are discussed toward the end of Foucault's *Discipline and Punish*, which also powerfully influenced Coetzee's novel, although it discusses the French Empire's historically later transformation.

The novel's redoubling of one historical and fictional reality in the other dissolves these realities' spatial and temporal 'belonging' on behalf of the "real's" spatial and temporal floating. As the subhumans and superhumans inhabit an indistinct space and time, they are by definition extraterritorial and exhistorical, i.e. they belong nowhere. This drives the "real" into an interminable longing – Lacan would say 'desire' – for a divine province that rejects all available historical realities as the places of its belonging. The "real's" desire never arrives at its destination. In one of his letters during the writing on *Barbarians*, Coetzee notes that the Magistrate's

> meeting with the barbarians was vacuous, no words were exchanged, the police are not simply evil, the girl refuses to betray her meaning to him, and finally the barbarians do not come. [. . .] This is a novel in which meaning is continually held back.
> (19 February 1979; quoted in Attwell 2014: 215)

Thus, the Magistrate's desire remains suspended. His "real" never arrives at its destination because of its "inner unfinalizability", i. e. its "capacity to outgrow, as it were, from within and to render *untrue* any externalizing and finalizing definition" (Bakhtin 1984: 59). The process of the "real's" incessant redefinition never comes to a halt by making its subject "renewable, substitutable, supplementary, and characterised by slippage" (Wicomb 2009: 20). As Greg Foster put it in his book *The Return of the Real*, one only can provisionally "uncover it in uncanny things" such as "the obscene vitality of the wound" or "the radical nihility of the corpse" (Foster 1994: 152, 166). It is precisely this that happens in *Barbarians:* the uncovering of the "real" in the wounds of the girl's body and the old man's corpse.

From consciousness to the body

The Magistrate is hardly in his nature a relentless searcher for the "grimaces" of the "real" in his reality (Lacan 1991: 148), but becomes such by force of exceptional circumstances. Before the state of exception affected his frontier, he was peacefully immersed in the cyclical time of nature in the way he imagines the barbarians are, "watch[ing] the sun rise and set, eat[ing] and sleep[ing] and [being] content" (Coetzee 1982b: 13). Placed "on the roof of the world", where "[f]rom the sky thousands of stars look down on us" (Coetzee 1982b: 5), he enjoyed the harmony of the subhuman and superhuman sphere, undisturbed by the violent intervention of human history. It is the torture chamber, introduced by martial law, that turns him into a man of conscience and raises consciousness of his Empire's injustice toward the 'barbarians'. This consciousness clearly distinguishes him from other imperial officials in the distant periphery such as the aforementioned Kurtz and the Officer or the chief tax-collector in Kafka's "Refusal", who act as the 'barbarians'' calm executors. The Magistrate, on the contrary, feels ashamed of his Empire's treatment of them.

> One of the strangest features of shame [. . .] is the way bad treatment of someone else, [. . .] someone else's embarrassment, stigma, debility, bad smell, or strange behaviour, seemingly having nothing to do with me, can so readily flood me–assuming I am a shame-prone person–with this sensation whose very suffusiveness seems to delineate my precise, individual outlines in the most isolating way imaginable. (Sedgwick 2003: 36–37)

Departing from such shame that humiliates him – because he realizes the discrimination generated by his "precise, individual outlines" – he develops an attitude of sympathetic imagination to the barbarians. Some two decades thereafter, another of Coetzee's characters, Elizabeth Costello, promotes "sympathetic imagination" (2004a: 80) as an alternative to reason, the typical "being of human thought" (2004a: 67). If reason is founded on human self-certainty, sympathetic imagination's departure point is the human "state of humility" (Durrant 2006: 131) before the creatures. Humiliated by the feeling of shame, the Magistrate thus displays *in nuce* that which Costello as a prominent writer will develop to the extreme, at least in her son's view:

> "But my mother has been a man," he persists. "She has also been a dog. She can think her way into other people, into other existences. I have read her; I know. It is within her powers. Isn't that what is most important about fiction: that it takes us out of ourselves, into other lives?" (2004a: 22–23)[11]

It deserves remembering here that, in Coetzee's own understanding as well, "writing is dialogic: a matter of awakening the countervoices in oneself and embarking upon speech with them" (1992: 65). As opposed to blood relatives who are allocated to us by birth, he claims, we sympathetically imagine such 'elective relatives' because "we may want to disown our real parents and claim for our self a much finer-sounding lineage" (Coetzee 1993: 5). Following this program, in *The Master of Petersburg*, for example, Coetzee imagines Dostoevsky's mourning over the son from his first marriage in order to articulate his own

---

11 Significantly, this opinion likens Ian McEwan's conviction on the importance of the ability to empathize in fiction. He entrusts to his interviewers that "fiction is a deeply moral form in that it is the perfect medium for entering the mind of another. I think it is at the level of empathy that moral questions begin in fiction" (Louvel et al. 1995: 4). I will return to this commitment to dialogism that connects McEwan with Coetzee in the last chapter.

grief over the death of his son Nicolas. "Coetzee is writing about the fictional Dostoevsky in himself" (Attwell 2015: 168). Attwell even claims that all Coetzee's intertextual references are engaged to cope with the consistent exposure of his reality to the visits of the "real" (2015: xx, 25–26). It is the "real's" unstoppable suffusion that gives them birth, not the postmodern frivolous playfulness. Coetzee's famous remark that in South Africa "there is now too much truth for art to hold, truth by the bucketful, truth that overwhelms and swamps every act of the imagination" (1992: 99) certainly endorses this thesis. It is this elusive truth, not only South African of course, with whose embarrassing swamp he tries to come to terms by means of his elective relatives.

However, if it is only our humiliating shrinking under the "flood" of shame that makes us sympathize with others, then these others are not really *elected* by us. On the contrary, their unexpected breakthrough demarcates our identity, delineates our "precise, individual outlines [. . .] in the most isolating way imaginable", and establishes our conscience and consciousness. Like David Lurie from *Disgrace* or Kafka's Josef K., the Magistrate used to be an inconsiderate womanizer who, taking advantage of his position, misused young girls by disregarding their bodily aversion to such an old man. Like Lurie and Josef K., he equally disregarded that these girls "felt insulted by [his] behaviour" (Coetzee 1982b: 152). In *Disgrace*, Lurie's sexual proclivities are associated with his daughter's rapists. In his daughter's view, his penetration is associated with killing (Coetzee 1999a: 158). In Lurie's own sudden insight, male sexuality has determined the course of history no less than male killing. "The seed of generation, driven to perfect itself, driving deep into the woman's body, driving to bring the future into being. Drive, driven" (Coetzee 1999a: 194). In *Barbarians*, male killing has another 'natural' mode of appearance too: the hunt, a passion which the Magistrate shares with Colonel Joll and which helps him to fortify his maleness. For a long time, the killing of animals has come so naturally to him as it does to Kafka's hunter Gracchus.

> I was a hunter; was there any sin in that? I followed my calling as a hunter in the Black Forest, where there were still wolves in those days. I lay in ambush, shot, hit my mark, flayed the skins from my victims: was there any sin in that? (Kafka 1988m: 260)

But the Magistrate cannot unconcernedly go on with the killing since "time has broken; something has fallen in upon me from the sky, at random, from nowhere" (Coetzee 1982b: 60). Frightened like Lurie by his formerly habitual 'killing activities' and suddenly flooded with shame for having participated in them, he first gives up shooting at a ram he has in his target (1982b: 54–55). Thereafter he also realizes:

What I have been doing all this time, pressing myself upon such flowerlike soft-petalled children – not only her, on the other one too? I should have stayed among the gross and decaying where I belong: fat women with acrid armpits and bad tempers, whores with big slack cunts. (1982b: 131)

This consciousness-raising of his formerly unreflected 'child abuse' is unthinkable without his prior Jesus-like self-humiliation before the girl's disfigured body, i.e. his washing of her feet (1982b: 40). The tortured girl awakens parental responsibility in the Magistrate's up to then recklessly consumptive attitude to his young concubines.[12] Arguing that already ahead of *Barbarians*, i.e. in *Dusklands*, Eugene Dawn stabs his son and Jacobus Coetzee brutalizes the Khoi child, Mike Marais puts forth the thesis that, in Coetzee's work, "the child signifies what history has corrupted, defaced, effaced [. . .]. In terms of the logic of the child-metaphor, history is the realm of abandonment, of parental irresponsibility" (Marais 2009: 27). Indeed, hinting to Freud's famous essay, Coetzee lets the Magistrate state: "Somewhere, always, the child is being beaten" (Coetzee 1982b: 108). The girl's tormented body becomes the principal "real" of his reality that challenges its discrimination. This body's resistance ignites his sympathetic imagination whose hunger for expansion develops in other directions too. For example, as an amateur archeologist and cryptographer, he strives to domesticate the "real" of barbarian cultures. But not solely the girl and barbarians, he tends to take into his protection and thus reintegrate into history all that it has abandoned, including the tiniest "beetles, worms, cockroaches, ants" as the "miracles of creation" (Coetzee 1982b: 144).[13] He even fears he

---

[12] In a letter of 18 September 1978, composed amid writing the novel, Coetzee remarks: "Am struck by my concern for my children's future. One would die for them. The behaviour strikes me as instinctual. This man [who would become the magistrate]: will he not break out of his passivity, his contentment at the moment when he sees the girl, as his child, threatened?" (Quoted in Attwell 2014: 210).

[13] As Zimbler has shown, in Coetzee's next novel *Life & Times of Michael K*, the hero's behavior, appearance and modes of being are dominated by the "insect world" (Zimbler 2014: 127–130), invoking Kafka's well-known predilection for infinitesimal creatures. Canetti pointed out this predilection's closeness to Chinese culture's passion for insects. Some centuries ago, the Chinese used to keep their cherished crickets in a nutshell on their chests and Kafka also preferred to raise the tiny beings to eye level, i.e. to elevate them instead of humiliating them by stooping down to them on the ground (Canetti 1969:100–103). The protagonist-narrator of Kafka's "Memoirs of the Kalda Railway" accordingly states: "You can see small animals clearly only if you hold them before you at eye level; if you stoop down to them on the ground and look at them there, you acquire a false, imperfect notion of them" (1976: 310). It is such elevation that Kafka undertakes with the vermin bug Gregor Samsa in his "Metamorphosis" and Coetzee, after him, with his 'humiliated insect' Michael K.

himself will fall out of history and undertakes respective measures against such oblivion:

> I cannot save the prisoners, therefore let me save myself. Let it at the very least be said, if it ever comes to be said, if there is ever anyone in some remote future interested to know the way we lived, that in this far outpost of the Empire of light there existed one man who in his heart was not a barbarian. (Coetzee 1982b: 140)

Jarad Zimbler claims that Coetzee, via his early 'heroes' such as Dawn, Jacobus Coetzee, Magda, and Magistrate, introduces the so-called "central intelligence" into South African fiction of the 1970s in order to return "the complexities of thought and feeling" (Zimbler 2014: 114) into the South African bare Manichean world. Although the French *roman nouveau* had at that time already eliminated such consciousness as the last refuge of a suspect bourgeois humanism, Coetzee revivifies this typical "nineteenth-century European bourgeois" (Zimbler 2014: 111) that is oriented toward the expansion of his intellectual horizon in his Magistrate, with the aim of negating the inhuman South African present (Zimbler 2014: 117).

Although interesting, this thesis disregards Coetzee's ambiguous attitude to the European culture. The European consciousness whose distinct reality persistently humiliates itself by its excursions into the obscure "real", simultaneously elevates itself through them into an agent of self-assertion, self-expansion, and self-aggrandizement. Therefore, it is innocent solely in its self-perception. As Michael Valdez Moses remarks, "[a]lthough the magistrate regards his behavior as benevolent, paternal, and humane, his solicitous attention to the Other cannot be separated from the sinister apparatus of torture that the Empire employs" (Valdez Moses 1993: 121). Elleke Boehmer in her turn noticed that, already in his *White Writing*, Coetzee theorized the uneasy consequences of the European colonizers' imaginative appropriation of the settled land (Boehmer 2011: 208). In this book, he speaks of the "self-defeating process of naming South Africa by defining it as non-Europe – self-defeating because in each particular case in which South Africa is identified to be non-European, it remains Europe, not South Africa, that is named" (1988b: 164). For Lacan, this catachrestic naming of the "real" by reality unavoidably amounts to a "missed encounter". Since Elizabeth Costello's 'sympathetic imagination' appropriates the animal "real" in the same way as the European reality occupies South Africa's "real", Coetzee also cautions that "sympathetic identifications have a fiction-like status" (Kurtz and Coetzee 2015: 134). That is to say, the Magistrate's sympathetic imagination conquers the girl's "real" in the same way that, as we will come to see in the last chapter, Briony's imagination colonizes other characters in McEwan's *Atonement* (Seaboyer 2005: 32).

By attributing this imperial consciousness to their fictional doppelgangers (the Magistrate, Elizabeth and Briony), Coetzee and McEwan carefully detach themselves from its expansionist ambitions. Their technique of outsmarting their doppelgangers recalls Kafka's discrete distancing from the traveling researcher in "The Penal Colony". Kafka makes him share his imperial attitude to other cultures with the German criminologist Robert Heindl who inspired the character, and Coetzee follows Kafka by making the Magistrate share his colonizing attitude with his own blueprint, the Swedish ethnologist Sven Hedin. If the Magistrate excavated the inscribed poplar slips like Hedin (Wittenberg and Highman 2015: 115), he did so, again like Hedin, to appropriate them for imperial history.

To prevent such development in *Barbarians*, Coetzee lets the Magistrate's insatiable desire for the expansion of his reality first stumble on the "real" of the girl's body. The deployed signifiers leave a surplus, an excess that resists elimination and heightens the Magistrate's fascination with the girl. His lust for knowledge is unstoppable and nor is it afraid of torturers (1982b: 158, 166–167). But her silent resilience to his curiosity induces his recurrent dreams and sexual indifference, i.e. the signals of *his own* body's rebellion against the further expansion of his consciousness. In these dreams and through them, "the child arrives; she arrives when the Magistrate is unable to welcome her, to respond to her with advance knowledge and so place her" (Marais 2009: 26). Disabling his consciousness's ability to provide adequate responses, his rebellious body leaves its signifiers in a 'longing' condition.

However, the inarticulate "real" fully overflows his articulate reality only after the Empire turns his body, on the model of the barbarian ones, into the surface for its humiliating and mutilating engravings. When he strove to translate these engravings through his meticulous palpation into the documents of imperial history, the girl's body responded by freeing its materiality from such imposed 'sublimation' – and his body responds in exactly the same way. Disgraced bodies lose contact with their consciousness, i.e. the ability to connect their signifiers with respective signifieds. Their disfigurement displaces them into a floating mental state resembling the insomniac's condition of Levinas's *il y a*. Elaborating on this traumatic existential mood (1987: 65–67), Levinas pointed out the possibility of the sudden disappearance of stable and solid things, which our experience of existence relies upon, into nothingness. Once our existence, in such traumatic circumstances, is forced to unmoor itself from its familiar world, we suddenly face bare being that turns our reality upside down. Lying "in the reek of old vomit", the Magistrate is finally reduced to "the most rudimentary needs of [his] body" (1982b: 154), eating "like a beggar" (1982b: 172), waiting "for the whistle that calls the dogs" (1982b: 170), and allowed to die only "like a dog in a corner" (1982b:

157). Like the defaced girl that he once took into protection, he is now stripped of human identity and reduced to the bare life of a miserable creature.

Being subjected to such a debasing metamorphosis into the "real" without reality, the Magistrate *via negationis* evokes Coetzee's thesis that ideas acquire their distinction only when they become "part of the personality, part of the self, ultimately indistinguishable from the self" (1993: 7). The Magistrate is, on the contrary, emptied step by step out of his personality, his 'self' is turned into a floating signifier catapulted out of history. Since history never banishes its inhabitants from its territory without previously injuring and tainting them, his plan to "make a living" like an "unthinking savage", i.e. "to live in time like fish in water, like birds in air, like children" (Coetzee 1982b: 177) was bound to fail. Those who have not freely elected their subhuman humiliation, cannot expect their superhuman elevation. "There will be no history", Colonel Joll tells him, "the affair is too trivial" (1982b: 153). Anyway, the frontier is too undignified, he claims, to be considered by history. The Colonel's assistant Warrant Officer Mandel puts his 'marginal episode' in a nutshell: "We keep no record of you" (1982b: 167). Without a record there is no history. Despite all his systematic efforts, the Magistrate does not succeed in reintegrating the excommunicated "real" into the historical reality. What he instead manages to stage is the capitulation of this reality before the flood of the "real". The barbarians won the day, ridiculing his ambitions to become their historian and making him realize: "There has been something staring at me in the face, and still I do not see it" (1982b: 206). No better definition of the "real" is imaginable: One can never see it because the "real" draws the boundaries of one's reality. In terms of Lacan's 'missed encounter' between the eye and the gaze, the reality's eye is by definition outsmarted by the "real's" gaze: "You never look at me from the place from which I see you" (Lacan 1978: 101).

Elective relatives: Providing the "real" with a substitute reality

If the Magistrate fails to integrate the "real" that disconcerts him into the historical reality, *Barbarians*' narrative authority appears to be much more efficient and successful in this regard. By ruining his protagonist-narrator's attempt at elevating himself through a consistent self-humiliation, Coetzee ultimately turns him into an instrument for one of his 'elective relative's' favorite strategies:

> Kafka developed a literary form for writing like this. One of its key elements was to focalize a third-person, matter-of-fact narration through a passive central character who, living

aslant degradation, had few or no beliefs, little or no affective disposition, little or no substance or personality at all – who was subjectively empty. (During 2014: 503)

The prefiguration of the Magistrate's emptiness by that of Kafka's focalizers make his individual identity boundaries multiply and resonate in an open-ended intertextual space, the prefigurations of which constantly invite postfigurations. This hall of echoes is the favorite room for maneuver of Coetzee's narrative authority that ceaselessly lures new elective relatives into its universe. Let us just recall here that a reserved observation of an empire's intervention against the supposed barbarian peril, alongside "The Great Wall of China" and "Penal Colony", inspires *The Heart of Darkness* as well.

The Magistrate's situation thus appears prefigured by at least three literary established relationships. Leaving aside "The Great Wall of China" for a moment, the relationship between the protagonist-narrator Marlow and the appointed 'exterminator of the brutes' Kurtz, anticipates both the relationship between the Researcher and the Officer in Kafka's story and that between the Magistrate and Colonel Joll in Coetzee's novel. While Kurtz, Officer and Joll advocate a violent exclusion of barbarians from Empire's territory, Marlow, Researcher and Magistrate prefer their tolerant integration. Considering that Kurtz, the Officer and Joll are firmly determined to prevent the poisoning of the sound imperial body by the degenerate foreigners' penetration into it, *Barbarians*' narrative authority lets the High Command from "The Great Wall of China" join their group. As opposed to them, Marlow, the Traveling Explorer, the Magistrate, and the humble stonemason from Kafka's story advocate a non-violent attitude to the people of different beliefs and habits.

Although all these relationships emerge from the *translatio imperii*'s self-reforming periods as delineated in Foucault's *Discipline and Punish*, they are very differently located both historically and geopolitically. Due to this, the relationship between the Magistrate and the Colonel, with its anyway blurred geopolitical and historical boundaries, opens itself towards additional connections that in their turn invite further transfers. Their template is the transfer of the Dutch colonial misadventure in South Africa to the American much later one in Vietnam, as carried out in *Dusklands* (Robinson 2012: 32–33). The more floating the rendering of one relationship, the more links it associates. Coetzee himself pushes his doppelganger from the *Diary of a Bad Year*, Señor C, into such sweeping transnational and transhistorical comparisons when he claims that the South African tortures as depicted in his *Barbarians* merely announced those of the American deterritorialized camps for 'barbarians' (2007: 171) or compares them with Britain's imposition of colonial rule (2007: 39–45). His lust for such (mis)appropriations moreover continues, blaming the official Australian measure of rejecting refugees for being "not dissimilar to Guantanamo Bay" (2007: 112). Australia, he says, refuses to acknowledge that today's 'barbarians' arrive to the continent "in much the same boats" as their much-desired hosts had done some time ago (2007: 113).

Through such smoothly concatenated transfers, both the protagonist-narrator and the setting of *Barbarians* get a rich compensation for their deterritorialization. They acquire substitute, widely dispersed imagined territories from which, in the final account, Coetzee's narrative authority benefits the most. Not only their stripping of geopolitical belonging, he also capitalizes on his own stripping of belonging to a particular literary reality, as demonstrated in the transformation of *Barbarians'* author into the *Diary*'s fictional doppelganger. In fact, Coetzee deprives all his novels' narrative authorities of their delimited territory, making them sheer "intermediaries" of intertextual exchanges (Graham 2006: 233). This general tendency becomes particularly visible in *Elizabeth Costello*, *Diary of a Bad Year* and *The Childhood of Jesus* in which intertextual spaces get the upper hand over physical ones (Mosca 2016: 129). But Clarkson's thesis that "[t]here is no author-narrator who prescribes a resolution to the collision of voices from a position of anonymous omniscience" (Clarkson 2009: 100) holds for Coetzee's entire oeuvre. His narrative authorities resemble Socratic midwives from Bakhtin's reading of Dostoevsky (1994: 110), who, without having satisfactory answers of their own, provoke others to form their "strong opinions" as Señor C does in *Diary* (Northover 2012: 46–47). Instead of proposing one opinion of their own or another, their mission is to set the floating terms for the exchange of others' opinions. If they are all unknowingly put into the narrative authority's terms, then its 'floating signifier' is removed from their horizons. Coetzee's adoption of an intermediary's role is therefore all but "an abdication from a position of authorial power", as Lucy Graham contends (Graham 2006: 233). She forgets that Socrates, who himself never revealed a single truth, ultimately acquired world renown for his art of withholding and postponing such revelations. As a loyal distant follower of his "destruction of false assumptions rather than the establishment of certain truths" (Northover 2012: 40), Coetzee managed to join the same 'hall of fame'.

His strong tendency to turn his novels into a marketplace of others' ideas is well known and he has openly acknowledged it in a number of interviews (1992: 65; Scott 1997: 89; Wachtel 2001: 44). As Northover has convincingly argued, all his novels are "dialogic in substance", even if they have "apparently monologic forms" such as *In the Heart of the Country*, *Waiting for the Barbarians* and *Disgrace* (Northover 2012: 47). They invite many others into their space to understand who they are, or who they are not, or who they want to be. Some time ago, Coetzee claimed that

> in the process of responding to the writers one intuitively chooses to respond to, one makes oneself into the person whom in the most intractable but also perhaps the most deeply ethical sense one wants to be. (1993: 7)

However, it was not *person* but, on the contrary, a *withdrawal* of it into a 'floating signifier' that he aimed at when he exempted himself from his South African relatives and attached himself to European writers such as Defoe, Dostoevsky, Conrad, Kafka, and Beckett. He hid his humiliating scarface behind their elevated ones. The "dominant moral impulse at work" in Coetzee's early fiction is the "insatiable hunger of all his protagonists" to escape the "shackles of their historical position" (Watson 1996: 23) and Coetzee certainly speaks also of himself when he describes the Magistrate as "a man of conscience" deeply ashamed by the existence of the "torture chamber" in his surrounding (1992: 363). This is after all confirmed by his parenthetic admittance

> that I, as a person, as a personality, am overwhelmed, that my thinking is thrown into confusion and helplessness, by the fact of human suffering in the world, and not only human suffering. These fictional constructions of mine are paltry, ludicrous defenses against that being-overwhelmed, and, to me, transparently so. (1992: 248)

As I have argued above, being-overwhelmed is the key modality in which the "real" pays visit to our reality. There is no doubt that this visit, in Coetzee's case, takes place in South Africa, especially if we consider the "perpetual anxiety" of the provincial subject frantically looking for 'elsewhere', which, as we have seen, permeates *Scenes from Provincial Life* (Attwell 2015: 26). As Attwell points out, Coetzee was never "comfortably settled" in the Cape Town in which he spent thirty years of his life (Attwell 2015: 26) but was all the time haunted by the diasporic feeling of non-belonging to his kin of exploiters and torturers (Jacobs 2016: 205). This deep shame for their crimes follows him like an obstinate shadow even after he surrenders to the fascinating power of 'elsewhere' and leaves South Africa for Australia – since, as he explains to his biographer, he "had not left South Africa [. . .] but come to Australia" (Kannemeyer 2012: 541). His systematic erasure of all political, racial, and social references to the South Africa of the 1970s and 1980s in his early novels (Elshamy 2018: 200–201) is generated precisely by this shame for their executive power in his country at the time. If he carefully avoided joining the street demonstrations in South Africa against the colonial supremacy of the whites over the blacks – whereas he readily joined those in the United States against the Vietnam War even though he was aware of the threat of imprisonment and concomitant banishment that indeed materialized – this is because in South Africa his "acceptance of historical guilt" for his ancestors and contemporaries, which deeply ashamed him, overshadowed his "desire for political change" (Head 2009: 23).

This overwhelming shame for the atrocities committed by his Afrikaner kin is the "real" that generates Coetzee's 'grimace'. Kafka described this disfigurement by the truth as "being dazzled [*Geblendet-Sein*] by truth: the light on the grotesquely grimacing retreating face is true, and nothing else" (1991: 79). His rendering of the truth in fact very accurately anticipates Lacan's rendering of the "real": the truth can be captured only in its "grimaces", i.e. deforming imprints which its sudden flashes leave behind in reality. As no one can survive a direct encounter with the light of the truth without "getting burnt", the artists' task is to find out "in the dark void a place where the beam of light can be intensely caught" (Kafka 1991: 86).

Dazzled by the shocking truth, Coetzee follows Kafka's agenda. In order to visualize and thus liberate himself from his embarrassing swamp, he looks for the protagonists and artists whose *Fratzengesichter* have intensely caught the beam of the truth's light. Yet this therapeutic agenda confronts a structural obstacle, which did not escape Kafka's attention. As he notoriously carefully noticed in his *Third Octavo Notebook*, the grimacing faces which an artist recognizes as his or her elective relatives do not exactly reveal to him or her *the* truth that has turned his or her own face into a grimace but only *a* truth that has not "been perceptible before" (1991: 86). This is since the respective faces have not yet been revealed from *this one* perspective, i.e. elected by *this one* kindred spirit. What Kafka is aiming at with his remark, is that the multifaceted grimacing faces adapt their truth to the one who elects them as his or her relatives. As the truth cannot be witnessed directly, it is necessarily "witnessed by adoption" (Hartman 1996: 9). It is therefore Coetzee's own 'grimace' that, unaware, sets the terms for his detection of others' 'grimaces' in the same way as Europe's blindness sets the terms for its detection of South Africa's truth or Elisabeth Costello's wounded condition for her detection of the truth of animals.

However, if we are electing our relatives under the guidance of *our* truth that keeps us in its grips, how can we expect these relatives to *liberate* us from it? In other words, if a specifically South African 'grimace of shame' sets the standard for the 'grimacing faces' of European writers – as if taking revenge on the Europeans for setting Europe as the unbeatable standard for their perception of South Africa – how can Coetzee expect 'elective relatives' to pull him out of his South African affiliations? Instead of making their truth speak for his, he unwillingly practices Benedict Anderson's "reversed ventriloquism" (Anderson 1991: 198), making his truth speak for theirs. It is worthwhile noticing that he paid respect precisely to Lacan's insight that humans cannot but be ignorant of the "real" that generates all their activities including speech (Coetzee 1992: 29). He obviously agrees that the writer cannot know "where am I when I write" (Coetzee 1992: 30). This might explain why he does not know that he *beforehand* measures his 'elective relatives' by the truth that he declares to have distilled from their studying as an *after-effect*.

Viewed from this angle, *Barbarians*' narrative authority benefits considerably from the same transfers whose failures crushed the Magistrate's reality. Whereas the Magistrate's encounter with the "real" ultimately engulfed his reality, the narrative authority's own "grimace" – all the time parasitizing on the Magistrate's one – conquered new realities via the adopted elective relatives. The more untranslatable the Magistrate's "real" proved to be, the more narrative authority's translations it required in order to be elucidated. The authority was thus permitted to meet its insatiable desire after the new realities, the same one that was forbidden to the Magistrate; the latter's subhuman "floating signifier" gave rise to the former's superhuman one. After Coetzee moved to Australia, his authority even surpassed its South African identification with English, German, and Russian writers through the introduction of "new south-south homologies, inter-cultural links and cross ocean interests" (Boehmer, Ng and Sheehan 2016: 195). With the Croatian family from *Slow Man*, the minor cultures of East Central Europe also entered its rapidly growing intertextual community of 'elective relatives'. According to Coetzee's unpublished paper 'Short Works: Reading, Intro to *Nietverloren*' of 2006, through the collapse of the Soviet-controlled Europe, which was simultaneous to the dismantling of apartheid in the country of his birth, even the countries such as South Africa, East Germany, Russia and Kyrgyzstan that had for half a century built walls to separate them from the world, rejoined the world community (Coetzee 2006a: 6) – the only one that Coetzee, who in the Jesus-novels included into it also the huge Hispanic hemisphere, considers as his home. As Rebecca Walkowitz pointed out,

> for Coetzee, it has always seemed inappropriate, both ethically and historically, to suggest that his writing is part of a unique national-language tradition or emerges from a coherent national community. (Walkowitz 2009: 572)

With respect to his swift canonization, Boehmer et al. remark that "[w]hat was once a recalcitrant and (on occasion) reverbative body of work had acquired mainstream credibility and accessibility" (Boehmer, Ng and Sheehan 2016: 199–200), following the path of the inscrutable and untranslatable European modernist works that had meanwhile achieved a worldwide circulation (Diepeveen 2003: 1–9). As Kafka's oeuvre unmistakably testifies to, the more untranslatable a work is, the more translations it stimulates. Coetzee himself invested sustained efforts in fostering the worldwide translation of his works (Boehmer 2005: 137–143) not only by providing materials for his archive at the Harry Ransom Center in Austin and adapting his works for musical and multimedia performances (Boehmer, Ng and Sheehan 2016: 197–198) but primarily by producing works "written for translation, born-translated" (Walkowitz 2009: 569). Projecting "comparative beginnings" (Walkowitz 2009: 572) and stimulating transnational contacts, as Walkowitz spells out, all his works are adapted to an age of multilingual circulation. Steeped in multiple loyalties and simultaneously attached to various national traditions, migrant destiny is their deliberate choice. With *Slow Man* and Jesus-novels, it even advances into the problem, which their protagonists face on daily basis (Jacobs 2017). It looks like Coetzee followed the advice given by his alter ego Elizabeth Costello to Paul Rayment in *Slow Man*, that he ought to make himself translatable

> [s]o that someone, somewhere *might* put you in a book. So that someone might *want* to put you in a book. Someone, anyone – not just me. So that you may be *worth* putting in a book [. . .] Become major, Paul. Live like a hero. That is what the classics teach us. Be a main character. Otherwise what is life for? (Coetzee 2006b: 229)

It remains to be seen whether Coetzee, by following this advice to make himself 'connectable' in the global intertextual space through the adaptation of his works to the "complexities and subtleties" of Western "great art" (Brennan 1989: 36–37) and the global processes of cultural and linguistic translation, whether he has not *adopted* that which he proclaims to have himself *adapted* to. Was the transnational literary reality which Coetzee, with the admirable diligence and doggedness of Kafka's 'mole' from "The Construction",[14] had put together as his only acceptable home – not eventually conquered by the 'grimace' of his South African reality? Are all his 'elected relatives' comfortably accommodated in it? For it has to be considered, for example, that, although Coetzee as an English-speaking Afrikaner is a dislocated member of the colonizers' breed in the mold of the Pole Joseph Conrad, the latter was a British citizen far removed from the colonies, whereas Coetzee as a South African citizen was at the heart of one of them. Kafka, for his part, did not belong to the breed of colonizers but, on the contrary, to the victims, and his German was a result of the Jewish assimilation into the breed of colonizers rather than, as with Coetzee's English, of his family's detachment from this breed. Further on, Kafka's father was a tyrant rather than a weakling like Coetzee's, and Kafka's mother did not operate as a link to the broader cosmopolitan world as did Coetzee's. Besides, the Jews of Kafka's (and Hofmannsthal's) time were exposed to insults and persecutions which, however atypical an Afrikaner Coetzee was, he never experienced. His sympathetic imagination discovered outsiders and 'degenerates' out of the shame of racial persecutors, not that of the persecuted "mangy race" as Kafka and Hofmannsthal. At the same time, Coetzee feels dislocated among the Afrikaner colonizers in a different

---

14 Willa and Edwin Muir translate the German title "Der Bau" as "The Burrow".

way to McEwan, for example, among the British ones. As opposed to Coetzee, English is McEwan's native tongue but he entered it as the son of a Scottish father who, due to the father's military postings to British colonial outposts, spent his early childhood in vivid contact with foreign languages. Contrary to Coetzee, he was born as the citizen of a colonizing empire, but, from the outset, his country's colonial past and present disturbed his British habitus.

Considering all these and other differences that need to be drawn when we discuss post-imperial writers, the transformation of Coetzee's oeuvre into the 'floating signifier' of Defoe's, Dostoevsky's, Conrad's, Kafka's, Hofmannsthal's, Musil's, or Beckett's works as well as, most recently, the Gospels (Jacobs 2017) is less "an *acknowledgement* [. . .] of literary paternity" (Coetzee 1993: 5, italics mine) than an *exercise* in it. By offering them protection in terms of his specifically South African 'migration drive', Coetzee banished all their aspects that are untranslatable in these terms into the province of the "real" and thus excluded them from his supposedly global reality. At the same time, this "zone of indistinction" of his became the abode of 'provincial' writers who were not born into English or raised in other European languages, who could therefore not attract the Western metropolitan taste and thus qualify for the curriculum and canon of world literature. As a result, even though Coetzee's transborder community of migrant voices aspired to "solidarity without exclusion, agency without possessiveness" (Walkowitz 2009: 580), it turns out to have been "overcoming *that* to join *this*" (Brouillette 2016: 91) not unlike 'provincial' communities of native voices. The transborder community's 'belonging to nowhere' suppressed these voices in the same way that the 'provincial' communities' 'belonging to somewhere' marginalized the migrant ones. Nevertheless, one should beware of championing the authenticity of 'provincials' who have allegedly ably eschewed the mechanisms of metropolitan consecration (Ahmad 1992: 45). On the contrary, it is precisely their godforsaken provinciality that is the most striking 'grimace' of literature's new reality, the untranslatable remnant of its worldwide circulation that expects to be rescued from oblivion. Returning to "The Construction" as a 'blueprint' for Coetzee's piecemeal and meticulous building of his intertextual reality, was Kafka's untiring constructor of his burrow's network of labyrinths not growingly 'grimaced' by an ever louder whistle of the thereby suppressed "real"?

9 Conscience on the Pillar of Shame: The Grace of the Graceless in *Disgrace*

Protection/repression: The fragile hierarchy of power relations

The center stage of *Barbarians* is taken by the clash between the Magistrate's soft colonialism, committed to the integration of barbarians into humanity, and Colonel Joll's hard colonialism that aims at their exclusion. As the Magistrate finally realizes, his and Joll's attitude to barbarians do not oppose but rather complement each other, since the former proves instrumental for Empire's easy times and the latter for its harsh times (Coetzee 1982b: 180). But their complicity is in fact deeper, as they always intersect and run parallel to each other in one and the same central character: as a hunter, the Magistrate exterminates animals; as a womanizer, he neglects his partners' preferences; as an archeologist, he strives to allocate an appropriate zone to the barbarian culture. According to some critics, although the relationships between Marlow and Kurtz in *The Heart of Darkness* and the Traveling Explorer and the Officer in "The Penal Colony" anticipate the relationship between the Magistrate and Joll, such a good cop, bad cop complicity is missing in them (Micali 2017: 14–15; Valdez Moses 1993: 121). However, under closer inspection, Marlow simultaneously shows tolerance towards the natives and derogates Kurtz's Intended when, at the very end of Conrad's novella, he spares her of Kurtz's final words; in his opinion, women are not up to facing the truth. The Traveling Explorer, for his part, although epitomizing Western tolerance for differences, nevertheless supports the use of extraordinary measures in penal colonies (Kafka 1988g: 171). In his view, the "poor, humble creatures" (Kafka 1988g: 191) or ugly, "submissive dogs" (Kafka 1988g: 165) that populate them do not deserve the same empathy as the Officer who represents the French Empire (Kafka 1988g: 167, 184). Thus, it is not only the case that tolerance is necessarily limited, but that it couples protection with repression.

While Coetzee worked on his novel, Edward Said's *Orientalism* (1978) came out, a ground-breaking investigation of the complicity between the growing Western scholarly interest in the Orient and the expanding Western appetite for its colonization. If we replace the Orient with the barbarians, then this is exactly what the Magistrate is aiming at: to create an exclusive "ghetto" for which, considering the immaturity of its inhabitants, human history assumes responsibility and provides protection to (Amselle 2003: xii). When Said flagged Marx's (in)famous adage that "They cannot represent themselves; they must be represented" as one of his book's epigraphs, he was targeting this dark side of the protected subjects' generosity towards the repressed ones. Their readiness for protection demonstrates an imperial superiority over the protected that is regularly endorsed by the repression of those who, stubbornly sticking to their 'backwardness', resist the offered 'cultivation' of their abilities. To put this in Althusserian terms, "ideological state apparatuses" are unimaginable without the presence of the "repressive" ones (Althusser 1971: 121–124). Those who are not reasonable enough to cooperate with their mentors, experience repression as attuned to their social location.

Keeping this in mind, at the beginning of *Barbarians*, the Magistrate teaches the tortured boy to be cooperative: "Listen: you must tell the officer the truth. That is all he wants to hear from you – the truth. Once he is sure you are telling the truth he will not hurt you" (Coetzee 1982b: 12). However, he omits from his lesson that this truth must be the one which the officer expects to hear. The Empire sets the terms of the truth, which the protected subjects must accept if they want to avoid incurring sanctions. Their harshness depends upon the established hierarchy of power relations between the human and animal, whites and blacks, or male and female, which through their intersections and/or conflations determine the value of particular subjects. In his treatise "On the Jewish question", for example, Marx solved this question by proposing the assimilation of the Jews into humanity and, although he never directly discussed the 'female question', one might arguably claim that he expected women to accept the same. But the integration of the 'blacks', 'degenerates', or 'barbarians', due to their perceived 'animally inborn idleness', proved to be a much more difficult task than that of the Jews or women. As Coetzee notices in his discussion of the topic, idleness is considered incorrigible (1988b: 18), which is why it must be exterminated. Whereas in *Dusklands* the identification of the natives with animals justifies their massacre in Nama village (Coetzee 1998b: 103, 195), in *Life & Times of Michael K* the same derogating identification of the main protagonist legitimates his extreme deprivation (Coetzee 2004b: 204–205).

In the setting of *Disgrace*, this fine-tuned network of power relations, whose protective and repressive aspects are unevenly distributed among the citizens, acquires geopolitical, racial, and social determinants that are systematically skipped in *Barbarians*. The location is clear from the very first paragraph: Windsor Mansions, Cape Town, post-apartheid South Africa. There is a hint to the race of both David Lurie's part-time prostitute Soraya who has a "honey-brown body" and his student-mistress who is designated as "Meláni: the dark one" (Coetzee 1999a: 18). However, do such racial determinants still rule the day in the freshly reshaped South African society? They seem to have been overshadowed by legal determinants that protect black private lives from harassment, such as that of Soraya, or black female bodies from abuse, such as that of

Melanie. They also enable black men to enjoy live TV-broadcasts of soccer games in their own languages (Coetzee 1999a: 75) or to become land proprietors and thus distance themselves "as much as possible from a history of wage labor or labor tenancy" (Attwell 2002: 335); the case in point is Petrus, the black land tenant on Lucy's farm. In the law's 'gray zone', i.e. on Lucy's farm 'in the heart of the country', even black raids and rapes are overlooked or kept secret (Coetzee 1999a: 108–109; 133–135). Gender determinants can also cut across racial ones, associating the rapists among the blacks with those among the whites and thus attributing to male sexuality the force to shape history as "a cyclic re-enactment of power and appropriation at every level" (Attwell 2002: 338). Finally, the blacks cease to be automatically associated with 'barbarians' since the black members of the university committee of inquiry, as their names suggest, demonstrate tolerance towards Lurie who is, on the contrary, intransigent and intolerant towards them (Coetzee 1999a: 47–58). In short, although *Disgrace* provides its characters with more or less clear political, racial, social, and sexual orientation determinants, the unstable hierarchy of power relations exposes their positions to a partial revision or complete dispossession.

The novel makes the power relations between males and females, privileged and underprivileged, whites and blacks, and humans and animals dethrone one another's supremacy on an almost daily basis. In a shaky state in the grip of *translatio imperii*, the protection of its citizens can, overnight, turn into repression. Like Kafka's post-imperial Czechoslovakia, Coetzee's post-apartheid South Africa is presented as the tyranny of one self-enclosed sphere against another, in which "everyone feels the grip on the neck" (Kafka 1953: 312). The separation of citizens from one another into a "sequestered and observed solitude" that ensures the "invisibility" of their private lives as the "guarantee of the order" of new disciplinary societies (Foucault 1977: 200–201), turns into the greatest peril for this order's maintenance. Protected citizens recklessly follow their agenda at the expense of the repressed ones. In the footsteps of Josef K., Lurie unconcernedly gives rise to his abundant sexual appetites for underprivileged women until the sudden loss of his privileged social status forces him to atone his transgressions. He pays weekly visits to Soraya with the same vehement possession drive as Josef K. has for Elsa or the Magistrate has for his concubines. Taking advantage of their social rank and privileges, they equally disregard their sexual object's preferences. Lurie is convinced of a woman's "duty" to share "more widely" her beauty, which he conceives as "the bounty she brings into the world" (Coetzee 1999a: 16). Her body, he thinks, does not belong to her but to all privileged men capable of adequately supporting their appetite for it. For Soraya, for instance, he likes buying presents (Coetzee 1999a: 5), which is why he cannot accept her decent withdrawal from his 'possession' and why, feeling offended, besides her body, he suddenly lays claim to her private life as well (Coetzee 1999a: 9–10).

After he is coerced to give her up, threatened by a charge of harassment, he compensates for this loss by seizing a much younger 'exotic', the dark Melanie with a gentle touch of "almost Chinese cheekbones" (Coetzee 1999a: 11), a perfect mélange of exotic constituents evidently superior to that of the lost Soraya. After the second 'coloured' lady thus enters the series of "his charges" (Coetzee 1999a: 12), race proves to be a welcome 'intensifier' of his sexual passions. In case of Melanie it is additionally 'spiced' by her young age, turning the middle-aged lover into a kind of "foster-father, step-father, shadow-father" (Coetzee 1999a: 6) to the girl. Throughout his life he was surrounded by women in different roles. "As mother, aunts, sisters fell away, they were replaced in due course by mistresses, wives, a daughter" (Coetzee 1999a: 7). However, unlike his absent graceless daughter who is protected from his aggression by her blood affiliation to him, the present gracious Melanie is dark, young, and his student, i.e. triply exposed to his power. This threefold dependence increases his excitement. Driven by this wind in his sails, he sets no limits to his thirst for her body even if it is, from her point of view, "undesired to the core" (Coetzee 1999a: 25).

Purgatory and atonement: From body to conscience

Once his transgression goes public, Lurie realizes with the kind assistance of his second ex-wife Rosalind that, despite the merciless command of Eros that shatters him to the bones, young girls ought to "be protected from the sight of their elders in the throes of passion" (Coetzee 1999a: 44). This surprising concession to the beings bereft of protection, which, after his atonement, will be followed by a much more extensive one (Coetzee 1999a: 190), almost sounds like a brief summary of the Magistrate's kindred admittance from *Barbarians*:

> There is no limit to the foolishness of men of my age. Our only excuse is that we leave no mark of our own on the girls who pass through our hands: our convoluted desires, our ritualized lovemaking, our elephantine ecstasies are soon forgotten, they shrug off our clumsy dance as they drive straight as arrows into the arms of men whose children they will bear, the young and vigorous and direct. (Coetzee 1982b: 179)

But before they are themselves exposed to political and social repression, the politically and socially protected subjects do not bother themselves with those whom they are repressing. The harsher their sudden exposure becomes, the deeper their repentance. Like the disempowered Magistrate, the dismissed Lurie discovers his long-suppressed fatherhood, which replaces the proud serial demonstration of his white male 'service to Eros' (Coetzee 1999a: 52).[1] Along with his sexual, racial, and institutional power, his "vanity and self-righteousness" are also affected (1999a: 47). His maleness is also deterritorialized in another important sense. His habit of looking at women as the 'dark objects of desire' cannot, of course, be applied to his daughter. Apart from living with an older "sad-looking" female partner, she is weighty, ample, with "none too clean fingernails", and "withdrawn from the field of love" into daily care for the garden and her dogs (Coetzee 1999a: 59–65). Neither she nor her friends are women that fit his aesthetic standards, which is why he switches from conversing with her on the topic of female beauty, addressed in the talk with Melanie, to that of maternal duty as, in Lurie's astonishing new opinion, the female life's ultimate purpose (Coetzee 1999a: 63).

Such a gradual disappearance of Lurie's up until then unprecedented male arrogance toward women after he was sanctioned by an extraordinary academic committee, stimulated Christopher Conti to compare him with Josef K. who likewise, slowly, activates the examination of his own conscience after his case before a peculiar examining tribunal went public. Indeed, Lurie is alerted by the committee's chair that "the body here gathered [. . .] has no powers" (Coetzee 1999a: 47), while Josef K. himself realizes that his is "not a case that's being tried in the normal court" (Kafka 2009: 67) but in a sort of purgatory. Both refuse to accept this purgatory's moral premises whose summary justice may be in force in the vestibules of law but not in its public courtrooms. Coetzee investigated these vestibules in *Life&Times of Michael K*, "an allegory of the persecuted outsider in flight from the tyranny of the modern security state" (Conti 2016: 474). However, unlike Michael K, both Josef K. and Lurie are socially and economically well-positioned individuals, enjoying all the privileges of protected citizens who reserve the vestibules of martial law for their repressed co-citizens. Yet, out of the blue, an unexpected switch in their states' shaky network of power relations catapults them out of their protected positions.

---

[1] The consciousness raising of a forgotten or suppressed parental responsibility is such a frequent topic in Coetzee's novels (next to *Barbarians* and *Disgrace*, for example, in *Foe, The Master of Petersburg, Age of Iron, Slow Man, The Childhood of Jesus, The Schooldays of Jesus*) that one might claim, as Mike Marais did, that he tries through his writing to save the child that has been abandoned by either a personal or collective history (Marais 2009: xiv). There is, of course, a parallel responsibility of dependents towards the parents, which, next to figuring in novels such as *In the Heart of the Country, Disgrace* and *Elizabeth Costello*, comes to the fore in Coetzee's creative indebtedness to Defoe, Dostoevsky, Kafka, and Beckett.

In his cogent comparison of Lurie's awakening conscience with that of Josef K.'s, Conti unfortunately skips Kafka's own purgatory that preceded Josef K.'s and inspired it, i.e. the extraordinary 'tribunal' that took place in the Askanischer Hof hotel in Berlin and was conducted by Felice's friend Grete Bloch. Accused of dishonesty toward Felice, Kafka kept silent all the time, as if thereby indicating that he did not acknowledge the 'tribunal' he was brought to. As he indeed made clear in his letter to Grete Bloch of October 1914, the only tribunal he was ready to acknowledge was that of his own conscience (Koch 2011: 53–54). No external accusation could beat the depth of his internal repentance, which fearlessly delivered itself to the authority of an upcoming all-embracing truth. Refusing to protect himself from this truth by accepting the external norms in force, Kafka's protagonist Josef K. declares an analogous readiness for the humiliating exposure of his conscience. The dishonored Lurie, in his turn, gradually coming to consciousness of his responsibility, feels equally ashamed and willing to suffer for his sin in expectation of the "verdict of the universe and its all-seeing eye" (Coetzee 1999a: 195). The service of his unprotected conscience to the truth-to-come thus replaces the former service of his privileged body to Eros.

In the same way that Kafka, as the author, endorses Josef K. in this switch from one unconditional service to the other, Coetzee, as the author, pushes Lurie's self-dispossessing agenda as if it were his own. According to Sarah Brouillete, it indeed *is* his own: the stubborn self-dispossession of his authorial identity that systematically progressed from one novel to another proved a rewarding technology, trapping "his readers in a series of unending debates" and thus fostering his career and encouraging his canonization (Brouillete 2007: 125). Conti (2016: 472–473), for his part, argues that, in both Kafka's and Coetzee's disintegrated world, bereft of an ultimate transcendental authority, these authors' self-tormenting conscience is promoted to the only all-embracing standpoint of redemption, overwhelmed by shame for the human race that cannot but humiliate some of its representatives. In this sense, the feeling that permeates *The Trial*'s final sentence "'Like a dog!', he said, it was as if the shame of it should outlive him" is the moving force of both Kafka's and Coetzee's writing. Their authors act as the victims who are deeply ashamed of belonging to the same race as their perpetrators. This indeed proved to be a very attractive standpoint of redemption that, galvanizing most diverse readers to attach themselves to it, managed to establish a highly influential transborder community of self-dispossessed subalterns.

Unlike their authors who had already covered the distance from the selfish devotion to their bodily drives to the altruist dedication to an all-encompassing truth before they started to write on their novels, the novel protagonists' conscience as awakened by the force of circumstances still has a long way to go. After having been compelled to replace a gracious urban mistress with the graceless farm-keeping daughter – whom he immediately entrusts that "being a father is a rather abstract business" (Coetzee 1999a: 63) – Lurie does not give up all his previous "vanity and self-righteousness" at once (Coetzee 1999a: 47). He still feels powerfully sexually attached to Melanie (Coetzee 1999a: 65), ironizing the committee's puritanical drive despite Lucy's attempt to distract him from his "heroically unbending" attitude (Coetzee 1999a: 66). No doubt, his strong reservations about the pressure put on the people who committed abuses to make full public disclosure of themselves, allude to the Truth and Reconciliation Commissions that were established throughout South Africa (including Cape Town) a year or two prior to his own hearing, set by Coetzee in 1997.

However, to understand his irritation's broader background, one has to recall Josef K.'s frustration with the officialdom of his country that "does not seek out guilt in the population but [. . .] is attracted by guilt" (Kafka 2009: 8–9). It pruriently leaves it to the subjects themselves to give substance and shape to their intuited guilt by coming forth with its piquant details. In Kafka's expert view, this focus upon a suspect person's 'soul' instead of deeds threatened to contaminate the established legal criteria with the arbitrary psychological deliberations of the examining magistrates, experts, witnesses, and committees. Their personal emotional involvement in deciphering the elusive 'evil intent' of the alleged abuser made their decisions biased, unpredictable, and deeply complicit (Ziolkowski 1997: 221). Underlining this complicity some half of a century thereafter, Foucault pointed out that a society's protected agencies use the illegality of moral abusers to pursue their own illegalities. "Delinquency visibly assumed its ambiguous status as an object and instrument for a police apparatus that worked against it and with it" (Foucault 1977: 283). Foucault concludes that within one and the same modern juridical frame, the capillary mechanisms of counter-law disqualify and invalidate the egalitarian law by turning it into a discriminatory inquisitorial machine (1977: 222–227). Applied to South Africa, the summary justice of its apartheid regime has not been overcome but instead resumed by the country's post-apartheid administration. If it reminds Lurie "too much of Mao's China" (Coetzee 1999a: 66), this is because the post-apartheid disciplinary approach to population has in fact moved the summary justice from the totalitarian regime's obscure periphery to the egalitarian society's daylight stage.

In this broader frame, Lurie's intransigent resistance to his country's martial law reminds us of Josef K.'s unbending resilience to the focus of the late Habsburg-reformed juridical system on his presumed criminal motivation rather than any verifiable crime. As such an unbridled "inventing [of] the criminal" (Wetzell 2000) amounts to a perilous abuse of the law in whatever country it takes place, both Josef and Lurie wage war against the dubious methods of their capillary surveillance. Whereas Josef rejects the advice of his "women helpers" (Kafka 2009: 77) to accept the tacit rules of new commonality and give up his selfish way of life, Lurie obstinately defends the free acting-out of his promiscuous desire for women because all of these experiences "enrich" him (Coetzee 1999a: 56) and make him a "better person" (Coetzee 1999a: 70). He thereby lightly skips the experiences of these women themselves, as Lucy rushes to remind him (Coetzee 1999a: 70), as well as his own experiences with women "who make no effort to be attractive" such as Lucy's friends (Coetzee 1999a: 72). As his daughter became "lost to men", he even reproaches himself for having possibly fathered her in a wrong way (Coetzee 1999a: 76). After moving to her farm, however, he realized that he ought to chase out such prejudices. "But he does not care to do so, or does not care enough" (Coetzee 1999a: 72). He still adheres to graceful beings, bracketing out of his world not solely graceless women but also animals which are of "a different order of creation" and should not be approached out of someone's feeling of guilt or fear of retribution (Coetzee 1999a: 74). If he is going to take care of them, then it is not in order "to make reparation for past misdeeds", preferring to remain himself, unreformed, i.e. attracted by beautiful women and haunted by voluptuousness (Coetzee 1999a: 77–78).

However, can he, as such a womanizer – "mad, bad, and dangerous to know", as Lucy ironically formulates (Coetzee 1999a: 77) – be of any use in this godforsaken countryside? Being "in disgrace", he might not be of any use at all (Coetzee 1999a: 85). He suddenly realizes that he is not only in his society's disgrace but, more importantly, in Eros's disgrace, quite like his middle-aged 'hero' Byron who "always looked to thirty as the barrier to any real or fierce delight in the passions" (Coetzee 1999a: 87). Eros abandons the bodies in the grip of disgrace, bringing the summer of their passions to a close. Only at this point, after his body has been given up by Eros, does Lurie begin to doubt whether Lucy had separated from him and turned away from men precisely because he acted as Eros' fierce servant, sacrificing his daughter to his devotion to the lost world of grace (Coetzee 1999a: 89–90).

From exemption to redemption: The grace of falling in disgrace

If the divine world of grace is gone with the arrival of the modern human society, then his devotion could not be but remedial. Whereas Josef K. tried to compensate for the lost transcendence by replacing it with his professional career, Lurie was, like Walter Benjamin's *flaneur*, dedicated to the salvation of its leftovers, in his case identified in female bodies as its unknowing transmitters. By collecting divine grace's remnants as stored in these bodies and piecing them together in his own body, he was pulling out the latter from its graceless self-enclosure into the sublime heights of an all-embracing body:

> In a sudden and soundless eruption, as if he has fallen into a waking dream, a stream of images pours down, images of women he has known on two continents, some from so far away in time that he barely recognizes them. Like leaves blown on the wind, pell-mell, they pass before him. *A fair field full of folk*: hundreds of lives all tangled with his.
> (Coetzee 1999a: 192)

Although Lurie's restorationist mission was guided by the difference between the graceful and the graceless rather than the useful and the useless as with Josef K.'s mission,[2] Coetzee's shares with Kafka's protagonist the same discriminatory conviction that 'higher objectives' exempt him from the moral law that holds for those who are doomed to take care of others (Conti 2016: 478). Having to care for others is the business of subalterns whom society confronts with repression instead of taking them into its protection; it has nothing to do with him. Yet, Coetzee asks in his conversation with Arabella Kurtz:

> What happens to justice [. . .] if we are free to ignore aspects of the past in the name of personal growth? At what point does the deployment of repression in the cause of personal fulfillment become culpable?
> (Kurtz and Coetzee 2015: 34)

After having experienced his society's repression and moved to the world of those exposed to it on a daily basis, it dawned on Lurie that his remedial mission of saving the lost grace of the world, which he stuck to for some time even on the farm, acted as a self-appointed "censor" that cleansed his world of those in disgrace completely on its own, i.e. without any "divine help" (Coetzee 1999a: 91). Through such a compensatory elevation of his graceless life to grace, the previous divine and symbolic "purgation" of human community through the elimination of scapegoats "was replaced by the purge", i.e. the removal of all graceless subjects from his life (Coetzee 1999a: 91). This is how humans act in the 'fallen' world as "cluttered with its own dregs" (Kafka 1988c: 24; trans. modified: *hochgeschüttet voll ihres Bodensatzes*). After the irrevocable compartmentalization of this world, reigned by "the watchfulness of all over all" (Coetzee 1999a: 91), its every unit feels strangled by the other (Kafka 1953: 312). In this "collection of separated individuals" (Foucault 1977: 201), every individual blindly follows his or her "imaginary norm" (Slaughter 2007: 215), guarding "himself [or herself] from being fixed by his [or her] fellow humans"

---

[2] One should recall that the thirty year-old Josef had his career ahead of him and not behind him as with the fifty-two year-old Lurie.

(Kafka 2012: 207). Unfortunately, an individual's exemption from his/her fellow humans spawns the latter's deprivation of his/her protection and grace.

In societies with a stable power hierarchy, individuals strive to consolidate the power of their selves at the expense of those bereft of power. In translational societies, which try to leave behind the tyranny of those in power, the selves that have unexpectedly fallen into disgrace promote self-disempowerment into their agenda. This might explain why Coetzee structured *Disgrace* as an inverted *Bildungsroman* based on the protagonist's disgraceful catharsis, "a novel which involves the forfeiture rather than consolidation of the protagonist's sense of self" (Marais 2009: 175). Disgraced and ashamed of his former vulture self, Lurie aims at an *ek-stasis*, a "position that is precisely not a position, which would therefore allow the self to be within the world while viewing it from nowhere within it" (Marais 2009: 178). Significantly enough, it is exactly this *ecstasy-belonging* that defines the political state of exception in Carl Schmitt's pioneering explanation: "the sovereign stands outside of the normally valid juridical order, and yet belongs to it" (1985: 7). This means that Lurie's self-exemption from the realm of the protected does not abolish the inequality between the protected and repressed – as it pretends to be doing – but establishes a new power asymmetry because an agency exempts itself from the same law to which it subjects all others. For this reason, Lurie's disempowerment amounts to a re-empowerment. If the law did not previously apply to him because he was protected and possessed privileges, now it does not apply for the reverse reason, i.e. because he is outside of its protection.

The final trigger for his humiliating descent into such a non-position is the three lads' raid on Lucy's farm during which she is raped and he is burnt and disfigured (Coetzee 1999a: 96–97). In this way, like the Magistrate, Lurie confirms Coetzee's credo:

> The body with its pains becomes a counter to the endless trials of doubt. [. . .] the suffering body takes this authority: that is its power. To use other words: its power is undeniable. (1992: 248)

He suddenly feels old, floating toward the end of his life (Coetzee 1999a: 107), and is indeed approached by Lucy as such, or, in a significant inversion of their roles, as a child (Coetzee 1999a: 103–104). In a sense, he indeed develops an infantile "sympathetic imagination" as a mirror-inversion of his previous neglect of his family obligations: he is full of understanding for "his little girl, guarding her from harm" (Coetzee 1999a: 104); he realizes that, pressed into the stiffened medium of the English language, "Petrus's story would come out arthritic, bygone" (Coetzee 1999a: 107); he is concerned about the sheep that Petrus aims to slaughter for his party (Coetzee 1999a: 126); his indifference to animals disappears and "tears flow down his face" before the superfluous canines that have to be killed (Coetzee 1999a: 143); he declares the bankruptcy of his attachment to the female's grace, sleeping with Bev Shaw, with whom he "never did dream he would sleep with" (Coetzee 1999a: 149); he falls into such a disgrace that he thinks of himself as a "figure from the margins of history" (Coetzee 1999a: 167); and, after his daughter transforms into a creature with "no cards, no weapon, no property, no rights, no dignity" (Coetzee 1999a: 205), his own denigration takes the form of "a mad old man who sits among the dogs singing to himself" (Coetzee 1999a: 212).

Only after one's self is debased to the degree of an abandoned animal bound for "a hole in the ground" (1999a: 189) can it qualify for an all-embracing point of redemption, which, to deserve its name, must include the most insignificant and miserable creatures. In *Elizabeth Costello*, Coetzee quotes one of his 'elected relatives", Hugo von Hofmannsthal's "Letter of Lord Chandos", in which the Lord entrusts Francis Bacon that

> even a negligible creature, a dog, a rat, a beetle, a stunted apple tree, a cart track winding over a hill, a mossy stone, count more for me than a night of bliss with the most beautiful, most devoted mistress. (Hofmannsthal 2004a: 226)

At the end of his trajectory, Lurie could, paradoxically enough, unreservedly subscribe to this statement. The unknown language of suffering animals and inanimate creatures is the greatest challenge for the human sympathetic imagination, which perhaps only an abandoned child can successfully meet. In Lurie's case, this is his daughter Lucy who, dictated by the pattern of an inverted *Bildungsroman*, from a certain point takes on his parental role by returning him into the role of a child (Coetzee 1999a: 103–105). "*My daughter*, he thinks; *my dearest daughter. Whom it has fallen to me to guide*" (Coetzee 1999a: 156; italics in original). She teaches him to replace his powerful male self with a weak infantile one that equally empathizes with all creatures, the differences between them notwithstanding. If the *Bildungsroman* charts the trajectory of an irrational youngster's integration into the rational world of adults, then the inverted *Bildungsroman* transforms an adult back into the child that refuses to position itself by making political decisions either for *this* or against *that*. For Lucy, Lurie's child, the battle of ideas is a typical male business. "I don't act in terms of abstractions" (Coetzee 1999a: 112). In a word, she is "[n]ot her father's girl, not any longer" (Coetzee 1999a: 105).

Nevertheless, whatever her opinion, the refusal to take positions is not an exclusively female attitude to life. Commenting on the shift from empires to state democracies, Coetzee's doppelganger from the *Diary of a Bad Year*, Señor C, presents the following reflection:

> In the days of kings, the subject was told: *You used to be the subject of King A, now King A is dead and behold, you are the subject of King B.* Then democracy arrived, and the subject was for the first time presented with a choice: *Do you (collectively) want to be ruled by Citizen A or Citizen B?* [. . .] most people, *ordinary* people are in their hearts inclined to choose neither. [. . .] *You have to choose*, says the state: *A or B?"* (Coetzee 2007: 8)

He clearly disapproves such *either-or* thinking: "Democracy does not allow for politics outside the democratic system. In this sense, democracy is totalitarian." (Coetzee 2007: 15) Therefore, the inversion of the *Bildungsroman*'s pattern in *Disgrace* reflects Coetzee's general predilection for a political non-position as embodied in the figure of Jesus (Vlies 2017: 51–74). Xiaoran Hu recently argued that

> Coetzee's novelistic discourse encapsulates a self-consciously formed withdrawal from taking any categorical political position as precisely an effective means of political participation. (Hu 2020: 976)

In Coetzee's several novels before *Disgrace*, this withdrawal from political positioning takes the shape of a voluntary parenthood that offers protection to an as-if-child but renounces repression over it. Consider the relationship between the Magistrate and the girl in *Barbarians*, Susan and Friday in *Foe*, or Mrs. Curren and Vercueil in *Age of Iron*. In *The Childhood of Jesus*, Coetzee goes even further in recognizing the child's authority in place of the father's, until in *The Schooldays of Jesus* the surrogate father ultimately turns into the child. Although David is educated in dance school, "it is eventually Simon who puts on the child's dance slippers and begins to learn to dance" (Hu 2020: 984). Lurie is Lucy's biological father, but the same parental relationship's inversion takes place in his adoption of her non-positional self.

Referring to Erasmus's Folly, Foucault's madness, and Lacan's unconscious as the counter-voices to the command of reason, Hu stresses the childlike non-position's subversive potential. Whereas those on the stage of political rivalry "must tell the truth", i.e. *partake* in it, Folly, madness, and the unconscious *set the terms* for the onstage political positioning, as testified by David who in the novel claims "I am the truth" (Coetzee 2014: 225). As is well known, Jesus indeed stated "I am the Way, and the Truth, and the Life" (John 14:6), meaning that whoever raises the claim for truth has to accept *his* premises for doing so. Acting off-stage, he adopts "a position that is precisely not a position" (Marais 2009: 178) and thus, anticipating the sovereign's *ecstasy-belonging* in the political state of exception, ensures an absolute, 'panoptic' control of subjects. "You never look at me from the place from which I see you" (Lacan 1978: 101). Therefore, contrary to Hu's main thesis in his otherwise illuminating article, the childlike non-position does not so much *subvert* power as it invisibly *seizes* it.

Both Davids' (Jesus' and Lurie's) unselfish "sympathetic imagination" act as an instrument of power over others.

Blaming and humiliating itself after the experienced disgrace, Lurie's conscience acts on behalf of the ultimate standpoint of redemption, "the universe and its all-seeing eye" (Coetzee 1999a: 195), in the same way that Jesus acted on behalf of the Father. The only way to the restoration of grace in a 'fallen' world, they testify, passes through a disgraceful self-dispossession. This way is taken by victims who are deeply ashamed of belonging to the same race as perpetrators, and especially so if for some time, as in Lurie's case, they themselves acted as wrongdoers. In fact, Lurie's atonement is strongly supported by his author's atonement for belonging to the kin of exploiters and torturers and concomitant exemption from it for the sake of 'higher objectives'. However, while Lurie's atonement followed the objective of collecting the remnants of grace as stored in female bodies, Coetzee aimed at "leaving something behind" "with a life of its own" (Coetzee 1999a: 63), i.e. artworks. It is only after the failure of Lurie's first mission of restoring grace in the world via women that he switches to his second, Coetzee-like one, i.e. working on an opera about Lord Byron and his mistress the Contessa Guiccioli. It is small wonder since, via Byron's "legions of countesses and kitchenmaids" that the writer "pushed himself into" (Coetzee 1999a: 160), Lurie atones for hundreds of women's lives that he himself had misused, via the Countess's suffering, he expiates the abuse of Melanie, and, via Byron's daughter Allegra who sings "Why have you forgotten me?" (Coetzee 1999a:186), he repents for his abandonment of Lucy.

But Coetzee eventually prevents Lurie from giving himself to the world as an author on his own by directing him instead, through an exchange of roles with Lucy, first to serve humankind as a child and then, through an exchange of roles with Petrus, even as a dog-man (1999a: 146).[3] He ends as an exemplary caretaker of discarded creatures, embarking on a mission that he initially dismissed as something reserved for graceless women. He previously expressed the opinion that caring for children is a woman's mission in the world, since men give birth to artworks (1999a: 63), but now he is happy that the fruit of Lucy's rape that was "meant to soil her, to mark her, like a dog's urine" (Coetzee 1999a: 199), will make him a grandfather (Coetzee 1999a: 217). After his degradation, he

---

[3] According to Philippou (2016: 220), taking care of dogs, in Coetzee's novels, often coincides with taking care of one's children. In *The Master of Petersburg* (Coetzee 1994: 80), Dostoevsky, while unraveling the mystery of his stepson's death, responds to a dog's howling and whimpering as something owed an "ethical responsibility". In *Age of Iron* (Coetzee 1998a: 7) Mrs. Curren writes to her daughter that what she owes to her as her biological child, she owes to any dog in need.

first tried to compensate for it on Coetzee's model, i.e. by finding a 'relative' (Byron) among the Western prominent writers, in order to connect his marginal story to the canon, i.e. "become major", as Costello advises Paul Rayment. But Coetzee drove his attempt into failure, like that of another unfortunate parent, Susan Barton from *Foe*, who was at pains to connect her and Friday's story to that of Defoe's *Robinson Crusoe* as the goal-directed Western-world's founding story. None of them succeeds in elevating himself or herself to divine grace by producing art with a life of its own. In lieu of atoning their sins in this sublime way, they must accept responsibility for debased beings by taking material care of them, such as Susan of the mutilated Friday or Lurie of discarded dogs. At the end, Lurie is even banished from the world of divine grace into the life of a disgraceful creature. His denigrating trajectory leads from a womanizer via an artist, parent, child, and dog-man to a discarded dog. When he, in the novel's final sentence, hands over a mutilated young dog for euthanasia, according to Chris Danta, he recognizes himself in the dog's vulnerable kin (Danta 2007: 734), which is punished by humans for its unbridled fertility, i.e. giving itself up to its "ungovernable impulses" – the same 'sin' he himself was punished for (Coetzee 1999a: 52). As humans must by definition control such impulses, he eventually gives up his humanity (O'Sullivan 2011: 133).

While Lurie's is thus growingly guided by a responsibility to the punished dogs, up to the point of merging with them, his author acts out of responsibility to the all-embracing Truth that does not allow for such identifications. As soon as we identify ourselves with an agency, we make ourselves identifiable by others and thus fall prey to our identification. Elizabeth Costello's son, reflecting on how his mother makes her readers fall prey to their identifications with her fictional agencies, compares her to "large cats that pause as they eviscerate their victim and, across the torn-open belly, give you a cold yellow stare" (Coetzee 2004a: 5). However, Costello's own identification with the animals as systematically killed by humans also testifies to a "reversed ventriloquism" (Anderson 1991: 198), i.e. her covered speaking for animals. As their truth is inaccessible, she witnesses it "by adoption" (Hartman 1996: 9) in order then, through her fictions and lectures, to impose it on humans. This invisible maneuver makes her daughter-in-law state "[s]he is trying to extend her inhibiting power over the whole community!" (Coetzee 2004a: 113)

> Her great hero Franz Kafka played the same game with his family. He refused to eat this, he refused to eat that, he would rather starve, he said. Soon everyone was feeling guilty about eating in front of him, and he could sit back feeling virtuous.   (Coetzee 2004a: 114)

In his correspondence with Paul Auster, Coetzee mentions his having come across Ernst Pawel's book on how Kafka's vegetarianism alienated him from his family to "the point when he began to take his meals by himself" (Pawel 1984; Auster and Coetzee 2014: 111). "Kafka, says Pawel, drew unconsciously upon Jewish dietary law to create for himself a set of rituals of an ascetic, self-punishing, and finally destructive nature" (Auster and Coetzee 2014: 111). In this way, he created an in-group of vegetarians as opposed to the 'banned' out-group of carnivores, presided over by his feared father (Auster and Coetzee 2014: 113).

To avoid such discrimination through identification, Coetzee's narrative authority eschews all identifications, developing a conscience deeply ashamed of all kinds of belonging. Belonging cannot but open a vicious circle of animosity, aggression, and violence that permeates centuries of South African history. "It was history speaking through them", comments Lurie on the raid on Lucy's farm. "A history of wrong. [. . .] It came down from the ancestors" (Coetzee 1999a: 156). "Booty; war reparations; another incident in the great campaign of redistribution" (Coetzee 1999a: 176). In the *Diary of a Bad Year*, Coetzee's doppelganger Señor C traces this vicious circle back to the arrival of Dutch settlers in the early colonial times, when they adopted "the same practice of raiding (raiding of livestock, raiding of women) that marked relations between bands or tribes already resident there" (2007: 104). Both blacks and whites departed from the "self-evident" premise, this is their land while all the others are outsiders and by this very fact deprived of their citizen rights. But to prove that they exclusively are the proper residents, they paradoxically adopted precisely these others' violent guideline that 'might makes right'. The delineated vicious circle of adopting the other's violent behavior by simultaneously blaming him for it, is how *translatio imperii* works in South Africa: it bereaves people of historical memory. They come to forget they had suffered under the same violence that they are today inflicting on others.

To avoid this exclusionary logic of gangs, which find their *raison d'être* in inventing and fighting ever new enemies (Kurtz and Coetzee 2015: 145), Coetzee's narrative authority refuses belonging to any of them. It exempts itself even from the South African literature, which proved unable "to move from elementary relations of contestation, domination, and subjugation to the vast and complex human world that lies beyond them" (Coetzee 1992: 98). However, it equally pulls itself out of belonging to its European 'elected relatives' such as Defoe, Dostoevsky, Conrad, Kafka, or Beckett, considering the European literatures' troublesome colonial heritage. No standpoint of redemption can satisfy Coetzee's narrative authority except for its conscience as overwhelmed by an interminable shame at its inevitable belonging to the divided humanity. The unconditional service of this authority's conscience to the truth-to-come takes the place of its characters' unconditional service to their group, even if the latter consists of the abandoned children and animals. After Lurie has beaten the "mentally and morally deficient" boy Pollux (Coetzee 1999a: 208), who had witnessed Lucy's rape in order "to learn" (Coetzee 1999a: 159)[4] and who was now peeping at her in her bathroom (Coetzee 1999a: 206), Lucy defends him. "I must have peace around me. I am prepared to do anything, make any sacrifice, for the sake of peace" (Coetzee 1999a: 208). If she wants to stay on the farm, that is, she must declare herself as belonging to the kin of its new proprietors and her offenders. It is the same 'capitulation' that Lurie subscribes to – belonging to the kin of sacrificed dogs for the sake of peace – when he gives up the mutilated young dog, "like a lamb", to euthanasia (Coetzee 1999a: 220). He thus gives up not only control over it but also over his own human life, which distinguished him from animal life as marked by "ungovernable impulses" (Coetzee 1999a: 52).

Yet neither such a radical exemption from belonging to the human race is good enough for Coetzee's narrative authority because, ultimately, it appropriates abandoned and wounded animals in the same selfish way as Elizabeth Costello. There is no such giving up of control over the other that does not amount to taking up a new form of control over it. Costello's identification with the tortured and exterminated animals has not really liberated her narrative authority but rather simulated such a liberation, while in fact solidifying it via the readers who were gained for it. This is exactly how the transformed, 'sacrificial' Lurie makes himself guilty of homogenizing an in-group, supposedly freed of control over others, as opposed to an out-group of control-keepers. Besides, his in-group drives "the utmost strangers into each other's arms, making them kin, kind, beyond all prudence" (Coetzee 1999a: 194) not unlike the one that penetrates all women bodies with one and the same seed "to bring the future into being" (Coetzee 1999a: 194).

As any grouping thus necessarily generates guilt toward those who are excluded from it, Coetzee's narrative authority develops an endlessly ashamed conscience that never tires of exempting itself out of it. Being extremely reluctant to get protection from one group at the price of another group's repression, this narrative authority eventually refuses both responsibility for his group's members and the guilt of those of another group. The only responsibility and guilt that it is willing to accept and to atone for is the Truth-to-come as the postponed standpoint of an all-encompassing redemption. As the characters who are involved in the vicious circle of mutual guilt overlook and ignore this common Truth, it cannot but be ashamed of them. Shame vs. guilt is therefore the

---

4 In *Barbarians*, as well, children are invited to participate in the spectacle of the Magistrate's abasement with the same 'educational' purpose of raising calm executors (Coetzee 1982b: 142).

final demarcation line between Coetzee's narrative authority and his characters: the authority accepts the shame for the characters' exclusion of others but relegates the guilt for such behavior to them. Discrimination is not its way of approaching others, which is why it, overwhelmed by shame, refuses to belong to them.

However not even this demarcation line is clear-cut, considering that the author's doppelgangers as well strive towards redemption through an exemption from the filthy human affairs, denying their guilt and responsibility in the way that their author does. A number of critics have noticed that Coetzee's protagonists, by foregrounding their feeling of shame at belonging to the kin of perpetrators, significantly suppress their sense of guilt for their misbehavior towards others.

> The preference for the word shame subtly shifts the burden of guilt to others, as when Mrs Curren blames the political leadership in *Age of Iron* or when the Magistrate blames Colonel Joll in *Waiting for the Barbarians*. (Conti 2016: 475)

In the same way, Señor C from the *Diary of a Bad Year* tries to transfer such denial of guilt to the British (Coetzee 2007: 44) or Germans: "*We have no blood on our hands, so why are we looked on as racists and murderers?*" (Coetzee 2007: 50; italics in original). But they shift guilt to others precisely because they sense it much deeper than they are consciously willing to allow. The same holds true for their author who has "negotiated guilt in a variety of ways so indirect as to avert attention from its existence, but so numerous in aggregate as to confirm, however obliquely, its great and undiminished personal gravity" (Robinson 2012: 39). Even if a person "feeling shame cannot be held responsible, guilty, for who he or she is", shame is intrinsically linked with the sense of guilt as the person who belongs to a guilty group eventually did "nothing to discredit, condemn, or oppose the practices of that group" (Tegla 2012: 972). Since being a white writer in South Africa was obviously a privileged condition, Coetzee's shame is "inseparable from the activity of literary production" (Bewes 2011: 137). This means that the same activity which pulled him out of the shackles of South African belonging, pushed him back into this belonging through an ever-stronger sense of guilt, which in its turn induced a more powerful shame. "[S]hame is an event of incommensurability: the simultaneous impossibility of identifying and disidentifying with one's own country" (Robinson 2012: 6). "The double-bind is thus complete: there is shame in being identified with the Afrikaners, and there is shame in separating oneself from them" (Robinson 2012: 16).

Applying this paradox to the relationship between Coetzee's narrative authority and its characters, it appears that the former is equally ashamed of being identified with the latter and of being separated from them. At the outset, the authority insists it is a *victim* of the guilt of which its character, through its disgraceful behavior to other characters, is a *bearer*. Thereafter it realizes that it behaves to its character in an even more exclusionary way than the latter behaves to others and that, therefore, it is an equal bearer of guilt. However, as the authority does not deny this guilt but puts its conscience on the pillar of shame to atone it, it draws closer to redemption than its character. The more openly one admits one's disgrace, the higher is the grace s/he approaches. This grace is the satisfaction which Coetzee's authorial conscience gets for the disgrace of its non-belonging, albeit only a provisional one, until the guilt for its consequences re-surmounts it.

10 From Lectures to Lessons and Back Again: The Deterritorialization of Transmission in *Elizabeth Costello*

Migration drive: Getting out of non-belonging

Embedding the lectures given by Coetzee in the late 1990s (1997, 1999b), *Elizabeth Costello* (2004a) consists of eight "lessons". By composing it in such a manner, for the first time, Coetzee turns fiction into "a kind of post-fictional reportage" (Boehmer 2011: 204–5) in which he, both directly and through his female incarnation, rewrites his own 'bio-text' rather than that of other authors or their novels. The first, third and fourth lessons play host to his own lectures, the second to his doppelganger's lecture on "The Future of the Novel", the sixth her lecture on "Witness, Silence, and Censorship", and in the eighth she 'sings' for the high bench of judges. In Lesson Two, Costello's former lover, the Nigerian writer Emmanuel Egudu, delivers a lecture on "The Novel in Africa", while in Lesson Five her sister, the medical missionary Blanche, delivers one on "The Humanities in Africa". Where Coetzee had initially tailored his lectures as fictions, he now shapes his fiction as lessons. By opening up lectures and fiction to each other in such a way, both genres bid farewell to their genuine, oral vs. written 'territories' of transmission by setting up a bridge to the territory of the other. Significantly, the narrator addresses the "bridging problem" (Coetzee 2004a: 1) faced by people whenever they are about to leave their domestic territory for "stranger shores" (Coetzee 2001) right at the book's beginning. The crucial question raised by such deterritorialization is: Why would one long for "stranger shores" if the territory where one resides feels like his or her home? It is only after this home, for whatever reason, bereaves someone of belonging that he or she 'knocks together' an imaginary bridge to reach another, presumably more homely territory. Such bridging is but a response to the political reconfiguration of common-being that deterritorialized many people without them "having done anything wrong" (Kafka 2009: 5).

Among many other places, Coetzee addresses this non-belonging's uncanny origin in his 1999 essay on Daniel Defoe, referring to the writer's significant sentence from the preface to his *Robinson Crusoe*:

> I can affirm that I enjoy much more solitude in the middle of the greatest collection of mankind in the world, I mean, at London, while I am writing this, than ever I could say I enjoyed in eight and twenty years confinement to a desolate island. (2001: 18)

This feeling of being outside of one's home but amidst of it – Defoe was knowingly hiding from bailiffs – explains why the narrator of *Elizabeth Costello* designates the situation, which he shares with the attendants of his lecture, as a "nowhere": a non-territory as the point of departure for "the far territory, where we want to be" (Coetzee 2004a: 1). A setting that we feel familiar with becomes a "nowhere" through its deterritorialization, either enforced or intentional. As all lectures take place in the lecture hall's artificial space by assembling unmoored individuals who are ready to undertake an imaginary journey to a "far bank" (Coetzee 2004a: 1), they prefigure the initial situation of fictions. Something must have gathered people at this "nowhere". However, the group of people attending lectures is spatially and temporally limited and directly involved in the happening. The addressees of the fictions, in contrast, are spatially scattered, temporally postponed and thus only indirectly affected. Unlike the bodily attendants of Coetzee's and Elizabeth Costello's *lectures*, the readers of their fictional *lessons* are disembodied, anonymous, and beyond the field of view. Whereas the lecturers simultaneously keep a keen eye on their attendants and expose themselves to their verdict,[1] the authors and readers are silently immersed in their activity in complete individual isolation. Being visually inaccessible to each other, they must imagine each other with the concomitant risk of thereby tailoring the other for one's provisional needs.

Therefore, when a fiction consists of lessons that in their turn embed lectures, the latter are delivered simultaneously to the *present direct* and to *absent indirect* addressees. Whereas both the lecturer and his or her attendants, so to say, stand under the stage lights, readers are sheltered in the dark auditorium. In the outcome, *Elizabeth Costello's* lessons expose their lectures' agencies, without them being aware of it, to their readership's observation and evaluation. While the introductory first-person plural of the first lesson's lecturer 'generously' encompasses his lecture's attendants, its readers have the opportunity to detect the background of lecturer's 'generosity'. The same bifurcation of addressees into those who are intended and those who are unintended that characterizes the "we" in *Costello's* first lesson holds true for the "you" of Kafka's "An Imperial Message". Its first sentence reads:

---

[1] In this sense, Costello's final "singing" for the panel of judges is both the culmination point and the hidden common denominator of all her former lectures. When she compares herself to a singing bird (Coetzee 2004a: 223), Coetzee obviously hints to the German verb *vorsingen*, which, among its various other meanings, refers to "putting one's abilities to a decisive test before a panel of judges" – and that is what her lectures have always been doing. In their essence, all lectures are hearings.

> The Emperor, it is said, has sent a message to you, the individual, the miserable subject, the insignificant shadow fled in the remotest distance before the imperial sun; the Emperor from his deathbed has sent a message to you alone. (Kafka 1988c: 24, trans. modified: *Der Kaiser – so heißt es – hat dir, dem Einzelnen, dem jämmerlichen Untertanen, dem winzig vor der kaiserlichen Sonne in die fernste Ferne geflüchteten Schatten, gerade dir hat der Kaiser von seinem Sterbebett aus eine Botschaft gesendet.*)

Being uttered by an oral transmitter of an old legend ("it is said"), it is directed at the Emperor's addressee of yesterday who – once vegetating on the given empire's remotest periphery and now, after many centuries, on that of a modern society – today feels abandoned by the highest authority of his or her world. However miserable these bygone and present "yous" happen to be, the storyteller still locates them within the area of his jurisdiction – which the reader of Kafka's parable is liberated from. As he or she no longer belongs to the transmitter's community, this distance enables him or her to *draw a lesson* from the transmitter's performance. As the community bond that authorizes the latter meanwhile vanished, the reader must interpret it alone. His or her responsibility for the lesson drawn in the situation of narration mirrors that of the "you" for the materialization of the Emperor's will in the narrated situation. In both cases, an agency that "lays much store" (Kafka 1988c: 24) on the accurate transmission of its closing statement faces its distant addressee, across a huge spatial and temporal gap, with the task of deciphering it.

As an emperor is usually considered God's envoy, the messenger is his ambassador, and the storyteller continues where the messenger's mission has failed, the transmission obviously takes the center stage in "An Imperial Message". Each agency is but a mediator for its forerunner's will. To carry on the transmission chain, the storyteller authorizes the "you" who sits at his or her window, ready for departure towards a "far bank", and this "you" therein summons the reader to identify with him or her. This summoning recalls Althusser's famous street scene in which the presumed police call of "Hey, you there!" reaches one's ear without this addressee being able to visualize the caller (Althusser 1971: 111–114).[2] Who is eventually targeted by this resonating "you" is the crucial question for all readers who must indirectly *imagine* their authors instead of directly *attending* their performance. Am I as a reader supposed to act as this voice's trustee

---

[2] As an agency that escapes viewer's gaze automatically associates a "religious authority" (Butler 1997: 109; Silverman 1988: 49), Althusser in his argument emphasizes religious institutions. However, if "the divine performative" lurks behind the interpellation (Butler 1997: 110), then both the Emperor's call (as that of God's envoy) and that of the Muses are its epitomes.

and is its truth worth it?[3] Considering that Kafka sacrificed the question of truth "for the sake of clinging to transmissibility" (Benjamin 1966: 763) – which makes messengers dominate his fictions (Benjamin 2007a: 117) – it is only understandable that the reader of "An Imperial Message" is tempted to continue the transmission chain and to recognize himself or herself in the "you".

This temptation is particularly irresistible if the indirect addressee happens to be an equally isolated 'dreamer' as the direct one, equally eager to leave the place to which he or she is allocated. Cut off from transcendental authorities, modern societies generate such individuals that abundantly engage in invention to rescue themselves from their banishment to the "remotest distance from the imperial sun" (Kafka 1988c: 24). As writers with Australian residence, both fictional Costello and factual Coetzee epitomize such *migration drive*. Recall the scene from the book in which Susan Moebius, when responding to Costello's claim that she and other women writers engaged "some inventing of our own", remarks that Costello hails from a "very far away" country, which makes her "reporting from the far edges" (Coetzee 2004a: 15). Costello's inventor Coetzee, for his part, moved to Australia shortly before publishing his fiction (2002), which locates him in the same category.

As Arjun Appadurai remarked, "the meanest and most hopeless of lives, the most brutal and dehumanizing of circumstances, the harshest of lived inequalities" are particularly "open to the play of the imagination" (Appadurai 1998: 54). Nobody feels more "stranded in the present" (Fritzsche 2004) than the provincial "spectral humans" (Butler 2004: 33); nobody is more responsive to the distant others' appeal than those who "have been subjected to the violence of others" in their surroundings (Butler 2004: 16). *Exposed to peripheral reality and therefore doomed to invention*: this is what links Costello and Coetzee with the interpellated "you" of "An Imperial Message". In his argument, Althusser associates the authorized agency of the street call "Hey, you there!" with the ringer of our doorbell who, when addressed with our question "Who's there?", laconically replies "Me!" (Althusser 1971: 112). That is to say, the interpellator assumes that the addressee will recognize his or her voice as the suppressed "voice of [his or her own] consciousness" (Butler 1997: 107). This will happen because this addressee already shares a sort of common history with the caller, which heightens his or her responsiveness to the resonating call. It is for this reason that Costello and Coetzee, as lecturers and lesson-givers, recognize themselves as

---

[3] For the impact of Althusser's theory of ideological interpellation on postmodern narrative theory, see Currie 1998: 38.

the faraway transmitters of Kafka's 'lesson' and that they, in their turn, tune their call to the ears of kindred 'distant dreamers'.

Displacement: Getting away from sovereignty in a disciplinary age

However, such adoption of an indistinct "you" for the promotion of one's missionary distinction turns out to be a controversial undertaking. If the divine call's addressee is indeterminate, how can anyone claim the status of its transmitter exactly for himself or herself? Elizabeth Costello says that she only transmits the "dictate" of the Muses to her readers (Coetzee 2004a: 199). "And what if the invisible does not regard you as its secretary?", is her judge's rejoinder to this claim (Coetzee 2004a: 201). Besides, in Althusser's conception, whoever recognizes himself or herself in such an anonymous interpellation falls prey to ideological entrapment. Foucault, in his turn, speaks of an "omnipresent and omniscient power that subdivides itself in a regular, uninterrupted way even to the ultimate determination of the individual" (1977: 197). This power assigns to "each individual" "his 'true' name, his 'true' place, his 'true' body" (Foucault 1977: 198), and in particular to the 'abnormal' ones (Foucault 1977: 199) who, without being properly placed in the cogwheels of its normative machine, might induce its crisis. The writers perfectly fit this description. Therefore, when Costello and Coetzee, identifying with the position offered to them by the disciplinary power's institutions, deliver their honorary university lectures, they consent to act as this power's operators.

Here is how Kafka, in aphorism 47 of his "Reflections on sin, suffering, hope, and the true way", describes the situation of the call's individual receivers in modern disciplinary societies:

> They were given the choice of becoming kings or the messengers of kings. As children do, they all wanted to be messengers. That is why there are nothing but messengers. They race through the world and, as there are no kings, shout their proclamations, now meaningless, to one another. (Kafka 2012: 192)

In such a pluralized world of individual proclamations, which bereaves people of an obliging truth or reality, the so-called omniscient authors who behave as the ultimate agents of truth prove to be the most manipulative messengers. The classic realists are famous for having narrated their novels from the sovereign position of lecturers. Realizing how inadmissible such an imposition is in the modern plural society, Kafka replaced realist 'lecturing' with an assembled community – i.e. teaching people from a 'divine' podium – with an invisible and "agentless" (Coetzee 1992: 144) addressing of distant readers. It is therefore not by chance that both Coetzee, in his factual lecture at Bennington College in 1997, and Costello, in her fictional lecture at Altona College in the spring of 1995 (Coetzee 2004a: 16), raise the same question: "What Is Realism?".[4] In both arguments,[5] the realism of today refuses to accept the consensual illusion of their lecture halls as its self-evident departure point. In Lesson Six, Costello states that "a body of balanced, well-informed modern folk in a clear, well-lit lecture venue" (Coetzee 2004a: 175) has its limits, which a writer who deserves the attribute of a "realist" must transgress. The "realism's" task today is to translate the consensual "we" of oral performances as the medium of 'sovereign power' into the dissensual "yous" of written transmissions as the medium of capillary surveillance.

To carry out this task, Coetzee's and Costello's lectures transform the firm bridge, which the storyteller from "An Imperial Message" still builds between the present and the past, into the fragile bridge of Kafka's eponymous parable (Kafka 1988j). That is to say, both Coetzee's and Costello's bridges collapse under the lecturers' iterative attacks in the same way that Kafka's bridge breaks down under those of a passerby. Opposing the realist denial of the spatial and temporal gap between the situation of narration and the narrated situation, they never tire of foregrounding it. Coetzee's lecturer for example states that "unless certain scenes are skipped over we will be here all afternoon. The skips are not part of the text, they are part of the performance" (Coetzee 2004a: 16). By exposing the

---

4 In the book version, Coetzee slightly revised his lecture and re-titled it as "Realism".
5 In this fiction, Coetzee's own interpretation of realism is, of course, less visible than Costello's. If we agree with Northover (2012: 41) that Costello's son "John, who shares both Coetzee's name and reserved nature, expresses many doubts about Costello's position that Coetzee himself may feel", we might take John's reflection on realism (1994a: 9) as Coetzee's own (keeping in mind that Coetzee regularly disowns all that appears to be his own). John's emphasis on the tying of all ideas "to the speakers by whom they are enounced" (Coetzee 1994a: 9) as realism's decisive quality matches Coetzee's emphasis on the crucial innovation of Kafka's 'realism': his drawing of all references to reality into the references to the agencies who make them (or self-references) (Coetzee 1992: 203). Does Coetzee consider himself to be this technique's inheritor? Indeed, behind his 'postmodern' immersion in intertextual relations, many commentators have noticed his enduring "realistic spirit" (Mulhall 2009: 159; Attridge 2004a: 201; Zimbler 2014: 200). For him, "the power of communicating the impact of the real is of primary importance to fiction" (Boehmer 2011: 206). "This interest in grappling with the real in Australia relates to other interests that have grown in prominence in his more recent, Australian-phase work – the interest in living from the heart, in the full-blooded body, and not only through the simulacra of the literary, to cite from Elizabeth Costello's eighth lesson (1994a: 205)." (Boehmer 2011: 206) Wicomb also insists that Coetzee does not abolish mimesis but merely questions its nature "as flagged by European realism" (Wicomb 2009: 12). "In its shifting relationship with language and representation, substitution insists on engagement with the real [. . .]" (Wicomb 2009: 16).

shortcomings of his performance, he systematically prevents his audience from reaching "a dreamlike state in which the time and space of the real world fade away, superseded by the time and space of the fiction" (Coetzee 2004a: 16). Contrary to the storyteller in "An Imperial Message" who in the end immerses his present addressee into the past – "But you sit at your window and dream it to yourself when the evening arrives" (Kafka 1988c: 24, trans. modified: *erträumst sie dir, wenn der Abend kommt*) – Coetzee's lecturer strategically breaks the realist illusion. If Kafka's storyteller invites the parable's dissensual readers into the consensus of his performance's audience, Coetzee's lecturer takes the opposite direction by driving his lecture's consensual attendants into the dissensual perspectives of scattered readers. He thus turns a lecture into a lesson whose absent author has to be invoked by means of the readers' individual memory archives.

His female incarnation, Costello, exposes herself to individual judgments of her attendants in an even more radical way. Her performance gradually unmasks the fragility and vulnerability of her authority by turning its attendants into what she calls "goldfishes", "circling the dying whale, waiting their chance to dart in and take a quick mouthful" (Coetzee 2004a: 6). The first among them is her son John – significantly, the author's namesake – who, as "a misfortunate child, lonely and unloved" (Coetzee 2004a: 4), for a long time exacted revenge upon his mother for having secluded herself for the sake of her writing and locked him and his younger sister out of the best part of her life (Coetzee 2004a: 5). Now, after having read all her books and learned to appreciate them, he is "overwhelmed with sadness" (Coetzee 2004a: 26) about his lonesome aging mother who is performing to the world as "an old, tired circus seal" (Coetzee 2004a: 3). She is now generally worshiped as "a mouthpiece for the divine", but she is, in his opinion, in fact "a god incarnated in the child, wheeled from village to village to be applauded, venerated" (Coetzee 2004a: 31). Nobody knows her better than him who attended her

> screaming at her children: *"You are killing me! You are tearing the flesh from my body!"* (He lay in the dark with his sister afterwards, comforting her while she sobbed; he was seven; it was the first taste of fathering.) (Coetzee 2004a: 30; italics in the original)

Since her arrival in Pennsylvania to receive her award, he indeed takes over her parental role by acting at once as the critic, protector and instructor of his widely celebrated mother.

The son's perspective is not the only one that weakens the force of Costello's authority. Other characters appear over the course of the action, such as John's wife, her sister Blanche, the novelist Emmanuel Egudu, the poet Robert Duncan and her mother's partner Mr Phillips among others, whose critical observations, comments and/or direct imprints on her soul and body compromise Costello as an agent of impartial commonality. Several years thereafter, Coetzee will not only deepen this contamination of the writer's authority but also apply it, more directly, to Señor C in the *Diary of a Bad Year* (2007) and 'John Coetzee' in *Summertime* (2009). In both works, a series of 'minor' characters who were involved in 'Coetzee's' everyday life in various pragmatic ways interrogate, ruin and dethrone his authority. In *Summertime*, his migrant life story is "reflected on, and also reflected in, the stories of five informants [. . .] themselves immigrants" (Jacobs 2017: 60–61). As indicated, this crumbling of 'Coetzee's' authority appears to be fully in line with John's (Coetzee 2004a: 9), his mother's (Coetzee 2004a: 19) and Coetzee's revised understanding of realism (Coetzee 1993: 7), the mission of which becomes dismembering an allegedly consensual reality into its conflicting individual "readings".

The best way to provoke dissent is to put emphasis on the consensual reality's discarded 'real'. "At the gate", before the ultimate panel of judges, Costello claims to have acted as the "secretary" of all those whom the so-called common reality had "consigned to invisibility", such as violated children and exterminated peoples but also murderers and violators (Coetzee 2004a: 203–204). Contrary to the realists of yesteryear who averted their eyes from such atrocities, she followed their subjects' and objects' calls, including those of the suffering animals "with whom I share the substrate of life" (Coetzee 2004a: 80). Instead of departing from common reality, she thus exhibited the 'real' that escapes its normative grip.

> There used to be a time, we believe, when we could say who we were. Now we are just performers speaking our parts. The bottom has dropped out. We could think of this as a tragic turn of events, were it not that it is hard to have respect for whatever was the bottom that dropped out [. . .] (Coetzee 2004a: 19)

Deprived of a firm bottom, in her view, reality dissolved into a mobile configuration of simulacra that excludes the 'real' as its enabling domain. For writers, whose "light souls" (2004a: 215) live an immaterial life, dismantling the simulacra to rescue this suppressed 'real' amounts to an imperative: "*Too literary, too literary! I must get out of here before I die!*" (2004a: 215, italics in original). In Coetzee's view, however, the 'real' "cannot simply be accessed regardless of a writer's location" (Boehmer 2011: 205). Each location within the incessantly shifting configuration generates a different 'real'. By responding to its call from an ever-new point of view and establishing a migrating point of view, Coetzee untiringly distances himself from the artifice of reality that surrounds him. After Althusser, whoever subjects himself or herself to the call from 'beyond' becomes a subject, i.e. acquires his or her self (Althusser 1971: 170–176). Coetzee thus subscribed to Elizabeth Costello's claim that writers' have many selves, none of them more fundamental or true than others.

> You might as well ask which is the true Elizabeth Costello: the one who made the first statement or the one who made the second. My answer is, both are true. Both. And neither. (Coetzee 2004a: 221)

Nevertheless, among the many voices of the 'real', whose calls she recognizes as worthy of response, those of the despised animals enjoy the privilege. She recalls Kafka's wounded ape Red Peter (Coetzee 2004a: 62), who delivers a lecture for human beings who have injured, abused and humiliated him (Kafka 1988e). As she points out in her lecture, the human race captures apes, transports them to specially arranged penal colonies (Coetzee 2004a: 74), and 'cultivates' them there until they accept its norms and rules in the same way that it normalizes its delinquents, 'degenerates', or provincial *enfants terribles* for that matter (2004a: 68). Whoever among them resists, gets exterminated on the model of the Macquarie Island penguin colony (Coetzee 2004a: 55) or the aboriginals of Tasmania (Coetzee 2004a: 203). Those who consent to and endure their domestication eventually please their tamers' idea of them (2004a: 43), as both Red Peter and the 'exotic' Egudu pretend to be doing, the latter performing Africa to the race of its merciless exploiters and slaveholders (Coetzee 2004a: 51). The same domesticating pattern applies to the writer from the former European colony, Costello, who is "wheeled from village to village to be applauded, venerated" (Coetzee 2004a: 31). Nonetheless, Egudu cautions that, however advanced and noble the language which he uses in his lectures and writings may be, the African voice, dance, song, rhythm, and touch continue to haunt and disconcert it from within (Coetzee 2004a: 44).[6] Laying bare this foreclosed 'real' of human reality, the subalterns and victims pay back their offenders and violators. In her son's view for example, in lieu of being a "comforting writer", Costello acts as "[o]ne of those large cats that pause as they eviscerate their victim and, across the torn-open belly, give you a cold yellow stare" (Coetzee 2004a: 5).

Red Peter equally exhibits his wound to the human beings that have it inflicted upon him (Kafka 1988e: 283) by reminding them of their cruelty. Costello strategically repeats his gesture in her own lecture (Coetzee 2004a: 71), although

---

[6] It is small wonder that, in her conversation with Costello, a Russian lady on the cruiser singles out precisely his voice as *the* source of Egudu's charm that makes women "shudder" (Coetzee 2004a: 57). In the *Diary of a Bad Year*, Coetzee's doppelganger Señor C supports Egudu's thesis of the re-surfacing suppressed origins of European culture by pointing out that the body-experience, systematically banished "into the music of European peasantry, of gypsies, of the Balkans and Turkey and Central Asia", returns to the rhythms of European high music in the late nineteenth and early twentieth centuries (Coetzee 2007: 136). The same happens to the music of the New World "via the music of the slaves who have lost their African roots. From North to South America, African rhythms spread over all of the West. [. . .] The colonizers end up being colonized" (Coetzee 2007: 137).

the human treatment of apes hurts her soul rather than her body as in Peter's case. Whereas he is the scapegoat of the humans who repent for their sins via his sacrifice, she as a writer epitomizes "the scapegoat of mankind", at least in Kafka's understanding (Kafka 1958: 386). Both reappear among their violators to alert them, through their 'exhibition', of their disregarded pain – Red Peter from firsthand experience and Costello from secondhand. As Chris Danta put it, "the word *scapegoat* requires the story of violence also to be told from the side of the animal victim or, if you like, from the point of view of our own animality" (Danta 2007: 723). We have to rescue the animal in ourselves that we have sacrificed to become humans rather than sacrificing it again as we are used to doing with the child in ourselves who is, like the animal, "the father to the man" (Coetzee 1992: 29). In the final chapter, while working on her statement for the panel of judges, Costello recalls the scene in which Odysseus, paying a visit to the kingdom of dead, sacrifices his favorite ram. Without directly naming it, Kafka's interpretation of writer's sacrificial mission in the human world appears to be crossing her mind:

> She could do the same, here and now: turn herself into a bag, cut her veins and let herself pour on to the pavement, into the gutter. For that, finally, is all it means to be alive: to be able to die. Is this vision the sum of her faith: the vision of the ram and what happens to the ram? Will it be good enough story for them, her hungry judges? (Coetzee 2004a: 211)

Does she intend to please the judges in the way that Kafka, in the follow-up to the same letter, claims that the writer pleases his or her readers: "He makes it possible for men to enjoy sin without guilt, almost without guilt" (Kafka 1958: 386)? If she would really wish to please the judges, she would disregard Kafka's ironic correction of "almost", which implies that, although readers are lulled into an illusion of being cleansed of guilt by the writer's sacrifice, the writer in fact, facing them from the wounded animal's perspective, presents them with their race as one of violators. Acting as an ambassador of the violated, Elizabeth Costello thus reiterates Red Peter's and Egudu's vindictive gestures.

"Extreme souls": The pitfalls of a writer's hypertrophied sensitivity

Although Costello focuses on Red Peter who is, like her, compelled to lecture to the race of violators, her extremely mobile sympathetic imagination is also capable of displacing her "into the existence of a bat or a chimpanzee or an oyster" (2004a: 80) as well as into the world of tiny creatures such as frogs, midges, and grasshoppers (2004a: 222). Like the narrator-protagonist of Hugo von Hofmannsthal's fiction "The Lord Chandos's Letter", which Kafka used to read "as a kindred text" (Blanchot 1992: 183), she is persistently haunted by the silenced voices of suffering animals. Coetzee revivifies Hofmannsthal's sensitive hero in the postscript to his book, in which he introduces the Lord's wife and Costello's namesake "Elizabeth C.". In her letter, Lady Chandos entrusts to Sir Francis Bacon that the letter, which her husband sent to him three weeks earlier is not the outcome of his temporary madness but of his enduring condition, which she can no longer bear. Her husband is convinced that he lives in a world of things and beings that are completely interchangeable and therefore bereft of any identity of their own: "Each creature is key to all other creatures" (2004a: 229). Having unadvisedly committed a massacre of rats by ordering his cellars to be lined with poison, he has recklessly torn apart this common tissue of life that connects him with other creatures. As a consequence, "the shrilling of the death cries" haunts his conscience (Hofmannsthal 2005: 123–124). Hofmannsthal's Lord Chandos thus anticipates Costello's hypertrophied responsiveness "to the 'twitchings' of creaturely life" (Vermeulen 2013: 660). From a distance of four hundred years, Coetzee makes her reincarnate Lord's belief that humans "share the substrate of life" (2004a: 80) with all earthly creatures, a belief so powerful that she could equally utter his words:

> I had the intuition that everything was symbolism and every creature a key to all the others, and I felt I was surely the one who could take hold of each in turn and unlock as many of the others as would open. (Hofmannsthal 2005: 120)

At the same time, she could equally well understand the Lord's upset wife and her namesake who complains that "words give way under your feet like rotting boards" (Coetzee 2004a: 228), that she cannot find a single word to rely on because "[a]*lways it is not what I say but something else*" (Coetzee 2004a: 228, italics in original), and that she feels bereft of a home in her language – "where is home, where is home?" (Coetzee 2004a: 228). At the outset of the seventeenth century, Lord Chandos's world of an "infinitely extending allegory" (Lamb 2011: 82) reminds us of Walter Benjamin's interchangeable world of humans and creatures as detected in the early German seventeenth century. In his *Origin of German Tragic Drama*, Benjamin established a tacit analogy between the German baroque and the 'fallen' world of his post-imperial present. His heightened sensitivity for the neglected language of creatures was corroborated by his equally sensible contemporaries, such as Kafka who, for example, states "[A]lmost every word that I write [. . .] I would thereupon like to withdraw or, even better, to erase" (Kafka 1965: 477) or Maurice Blanchot who remarks: "As soon as something is said, something else needs to be said. [. . .] There is no rest" (Blanchot 1995d: 22). Several decades thereafter, at the beginning of the new millennium, Elizabeth Costello resumes their deep sense of homelessness in a language that has irreparably broken its words as the loyal mirrors of the world (Coetzee 2004a: 80). This language's "bottom has dropped out", making us "just performers speaking our parts" and depriving us of certainty as to how and whether at all our performance will be understood by other performers speaking their parts (Coetzee 2004a: 21). To prevent such misunderstanding, Elizabeth Costello invests effort to understand these others by developing, on the model of Hofmannsthal, Kafka, Benjamin and Blanchot, an all-embracing sympathetic imagination. "It is the otherness that is the challenge. Making up someone other than yourself" (Coetzee 2004a: 12).

But, due to the modern individualized experiences, the otherness does not challenge everyone equally. Because Lord Chandos believes that what is "at one moment a dog" is "at the next a vessel of revelation" (Coetzee 2004a: 229), "a dog, a rat, a beetle" counts more for him than "a night of bliss with the most beautiful, most devoted mistress" (2004a: 226). At the same time, his wife wonders how "can I live with rats and dogs and beetles crawling through me day and night, drowning and gasping, scratching at me, tugging me, urging me deeper and deeper into revelation – how?" (Coetzee 2004a: 229). In her view, not everyone is up to such challenge but only *extreme souls* (Coetzee 2004a: 228) who are, following in the footsteps of Jesus,[7] willing and capable to take upon themselves the suffering of others. As if confirming this sacrificial disposition of his mother, John Bernard imagines her

> in her big double bed, crouched, her knees drown up, her back bared. Out of her back, out of the waxy, old person's flesh, protrude three needles: not the tiny needles of the acupuncturist or the voodoo doctor but thick, grey needles, steel or plastic: knitting needles. The needles have not killed her, there is no need to worry about that, she breathes regularly in her sleep. Nevertheless, she lies impaled. (Coetzee 2004a: 26)

As Althusser's above-delineated theory of interpellation suggests, one does not welcome the urge of others, let alone displace oneself into their mindsets, without himself or herself being in an analogous position. This raises the question of

---

[7] The interest in Christ's figure, which culminated in *The Childhood of Jesus* and *The Schooldays of Jesus*, is continuous in Coetzee's work (see for example 1992: 337–338; 2012: 294). For example, we already meet Jesus, although apocryphally, in *Barbarians* when the Magistrate washes the girl's feet (Coetzee 1982b: 40), whereas the addressing of his figure in *Elizabeth Costello* directly anticipates the topic of the two Jesus novels: "Why a Christ dying in contortions rather than a living Christ? A man in his prime, in his early thirties, what do you have against showing him alive, in all his living beauty?" (Coetzee 2004a: 138).

whether one's personal pain does not distort that of the other instead of transmitting it. Consider, for example, when Lord Chandos's confuses his wife's body with that of a siren or dryad (Coetzee 2004a: 227). At the other end of the same spectrum, the suppression of one's experience can be transformed into an aversion to that of the other, as in Costello's disgust at Paul West because of the painful experience from her youth (Coetzee 2004a: 165–167; 179), or in the Gothic prohibition of Christ's bodily beauty (Coetzee 2004a: 138–139), or in the African culture's erasure of the European celebration of the erotic body (Coetzee 2004a: 140–141).

What intensifies such a distorting "filtering" of the sufferer's call is the authority that, in Althusser's interpretation, resonates in his or her voice (Althusser 1971: 170–176). The authority that Costello's schooled sensitivity discerns in the voices of violated animals is in the first place Kafka's. Seen from this angle, her acceptance of their call is but "a belated and redoubled scene, one which renders explicit a founding submission for which no such scene would prove adequate" (Butler 1997: 111). Kafka is the founding father of the modern European literature's submission to the suffering of animals. By subjecting herself to animal voices, Costello, as an Australian writer, in fact seeks his literary company. By adding Hofmannsthal to her 'elective affiliations', Coetzee pushes her spontaneous analogy between the Australian 'outsider postmodernism' and the European 'outsider modernism' (both focused on the question of realism) a step further. Kafka himself embraced Hofmannsthal's vision of the modern writer as someone who, banished by his age in the place of the dogs (Hofmannsthal 1979: 66), "must not close his eyes to any creature, to any thing, to any phantom, to any spectral product of a human brain" (Hofmannsthal 1979: 67). Indeed, Hofmannsthal's doppelganger Lord Chandos was determined to learn "a language of which I know not one word, a language in which mute things speak to me" in order to prepare himself to use it someday when he will be "standing before an unknown judge" (Hofmannsthal 2005: 127–128). Walking in his footsteps, Coetzee's doppelganger Elizabeth Costello is, after having learned the language of dumb beings, now standing before the judges (Wanberg 2016: 158). It is in this indirect way that Coetzee lets Hofmannsthal enter her "analogical filter".

But by introducing him directly in the postscript to *Elizabeth Costello*, Coetzee demonstrates a remarkable disposition for the analogical filtering of his own inspirational call that surpasses even that of his doppelganger. Composing his *Letter* at the beginning of the new century, in 1902, Hofmannsthal established a spontaneous analogy to Lord Chandos's beginning in 1603, when the age of baroque allegory was replaced by the age of empiricism and an analogical understanding of language gave way to a representational one.[8] As an addict of the outgoing age, Lord Chandos predicted the aberrations of the coming one at the very inception of its triumphant march in the same way that Hofmannsthal had a presentiment of these aberrations at the outset of the twentieth century (Wanberg 2016: 156). In 2003, at the start of the new millennium, Coetzee, for his part, establishes an analogy with Hofmannsthal's age with the same intention of announcing the forthcoming crisis in global progress. Whereas Hofmannsthal claimed that the rule of human language silenced the voices of creatures, Coetzee seems to be indicating that the spreading languages of the centers imperil those of the peripheries that feel, in their terms, unhomely. To escape this peril, peripheries employ the languages of their violators in the same subversive manner in which Red Peter as a lecturer or Lord Chandos as a poet employ human language. Like her 'literary relatives' Lord Chandos, Red Peter, Hofmannsthal, and Kafka – or her author Coetzee for that matter – Costello is at pains to excavate the animal, "indigenous and oral roots" (Coetzee 2004a: 154) of European languages, banished by European violators into the indistinct zones of their realities. The filtering of her excavation through these relatives eventually constructs a transborder community of the past-oriented 'bridge-builders' or 'analogy-drawers'. Collapsing the bridge to their present communities, these ventriloquists of subalterns who were victimized by their communities establish a bridge to their remote 'relatives'. Through their "agentless" interpellation, they introduce an assembly of anachronous, uprooted affiliates. However, this scattered community as based on 'elective affiliations' results from the same discriminatory filtering as its homogeneous forerunner because the anchored community members are now excluded from it in the same way that the unmoored ones were from the latter.

"Negative capability": The endless mission of transmission

As Coetzee's female doppelganger, Costello is in a trickier position than Hofmannsthal's male doppelganger, Lord Chandos, who, like his author, is a European aristocrat. To indicate this, Coetzee introduces the Lord's wife, Elizabeth, who addresses the avatar of the new empiricist age, Francis Bacon, to rescue her from her husband's boundless devotion to creatures. Costello is placed under similar pressure by her compatriots to obey her indigenous roots and she

---

8 This is of course the central topic of Foucault's *The Order of Things* that is in the background of this novel in the same way that Foucault's *Discipline and Punish* is in the background of *Barbarians*. The incapability of all new ages to get rid of their 'relinquished' forerunners is the persistent source of Coetzee's fascination.

likewise seeks refuge from it in European literature (Wanberg 2016: 154). Costello's author, in his turn, J. M. Coetzee, who in the 1960s and 1970s was publicly expected to acknowledge his "South African paternity" (Coetzee 1993: 7), escaped from this pressure in a similar way. However, at the same time, Costello is, like him, sceptical of the European 'progress' as it generated colonialism and is now drawing her into the institutional "networks of criticism, publishing houses, centers for translation and distribution, as well as literary awards" and dictating to her what she must write (Wanberg 2016: 154). To protect herself from such developments, after having taken refuge from the Australian periphery in the European center, she finds a new refuge from the latter in the work of Kafka, an internal outsider who was consistently dismantling Europe's dark side. Through such meandering – like Coetzee but unlike Hofmannsthal – Elizabeth Costello is grappling with two equally unacceptable pressures, that of the addicts to the past in the periphery and that of the advocates of the progress in the center. Instead of choosing between them, she never tires of dismantling one within the other.

It deserves attention that Lady Chandos's letter, which testifies to her fear of her husband's perilous insanity, was written on the day and month of the attacks on the Twin Towers ("11 September, AD 1603"; Coetzee 2004a: 230). Epitomizing a fanatic addiction to the past as a refuge from galloping globalization, they took place barely two years before the publication of *Elizabeth Costello*, leaving their watermarks upon its 'skin'. Like Lady Chandos, both Costello and Coetzee abhor such fanaticism, the daily pressure of which they experience in their resident countries. Costello is, for example, equally reserved towards Egudu's African 'fundamentalism' (Coetzee 2004a: 46) and her sister's Christian intolerance and rigidity (Coetzee 2004a: 138). But again, like Lady Chandos, she wants to alert the 'progressive' world that, by disregarding them, it averts its eyes from the dark side of its own 'progress'. As "the being of a certain spectrum of human thinking" (Coetzee 2004a: 67), reason not only has its limits but also horrible consequences. Through Costello's neither-nor attitude, Coetzee simultaneously dismantles the background of its triumphant march and detaches himself from Hofmannsthal's endorsement of irrationalism. The Austrian writer's addiction to the past as *against* the present is not an option as it painfully recalls his peripheral domiciles' (i.e. South Africa's and Australia's) convulsive defensive reactions. As a replacement, Costello engages an *internal* resistance or acute awareness of the past *within* the present, periphery *within* the center, or the other *within* the self.

This gives her what one among her judges dubs "negative capability" – a persistent keeping of human beliefs, opinions, and prejudices at bay (Coetzee 2004a: 200). Since she composes her works as a "secretary of the invisible"

(Coetzee 2004a: 199), "a belief is a resistance, an obstacle" (Coetzee 2004a: 200) that prevents her from discerning the call of another belief and thus in comprehending the whole scope of truth. Through such emptying of herself of all beliefs, opinions and convictions, she acts as a distant descendant of Socrates's 'dialectic negation'.

> For all Socrates's emphasis on reason and knowledge, the results of his reasoning in the early Platonic dialogues were entirely negative, the destruction of false assumptions rather than the establishment of certain truths. It is also important to keep in mind the Socratic paradox that he alone is wise since he alone knows that he knows nothing. Elizabeth Costello shares these essentially negative Socratic characteristics.
> (Northover 2012: 40)

Like Socrates, Costello enters many personal truths in order to negate them one after the other in favour of an interpersonal truth that they are systematically overlooking. In this regard, Kafka again seems to have been acting as a relay. As he put it in one of his aphorisms, it is impossible to know the truth in any other form but a lie (Kafka 2012: 196), which is why one must always say no to this lie: "to say no [to it] is to say yes [to the truth]" (Kafka 2012: 208). He might have learned this "negative capability" from Socrates who considered himself a midwife of the truth that switches from one person to the other but reaches its destination in none of them. As Costello's son John insists, while uncovering the secret of his mother's fascinating authorial power, she equally tirelessly visited ever new individual truths: "Isn't that what is most important about fiction: that it takes us out of ourselves, into other lives?" (Coetzee 2004a: 22–23).

She obstinately makes females and males (Coetzee 2004a: 22), humans and animals (Coetzee 2004a: 76–77), humans and gods (Coetzee 2004a: 184–192), religion and art (Coetzee 2004a: 136–141), the juridical and the literary (Coetzee 2004a: 220–221), and literary imagination and philosophical reason (Coetzee 2004a: 78–80) perform each other. After all, already her guide, Socrates contagiously entangled fiction and philosophy as he never stated the truth but pushed others to abort it in this way, consistently acting as Plato's 'performer'. Bakhtin contends that

> [i]n the Socratic dialogue the idea is organically combined with the image of a person, its carrier (Socrates and other essential participants in the dialogue). The dialogic testing of the idea is simultaneously also the testing of the person who presents it.   (1984: 111–112)

Through the introduction of Socrates and his interlocutors, Plato uncovers the philosophical discourse's fictional roots, depriving us of certainty whether the presented ideas are "those of the historical Socrates or of himself" (Press 1993: 1). How can we distinguish reason from imagination if they steadily interfere and resonate in one another? Plato effaces his truth through Socrates's performance and Socrates, in his turn, through that of his interlocutors:

> [The dialogues] present a world dominated by the figure of Socrates, who both is and is not the dialogical Socrates, who is interrogative (not assertive), ironic (distanced, self-effaced), and aporetic (troubled, doubtful). (Press 1993: 7)

Coetzee translates Plato's fictionalized philosophy into philosophical fiction by allowing the lecturing novelist Costello to perform his complex and contradictory ideas in the same polemically sharpened, unilateral way as the conversing philosopher Socrates performs Plato's (Mosca 2016: 134). In the staged debates, doppelgangers present their ideas with a "relentless determination" (Puchner 2011: 1) that is all but endorsed by their withdrawn and much more reluctant authors. In lieu of "strong opinions" (Coetzee 2007: 1), Plato and Coetzee cultivate never-ending thought that, as Attridge puts it, generates "the event" of "testing, of self-questioning, and not the outcome", i.e. truth (Attridge 2004a: 205).

The highest ideal for such fictional philosophy is the "negative capability" that pushes individual identities to exempt themselves ever anew from their distorted incarnations by following the lead of "I am what I am not". As long as one is what others expect him or her to be, one cannot feel at home in such an identity. Since Elizabeth Costello is a self-effacing novelist that only gives birth to her characters' truths, once placed in the lecture hall where the attendants expect her to present her own truth, she feels like a distorted incarnation of herself. Her son is the first to realize his mother's uneasiness with lecturing: "A strange ending to a strange talk, he thinks, ill-gauged, ill-argued. Not her *métier*, argumentation. She should not be here" (Coetzee 2004a: 80). She herself feels extremely ill at ease with her Amsterdam lecture on "Witness, Silence, and Censorship", which she is expected to deliver in the attendance of Paul West, an author who, to her horror, did not hesitate to meticulously lay bare the evil in his book on Hitler (Coetzee 2004a: 157–158). She is convinced that evil's nasty manifestations should not be publicly revealed (Coetzee 2004a: 167–169; 173).[9] At the same time, she asks herself, is she not resisting West's publicizing of the evil because she stubbornly concealed throughout her life that she had been, as a young girl, corporeally exposed to it (Coetzee 2004a: 165–166; 179)? Drawn into an unbearable pro et con, she eventually loses her track (Coetzee 2004a: 175–176):

---

[9] The dissent between West and Costello concerning the public presentation of evil anticipates that between J. M. Coetzee, who is against such presentation (Coetzee 1992: 363), and his doppelganger, Señor C from the *Diary of a Bad Year*, who advocates it (Coetzee 2007: 171). The analogy-building in Coetzee's translational oeuvre never comes to an end.

> She should not have come. Conferences are for exchanging thoughts, at least that is the idea behind conferences. You cannot exchange thoughts when you do not know what you think. (Coetzee 2004a: 181)

But even as a self-effacing, Socrates-like novelist she never feels at home. When she arrives "at the gate", she has the strong feeling of a worn-out, second-hand setting, a remote and poor simulacrum of *opera buffa*, Stalin's gulags, Nazi camps (Coetzee 2004a: 197), or Kafkaesque scenery for that matter, but "reduced and flattened to a parody" (Coetzee 2004a: 209). Such mocking exhibitions of cultural and literary *clichés*, displaced to the edge of the world, are meant, she thinks, "to teach pilgrims a lesson" (Coetzee 2004a: 209). If pilgrims that passed a long way to arrive to such miserable simulacra tend to make out of them a constitutive part of the world – and Costello regards this as the novelist's mission – they have to push the petty inhabitants of these simulacra to get out of their fake terms. Coetzee confronts his doppelganger with this task in the novel *Slow Man*, in which he introduces her as the author of the novel's main protagonist Paul Rayment (Coetzee 2006b: 79). She rings the doorbell and enters the life of her character that seems to have reached a dead end or at least aberration. As a sexagenarian, with an invalidated body and exhausted soul, he is on his way – a topic of Plato's Phaedrus that he "used to own" (Coetzee 2006b: 53)[10] – to experiencing 'true love' for the first time. Costello is disappointed with such a development in her protagonist's life because "stories like that are two a penny. You will have to make a stronger case for yourself" (Coetzee 2006b: 82).

Her devaluation of his scheduled life story is almost a mirror-image of a scene from Coetzee's earlier novel *Foe* (1986), in which the eponymous writer rejects the life story of the female castaway Susan because, in the form proposed by her, it would betray the readers' and, in particular, booksellers' expectations (Coetzee 1987: 116–117). Susan, for her part, realizes that her life will remain insubstantial if she does not manage to transmit her story unaltered to future generations. Although she lacks the art required for accomplishing this, she resolutely refuses "lies told about me" (Coetzee 1987: 40), i.e. Foe's making whatever he fancies of her story (Coetzee 1987: 123). Whereas *Foe*'s action is set at the beginning of the eighteenth century, at the time when no one could imagine a woman as the author of her story,[11] *Slow Man*'s action takes place in

---

10 Although the narrator does not name Plato's dialogue that Rayment "used to own", the illustration on the book's cover, as he depicts it, unmistakably refers to *Phaedrus* 253d-254e. In addition, Rayment draws a clear parallel between this book and the "book of his life" (Coetzee 2006b: 53).

11 Foe could not imagine her as his story's hero either (Defoe's Robinson Crusoe is knowingly a male) but the captain to whom she entrusts her story enthusiastically welcomes the prospect

contemporary Australia, which allows for the reversal of gender roles: a woman is now the author and a man is her hero. But the outcome is the same as she pushes him to tailor his life to her elite authorial criteria and he refuses to obey her demand. Her novels and articles are boring him, she is bothering him in his own apartment, which legitimizes his wondering how dare this "grey-haired, grey-faced" woman with a "bad heart" and breathing difficulties, how dare she "[tell] him how to run his life!" (Coetzee 2006b: 82).

"What case would you prefer me to make?" he says. "What story could make me worthy of your attention?"

> "How must I know? Think of something."
> Idiot woman! He ought to throw her out.
> "Push!" she urges.
> Push! Push what? "*Push!*" is what you say to a woman in labour.   (Coetzee 2006b: 83)

As Northover rightly suggests, "her asking him to 'push' alludes to her role of Socratic midwife" (2012: 50). However, she does not press him to "give birth to virtuous ideas" – as Northover (2012: 50) asserts probably because the philosopher Socrates would do so – but, since she is a literary author, demands him to get out of literary *clichés* in shaping his life. If characters have "a degree of independence from their author", then this is not because they are "self-originating" (Northover 2012: 50) but, on the contrary, originating in worn-out literary patterns as second-hand fictional creatures. "*'Too literary!'* she thinks again. A curse on literature!" (Coetzee 2004a: 225). With such derivative fictional creatures, no writer can reach originality. In the novel's very last sentence, the doorkeeper indeed entrusts to Elizabeth Costello that, despite her worldwide pilgrimage and tireless bridge-building, her life remained a pale copy of innumerable other lives: "We see people like you all the time" (Coetzee 2004a: 225).

When Rayment, wondering how to rid himself of "this madwoman", inquires of Elizabeth Costello as to who he is to her and why did she pick him as her hero, she replies: "You came to me" and "I am not in command of what comes to me" (Coetzee 2006b: 81). This reply returns us to the sudden interpellation of an author by her character, to which she only responds if she recognizes herself in it. What links Costello with Rayment, paving the way for this recognition, is the Australian residents' sense of double homelessness. They had left behind their European homes to settle in a country, which proved to already be the home of aboriginals who despise and mock them (Coetzee 2006b: 66).

---

of its publishing. However, he is also convinced that the "booksellers will hire a man to set your story to rights" (Coetzee 1987: 40).

Even though they tend to suppress this by denying the aboriginals, they in fact live a doubly dislocated life, carrying along their histories in a country that does not belong to them (Coetzee 2006b: 49–52). But there is a further, more personal reason why Rayment's interpellation might have drawn Costello's attention. His desperate desire to adopt another family's child by acting as its protector (Coetzee 2006b: 44–45; 73), which emerged out of regret for his fatherless life, is starkly reminiscent of her desire to take into her authorial protection a hurt and humiliated 'minor', which in its turn came into being out of regret for her own neglected 'minors'. "Twice married" and divorced (Coetzee 2006b: 120), she also consistently hurt and humiliated them (Coetzee 2004a: 4; 30). As they used to "make tiny whining sounds" in front of her study room's locked door (Coetzee 2004a: 4), it is maybe not purely by accident that she, at the gate, has the vision of "an old dog" with scars "from innumerable manglings" that is blocking her way to another world (Coetzee 2004a: 224).

If Rayment, as a man with a nationally and religiously hybrid European origin, a triple immigration experience and an unhappy childless marriage behind him, becomes a minor then his substitute son, Drago Jokić, is a representative of a minor post-Cold War East-Central European country, Croatia, which has adopted West European modernization in the distorted form of "hybrid capitalism". The political emancipation of East-Central European minor cultures has special significance for Coetzee since it ran parallel to that of the post-apartheid South Africa and, like the latter, "opened the floodgates for gangsters, racketeers and swindlers of every stripe, now free to engage in all kinds of unscrupulous and unlawful behaviour" (Boehmer, Ng & Sheehan 2016: 198). Indeed, Drago eventually forges Rayment's prized Fauchery photographs, inserting his father into the authentic scene of the Australian nineteenth-century migrant history (Coetzee 2006b: 218). Through such fraud, he refuses to act as Rayment's authored puppet in the same way that his substitute father refuses to act as an object of Costello's authoring: "You make up stories and bully us into playing them out for you" (Coetzee 2006b: 117).

In this novel of concatenated supplements (Derrida 1991: 176–177), the behavior of one character unknowingly operates as a disfiguring mirror of the other character's behavior. Characters are sentenced to lives of *protégés* that are "reflecting and distorting, miming and masking, like and unlike" the life of their protectors (Wicomb 2009: 12). Due to the unavoidable betrayal of the substitute father by the substitute son, the protection fails to reach its destination, eliminating the substitution. Commenting on his "three doses of the immigrant experience" (the migration of his Dutch-French parents from France to Australia, his return to France, and then coming back to Australia; Coetzee 2006b: 192), Rayment reveals an irrevocable non-belonging as its result: "I am not the *we* of anyone" (Coetzee 2006b: 193) and "*I am hollow at the core*" (Coetzee 2006b: 198; italics in original). Each attempt to get out of this substitute life into the authentic one merely spawns a new substitution:

> In its shifting relationship with language and representation, substitution insists on engagement with the real which is, however, shown to be heterogeneous, shifting, elusive and illusionary. (Wicomb 2009: 16)

Once it proves to be embarrassingly fake, each substitute gives rise to a new one. After Rayment's rejection of the prosthesis as a replacement for his lost leg, Drago builds for him a recumbent tricycle (Coetzee 2006b: 255). This infinite regression from one substitute to another is *Elizabeth Costello*'s and *Slow Man*'s rejoinder to the claim of European realism as the transmitter of the true reality. In these novels, transmission never arrives at its destination but therefore precisely remains a mission.

Translated into the writers' terms: As soon as the major European literatures proved to be an unsatisfactory substitute for the minor South African resp. Australian literatures, Coetzee launched a search for their excluded minors, such as Dutch, Polish, and Spanish literatures and even apocryphal Gospels for that matter (Boehmer, Ng & Sheehan 2016: 196–200; Mosca 2016: 135–137; Jacobs 2017: 68–69). Like Costello's, his 'negative capability' shifts from one substitute to the other. In the footsteps of Kafka who gave up the truth but not its "transmissibility" (Benjamin 1966: 763), the reiterated missed encounter with the 'real' turns transmission into a mission. Like Costello's, Coetzee's steadily migrating narrative authority teaches his characters and readers a "lesson to which" they "cannot be blind and deaf" (Coetzee 2006b: 198) and which might be rendered as the centers' (in)famous message to their peripheries: "Catch on the transmission of the 'real' in order to get out of your entrapment into the substitute reality!". Therefore, not only is Paul Rayment expected to "push" in order to leave behind the literary simulacrum of his life but, in the first place, the readers who, if they want to draw a proper lesson from their reading, must negate the fake ones one after another. Eventually, they never get this 'proper lesson', but acquire the negative capability of fighting off its forgeries. In this way, *Elizabeth Costello* bids farewell to the limited consensus of lecture-hall communities by teaching its scattered readers how to outmaneuver it for the benefit of a community-to-come. Getting rid of the sovereign power's settled "we", the 'novel' replaces it with the disciplinary power's mobile "we". Instead of being renounced, "we" is thus silently maintained and reaffirmed at the expense of those bereft of intellectual mobility.

Appendix

Appendix

Deprived of Protection: The Ethico-Politics of Authorship in Ian McEwan's *Atonement*

As Derrida never tired of repeating, it is not regular states but exceptional states that are caused by the collapse of our familiar world that confront us with the necessity of ethical decisions (Derrida 1993; 1992c; 13–14; 2005b: 155). As long as the world is *mine*, I do not experience the other's otherness and, therefore, nor its ethical challenge. My world must fall into mischief, come out of sync, or disappear beyond my horizon in order for me to become aware of my responsibility toward the other (as the *other*). As the cases of the Magistrate and David Lurie demonstrate, my defenselessness is *the* very condition for my bearing the other.

Considering this key point in Derrida's deconstructive ethics, it is understandable that he paid great attention to the last line of Paul Celan's poem *Große, glühende Wölbung* (Vast, Glowing Vault): "Die Welt ist fort, ich muss dich tragen" (The world is gone, I must carry you) (2005a; 2005b: 155; 2011: 104–105, 169–170, 266–268). In a long and elaborate series of reflections, Derrida argues that once my familiar world has gone, a wholly-other (*tout autre*) world opens up that enables me to remember, yet never to fully appropriate, the one that has disappeared. Being at the same time a condition of my *possibility* and an *impossibility*, this reverberating world of the past escapes me. From the moment of its withdrawal from my familiar horizon, it operates as a persistent challenge to the time and space of my belonging as well as to the rule of my cognition and behavior. In fact, through its interventions, its radical otherness disturbs all that appears familiar to me from the very beginning of Derrida's philosophy (Derrida 1982: 29–69). However, in its later and more explicitly "ethical" phase, this evasive alterity acts as a disruptive constituent of mine, which bereaves me both of mastery over myself and over the other. The state of exception thus gradually substitutes the regular one. From now on, my freedom is handed over to this haunting 'elsewhere', becoming "a freedom without autonomy, a heteronomy without servitude" (Derrida 2005b: 152). I am invited to invent the new rule of cohabitation with it, which cannot but betray the rule of the world that I belong to. "You have to betray [the world you belong to] in order to be truthful [to the world that displaces you into an 'elsewhere']" (Derrida 2003: 11).

> There are ethics precisely because there is this contradiction . . . [. . .] I have to respond to two injunctions, different and incompatible. That's where responsibility starts. [. . .] This is very dangerous and you have no guarantee. [. . .] Ethics is dangerous.   (Derrida 2003: 32–33)

Next to the immediate *political* responsibility toward others inside my given world there is thus this infinite *ethical* responsibility toward the evasive and powerfully resonant alterity outside my world, which in Derrida's understanding enjoys unquestionable priority. He accordingly states that *das Unheimliche* (in the sense of both the uncanny and unhomely) is "in a certain way the only thing which interests me" (Derrida 2003: 33–34). Indeed, his thinking is consistently oriented by the diasporic injunctions of this exilic otherness that invites him to an uneasy cohabitation. For the Derrida of the 1990s, such resonant calls to responsibility 'from the other shore' are epitomized by the radically undecidable meaning of literature. Since it is impossible to determine the identity of its acts, literature establishes a peculiar community in which "we know in common that we have nothing in common" (Derrida 2001: 58). As opposed to political communities with identifiable criteria of belonging, the only thing that unites such an ethical community is unconditional hospitability to literature's absolute alterity (Derrida 2000b: 83). Yet precisely because it eliminates "common belonging", Derrida allocates it the prestigious status of the "New International" (Derrida 1994b: 85). Being "never at home" in its "ecstatic process", the New International "receives its determination from something other than itself" (Derrida 2000a: 28), i.e. from literature's haunting otherness. Since literature thus becomes *the* "heir to the spirit of the Enlightenment which must not be renounced", its operations commit all other communities to a remorseless "transformation, re-evaluation and self-reinterpretation" (Derrida 1994b: 88).

It is this "new Enlightenment for the century to come" (Derrida 1994b: 90), i.e. an Enlightenment that is itself persistently enlightened by literature as regards its "infinite task", that Derrida unconditionally attaches himself to. In his philosophy, literature remains completely spared of deconstruction, whereas all other (id)entities are subjected to it. In the same sense in which he criticized Levinas's concept of ethics for not having taken into consideration its philosophical and historical "memory" that would necessarily condition it (Derrida and Labarrière 1986: 76), he could himself be criticized for having neglected the long philosophical and historical tradition of his rendering of literature in order to keep its urge untainted.[1] As I have already argued elsewhere (Biti 2016: 283), although Derrida

---

[1] This means that Derrida's understanding of literature (though not always uncritically, as I will indicate in short) spontaneously adopts the early German Romanticist literary opposition to Kant's philosophical transcendentalism. Because he tacitly adopts this overturn of philosophy's supremacy over literature – instead of reworking it as he regularly does with other oppositions – transcendentalism resurfaces in his rendering of literature. He significantly highlights the importance of the (new) Enlightenment, making now literature into its chief representative. If, in the Enlightenment doctrine, philosophical ratio assumed divine traits, the same authority

had repeatedly drawn attention to the possibility of a violent implementation of such an absolute 'command from beyond' (Derrida 1997: 65),[2] of its perilous proximity to 'the bad, even to the worst' (Derrida 1992d: 28),[3] whenever this 'command' was epitomized by literature, he nonetheless reiterated its welcome reevaluating character. Tending to deny literature's political investments, he ethically sanitized its High Address.

I take this eminently ethical understanding of literature by Derrida to be silently healing the political experience of defenselessness that, in the aftermath of the Second World War, powerfully affected some intellectual circles in post-imperial and post-colonial Europe. The prolongation of the turbulent interwar state of exception into the posttraumatic after-war Europe deepened the feeling of unprotectedness among the particularly sensitive intellectuals in both imperial countries and/or their (former) colonies. Whereas Derrida, as an Algerian Jew, might be attributed to the latter group, Maurice Blanchot for example, who in his youth collaborated with an anti-Semitic regime, testifies to the former group's vulnerability to exceptional conditions.[4] Irrespective of whether this vulnerability was political, as in the first instance, or ethical, as in the second,

---

is now allocated to literature: "God looks at me and I don't see him and it is on the basis of this gaze that singles me out [ce regard qui me regard (Derrida 1992b: 59, 67, 87)] that my responsibility comes into being" (Derrida 1995b: 51, 67, 91). In the ultimate analysis, however, Derrida places such divinization of literature at the service of deconstruction as its protector. For instance, he unhesitatingly declares that "deconstruction is justice" (Derrida 1992d: 15).

2 Derrida explicitly warns that pure face-to-face communication with the Other (i.e. without the mediation of the "small [political] other") might result in perilous consequences, i.e. the impossibility of distinguishing between good and evil, love and hate, giving and taking etc. (1997: 66).

3 Published as a separate book *a posteriori*, the French original contains an addition that is even more explicit in this regard: "Abandonnée à elle seule, l'idée incalculable et donatrice de la justice est toujours au plus près du mal, voire du pire car elle peut toujours être réappropriée par le calcul le plus pervers" (Derrida 1994a: 61).

4 For Blanchot's collaboration see Haase and Large 2001: 85–95. As demonstrated in the third chapter, in his lucid reading of Blanchot's "thought from outside", Foucault pointed to the post-traumatic character of Blanchot's attraction by "an absence that pulls as far away from itself as possible [. . . and that] has nothing to offer but the infinite void" (Foucault 1987: 28). This powerful attraction to the inarticulate 'outside' makes him negligent of the politically articulated order *inside* the world, which is extremely dangerous because the inarticulate outside, through its endless withdrawal, gradually removes the attracted person from his or her political articulation (Foucault 1987: 34), making his or her past, kin and whole life non-existent (Foucault 1987: 28). Nonetheless, Blanchot was (like Derrida) deeply fascinated with the dispossessed of protection (Foucault 1987: 41, 45), which ultimately drove him to render literature (like Derrida) as the most proper caretaker of theirs.

it drove its victims to establish a 'literary community' as the shelter for their scattered imagined allies.

Although the British novelist Ian McEwan belonged to a different geopolitical, social and cultural milieu, he nevertheless felt motivated to join this "literary community" of ethically disconcerted post-imperial intellectuals. Sebastian Groes convincingly argues that McEwan's early works "gave voice to an anxiety about social, cultural and moral decline after the end of Britain's imperial power had become vividly apparent" (2009a: 6). Groes also addresses the systematic disconnection of the public and private that characterized the fatherless post-war childhood of both McEwan himself and his hero Henry Perowne (in *Saturday*) (Groes 2009b: 108). Formative of the writer's youth, the frequent military service of McEwan's father at various outposts of Britain's colonies additionally induced his continual geographical, cultural, psychological and linguistic displacement (Groes 2009a: 5). In my interpretation, this deeply divided and guilt-ridden constellation of post-imperial Britain gave rise to the ethical profile of literature in McEwan's work, akin to (and at the same time different from) that in the works of Derrida and Blanchot. Being developed by a novelist in the first place, McEwan's understanding of literature acquires its final form in the complex narrative construction of his 'literary acts'. However, in order to uncover the suppressed traumatic germ at their basis I will open my analysis of *Atonement* with its central characters' significant feeling of defenselessness.

It deserves attention that the loss of parental care that severely affected the infants in *The Cement Garden* strikes the dependents in *Atonement* with unabated fierceness.[5] In this novel, not only the Tallis family's children grow up dispossessed of parental devotion. Father Jack is continually physically absent due to his political engagements and (secret) love affairs in London, while mother Emily absents herself from her children' lives because of her frequent migraines. The oldest among the three children and the only son, Leon, refuses to assume his

---

5 As indicated above, Henry Perowne in *Saturday* also recalls his fatherless childhood (McEwan 2005: 194) and is deeply disquieted by the disaggregation of his mother's mind (McEwan 2005: 158–167; 273–275). Some critics have addressed McEwan's own parentless childhood years (from the age of eleven to eighteen) in this context but it would certainly be misplaced to read McEwan's novels exclusively through these optics. In them, defenselessness reflects the condition of world and literature much more than his individual and personal problems. Both the post-imperial world and literature are deprived of transcendental authorities. I therefore agree with those critics who claim that, inasmuch as McEwan consistently searches for an ethically responsible literary form, his novels develop truth-oriented as opposed to relativist postmodern poetics (Elam 2009, Alden 2009). In this regard, they reflect the main concern of Kafka's and Coetzee's works.

father's responsibility, at least from his sister Cecilia's perspective (McEwan 2001: 102–103). Since their grandfather Harry was a farm laborer's son who changed his name and whose birth and marriage were not recorded, Cecilia experiences her family tree as wintry, bare, and rootless (McEwan 2001: 109). She sorely misses her father's authority that, even if she disagrees with him, centers her world (McEwan 2001: 46–47). The same goes for her younger sister, the novel's central character Briony (McEwan 2001: 122), in whose view her father must know the truth but is sadly inaccessible (McEwan 2001: 285–286). Deprived also of her mother's care, she either requires mothering from her older sister (McEwan 2001: 103) or isolates herself on her artificial island in an artificial lake (McEwan 2001: 163). She spends her time alone in her "intact inner world", always off and away in her mind (as her mother Emily perceives her, McEwan 2001: 68).

Even more shaken than the Tallis children are the Quincey children, cousins from the north on a visit to the Tallis' household, because of their parents' divorce and neglect (McEwan 2001: 57–59). Parental disregard is thus the general experience of infants in *Atonement*. The epitome of the fatherless childhood, however, is that of Robbie, the son of the Tallis' servants who was abandoned by his gardener father as a six years-old child (McEwan 2001: 122) and thereupon found in Jack Tallis a benevolent surrogate father to support his schooling. Unfortunately, it turns out that even the Tallises renounce him. As a result of the return of this trauma, he desperately longs for his own father, dead or alive, to center his life. Moreover, he powerfully desires the role of the father for himself (McEwan 2001: 241). That is to say, precisely as an abandoned child, whose rejection was reinvigorated by his surrogate family, Robbie strongly inclines to take into protection various helpless dependents.[6] His passionate attachment to them is striking (even more so if we consider that it is established by Briony as the narrator *and* the implied author as this narrator's shaper). First, he bravely saves Briony from the river (2001: 230–231). Then, he rescues the disappeared Quincey brothers by carrying "Pierrot on his shoulders and Jackson in his arms" back into the Tallises' house (McEwan 2001: 262). Finally, in the disjointed world of war, devoid of God – a chaotic inversion of the poetic order that characterized his study time (McEwan 2001: 264) – a severed child's leg in a tree does not let him go (McEwan 2001: 191–192, 202, 262). It reminds him of a Flemish woman with a terrified child in her arms (McEwan 2001: 236–238) for whose dismemberments he somehow feels responsible:

---

[6] In this regard, his acting is an internal echo of McEwan's narrative acting that, as delineated above, equally tends to provide a shelter to the defenseless characters and readers. McEwan's sheltering of the defenseless, in its turn, repeats those of Kafka and Coetzee.

> He must go back and get the boy from the tree. (. . .) Gather up from the mud the pieces of burned, striped cloth, the shred of his pyjamas, then bring him down, the poor pale boy, and make a decent burial. (McEwan 2001: 263)

Haunted by the abandonments he was victimized by, Robbie proves to be affectively committed to victims. If we try to translate the aforementioned poem by Celan into his own ethical terms, the outcome might read: because my familiar "world is gone" "I must carry you" as a random, collateral victim whom I happened to meet in a world out of joint. For who if not I myself am the ultimate addressee of your appeal? The war as the paradigmatic state of exception disqualifies inherited rules that the so-called grand history instructs us to adhere to. They lose their former validity:

> Who could ever describe this confusion, and come up with the village names and the dates for the history books? And take the reasonable view and begin to assign the blame? No one would ever know what it was like to be here. Without the details there could be no larger picture. (McEwan 2001: 227)

In a world deprived of universal protection, in which therefore "everyone [came to be] guilt[y] and no one was", because "we witnessed each other's crimes" (McEwan 2001: 261), infers Robbie, one of us who is guilty has to take the responsibility for "burying the innocent" and letting "no one change the evidence" (McEwan 2001: 262–263). This is why he – silently endorsed by the narrator, Briony, behind him and the implied author behind her – attentively records occurrences that do not match the so-called accounts of general historical interest. In a world thrown into the state of exception, the criteria of historical and moral 'recordability' are left to individual responsibility. It would be immoral to take them at their face value.

Robbie's delineated strategy of taking care of apparently insignificant occurrences, apart from resounding Briony's and the author's, is all but unique in the highly turbulent interwar time devoid of secure belonging. Crafted as his character is, its ethical attitude establishes elective affinities with that of some renowned 'external' contemporaries.[7] To mention the most famous one, in the immediate aftermath of the First World War Ludwig Wittgenstein declared that the human world's ultimate sense lies outside its inhabitants'

---

[7] The abundance of intertextual references in McEwan's work is notorious (Cormack 2009; Marcus 2009; Groes 2009a, 2009b). However, correspondence between Robbie's ethical orientation and that of some prominent interwar thinkers does not so much originate in McEwan's intertextual strategy as in the ethical disposition of his oeuvre, which was generated by the same experience of defenselessness as felt by Robbie. Once again, Robbie appears as the author's doppelganger.

horizon (Wittgenstein 2016: 6.41), which is why it remains impenetrable to them. All they can do is attentively gather its indices. The same ruined world has also driven Walter Benjamin to replace historian with the "chronic" who lets "nothing that ever happened" go unnoticed (Benjamin 1977d: 252). In his "Theses on the Philosophy of History", one of the key documents of the same chaotic interwar time that affects the world of *Atonement*, Benjamin stated that any trifle might prove to be important for the final account to come (1977d: 252). In his notes from the same state of exception, finally, Mikhail Bakhtin similarly concluded: "There is nothing absolutely dead; every meaning will experience the holiday of its rebirth" (Bakhtin 1979: 373).

While it establishes the delineated multidirectional correspondences, Robbie's ethical reasoning in the midst of the war operates as a sort of transmitter between the *prewar* thinkers and Briony's and McEwan's *postwar* ethics. The overlapping of these two states of exception points to their troubling continuity. McEwan is as equally guilt-ridden as Derrida who "always feels guilty" (Derrida 2003: 48–49) and both of them in a way subscribe to Robbie's war statement: "Let the guilty bury the innocent, and let no one change the evidence" (McEwan 2001: 262–263). Even if McEwan attributes the glorification and sanctification of Robbie's character to the atonement of his narrative shaper Briony, thus keeping aloof from both doppelgangers of him, he nonetheless engages their war commitment to the innocents to undo the contemporary heroic myths (Elam 2009: 44).[8] His meticulous care for the seemingly insignificant details of the past – as induced among other things by personal indebtedness to his father as a Second World War veteran who served at Dunkirk[9] – refuses to take recent historical fictions at their word (Alden 2009: 60–61).

Even though Robbie's and Briony's remorseful attachment to the victims anticipates in many important aspects the authorial ethical strategy in *Atonement*, they are both simultaneously exposed as selfish. This is how correspondences operate in this novel: they continually turn those who know better into the duped, truths into illusions, and vice versa. While the narrator and author expose their characters as their inferiors – 'almost the same but not quite' – these inferiors make their superiors reproduce their fallacies. All are entrapped within a persistently devaluing and revaluing web of correspondences which is

---

8 For the parallel profile of Briony's and McEwan's commitment to the meticulous reconstruction of the past, see Finney 2002.
9 In his reply to accusations of plagiarism, McEwan addresses "his weighty obligation to strict accuracy. In writing about wartime especially, it seems like a form of respect for the suffering of a generation conscripted into a nightmare" (*The Guardian*, April 1, 2006).

why, ultimately, the reader has nobody left to rely on.[10] As one critic put it, *Atonement* "continuously wrong-foots the reader, brutally punishing us for our willingness to suspend our disbelief" (Groes 2009a: 4). The author never stops ethically exempting himself from his doppelgangers, but he nonetheless re-enacts their moral and cognitive aberrations; and the same happens to his reader. In sum, *Atonement* draws its characters, narrator, author, and readers into the frenetic pursuit of the final *ethical* truth but repeatedly entraps them in this truth's provisional *political* surrogates.

Anyhow, for those who are remorsefully attached to this truth, no worse a delusion than the selfish withdrawal into one's own artificial world is imaginable. Instead of ethically extending the politically established world, it tyrannically restricts it. In the novel, this kind of behavior represents *young* Briony, who thereby inconspicuously acts as the doppelganger of the author's delusive youth.[11] But this is not her only blind spot because she also instinctively reproduces her evasive mother who finds refuge either in her migraine, selfish "peace of mind" (McEwan 2001: 71), or complete disregard of upcoming war dangers as anticipated in her husband's secret file "Eventuality Planning" (McEwan 2001: 122). As testified by Briony's youthful melodrama *The Trials of Arabella*, her desire to compensate for her family's disintegration through the creation of literary illusion beats even that of her mother. The teenager enjoys exerting absolute control over her artificial world, which is why she keeps the complexities of the surrounding reality at a safe distance from it. Next to her mother and young McEwan, she equally echoes young Robbie at the time of his Cambridge professors who "revered the free, unruly spirits" of poets (McEwan 2001: 264). Mature Briony is therefore at pains to liberate herself from her youthful blind spots. But instead of the desired liberation, in an informed reader's perspective, she accomplishes only a reduplication of Robbie's and McEwan's maturation.

At the moment when Robbie chooses to study medicine, he equally exempts himself from the attitude to literature that was induced by his education at Cambridge (McEwan 2001: 91).[12] But it turns out, retroactively, that he thereby merely

---

10 In previous chapters, the same mutual exposure of delusions has been detected in various asymmetric relationships in Kafka's and Coetzee's works.
11 McEwan (2002) confesses that in his early collections of stories "[m]y female characters became the repository of all the goodness that men fell short of. In other words, pen in hand, I was going to set my mother free" (2002: 41–42), i.e. from the mistreatment of his father.
12 Before this distancing, literature visibly affected his way of thinking, for example the conversations and letters that he shared with Cecilia (the obscene one is obviously inspired by D. H. Lawrence; see Marcus 2009: 91). Robbie is said to have finished English literature at Cambridge at the time of Professor Leavis (McEwan 2001: 91), who knowingly claimed the preeminence of Literary Studies as a "strong humane center" over increasingly "specialist studies" as

fulfilled the elderly Briony's wish to transform her literature through her expiating medical care. While Robbie's literary maturing thus echoes Briony's, her nursing remorsefully resumes Cecilia's damaged course of life. In this novel's entrapping hall of mirrors, all emancipations are destined to fail. At the end of the day, Briony's conviction that she would be a better writer for having gone through a difficult life experience unwittingly turns Robbie's conviction that "he would be a better doctor for having read literature" upside down (McEwan 2001: 93). Through Robbie's delusions, Briony realizes that the vicissitudes of reality only exist to serve the ennoblement of her literature. She accordingly refutes the 'Leavisite' right of reality to arrogate to itself the primary ontological position (McEwan 2001: 371). The only task of life is to aggravate and thus refine the mission of literature. Yet in the "wrong-footing strategy" of this novel, even Briony's "suspension of disbelief" in literature is destined to be punished.

This disillusionment by Briony deserves more detailed elaboration. The redrawing of her life's originally envisaged design – nursing instead of university – makes Briony abandon the writerly self-confinement of "the earnest, reflective child" that she was by considering in her subsequent literary attempts other, previously neglected points of view (McEwan 2001: 41). The grown-up Briony trusts she was "so worldly now as to be above such nursery-tale ideas as good and evil", launching instead a search for "some lofty, god-like place, from which all people could be judged alike, not pitted against each other, as in some life-long hockey match, but seen noisily jostling together in all their glorious imperfection" (McEwan 2001: 115). In her retroactive view, literary maturing implies rejecting authorial anger toward fellow beings in favor of an endless compassion for them. To achieve such impartiality, she replaces "direct and simple" stories that were destined to telepathically "send thoughts and feeling from her mind to her reader's" (McEwan 2001: 37) with a more complex and encompassing kind of narrative prose, which transcends easy genre determinations. To term it a story is "such an inadequate word" for it (McEwan 2001: 281) but neither "novella" (McEwan 2001: 318) nor "little novel" (McEwan 2001: 320) really fit. By stubbornly exempting herself from the role of a dupe, which she was continually lured into, Briony never stops drafting and redrafting this prose in the course of almost six decades until it acquires the given novelistic profile of *Atonement*.

But did she really renounce her adolescent phantasies about the "godly power of creation" (McEwan 2001: 76) once she had realized that to "enter a

---

its mighty rivals (Leavis 1969: 3). With him, literature wiped its hands clean of any political interest by rendering its representation of reality all-encompassing. As already indicated, not only Robbie's and Briony's but also McEwan's maturing help them 'emancipate' themselves from this illusion.

mind and show it at work, or being worked on, and to do this in a symmetrical design – this would be an artistic triumph" (McEwan 2001: 282)? By adhering to this belief, was she not again driven into Robbie's opinion:

> Rise and fall – this was the doctor's business, and it was literature's too. He was thinking of the nineteenth-century novel. Broad tolerance and the long view, an inconspicuously warm heart and cool judgement . . . [?]   (McEwan 2001: 93)

Or, by achieving this "triumph", has she not fallen victim of McEwan's temporary admiration for the nineteenth century novel's shifting points of view, which he seems to have distanced himself from in *Atonement*?[13] In a word, was she not silently dispossessed of the unbiased authorship she was heading to?[14] Since the impartially shifting points of view are invisibly filtered through Briony's selfish representation from the novel's very outset, the implied author seems to be suggesting behind her back that impartiality and selfishness make an inextricable couple. Briony involuntarily intertwines them all the time.

Already as a teenager, she considers writing a story about the scene by the fountain by representing the scene from three different and equally valid points of view (McEwan 2001: 40). As a guilt-ridden old woman whose memory and reasoning ability are on the brink of the incapacitation, she realizes, on the contrary, that the engagement of the different points of view testifies to her cowardice toward the others more than to her altruism. By exempting herself from being duped by her youthful revenge, she moved into another, genetic entrapment. While through her meandering she consistently avoided facing the truth, she was repeating her mother who, by keeping herself away from confrontations with her husband (2001: 148–149), only strove for her own comfort (McEwan 2001: 71). If young Briony was predetermined by her mother's evasiveness, old Briony is captured by her disinterestedness. Despite her entire literary maturing, she does not accomplish individuality. Her creative authorial strategy turns out to have been governed by her genetically programmed mind: "It was not the backbone of a story that she lacked. It was backbone" (McEwan 2001: 320). Her narrative did not follow from her *mind*'s literary self-reflection and

---

13 On this admiration see the interview given to David Lynn 2007. According to Elam, by dismantling Briony's illusions, McEwan alerts his readers to not unreservedly trust the strategy he has chosen in this novel (Elam 2009: 23). The same could be said, of course, of Coetzee's dismantling of Elizabeth Costello's illusions.

14 Marcus remarks that "the novelist's imaginative entry into other minds can never obviate the fact that these minds are, ultimately, his or her own creation" (2009: 94). Seaboyer endorses this by stating that "Briony may be claiming to attempt to atone for her sin against Robbie, but she may also be accused of 'colonising' him for the sake of her writing" (2005: 32).

genre considerations (McEwan 2001: 37, 41, 45, 115, 159–160, 280–282), but from her *brain*'s inborn disposition.[15] Is each and every literary emancipation predetermined to be deluded in such a way? Can McEwan, as Briony's 'protector', prevent such subterraneous dispossession of his authorial sovereignty?

In fact, both the young and mature Briony victimize the uneasy truth, 'slash its nettles' (McEwan 2001: 76) to please those who desperately need the illusion, such as the deathly wounded soldier who longed for true love (McEwan 2001: 206) or the literary audience that attaches itself to common sense or love stories (McEwan 2001: 76, 169–170, 308). But, more than anybody else, she herself is addicted to illusions. If she consistently identified with those in need of illusions, she did it for the same reason that Robbie identified with those in need of protection. By forcing them into the role of victims, she made them epitomize her own wishful status. By making Lola the victim of Robbie's desire despite her obvious hesitations to clearly identify the rapist (McEwan 2001: 168), she punished Robbie for failing to act toward her in the same way. Or, in an equally compensatory manner, after a half a dozen different drafts of her manuscript in an almost 60-year assignment (McEwan 2001: 369), she resumes the happy love story from the beginning of her career, calmly falsifying the facts that Robbie died of septicaemia and Cecilia was killed by a bomb (McEwan 2001: 370–371).

To sum this up, not only the young but also the grown-up Briony refuses to face the dispossessing truth. In her writerly strategy, protecting herself in the guise of others maintains the upper hand. Toward the end of her life, she compulsively repeats "I was trying not to think about it", or "I could hardly face that now" (McEwan 2001: 358), or "I no longer possess the courage of my pessimism" (McEwan 2001: 371). Equally, during the wedding ceremony in the Church of the Holy Trinity on Clapham Common, not only does she miss the opportunity to proclaim in public the crime that Paul, Lola and she committed but she convinces herself to keep silent even though she recognizes in Lola a "little mistress of histrionics" (McEwan 2001: 146) or, much later, "the stage villain" who is "heavy on the make-up" (McEwan 2001: 358). After all, Lola imposed herself on Briony's

---

[15] For the replacement of modernist 'mind' with postmodernist 'brain' in McEwan's novels, see Head 2007: 192. It deserves attention that the old-aged Briony (who narrates the novel) suffers from a neurological disease like Perowne's mother and Braxton in *Saturday*, and McEwan's own mother for that matter. That is to say, as any political regular state can at any time be destroyed by the state of exception that hideously inhabits it, the same can happen to any personal 'regular state'. The perspective of personal memory's eradication makes, both in Briony's (Elam 2009: 42–43) and McEwan's view (Marcus 2009: 95), the meticulous storage of its 'innocent victims' equally central as is the above addressed storage of the seemingly insignificant details of political states of exception.

life by pushing her to deliver Paul, the attacker and Lola's future husband, to safety. Although Lola heavily ruined her life's opportunities in much the same way that Lola's mother Hermione damaged her mother's, Briony nonetheless takes her into her protection. This is because, as such a generous protector of others, she pointed out *their* dependency by preventing them from uncovering *her own*. "What sense or hope or satisfaction could a reader" or anybody else draw from telling the truth, asks Briony, seemingly out of concern for others (McEwan 2001: 371), but she in fact avoids telling it in order to keep *her wounds* protected. Yet by dismantling Briony as the "little mistress of histrionics" like Lola, the author dooms her strategy to failure. Lola overwhelms her despite Briony's effort to keep her under surveillance.

As I have already indicated, mature Briony's care for the unprotected acts as the doppelganger of mature McEwan's ethical strategy. Both distance themselves from their deluded literary youth but the author, in shaping his own literary transformation, 'parenthesizes' that of his doppelganger. By dismantling the selfishness of Briony's mentoring he surreptitiously renders his caretaking superior. He pretends not to be entrapped in her delusions as she is in those of her characters. If her narrative atones – and the title, that is by definition in the implied author's competence, leaves no doubt about this – his narrative does not. Such an interpretation of authorial strategy goes against the grain of the mainstream reception of *Atonement*, which claims that from its very epigraph to deep into its narrative strategy the novel cautions against the illusion of literature's neutrality (Kemp 2001; Elam 2009; Alden 2009; Finney 2002; Marcus 2009; Groes 2009b). I on the contrary claim that by exposing the political entrapment of Briony's literature, the author ethically exempts his own literature from it. Like Derrida who spares (his rendering of) literature of the same reevaluation to which this literature subjects the whole world, McEwan exempts (his technique of) authorship from the same devaluation that all his figures must undergo. To recall my argument from the beginning, he gives his authoring operation the traits of an 'evasive alterity'. Strategically withdrawn into an 'elsewhere', he protects characters and readers from a non-place that eludes to their protection.

In *Atonement*, even Briony as narrator remains hidden until the novel's very epilogue, which transfers the readers into the much later situation of writing. Once introduced into it, the reader is asked to reevaluate all that s/he has learned hitherto, especially if s/he has failed to notice earlier references to the situation of writing (McEwan 2001: 41, 162) or Briony's critical reflection on the literary practice of her youth (McEwan 2001: 281–282). As opposed to the explicitness of this switch to the first-person narrative with all its far-reaching consequences, the implied author's deactivating operations are carried out in the background of the reader's attention. They assume, firstly, the form of intertextual hints, such as those to Jane Austen in the epigraph, to Woolf's modernist novelistic agenda in Briony's *Two Figures by a Fountain*, and to the nineteenth century novel's shifting point of view in the final version of Briony's narrative, in addition to the scattered and more or less cloaked hints at *Twelfth Night, Clarissa, What Maisie Knew*, D. H. Lawrence, T. S. Eliot and other works and writers. Secondly, as already indicated, by pointing out Briony's need to please herself through the others[16] and by disclosing in the background of her fiction either her selfish interests[17] or genetically inherited habits, the implied author questions the sovereignty of Briony's literary action. Finally, in the epilogue the reader realizes that Briony was legally prevented from publicizing the crime that Paul, Lola and she committed as long as her fellow criminals were alive (McEwan 2001: 368–370) and, even more importantly, that she can no longer postpone the publishing of her novel because of the quickly approaching incapacitation of her memory. In all these various and subtly combined ways, the implied author turns Briony's writing into an inferior Doppelgänger of his own. That is to say, while claiming to provide protection to others as situated both within and outside her fictional universe, she unwittingly redoubles them, enmeshes herself into their particular interests, distorts them and falsifies them for the sake of her personal pleasure.

Briony thus proves overtaken by the figures that she was at great pains to appropriately store in her fictional shelter. However the question has to be raised as to whether the author himself, while exposing the selfishness of Briony's literary action, manages to avoid its repetition. The strategy he engages to accomplish this is to give expression to the aspects that Briony's narrative has bereft of voice, to place himself at the service of an 'elsewhere' that Briony's fiction has left behind. It is through such resumption of 'diasporic injunctions' that his authorship escapes to be identified. However, because he assumes responsibility for that which Briony's 'truth' has forced into exile, he must '*betray' her truth* in the same way that she has previously 'betrayed' the truth of others. In accordance with Derrida's ethics, which renders this responsibility toward the 'exilic alterity' both superior and infinite, this novel turns 'betrayal' of one's fellow beings into its imperative strategy, demanding from characters, the

---

[16] For example, the soldier with a missing head's side Luc Cornet (who is aged eighteen, like Briony while she nurses him) asks Briony if her sister is now happily married. She responds "They will be soon" and lets this happen in her fiction as if to please him (McEwan 2001: 305–310). But it is of course not only him whom she pleases with her happy love story.

[17] For instance, she punishes Lola for stealing her role in *Arabella*, Cecilia for stealing Robbie from her, and Robbie for choosing Cecilia instead of her.

narrator, the author, and readers that they ceaselessly 'betray' those with whom they share the world. This is why, precisely by 'ethically' exempting himself from Briony's 'political' perspective, the author must also repeat her 'betrayal' of others.

To return to my introductory thesis, the establishment of the reevaluation as the central agenda in the novel's agencies uncovers the post-imperial state of exception as the place of origin of McEwan's works. After the collapse of the long-lasting imperial world, the post-imperial world's distribution of values ran amok, making its inhabitants into repeated dupes. This explains why in *Atonement* the scene by the fountain, for example, undergoes incessant reevaluation through the changing perspectives that never stop 'stranding' one another of its protagonists, its witnesses, the writer and the reader (like Cyril Connolly). Likewise, why the character of young Briony is subjected to an equally merciless redescription from the perspective of her mother, sister and Robbie. The same holds for Jack Tallis through the perspectives of his wife, two daughters and Robbie. The truth of all characters becomes the object of a persistent 'betrayal', all the more so if one considers Briony's underlying and invisible perspective as additionally oscillating between her role as the protagonist and her capacity as the narrator. The characters are consecutively exposed to each other's, the narrator's, and the author's questioning in the name of an 'ultimate' truth that escapes them all.

As I stated in the introduction, only this *elusive literary truth* – typical of the exceptional states' passionate attachment to their commanding 'exterior' – undergoes no questioning at all. It reigns supreme not only within the novel but, because of *Atonement*'s rich intertextual resonances, far beyond it. Both the epigraph that 'grafts' this novel onto the British mainstream tradition and the introduction of Briony's situation of writing, that for its part 'frames' her fiction, testify to this elusive truth's all-pervasiveness. In Derrida's interpretation, neither *grafts* nor *frames* fully belong to that which they transfigure (Derrida 1988: 9; Derrida 1987b: 9). Like "supplements", while completing the presence of an entity, they simultaneously "mark an absence" (Derrida 1976: 144) and, in this way, open an "indefinite process" (Derrida 1976: 281) of supplementation. Placed as they are, "neither inside nor outside" (Derrida 1987b: 9), they exempt themselves from that which they transfigure. In Giorgio Agamben's interpretation, exactly the same atopic in-betweenness characterizes that which he calls the "state of exception" that:

> is neither internal nor external to the juridical order, and the problem of defining it concerns precisely a threshold, or a zone of indifference, where inside and outside do not exclude each other but rather blur with one another. (Agamben 2005a: 27)

Because such a state of exception, as I claimed at the outset, induces the authorial operation of McEwan's novel, the grafting of its outside onto its inside cannot but be interminable. In the same manner that the situation of Briony's writing transfigures all that she has written, the situation of McEwan's authoring of her transfigures all of her writing. This is how persistent reevaluation, in the spirit of Derrida's "New International", becomes the law of reading *Atonement*.

Whenever an ethical agenda establishes itself as a law, it expects all whom it addresses to respect this law, i.e. to accept the role of one of its instances. *Tua res agitur, tua fabula narratur* operates as the binding force of literary community, the chief manner in which it mobilizes its allies. It therefore drives not only this novel's narrator but also its author into an almost compulsive multiplication of their doppelgangers. If Briony's exposed narrative politics turns these doppelgangers into the devices of her atonement, McEwan's hidden politics of authoring turns them into the polygons of his self-healing protection. The difference between these two politics is that the feeling of guilt that sets in motion the author's is not self-induced as Briony's but inflicted by the post-imperial state of exception that he, as a somewhat dislocated member of an imperial nation, was 'born into'. Yet although he therefore, like Derrida, felt that he was continually guilty, his literary protection of those whom he found to be in need of protection did not eliminate the imperialism that gave rise to his 'guilt'. As all ethical re-descriptions unwittingly reintroduce the political asymmetry that they are at pains to neutralize, McEwan's politics of authoring ultimately reaffirmed this imperialism.[18] Not in spite of his intended exemption from the power relationship but precisely through this exemption, his ethical reconfiguration of literature has reestablished the authorial supremacy. It is in this regard that McEwan demonstrates his affiliation to post-imperial literature.

---

[18] On the political and historical background of the 'protectoral' re-description of imperialism, see Amselle 2003: 12–13.

References

Adorno, Theodor Wiesengrund (1978) *Minima Moralia: Reflections on Damaged Life*, trans. Edmund F. N. Jephcott (London: Verso).
Adorno, Theodor Wiesengrund (2001) *Problems of Moral Philosophy*, trans. Rodney Livingstone (Stanford, CA: Stanford University Press).
Agamben, Giorgio (1998) *Homo Sacer: Sovereign Power and Bare Life*, trans. Daniel Heller-Roazen (Stanford, CA: Stanford University Press).
Agamben, Giorgio (1999a) "Absolute Immanence," in *Potentialities: Collected Essays in Philosophy*, trans. and ed. Daniel Heller-Roazen (Stanford, CA: Stanford University Press), 220–243.
Agamben, Giorgio (1999b) "Bartleby, Or On Contingency," in *Potentialities: Collected Essays in Philosophy*, trans. and ed. Daniel Heller-Roazen (Stanford, CA: Stanford University Press), 243–275.
Agamben, Giorgio (2005a) *State of Exception*, trans. Kevin Attell (Chicago: The University of Chicago Press).
Agamben, Giorgio (2005b) *The Time that Remains: A Commentary on the Letter to the Romans*, trans. Patricia Dailey (Stanford, CA: Stanford University Press).
Agamben, Giorgio (2009) *The Signature of All Things: On Method*, trans. Luca D'Isanto with Kevin Attell (New York: Zone Books).
Agamben, Giorgio (2010) *Nudities*, trans. David Kishik and Stefan Pedatella (Stanford, CA: Stanford University Press).
Ahmad, Aijaz (1992) *In Theory: Classes, Nations, Literatures* (London and New York: Verso).
Albrecht, Andrea (2005) *Kosmopolitismus: Weltbürgerdiskurse in Literatur, Philosophie und Publizistik um 1800* (Berlin and New York: De Gruyter).
Alden, Natasha (2009) "Words of War, War of Words: *Atonement* and the Question of Plagiarism," in *Ian McEwan: Contemporary Critical Perspectives*, ed. Sebastian Groes (London and New York: Continuum), 57–69.
Alexander, Jeffrey (2012) *Trauma: A Social Theory* (Cambridge and Malden, MA: Polity).
Alt, Peter-André (2005) *Franz Kafka: Der ewige Sohn: Eine Biographie* (Munich: C. H. Beck)
Althusser, Louis (1971) "Ideology and Ideological State Apparatuses: Notes towards an Investigation," in *Lenin and Philosophy and Other Essays*, trans. Ben Brewster (London: Monthly Review Press), 121–176.
Amselle, Jean-Loup (2003) *Affirmative Exclusion: Cultural Pluralism and the Rule of Custom in France*, trans. Jean-Marie Todd (Ithaca, NY: Cornell University Press).
Anderson, Benedict (1991) *Imagined Communities: Reflections on the origin and spread of nationalism*, rev. and ext. edition (London: Verso).
Apter, Emily (1995) "Comparative Exile: Competing Margins in the History of Comparative Literature," in *Comparative* Literature *in the Age of Multiculturalism*, ed. Charles Bernheimer (Baltimore and London: Johns Hopkins University Press), 86–97.
Apter, Emily (2013) *Against World Literature: On the Politics of Untranslatability* (London and New York: Verso).
Appadurai, Arjun (1998) *Modernity at Large: Cultural Dimensions of Globalization* (Minneapolis: University of Minnesota Press).
Arendt, Hannah (1979) *The Origins of Totalitarianism* (San Diego: Harcourt, Brace and Jovanovich).

Arendt, Hannah (1990) *On Revolution* (London: Penguin).
Arendt, Hannah (2007) "Walter Benjamin: 1892–1940," in Walter Benjamin, *Illuminations*, trans. Harry Zohn (New York: Schocken Books), 1–59.
Attridge, Derek (2004a) *J. M. Coetzee and the Ethics of Reading: Literature in the Event* (Chicago and London: The University of Chicago Press).
Attridge, Derek (2004b) *The Singularity of Literature* (London and New York: Routledge).
Attridge, Derek (2008) "Introduction," in John Maxwell Coetzee, *Inner Workings 2000–2005* (New York: Penguin).
Attwell, David (2002) "Race in *Disgrace*," *Interventions* 4.3, 331–341.
Attwell, David (2014) "Writing Revolution: The Manuscript Revisions of J. M. Coetzee's *Waiting for the Barbarians*," *Life Writing* 11.2, 201–216.
Attwell, David (2015) *J. M. Coetzee and the Life of Writing: Face to Face with Time* (Oxford: Oxford University Press).
Ausenda, Giorgio (1995) *After Empire: Towards an Ethnology of Europe's Barbarians* (San Marino: The Boydell Press).
Auster, Paul and Coetzee, John Maxwell (2014) *Here and Now: Letters 2008–2011* (Vintage: London).
Badiou, Alain (2003) *Saint Paul: The Foundation of Universalism*, trans. Ray Brassier (Stanford, CA: Stanford University Press).
Bakhtin, Mikhail (1979) *Estetika slovessnogo tvorchestva*, ed. Sergey Bocharov (Moscow: Iskusstvo).
Bakhtin, Mikhail (1981) *The Dialogic Imagination: Four Essays by M. M. Bakhtin*, trans. Michael Holquist and Caryl Emerson, ed. Michael Holquist (Austin: Texas University Press).
Bakhtin, Mikhail (1984) *Problems of Dostoevsky's Poetics*, trans. Caryl Emerson. (Massachusetts: University of Minnesota Press).
Bakhtin, Mikhail (1990) *Art and Answerability: Early Philosophical Essays by M. M. Bakhtin*, ed. and trans. Michael Holquist and Vadim Liapunov (Austin: Texas University Press).
Bakić-Hayden, Milica (1995) "Nesting Orientalisms: The Case of Former Yugoslavia," *Slavic Review* 54.4, 917–931.
Bales, Kevin (1999) *Disposable People: New Slavery in the Global Economy* (Berkeley and Los Angeles and London: University of California Press).
Banfield, Ann (1991) "L'Écriture et le non-dit," *Diacritics* 21.4, 21–31.
Banfield, Ann (2005) "*Écriture*, Narration and the Grammar of French," in *Narrative: From Malory to Motion Pictures*, ed. Jeremy Hawthorn (London: Edward Arnold), 1–24.
Barkey, Karen (1996) "Thinking about Consequences of Empire," in *After Empire: Multiethnic Societies and Nation-Building. The Soviet Union and the Russian, Ottoman, and Habsburg Empires*, eds. Karen Barkey and Mark van Hagen (Boulder and Oxford: Westview Press), 99–114.
Barthes, Roland (1977) "The Death of the Author," in *Image – Music – Text*, trans. S. Heath (London: Fontana), 142–148.
Bauman, Zygmunt (1998) *Globalization: The Human Consequences* (Cambridge: Polity).
Bauman, Zygmunt (2004) *Europe: An Unfinished Adventure* (Cambridge: Wiley).
Beebee, Thomas (2011) "What in the world does Friedrich Nietzsche have against Weltliteratur?," *Neohelicon* 38, 367–379.
Begam, Richard (1992) "An Interview with J. M. Coetzee," *Contemporary Literature* 33.3, 419–431.
Beißner, Friedrich (1952) *Der Erzähler Franz Kafka* (Stuttgart: Kohlhammer).

Beller, Stephen (1989) *Vienna and the Jews, 1867–1938: A Cultural History* (New York and Cambridge: Cambridge University Press).
Benjamin, Walter (1966) *Briefe* II (Frankfurt am Main: Suhrkamp).
Benjamin, Walter (1969) "Theses on the Philosophy of History," in *Illuminations*, trans. Harry Zohn (New York: Schocken), 253–264.
Benjamin, Walter (1974) "Der Begriff der Kunstkritik in der deutschen Romantik," in *Gesammelte Schriften*, vol. I-1, eds. Rolf Tiedemann and Hermann Schweppenhäuser (Frankfurt am Main: Suhrkamp), 7–122.
Benjamin, Walter (1977a) "Die Aufgabe des Übersetzers," in *Illuminationen: Ausgewählte Schriften*, ed. Siegfried Unseld (Frankfurt am Main: Suhrkamp), 50–63.
Benjamin, Walter (1977b) "Erfahrung und Armut," in *Illuminationen: Ausgewählte Schriften*, ed. Siegfried Unseld (Frankfurt am Main: Suhrkamp), 291–297.
Benjamin, Walter (1977c) "Goethes *Wahlverwandtschaften*," in *Illuminationen. Ausgewählte Schriften*, ed. Siegfried Unseld (Frankfurt am Main: Suhrkamp), 63–135.
Benjamin, Walter (1977d) "Über den Begriff der Geschichte," in *Illuminationen: Ausgewählte Schriften*, ed. Siegfried Unseld (Frankfurt am Main: Suhrkamp), 251–261.
Benjamin, Walter (1979) "Doctrine of the Similar," trans. Knut Tarkowski, *New German Critique* 17, 60–69.
Benjamin, Walter (1980a) "Der Ursprung des deutschen Trauerspiels," in *Gesammelte Schriften*, vol. I-1, eds. Rolf Tiedemann and Hermann Schweppenhauser (Frankfurt am Main: Suhrkamp), 203–430.
Benjamin, Walter (1980b) "Über das mimetische Vermögen," in *Gesammelte Schriften*, vol. II-1, eds. Rolf Tiedemann and Hermann Schweppenhäuser (Frankfurt am Main: Suhrkamp), 210–213.
Benjamin, Walter (1980c) "Über einige Motive bei Baudelaire," in *Gesammelte Schriften*, vol. I-2, eds. Rolf Tiedemann and Hermann Schweppenhäuser (Frankfurt am Main: Suhrkamp), 605–653.
Benjamin, Walter (1980d) "Zentralpark," in *Gesammelte Schriften*, vol. I-2, eds. Rolf Tiedemann und Hermann Schweppenhauser (Frankfurt am Main: Suhrkamp), 655–690.
Benjamin, Walter (1980e) "Zur Kritik der Gewalt," in *Gesammelte Schriften*, vol. II-1, eds. Rolf Tiedemann and Hermann Schweppenhäuser (Frankfurt am Main: Suhrkamp), 179–204.
Benjamin, Walter (2004) "The Task of the Translator," in *The Translation Studies Reader. Second Edition*, trans. Harry Zohn (revised), ed. Lawrence Venuti (New York and London: Routledge), 75–83.
Benjamin, Walter (2007a) "Franz Kafka: On The Tenth Anniversary of His Death," in *Illuminations*, trans. Harry Zohn (New York: Schocken Books), 111–141.
Benjamin, Walter (2007b) "On Some Motifs in Baudelaire," in *Illuminations*, trans. Harry Zohn (New York: Schocken Books), 155–200.
Benjamin, Walter (2007c) "Some Reflections on Kafka," in *Illuminations*, trans. Harry Zohn (New York: Schocken Books), 141–145.
Benjamin, Walter (2009) *The Origin of German Tragic Drama*, trans. John Osborne (London: Verso).
Berend, Ivan T. (1998) *Decades of Crisis: Central and Eastern Europe before World War II* (Berkeley and Los Angeles and London: University of California Press).
Bergengruen, Maximilian (2016) "*Vor dem Gesetz* sind alle Staatsbürger gleich? Rechtsgrundsatz und Gesetzesfiktion in Kafkas Türhüter-Legende," *Deutsche Vierteljahrsschrift für Literaturwissenschaft und Geistesgeschichte* 90.3, 415–434.

Bewes, Timothy (2011) *The Event of Postcolonial Shame* (Princeton: Princeton University Press).
Bhabha, Homi (1994) *The Location of Culture* (London and New York: Routledge).
Biti, Vladimir (2020) „Post-imperial Europe: Integration through Disintegration," *European Review* 28.1, 62–75.
Biti, Vladimir (2016) *Tracing Global Democracy: Literature, Theory, and the Politics of Trauma* (Berlin and Boston: De Gruyter).
Biti, Vladimir (2018) *Attached to Dispossession: Sacrificial Narratives in Post-imperial Europe* (Leiden and Boston: Brill).
Blanchot, Maurice (1949) *La Part du feu* (Paris: Gallimard).
Blanchot, Maurice (1969) *L'Entretien infini* (Paris: Gallimard).
Blanchot, Maurice (1980) *L'Écriture du désastre* (Paris: Gallimard).
Blanchot, Maurice (1983) *La Communauté inavouable* (Paris: Minuit).
Blanchot, Maurice (1986) *Michel Foucault tel que je l'imagine* (Saint-Clément: Fata morgana).
Blanchot, Maurice (1987) "Michel Foucault as I Imagine Him," in *Foucault/Blanchot*, trans. Jeffrey Mehlman (New York: Zone).
Blanchot, Maurice (1992) *The Space of Literature*, trans. Ann Smock (Lincoln and London: University of Nebraska Press).
Blanchot, Maurice (1993) *The Infinite Conversation*, trans. Susan Hanson (Minneapolis: University of Minnesota Press).
Blanchot, Maurice (1995a) "Literature and the Right to Death," in *The Work of Fire*, trans. Charlotte Mandell (Stanford, CA: Stanford University Press), 300–344.
Blanchot, Maurice (1995b) "Reading Kafka," in *The Work of Fire*, trans. Charlotte Mandell (Stanford, CA: Stanford University Press), 1–11.
Blanchot, Maurice (1995c) "The Language of Fiction," in *The Work of Fire*, trans. Charlotte Mandell (Stanford, CA: Stanford University Press), 74–84.
Blanchot, Maurice (1995d) *The Work of Fire*, trans. Charlotte Mandell (Stanford, CA: Stanford University Press).
Blanchot, Maurice (1995e) *The Writing of the Disaster*, trans. Ann Smock (Lincoln and London: University of Nebraska Press).
Blanchot, Maurice (1997) *Friendship*, trans. Elizabeth Rottenberg (Stanford, CA: Stanford University Press).
Boehmer, Elleke (2005) *Colonial and Postcolonial Literature: Migrant Metaphors* (Oxford: Oxford University Press).
Boehmer, Elleke (2011) "J. M. Coetzee's Australian Realism," in *Postcolonial Poetics: Genre and Form*, eds. Patrick Crowley and Jane Hiddleston (Liverpool: Liverpool University Press), 202–218.
Boehmer, Elleke and Ng, Lynda and Sheehan, Paul (2016) "The world, the text and the author: Coetzee and untranslatability," *European Journal of English Studies* 20.2, 192–206.
Brennan, Timothy (1989) "Cosmopolitans and Celebrities," *Race and Class* 31, 1–19.
Broch, Hermann (1974) *Hofmannsthal und seine Zeit: Eine Studie* (Frankfurt am Main: Suhrkamp).
Brouillette, Sarah (2007) *Postcolonial Writers in the Global Literary Marketplace* (Basingstoke: Palgrave Macmillan).
Brouillette, Sarah (2016) "Global Literary Marketplace," in *Bourdieu and Postcolonial Studies*, ed. Raphael Dalleo (Liverpool: Liverpool University Press), 80–101.

Brown, Wendy (2006) *Regulating Aversion: Tolerance in the Age of Identity and Empire* (Princeton and New Jersey: Princeton University Press).
Brubaker, Rogers (1992) *Citizenship and Nationhood in France and Germany* (Cambridge, MA and London: Cambridge University Press).
Brubaker, Rogers (1996) *Nationalism Reframed: Nationalism and the national question in the New Europe* (Cambridge and New York: Cambridge University Press).
Butler, Judith (1997) *The Psychic Life of Power: Theories in Subjection* (Stanford, CA: Stanford University Press).
Butler, Judith (2004) *Precarious Life: The Powers of Mourning and Violence* (London and New York: Verso).
Butler, Judith (2012) *Parting Ways: Jewishness and the Question of Zionism* (New York: Columbia University Press).
Butler, Judith (2013) *Dispossession: The Performative in the Political. Conversations with Athena Athanasiou* (Cambridge, MA: Polity Press).
Calvino, Italo (1986) "Levels of Reality in Literature," in *The Uses of Literature*, trans. Patrick Creagh (New York: Harcourt & Brace), 101–124.
Canetti, Elias (1969) *Der andere Prozeß: Kafkas Briefe an Felice* (Munich: Hanser).
Caruth, Cathy (1996) *Unclaimed Experience: Trauma, Narrative, and History* (Baltimore and London: Johns Hopkins University Press).
Cassin, Barbara (2014) "Introduction," in *Dictionary of Untranslatables: A Philosophical Lexicon*, ed. B. Cassin, trans. Emily Apter, Jacques Lezra, and Michael Wood (Princeton: Princeton University Press), xvii–xx.
Chakrabarty, Dipesh (2000) *Provincializing Europe: Postcolonial Thought and Historical Difference* (Princeton and Oxford: Princeton University Press).
Citton, Yves (2009) "Political Agency and the Ambivalence of the Sensible," in *Jacques Rancière: History, Politics, Aesthetics*, eds. Gabriel Rockhill and Philip Watts (Durham and London: Duke University Press), 120–140.
Clarkson, Carrol (2009) *J. M. Coetzee: Countervoices* (London: Palgrave Macmillan).
Coetzee, John Maxwell (1982a) *In the Heart of the Country* (London: Penguin).
Coetzee, John Maxwell (1982b) *Waiting for the Barbarians* (New York: Penguin).
Coetzee, John Maxwell (1984) *Truth in Autobiography: Inaugural Lecture* (Capetown: University of Cape Town).
Coetzee, John Maxwell (1987) *Foe* (New York: Penguin).
Coetzee, John Maxwell (1988a) "The novel today," *Upstream* 6.1, 2–5.
Coetzee, John Maxwell (1988b) *White Writing: On the Culture of Letters in South Africa* (New Haven: Yale University Press).
Coetzee, John Maxwell (1992) *Doubling the Point: Essays and Interviews*, ed. David Attwell (Cambridge, MA and London: Harvard University Press).
Coetzee, John Maxwell (1993) "Homage," *Threepenny Review* 53, 5–7.
Coetzee, John Maxwell (2008) *Inner Workings 2000–2005* (New York: Penguin).
Coetzee, John Maxwell (1994) *The Master of Petersburg* (London: Vintage).
Coetzee, John Maxwell (1997) *What is Realism?* (Bennington, VT: Bennington College).
Coetzee, John Maxwell (1998a) *Age of Iron* (London and New York: Penguin).
Coetzee, John Maxwell (1998b) *Dusklands* (London: Vintage).
Coetzee, John Maxwell (1999a) *Disgrace* (London: Secker & Warburg).

Coetzee, John Maxwell (1999b) *The Lives of Animals*, with Marjorie Garber, Peter Singer, Wendy Doniger, and Barbara Smuts, ed. Amy Gutman (Princeton: Princeton University Press).
Coetzee, John Maxwell (2001) *Stranger Shores: Literary Essays 1986–1999* (New York: Penguin).
Coetzee, John Maxwell (2004a) *Elizabeth Costello* (London: Vintage).
Coetzee, John Maxwell (2004b) *Life & Times of Michael K.* (London: Penguin).
Coetzee, John Maxwell (2006a) "Short Works: Reading, Intro to *Nietverloren*," HRC. Container.
Coetzee, John Maxwell (2006b) *Slow Man* (London: Vintage).
Coetzee, John Maxwell (2007) *Diary of a Bad Year* (London: Vintage).
Coetzee, John Maxwell (2012) *Scenes from Provincial Life: Boyhood. Youth. Summertime* (New York: Penguin).
Coetzee, John Maxwell (2014) *The Childhood of Jesus* (London: Vintage).
Coetzee, John Maxwell (2016) *The Schooldays of Jesus* (London: Vintage).
Cohen, Gary B. (2013) "Our Laws, Our Taxes, and Our Administration: Citizenship in Imperial Austria," in *Shatterzone of Empires: Coexistence and Violence in the German, Habsburg, Russian and Ottoman Borderlands*, eds. Omer Bartov and Eric D. Weitz (Bloomington and Indianapolis: Indiana University Press), 103–121.
Conti, Christopher (2016) "The trial of David Lurie: Kafka's courtroom in Coetzee's *Disgrace*," *Textual Practice* 30.3, 469–492.
Cormack, Alistair (2009) "Postmodernism and the Ethics of Fiction in *Atonement*," in *Ian McEwan: Contemporary Critical Perspectives*, ed. Sebastian Groes (London and New York: Continuum), 70–82.
Cornwall, Mark (2006) "The Habsburg Monarchy," in *What is a Nation? Europe 1879–1914*, eds. Tymothy Baycroft and Mark Hewitson (Oxford and New York: Oxford University Press), 171–192.
Currie, Mark (1998) *Postmodern Narrative Theory* (New York: Palgrave Macmillan).
Danta, Chris (2007) "'Like a dog . . . like a lamb': Becoming Sacrificial Animal in Kafka and Coetzee," *New Literary History* 38.4, 721–737.
Deleuze, Gilles (1986) *Foucault* (Paris: Minuit).
Deleuze, Gilles (1994) *Difference and Repetition*, trans. Paul Patton (New York: Columbia University Press).
Deleuze, Gilles (1998) *Essays Critical and Clinical*, trans. by Daniel W. Smith and Michael A. Greco (London: Verso).
Deleuze, Gilles (2005) "Immanence: A Life," in *Pure Immanence: Essays on a Life*, trans. Anne Boyman (New York: Zone Books), 25–35.
Deleuze, Gilles and Guattari, Félix (1983) *Anti-Oedipus: Capitalism and Schizophrenia*, vol. 1, trans. Robert Hurley, Mark Seem, and Helen Lane (Minneapolis: University of Minnesota Press).
Deleuze, Gilles and Guattari, Félix (1986) *Kafka: Toward a Minor Literature*, trans. Dana Polan (Minneapolis: University of Minnesota Press).
Deleuze, Gilles and Guattari, Félix (1987) *A Thousand Plateaus: Capitalism and Schizophrenia*, vol. 2, trans. Brian Massumi (Minneapolis: University of Minnesota Press).
Deleuze, Gilles and Guattari, Félix (1994) *What Is Philosophy?*, trans. Graham Burchell and Hugh Tomlinson (London and New York: Verso).
De Man, Paul (1984) "Autobiography as De-Facement," in *The Rhetoric of Romanticism* (New York: Columbia University Press), 67–81.

Derrida, Jacques (1976) *Of Grammatology*, trans. Gayatri C. Spivak (Baltimore: Johns Hopkins University Press).
Derrida, Jacques (1981a) *Dissemination*, trans. Barbara Johnson (Chicago: The University of Chicago Press).
Derrida, Jacques (1981b) *Positions*, trans. Alan Bass (Chicago: The University of Chicago Press).
Derrida, Jacques (1982) "Ousia and Grammē: Note on a Note from *Being and Time*," in *Margins of Philosophy*, trans. Alan Bass (Chicago: The University of Chicago Press), 29–67.
Derrida, Jacques (1985) "Préjugés – devant la loi," in Derrida, Jacques, Vincent Descombes, Garbis Kortian, Philippe Lacoue-Labarthe, Jean-François Lyotard, and Jean-Luc Nancy, *La faculté de juger* (Paris: PUF), 87–139.
Derrida, Jacques (1987a) *The Other Heading*, trans. Pascale-Anne Brault and Michael B. Naas (Bloomington and Indianapolis: Indiana University Press).
Derrida, Jacques (1987b) *The Truth in Painting*, trans. Geoffrey Bennington and Ian McLeod (Chicago: The University of Chicago Press).
Derrida, Jacques (1988) *Limited Inc.*, trans. Jeffrey Mehlman and Samuel Weber (Evanston, Ill.: Northwestern University Press).
Derrida, Jacques (1991) "The Double Session," trans. Barbara Johnson, in Kamuf, Peggy, ed. *A Derrida Reader: Between the Blinds* (New York, London and Toronto: Harvester Wheatsheaf), 171–199.
Derrida, Jacques (1992a) "Before the Law," *Acts of Literature*, trans. Avital Ronell and Christine Roulston, ed. Derek Attridge (London: Routledge), 183–220.
Derrida, Jacques (1992b) *Donner la mort. L'Éthique du don: Jacques Derrida et la pensée du don*. eds. Jean-Michel Rabaté and Michael Wetzel (Paris: Transition).
Derrida, Jacques (1992c) *Given Time – I, Counterfeit Money*, trans. Peggy Kamuf (Chicago: The University of Chicago Press).
Derrida, Jacques (1992d) "The Force of Law: The 'Mystical Foundation of Authority'," in *Deconstruction and the Possibility of Justice*, trans. Mary Quaintance, eds. David Carlson, Drucilla Cornell, and Michael Rosenfeld (New York: Taylor & Francis), 3–67.
Derrida, Jacques (1992e) "This Strange Institution Called Literature," in *Acts of Literature*, ed. Derek Attridge (London and New York: Routledge), 33–75.
Derrida, Jacques (1993) *Aporias: Dying-Awaiting (One Another at) "the Limits of Truth"*, trans. Thomas Dutoit (Stanford, CA: Stanford University Press).
Derrida, Jacques (1994a) *Force de loi: Le «Fondement mystique de l'autorité»* (Paris: Galilée).
Derrida, Jacques (1994b) *Specters of Marx: The State of Debt, the Work of Mourning & and the New International*, trans. Peggy Kamuf (London and New York: Routledge).
Derrida, Jacques (1995a) *Points: Interviews 1974–1994*, ed. Elisabeth Weber (Stanford: Stanford University Press).
Derrida, Jacques (1995b) *The Gift of Death*, trans. David Wills (Chicago: The University of Chicago Press).
Derrida, Jacques (1997) *Adieu*. Paris: Galilée.
Derrida, Jacques (2000a) *Demeure: Fiction and Testimony*, trans. Elizabeth Rottenberg (Stanford, CA: Stanford University Press).
Derrida, Jacques (2000b) *Of Hospitality*, trans. Rachel Bowby (Stanford, CA: Stanford University Press).
Derrida, Jacques (2001) *A Taste for the Secret*, ed. G. Donnis and W. Webb, trans. G. Donnis (Cambridge: Polity).

Derrida, Jacques (2003) "Following theory," in Derrida, Jacques and Frank Kermode, and Toril Moi, and Christopher Norris, *Life.after.theory*, ed. Michael Payne and John Schad (London and New York: Continuum), 1–52.

Derrida, Jacques (2005a) "Rams: Uninterrupted Dialogue – Between Two Infinities, the Poem," in *Sovereignties in Question: The Poetics of Paul Celan*, eds. Thomas Dutoit and Outi Pasanen (New York: Fordham University Press), 135–163.

Derrida, Jacques (2005b) *Rogues: Two Essays on Reason*, trans. Pascale Ann Brault and Michael Naas (Palo Alto, CA: Stanford University Press).

Derrida, Jacques (2008) "How to Avoid Speaking: Denials," in *Psyche: Inventions of the Other*, trans. Ken Frieden and Elizabeth Rottenberg (Stanford: Stanford University Press), 143–196.

Derrida, Jacques (2011) *The Beast and the Sovereign*, vol. 2, trans. Geoffrey Bennington (Chicago: The University of Chicago Press).

Derrida, Jacques and Pierre-Jean Labarrière (1986) *Altérités* (Paris: Osiris).

Diepeveen, Leonard (2003) *The Difficulties of Modernism* (New York: Routledge).

Dodd, William J. (1992) *Kafka and Dostoevsky: The Shaping of Influence* (Basingstoke: Macmillan).

Du Bois, William E. B. (1990) *The Souls of Black Folk* (New York: Vintage).

During, Simon (2014) "Postcolonial Aesthetic," PMLA 129.3, 498–503.

Durrant, Sam (2006) "J. M. Coetzee, Elizabeth Costello, and the Limits of the Sympathetic Imagination," in *J. M. Coetzee and the Idea of the Public Intellectual*, ed. Jane Poyner (Athens, Ohio: Ohio University Press), 118–134.

Elam, Julie (2009) *Ian McEwan's* Atonement: *A Reader's Guide* (London and New York: Continuum).

Elshamy, Nashwa Mohammad (2018) "Travelling Concepts in J. M. Coetzee's Apartheid and Post-apartheid Novels," *Critical African Studies* 10.2, 196–211.

Eshel, Amir (2012) *Futurity: contemporary literature and the quest for the past* (Chicago: The University of Chicago Press).

Esposito, Roberto (2011) "The Person and Human Life," in *Theory after 'Theory'*, eds. Jane Elliott and Derek Attridge (London and New York: Routledge), 205–220.

Evans, R. J. W. (2006) *Austria, Hungary, and the Habsburgs: Essays on Central Europe c. 1683–1867* (Oxford: Oxford University Press), 134–146.

Fanon, Frantz (1967) *Black Skin, White Masks*, trans. Charles Lam Markmann (New York: Grove Weidenfeld).

Finney, Brian (2002) "Briony's Stand against Oblivion: Ian McEwan's *Atonement*," in *Journal of Modern Literature* 27.3, 68–82.

Foster, Greg (1994) *The Return of the Real: The Avant-garde at the End of the Century* (Cambridge, MA: MIT Press).

Foucault, Michel (1971) *The Order of Things: An Archeology of the Human Sciences*, trans. Alan Sheridan (New York: Pantheon).

Foucault, Michel (1977) *Discipline and Punish: The Birth of the Prison*, trans. Alan Sheridan (New York: Vintage).

Foucault, Michel (1984) "Nietzsche, Genealogy, History," in *The Foucault Reader*, ed. Paul Rabinow, trans. Donald F. Bouchard (New York: Pantheon), 76–101.

Foucault, Michel (1987) "Maurice Blanchot: The Thought from Outside," in *Foucault/Blanchot*, trans. Brian Massumi (New York: Zone), 7–60.

Foucault, Michel (2001) "Pouvoirs et stratégies" (entretien avec J. Rancière). *Dits et écrits*, vol. II (Paris: Gallimard), 418–428.
Freud, Sigmund (1947) *Zur Psychopathologie des Alltagslebens. Gesammelte Werke*, vol. 4, in cooperation with Marie Bonaparte, eds. Anna Freud, Edward Bibring, Willi Hoffer, Ernst Kris, and Otto Isakower (London: Imago).
Freud, Sigmund (1975) „Notiz über den 'Wunderblock'," in *Studienausgabe*, vol. 3: *Psychologie des Unbewussten* (Frankfurt am Main: Fischer), 363–369.
Freud, Sigmund (2001) "Massenpsychologie und Ich-Analyse," in *Gesammelte Werke in achtzehn Bänden*, vol. 13 (Frankfurt am Main: Fischer), 73–165.
Freud, Sigmund (2003) "Der Mann Moses und die monotheistische Religion". *Studienausgabe*, vol. 9: *Fragen der Gesellschaft/ Ursprünge der Religion*, eds. Alexander Mitscherlich, Angela Richards, and James Strachey (Frankfurt am Main: Fischer), 455–581.
Freud, Sigmund (2005) "Das Unheimliche," in *Gesammelte Werke*, vol. XII: *Werke aus den Jahren 1917–1920*, in cooperation with Marie Bonaparte, eds. Anna Freud, Edward Bibring, Willi Hoffer, Ernst Kris, and Otto Isakower (London: Imago), 229–268.
Friedman, Lawrence M. (2000) "Lexitainment – Legal Process as Theater," in *DePaul Law Review* 50.2, 539–558.
Fritzsche, Peter (2004) *Stranded in the Present: Modern Time and the Melancholy of History* (Cambridge, MA and London: Harvard University Press).
Gasché, Rodolphe (2009) *Europe or the Infinite Task: A Study of a Philosophical Concept* (Stanford: Stanford University Press).
Gilroy, Paul (1993) *The Black Atlantic: Modernity and Double Consciousness* (Cambridge, MA: Harvard University Press).
Graham, Lucy (2006) "Textual Transvestism: The Female Voices of J. M. Coetzee," in *J. M. Coetzee and the Idea of the Public Intellectual*, ed. Jane Poyner (Athens, Ohio: Ohio University Press), 217–236.
Gray, Richard T. et al. (2005) *A Franz Kafka Encyclopedia* (Westport, CT: Greenwood Publishing Group).
Groes, Sebastian (2009a) "A Cartography of the Contemporary. Mapping Newness in the Work of Ian McEwan," in *Ian McEwan: Contemporary Critical Perspectives*, ed. Sebastian Groes (London and New York: Continuum), 1–12.
Groes, Sebastian (2009b) "Ian McEwan and the Modernist Consciousness of the City in *Saturday*". *Ian McEwan: Contemporary Critical Perspectives*, ed. Sebastian Groes (London and New York: Continuum), 99–114.
Guha, Ranajit (2002) *History at the Limit of World-History* (New York: Columbia University Press).
Haase, Ulrich and Large, William (2001) *Maurice Blanchot* (London and New York: Routledge).
Habermas, Jürgen and Derrida, Jacques (2003) "February 15, or What Binds Europeans Together: a plea for a common foreign policy, beginning in the core of Europe," *Constellations* 10.3, 291–297.
Hanson, Stephen E. (2010) *Post-Imperial Democracies: Ideology and Party Formation in Third Republic France, Weimar Germany, and Post-Soviet Russia* (Cambridge and New York: Cambridge University Press).
Hartman, Geoffrey (1996) *The Longest Shadow: In the Aftermath of the Holocaust* (Bloomington: Indiana University Press).
Head, Dominic (2007) *Ian McEwan* (Manchester: Manchester University Press).

Head Dominic (2009) *The Cambridge Introduction to J. M. Coetzee* (Cambridge and New York: Cambridge University Press).
Hegel, Georg Wilhelm Friedrich (1896) *Philosophy of Right*, trans. Samuel Waters Dyde (London: George Bell and Sons).
Hegel, Georg Wilhelm Friedrich (1975) *Aesthetics: Lectures on Fine Art*, vol. 1, trans. Thomas Malcolm Knox (Oxford University Press: Oxford).
Hegel, Georg Wilhelm Friedrich (1982) *Lectures on the Philosophy of World History. Introduction: Reason in History*, ed. Johannes Hoffmeister, trans. Hugh Barr Nisbet (Cambridge: Cambridge University Press).
Hegel, Georg Wilhelm Friedrich (2011) *The Phenomenology of Mind*, trans. James Black Baillie (New York: Dover).
Herder, Johann Gottfried (1989) *Ideen zur Philosophie der Geschichte der Menschheit*, ed. Martin Bollacher, in *Werke in zehn Bänden*, vol. 6, ed. Martin Bollacher et al. (Frankfurt am Main: Deutscher Klassiker Verlag).
Hirsch, Marianne (2012) *The Generation of Postmemory: Writing and Visual Culture after the Holocaust* (New York: Columbia University Press).
Hobsbawm, Eric J. (1996) "The End of Empires," in *After Empire: Multiethnic Societies and Nation-Building: The Soviet Union and the Russian, Ottoman, and Habsburg Empires*, eds. Karen Barkey and Mark van Hagen (Boulder, CO and Oxford: Westview Press), 12–16.
Hofmannsthal, Hugo von (1979) "Der Dichter und diese Zeit," in *Reden und Aufsätze I* (1891–1913), *Gesammelte Werke in zehn Einzelbänden*, vol. 8, ed. Bernd Schoeller (Frankfurt am Main: Suhrkamp), 54–82.
Hofmannsthal, Hugo von (1980) "Wert und Ehre deutscher Sprache," in *Reden und Aufsätze III* (1925–1929), *Gesammelte Werke in zehn Einzelbänden*, vol. 10, ed. Bernd Schoeller (Frankfurt am Main: Suhrkamp), 128–134.
Hofmannsthal, Hugo von (2005) *The Lord Chandos Letter and Other Writings*, trans. Joel Rotenberg (New York: The New York Review of Books).
Hu, Xiaoran (2020) "J. M. Coetzee: politics of the child, politics of nonposition," *Textual Practice* 34.6, 975–993.
Hunt, Lynn (1984) *Politics, Culture, and Class in the French Revolution* (Berkeley: University of California Press).
Husserl, Edmund von (1954) *Die Krisis des europäischen Menschentums und die Philosophie* (The Hague: Nijhoff).
Jacobs, Johann U. (2016) *Diaspora and Identity in South African Fiction* (Durban: University of KwaZulu-Natal Press).
Jacobs, Johann U. (2017) "A Bridging Fiction: The Migrant Subject in J. M. Coetzee's *The Childhood of Jesus*," *Journal of Literary Studies* 33.1, 59–75.
Janouch, Gustave (1968) *Gespräche mit Kafka* (Frankfurt am Main: Fischer).
Johansson, Perry (2012) *Saluting the yellow emperor: a case of Swedish sinography* (Leiden: Brill).
Judson, Pieter (2016) *The Habsburg Empire: A New History* (Cambridge, MA and London: The Belknap Press of Harvard University Press).
Kafka, Franz (1953) "Fragmente aus Heften und losen Blättern," in *Hochzeitsvorbereitungen auf dem Lande und andere Prosa aus dem Nachlass*, ed. Max Brod (New York: Schocken), 224–418.
Kafka, Franz (1958) *Briefe 1902–1924*, ed. Max Brod (Frankfurt am Main: Fischer).

Kafka, Franz (1958a) „Brief an den Vater," in *Hochzeitsvorbereitungen auf dem Lande* (Frankfurt am Main: Fischer), 162–223.
Kafka, Franz (1964) *Tagebücher 1910–1923*, ed. Max Brod (Frankfurt am Main: Fischer).
Kafka, Franz (1965) *Briefe an Felice und andere Korrespondenz aus der Verlobungszeit*, eds. Erich Heller and Jürgen Born (Frankfurt am Main: Fischer).
Kafka, Franz (1976) *The Diaries 1910–1923*, ed. Max Brod, trans. Oseph Kresh and Martin Greenberg (New York: Schocken Books).
Kafka, Franz (1980) "'Er'. Aufzeichnungen aus dem Jahre 1920," in *Beschreibung eines Kampfes: Novellen, Skizzen, Aphorismen aus dem Nachlass, Gesammelte Werke*, vol. 5, ed. Max Brod (Frankfurt am Main: Fischer), 216–222.
Kafka, Franz (1983) *Briefe an Milena*, ed. Jürgen Börn und Michael Müller (Frankfurt am Main: Fischer).
Kafka, Franz (1986a) "Betrachtungen über Sünde, Leid, Hoffnung und den wahren Weg," in *Hochzeitsvorbereitungen auf dem Lande* (Frankfurt am Main: Fischer), 30–40.
Kafka, Franz (1986b) "Das dritte Oktavheft," in *Hochzeitsvorbereitungen auf dem Lande* (Frankfurt am Main: Fischer), 52–78.
Kafka, Franz (1986c) "Das erste Oktavheft," in *Hochzeitsvorbereitungen auf dem Lande* (Frankfurt am Main: Fischer), 41–48.
Kafka, Franz (1988a) "A Country Doctor," in *The Complete Stories*, trans. Willa and Edwin Muir (New York: Schocken Books), 249–261.
Kafka, Franz (1988b) "A Hunger Artist," *in The Complete Stories*, trans. Willa and Edwin Muir (New York: Schocken Books), 300–310.
Kafka, Franz (1988c) "An Imperial Message," in *The Complete Stories*, trans. Willa and Edwin Muir (New York: Schocken Books), 24.
Kafka, Franz (1988d) "An Old Manuscript," in *The Complete Stories*, trans. Willa and Edwin Muir (New York: Schocken Books), 455–457.
Kafka, Franz (1988e) "A Report to an Academy," in *The Complete Stories*, trans. Willa and Edwin Muir (New York: Schocken Books), 281–291.
Kafka, Franz (1988f) "Before the Law," in *The Complete Stories*, trans. Willa and Edwin Muir (New York: Schocken Books), 22–23.
Kafka, Franz (1988g) "In the Penal Colony," in *The Complete Stories*, trans. Willa and Edwin Muir (New York: Schocken Books), 165–192.
Kafka, Franz (1988h) „Investigations of a Dog," in *The Complete Stories*, trans. Willa and Edwin Muir (New York: Schocken Books), 310–346.
Kafka, Franz (1988i) "On parables," in *The Complete Stories*, trans. Willa and Edwin Muir (New York: Schocken Books), 506–507.
Kafka, Franz (1988j) "The Bridge," in *The Complete Stories*, trans. Willa and Edwin Muir (New York: Schocken Books), 449.
Kafka, Franz (1988k) "The Cares of a Family Man," in *The Complete Stories*, trans. Willa and Edwin Muir (New York: Schocken Books), 469–470.
Kafka, Franz (1988l) "The Great Wall of China," in *The Complete Stories*, trans. Willa and Edwin Muir (New York: Schocken Books), 266–279.
Kafka, Franz (1988m) "The Hunter Gracchus," in *The Complete Stories*, trans. Willa and Edwin Muir (New York: Schocken Books), 256–265.
Kafka, Franz (1988n) "The News of the Building of the Wall: A Fragment," in *The Complete Stories*, trans. Willa and Edwin Muir (New York: Schocken Books), 280–282.

Kafka, Franz (1988o) "The Problem of Our Laws," in *The Complete Stories*, trans. Willa and Edwin Muir (New York: Schocken Books), 482–483.
Kafka, Franz (1988p) "The Refusal," in *The Complete Stories*, trans. Willa and Edwin Muir (New York: Schocken Books), 295–300.
Kafka, Franz (1991) *The Blue Octavo Notebooks*, ed. Max Brod, trans. Ernst Kaiser and Eithne Wilkins (Boston: Exact Change).
Kafka, Franz (1994a) "Beim Bau der chinesischen Mauer," in *Beim Bau der chinesischen Mauer und andere Schriften aus dem Nachlass. Gesammelte Werke in zwölf Bänden*, vol. 6, ed. Hans-Gerd Koch (Frankfurt am Main: Fischer), 65–80.
Kafka, Franz (1994b) *Der Proceß*, in der Fassung der Handschrift, *Gesammelte Werke in zwölf Bänden*, vol. 3, ed. Hans-Gerd Koch (Frankfurt am Main: Fischer).
Kafka, Franz (2008) *Dearest Father*, trans. Hannah and Richard Stokes (London: Oneworld Classics).
Kafka, Franz (2009) *The Trial*, trans. Mike Mitchel (Oxford and New York: Oxford University Press).
Kafka, Franz (2012) "Aphorisms," in *A Hunger Artist and Other Stories*, trans. Joyce Crick, ed. Ritchie Robertson (Oxford: Oxford University Press), 188–209.
Kannemeyer, John Christoffel (2012) *J. M. Coetzee: A Life in Writing*, trans. Michiel Heyns (Melbourne and London: Scribe).
Kant, Immanuel (2006) *Political Writings*, ed. Hans Siegbert Reiss, trans. Hugh Bart Nisbet (Cambridge: Cambridge University Press).
Kant, Immanuel (2007) *Critique of Judgment*, trans. James Creed Meredith, rev. Nicholas Walker (Oxford and Cambridge: Cambridge University Press).
Kemp, Peter (2001) "*Atonement* by Ian McEwan," in *The Sunday Times*, September 16.
Keyder, Caglar (1996) "The Ottoman Empire," in *After Empire: Multiethnic Societies and Nation-Building. The Soviet Union and the Russian, Ottoman, and Habsburg Empires*, eds. Karen Barkey and Mark van Hagen (Boulder, CO and Oxford: Westview Press), 30–44.
Koch, Hans-Gerd (2011) *Geteilte Post: 28 Briefe an Grete Bloch* (Marbach am Neckar: Deutsche Schillergesellschaft).
Koch, Manfred (2002) *Weimarer Weltbewohner: Zur Genese von Goethes Begriff 'Weltliteratur'* (Tübingen: Niemeyer).
Kojève, Alexandre (1952) "Les romans de la sagesse," *Critique* (Clandeboye, Man) 60, 387–397.
Kożuchowski, Adam (2013) *The Afterlife of Austria-Hungary: The Image of the Habsburg Monarchy in Interwar Europe* (Pittsburgh: University of Pittsburgh Press).
Kraus, Karl (1898) *Eine Krone für Zion* (Vienna: Frisch).
Kristeva, Julia (1991) *Strangers to Ourselves*, trans. Leon S. Roudiez (London: Columbia University Press).
Kristeva, Julia (1993) *Nations without Nationalism*, trans. Leon S. Roudiez (New York: Columbia University Press).
Kundszus, Winfried (1964) "Erzählhaltung und Zeitverschiebung in Kafkas 'Prozeß' und 'Schloß'," *Deutsche Vierteljahrsschrift für Literaturwissenschaft und Geistesgeschichte* 38, 192–207.
Kundszus, Winfried (1970) "Erzählperspektive und Erzählgeschehen in Kafkas 'Prozeß'," *Deutsche Vierteljahrsschrift für Literaturwissenschaft und Geistesgeschichte* 44, 306–317.
Kurtz, Arabella and Coetzee, John Maxwell (2015) *The Good Story: Exchanges on Truth, Fiction, and Psychotherapy* (London: Vintage).

Lacan, Jacques (1978) *The Four Fundamental Concepts of Psycho-Analysis*, trans. Alan Sheridan (New York: Norton).
Lacan, Jacques (1987) *The Seminar. Book I: Freud's Papers on Technique, 1953–1954*, trans. John Forrester, ed. Jacques-Alain Miller (Cambridge: Cambridge University Press).
Lacan, Jacques (1988) *The Seminar. Book II: The Ego in Freud's Theory and in the Technique of Psychoanalysis, 1954–1955*, trans. Sylvana Tomaselli, ed. Jacques-Alain Miller (Cambridge: Cambridge University Press).
Lacan, Jacques (1991) *Le Séminaire. Livre XVII: L'envers de la psychanalyse, 1969–70*, ed. Jacques Alain Miller (Paris: Seuil).
Lacan, Jacques (2006) *Écrits*, trans. Bruce Fink in collaboration with Héloïse Fink and Russell Grigg (New York: Norton).
Lamb, Jonathan (2011) "Sympathy with Animals and Salvation of Soul," *The Eighteenth Century* 52.1, 69–85.
Leavis, Frank R. (1969) *English Literature in Our Time and the University: The Clark Lectures 1967* (London: Chatto and Windus).
Levinas, Emmanuel (1969) *Totality and Infinity*, trans. Alphonso Lingis (Pittsburgh: Duquesne University Press).
Levinas, Emmanuel (1986) "The Trace of the Other," in *Deconstruction in Context*, trans. Alphonso Lingis, ed. Mark C. Taylor (Chicago: The University of Chicago Press), 345–359.
Levinas, Emmanuel (1987) *Existence and Existents*, trans. Alphonso Lingis (Pittsburgh: Duquesne University Press).
Levinas. Emmanuel (1990) *Difficult Freedom: Essays on Judaism*, trans. Seán Hand (Baltimore: Johns Hopkins University Press).
Levinas, Emmanuel (1996) "Transcendence and Height," in *Basic Philosophical Writings*, trans. Peter Atterton et al., eds. Adriaan T. Peperzak, Simon Critchley, and Robert Bernasconi (Bloomington: Indiana University Press), 11–33.
Lévi-Strauss, Claude (1987) *Introduction to the Work of Marcel Mauss*, trans. F. Baker (London: Routledge).
Liska, Vivian (2017) *German-Jewish Thought and Its Afterlife* (Bloomington: Indiana University Press).
Liska, Vivian and Naomi Conen (2014) "A same other, another same: Walter Benjamin and Maurice Blanchot on translation," *The German Quarterly* 87.2, 229–245.
Litowitz, Douglas E. (2002) "Franz Kafka's Outsider Jurisprudence," *Law and Social Inquiry* 27.1, 103–137.
Loomba, Ania (1998) *Colonialism/Postcolonialism* (New York: Routledge).
Louvel, Liliane, Gilles Ménégaldo, and Anne-Laure Fortin (1995) "An Interview with Ian McEwan" (conducted November 1994), *Études Britanniques Contemporaines* 8, 1–12.
Luhmann, Niklas (1986a) "Das Kunstwerk und die Selbstreproduktion der Kunst," in *Stil: Geschichte und Funktion eines kulturwissenschaftlichen Diskurselement*s, eds. Hans Ulrich Gumbrecht and Karl Ludwig Pfeiffer (Frankfurt am Main: Suhrkamp), 620–672.
Luhmann, Niklas (1986b) "Intersubjektivität oder Kommunikation: Unterschiedliche Ausgangspunkte soziologischer Theoriebildung," *Archivio di Filosofia* 54, 41–60.
Luhmann, Niklas (1989) "Individuum, Individualität, Individualismus", in *Gesellschaftsstruktur und Semantik: Studien zur Wissenssoziologie der modernen Gesellschaft*, vol. 3 (Frankfurt am Main: Suhrkamp), 149–258.

Luhmann, Niklas (1990a) "Das Erkenntnisprogramm des Konstruktivismus und die unbekannt bleibende Realität," in *Soziologische Aufklärung: Konstruktivistische Perspektiven*, vol. 5 (Opladen: Westdeutscher Verlag), 31–58.
Luhmann, Niklas (1990b) "Weltkunst," in *Unbeobachtbare Welt: Über Kunst und Architektur*, eds. Dirk Baecker and Frederic D. Bunsen and Niklas Luhmann (Bielefeld: Haux), 7–45.
Luhmann, Niklas (1995) *Die Kunst der Gesellschaft* (Frankfurt am Main: Suhrkamp).
Luhmann, Niklas (1997) *Die Gesellschaft der Gesellschaft* (Frankfurt am Main: Suhrkamp).
Lynn, David (2007) "A Conversation with Ian McEwan", *Kenyon Review* 29.3, 38–51.
Marais, Mike (2009) *The Secretary of the Invisible: The Idea of Hospitality in the Fiction of J. M. Coetzee* (Amsterdam and New York: Rodopi).
Marcus, Laura (2009) "Ian McEwan's Modernist Time: *Atonement* and *Saturday*," in *Ian McEwan: Contemporary Critical Perspectives*, ed. Sebastian Groes (London and New York: Continuum), 83–98.
Matar, Anat (2018) "Maurice Blanchot: Modernism, Dissidence and the Privilege of Writing," *Critical Horizons: A Journal of Philosophy and Social Theory* 19.1, 67–80.
McEwan, Ian (1992) *Black Dogs* (London: Vintage).
McEwan, Ian (2001) *Atonement* (London: Vintage).
McEwan, Ian (2002) "Mother Tongue – A Memoir," in *On Modern British Fiction*, ed. Zachary Leader (Oxford: Oxford University Press).
McEwan, Ian (2005) *Saturday* (London: Jonathan Cape).
Micali, Simona (2017) "Aspettando i barbari. Conrad, Kafka, Coetzee," *Between* 7.14, 1–23.
Mignolo, Walter (2000) "The Many Faces of Cosmo-Polis: Border Thinking and Critical Cosmopolitanism," *Public Culture* 12.3, 721–748.
Mosca, Valeria (2016) "Ideas and embodied souls: Platonic and Christian intertexts in J. M. Coetzee's *Elizabeth Costello* and *The Childhood of Jesus*," *European Journal of English Studies* 20.2, 127–138.
Motyl, Alexander J. (1996) "Thinking about Empire," in *After Empire: Multiethnic Societies and Nation-Building. The Soviet Union and the Russian, Ottoman, and Habsburg Empires*, eds. Karen Barkey and Mark van Hagen (Boulder, CO and Oxford: Westview Press), 19–29.
Müller-Seidel, Walter (1986) *Die Deportation des Menschen: Kafkas Erzählung "In der Strafkolonie" im europäischen Kontext* (Stuttgart: Metzler).
Mulhall, Stephen (2009) *The Wounded Animal: J. M. Coetzee & the Difficulty of Reality in Literature & Philosophy* (Princeton, NJ: Princeton University Press).
Musil, Robert (2014) *Der Mann ohne Eigenschaften* (Reinbek: Rowohlt).
Nietzsche, Friedrich (1980) *Ecce homo. Sämtliche Werke*, vol. 6, eds. Giorgio Colli and Massimo Montinari (Berlin: De Gruyter).
Nietzsche, Friedrich (1996) *On the Genealogy of Morals: A Polemic*, trans. Douglas Smith (Oxford and New York: Oxford University Press).
Nietzsche, Friedrich (2010) *The Joyful Wisdom*, trans. Thomas Common (Adelaide: Ebooks).
Northover, Richard Alan (2012) "Elizabeth Costello as a Socratic Figure," *English in Africa* 39.1, 37–55.
O'Sullivan, Michael (2011) "Giving Up Control: Narrative Authority and Animal Experience in Coetzee and Kafka," *Mosaic: a journal for the interdisciplinary study of literature* 44.2, 119–135.
Pawel, Ernst (1984) *The Nightmare of Reason: A Life of Franz Kafka* (New York: Farrar Straus Giroux).

Penner, Dick (1986) "Sight, blindness and double thought in J. M. Coetzee's *Waiting for the Barbarians,*" *World literature written in English* 26.1, 34–45.
Philippou, Eleni (2016) "Dogs, Horses, and Red Herrings: The Animal in J. M. Coetzee's *The Childhood of Jesus,*" *Critique: Studies in Contemporary Fiction* 57.2, 217–227.
Politzer, Heinz (1962) *Franz Kafka: Parable and Paradox* (Ithaca, NY: Cornell University Press).
Povinelli, Elisabeth (2011) *Economies of Abandonment: Social Belonging and Endurance in Late Liberalism* (Durham and London: Duke University Press).
Press, Gerald A. (1993) "Introduction," in Press, Gerald A., ed., *Plato's Dialogues: New Studies and Interpretations* (Lanham, MD: Rowman and Littlefield).
Probyn Elspeth (1996) *Outside Belongings* (London and New York: Routledge).
Promitzer, Christian (2003) "The South Slavs in the Austrian Imagination: Serbs and Slovenes in the Changing View from German Nationalism to National Socialism," *Creating the Other: Ethnic Conflict and Nationalism in Habsburg Central Europe*, ed. Nancy M. Wingfield (New York and Oxford: Berghahn Books), 183–215.
Puchner, Martin (2011) "J. M. Coetzee's Novels of Thinking," *Raritan* 30.4, 1–12.
Rancière, Jacques (1999) *Disagreement: Politics and Philosophy*, trans. Julie Rose (University of Minnesota Press: Minneapolis).
Rancière, Jacques (2004) *The Flesh of Words: The Politics of Writing*, trans. Charlotte Mandell (Stanford: Stanford University Press).
Renan, Ernest (2006) "What Is a Nation," in *Becoming National: A Reader*, eds. Geoff Eley and Ronald Grigor Suny (Oxford and New York: Oxford University Press), 41–55.
Robertson, Richie (2009) "Introduction," in Kafka, Franz, *The Trial*, trans. Mike Mitchel (Oxford and New York: Oxford University Press), xi–xxvi.
Robinson, Forrest G. (2012) "Writing as Penance: National Guilt and J. M. Coetzee," *Arizona Quarterly: A Journal of American Literature, Culture, and Theory* 68.1, 1–54.
Rosa, Hartmut et al. (2010) *Theorien der Gemeinschaft zur Einführung* (Hamburg: Junius).
Roth, Joseph (2002) *The Radetzky March*, trans. Michael Hofmann (London: Granta Books).
Ryan, Michael (1982) *Marxism and Deconstruction: A Critical Articulation* (Baltimore: Johns Hopkins University Press).
Said, Edward (1978) *Orientalism* (New York: Vintage).
Samolsky, Russell (2011) *Apocalyptic Futures: Marked Bodies and the Violence of the Text in Kafka, Conrad, and Coetzee* (New York: Fordham University Press).
Schenk, Frithjof Benjamin (2013) "Travel, Railroads, and Identity Formation in the Russian Empire," in *Shatterzone of Empires: Coexistence and Violence in the German, Habsburg, Russian and Ottoman Borderlands*, eds. Omer Bartov and Eric D. Weitz (Bloomington: Indiana University Press), 136–151.
Schlegel, August Wilhelm (1965) *Geschichte der romantischen Literatur. Kritische Schriften und Briefe*, vol. 4, ed. Edgar Lohner (Stuttgart: Kohlhammer).
Schmitt, Carl (1985) *Political Theology*, trans. George Schwab (Cambridge: MIT Press).
Schmitt, Carl (1995) *Staat, Großraum, Nomos* (Berlin: Duncker & Humblot).
Schuman, Rebecca (2012) "'Unerschütterlich': Kafka's *Proceß*, Wittgenstein's *Tractatus*, and the Law of Logic," *The German Quarterly* 85.2, 156–172.
Scott, Joanna (1997) "Voice and Trajectory: An Interview with J. M Coetzee," *Salmagundi* 114–115, 82–102.
Seaboyer, Judith (2005) "Ian McEwan: Contemporary Realism and the Novel of Ideas," in *The Contemporary British Novel*, eds. James Acheson and Sarah C. E. Ross (Edinburgh: Edinburgh University Press), 23–34.

Sedgwick, Kosofsky Eve (2003) *Touching Feeling: Affect, Pedagogy, Performativity* (Durham, NC: Duke University Press).
Silverman, Kaja (1986) *The Threshold of the Visible World* (New York and London: Routledge).
Silverman, Kaja (1988) *The Acoustic Mirror: The Female Voice in Psychoanalysis and Cinema* (Bloomington: Indiana University Press).
Slaughter, Joseph R. (2007) *Human Rights, Inc.* (New York: Fordham University Press).
Starr, Peter (1995) *Logics of Failed Revolt: French Theory after May '68* (Stanford: Stanford University Press).
Stern, David G. (1996) *Wittgenstein on Mind and Language* (New York: Oxford University Press).
Stölzl, Christoph (1975) *Kafkas böses Böhmen: Zur Sozialgeschichte eines Prager Juden* (Munich: Text+Kritik).
Stourzh, Gerald (1994) "Ethnic Attribution in Late Imperial Austria: Good Intentions, Evil Consequences," in *The Habsburg Legacy: National Identity in Historical Perspective*, eds. Ritchie Robertson and Edward Timms (Edinburgh: Edinburgh University Press), 67–83.
Tegla, Emanuela (2012) "*Age of Iron*: The Collective Dimension of Shame and of Responsibility," *Journal of Southern African Studies* 38.4, 967–980.
Teubner, Günther (2012) "Das Recht vor seinem Gesetz: Franz Kafka zur (Un-)Möglichkeit einer Selbstreflexion des Rechts"; "The Law before Its Law: Franz Kafka on the (Im-)Possibility of Law's Self-Reflection" (parallel English trans. by Alison Lewis), *Ancilla Iuris*, 176–203.
Thum, Gregor (2013) "Megalomania and Angst: The Nineteenth-century Mythicization of Germany's Eastern Borderlands," in *Shatterzone of Empires: Coexistence and Violence in the German, Habsburg, Russian and Ottoman Borderlands*, eds. Omer Bartov and Eric D. Weitz (Bloomington: Indiana University Press), 42–60.
Todorova, Maria (1997) *Imagining the Balkans* (New York and Oxford: Oxford University Press).
Valdez Moses, Michael (1993) "The Mark of Empire: Writing, History, and Torture in Coetzee's *Waiting for the Barbarians*," *The Kenyon Review* 15.1, 115–127.
Vallury, Raji (2009) "Politicizing Art in Rancière and Deleuze: The Case of Postcolonial Literature," in *Jacques Rancière: History, Politics, Aesthetics*, eds. Gabriel Rockhill and Philip Watts (Durham and London: Duke University Press), 229–249.
Vermeulen, Pieter (2013) "Abandoned Creatures: Creaturely Life and the Novel Form in J. M. Coetzee's *Slow Man*," *Studies in the Novel* 45.4, 655–674.
Vlies, Andrew van der (2017) *Present Imperfect: Contemporary South African Writing* (Oxford: Oxford University Press).
Wachtel, Eleanor (2001) "The Sympathetic Imagination: A Conversation with J. M. Coetzee," *Brick* 57, 37–47.
Walkowitz, Rebecca L. (2009) "Comparison Literature," *New Literary History* 40.3, 567–85.
Wanberg, Kyle (2016) "The writer's inadequate response: *Elizabeth Costello* and the influence of Kafka and Hofmannsthal," *European Journal of English Studies* 20.2, 152–165.
Watson, Stephen (1996) "Colonialism and the Novels of J. M. Coetzee," in *Critical Perspectives on J. M. Coetzee*, eds. Graham Huggan and Stephen Watson (London: Macmillan Press), 13–36.
Weber, Samuel (2010) *Benjamin's –abilities* (Boston and Harvard: Harvard University Press).
Wetzell, Richard F. (2000) *Inventing the Criminal* (Chapel Hill: University of North Carolina Press).
Wicomb, Zoë (2009) "*Slow Man* and the Real: A Lesson in Reading and Writing," *JLS/TLW* 25.4, 7–24.

Wiedemann, Conrad (1993) "Deutsche Klassik und nationale Identität: Eine Revision der Sonderwegs-Frage," in *Klassik im Vergleich*, ed. Wilhelm Voßkamp (Stuttgart: Metzler), 541–569.
Wittenberg, Herman and Highman, Kate (2015) "Sven Hedin's "Vanished country": setting and history in J. M. Coetzee's *Waiting for the barbarians,*" *Scrutiny2* 20.1, 103–127.
Wittgenstein, Ludwig (1980) *Notebooks 1914–1916*, eds. G. H. von Wright and G. E. M. Anscombe (Chicago: The University of Chicago Press).
Wittgenstein, Ludwig (2016) *Tractatus Logico-Philosophicus* (London: Chiron Academic Press).
Wolff, Larry (2013) "The Traveler's View of Central Europe: Gradual Transitions and Degrees of Difference in European Borderlands," in *Shatterzone of Empires: Coexistence and Violence in the German, Habsburg, Russian and Ottoman Borderlands*, eds. Omer Bartov and Eric D. Weitz (Bloomington: Indiana University Press), 23–41.
Zahra, Tara (2010) "Imagined Noncommunities: National Indifference as a Category of Analysis," *Slavic Review* 69.1, 93–119.
Zimbler, Jarad (2014) *J. M. Coetzee and the politics of style* (New York: Cambridge University Press).
Ziolkowski, Theodore (1997) *The Mirror of Justice: Literary Reflections of Legal Crises* (Princeton and Oxford: Princeton University Press).

Index

Abu Ghraib/Guantanamo Bay 165, 174
Adoption
– 'analogical filter' 25, 210–211
– appropriation 23, 170, 178, 182
– assimilation 180–181
– of children 217
– subversion through 34, 97, 131, 141, 150
– witnessing by 176
Adorno, Theodor Wiesengrund 134–135
Africa/n 1, 30, 155, 157, 161, 198, 206, 212
Afrikaner 7, 13, 15, 153–154, 156, 197
– National Party 155–156
– nationalism 154
– settlers 154
Agamben, Giorgio 6, 8, 15, 17–18, 34, 44, 47–49, 51–52, 56, 60–62, 75, 78, 88–89, 94–97, 103, 128, 134, 234
Ahmad, Aijaz 179
Albania/n 32
Albrecht, Andrea 46
Alden, Natasha 224, 227, 232
Alexander the Great 115
Alexander, Jeffrey 57
Alexander, King 31
Alt, Peter-André 162
Althusser, Louis 107, 123, 181, 200–202, 205, 209–210
America/n 153, 164–165, 175
Amselle, Jean-Loup 180
Anderson, Benedict 9–10, 102, 176, 193
Animal 79
– abandoned 24, 190, 195
– ape 24, 128, 205–207
– bat 207
– beetle 169, 190, 209
– bird 199
– caged 98, 111
– cat 183, 206
– cockroach 169
– cricket 169
– death cries of 128, 208–210
– dog 37, 115–116, 127, 184–185, 190, 192–193, 195, 209, 217
– fish 132

– fox 132
– frog 159, 207
– grasshopper 207
– horse 2, 115
– vs. human 37–38
– hunt or killing of 22, 133, 168, 180, 193
– idleness 181
– insect 20, 133, 169
– jackdaw 159
– lamb 195
– lobster 133
– midge 207
– mole 198, 149
– mouse 132
– ox 159
– oyster 207
– penguin 206
– poisoned 208
– pork 122
– ram 207
– rat 133, 190, 208–209
– scapegoat 207
– seal 204
– sheep 190
– spider 127
– suffering 24, 210
– tortured 4
– turkey 122
– vermin 129
– voices of 128, 192, 208–210
– worm 122, 135, 169
– wounded 195, 207
Antonescu, Ion 31
Apartheid 163–164, 181–182, 186
Appadurai, Arjun 9, 31–32, 66, 126, 201
Apter, Emily 10, 56
Arab/ian 162
Arendt, Hannah 53, 59, 150
Aristotle 61
Attridge, Derek 40, 146, 149, 203, 214
Attwell, David 166, 168–169, 175, 182
Ausenda, Giorgio 159
Austen, Jane 233

Auster, Paul 154, 194
Australia/n 164–165, 175, 203, 216–217
– vs. Europe 210, 212
– vs. US 174, 201
Austria/n 13, 30, 83, 130, 152
Author-character relationship 4, 21, 197
– absent author 19–21, 74–75, 131
– assignee 20, 110–125
– division between vs. within them 2
– doppelganger 2, 8, 24, 26, 93–94, 96–98, 119–120, 157, 171, 210–211, 226, 228, 232, 235
– entanglement 21, 129, 131, 227
– ethics 227–228, 232
– mutual responsibility 4, 216
– narrator 2, 107–108, 115, 120, 129, 225
– politics 6–8, 133, 235
– selfish to one another 4, 26, 233
Authority
– Absent God 80, 148
– 'agentless' 19, 123, 202, 211
– call or interpellation of 123
– 'command from beyond' 8, 223
– dethroned 205
– elevated through humiliation 149, 172
– equivocal 7
– exempted 97, 102, 218, 232
– fragile 204
– High Address 223
– "high command" 19–20
– narrative 2, 7, 19, 100–109, 127, 135, 141–142, 157, 173–174, 177, 194–196, 218
– ruined 205
– "secretary of the invisible" 108, 202, 212
– self-dispossessing 8, 127
– sheltering 225
– standpoint of redemption 24, 185, 192
– supreme or ultimate 19, 71, 102, 235
– transcendental 61, 63, 185, 224
– transmitter of the Muses 202

Bacon, Francis 25, 208
Badiou, Alain 36
Bakhtin, Mikhail 2, 4, 97, 138–139, 145, 165–166, 174, 227
Bakić-Hayden, Milica 30

Bales, Kevin 58
Balkans 30, 206
Baltic 30
Banfield, Ann 75
Barkey, Karen 32, 34
Barthes, Roland 75
Baudelaire, Charles 49
Bauer, Felice 93–94, 185
Bauman, Zygmunt 40, 66
Beckett, Samuel 5, 175, 179, 194
Beebee, Thomas 9–10
Begam, Richard 162
Beißner, Friedrich 97
Beller, Stephen 11, 12, 45, 67
Belonging
– deprived or bereft or stripped of 6, 57, 130, 174
– detached from 157
– divided 7
– ecstasy (ex-stasis)-b. 189, 192
– vs. longing 7, 10, 21, 34–35, 38, 49, 55, 130
– mixed 158
– vs. non-belonging 7, 38, 57, 156–159, 175
– to nowhere 179, 199
– shame of 185, 192–196
– to somewhere 179
Benjamin, Walter 3, 11–12, 15–18, 44–58, 73–80, 88–90, 96, 111–112, 115–116, 127–128, 134, 150, 188, 208–209, 218, 227
Bentham, Jeremy 102
Berber 162
Berend, Ivan 31–32
Bergengruen, Maximilian 86–87, 105
Bergson, Henri 49
Berlin 11, 93, 185
Bewes, Timothy 99, 196
Bhabha, Homi 5, 10, 15–16, 29, 33, 43–58, 117, 123, 132, 150
Biko, Steven 161
Biti, Vladimir 8, 222
Blanchot, Maurice 16–18, 41, 59–67, 73–82, 88–90, 96, 127, 208–209, 223
Bloch, Grete 93–94, 147, 185
Body 206
– aging 183

– all-embracing 188
– vs. conscience 22, 183–186
– corpse 166
– disfigured 22, 169, 171
– disgraced 150, 171
– erotic 183–184, 210
– female 182, 188, 192
– girl's 22, 166
– Gothic prohibition of 210
– graceless 183–184, 186–188
– gracious 183, 186–188
– mutilated 22, 150, 209
– privileged 185
– rebellion 171
– suffering 189
– surface for engravings 22
– tortured 150, 169, 209
– woman's 182–183
– wounded 166, 206
Boehmer, Elleke 170, 177–178, 203, 205, 217–218
Bosnia and Herzegovina 32
British 164, 178
– colonialism 13, 153
– Commonwealth 5
– habitus 14, 179
– identity 14
– patriotism 155
– Union Party 155
Broch, Hermann 12
Brod, Max 53, 98, 108, 113, 145
Brouillette, Sarah 179, 185
Brown, Wendy 57
Brubaker, Rogers 11, 15, 30, 32, 35, 56, 126
Budapest 31
Bulgaria/n 32
Bush, George W. 164
Butler, Judith 6, 34, 57, 148, 200–201
Byron, Lord 192–193

Calvino, Italo 141
Canberra 164
Canetti, Elias 93, 149, 169
Cape Town 154, 162, 175, 181
Caruth, Cathy 136
Cassin, Barbara 49
Catholic/Catholicism 12, 154

Cervantes, Miguel 5
Chakrabarty, Dipesh 29
Child 79, 192
– abandoned 25, 169, 184, 225–226
– abuse 169
– adopted 217
– beaten 169, 195
– dismembered 225–226
– incarnated god 204
– misfortunate 204
– neglected 217
– non-position 191
– participant in violence 195
– sacrificed 187, 217, 226
– tortured 169
– violated 24, 169
China/Chinese 19, 74, 84, 162, 164–165, 183
– Chang-Kai-check 163
– Great Wall 19–20, 84, 100–101, 108
– Han 162
– vs. Huns 101
– Lop Nor 162
– Lou-lan 163
– Mao Zedong 186
– Ming 100
– vs. Mongols 100, 162–163
– Qin 100
– Qing 163
– Tibet 163
– unification 100–101
– vs. Uyghurs 163
– Xinjiang 163
Christian/ity 135, 212
Citton, Yves 79
Clarkson, Carrol 174
Coetzee, John Maxwell 1, 3–4, 6, 7–9, 13, 21–25, 123
– *Age of Iron* 4, 184, 191–192, 196
– *Boyhood* 147, 156
– *Diary of a Bad Year* 157, 164, 173–174, 191, 194, 196, 206, 214
– *Disgrace* 3–4, 23–24, 106, 168, 174, 180–197
– *Doubling the Point* 83, 108, 132, 153–154, 165, 167–168, 174, 177, 202–203, 209, 214
– *Dusklands* 132, 153, 158, 162, 169, 173, 181

- *Elizabeth Costello* 4, 24–25, 108, 167, 174, 184, 190, 193, 198–218
- *Foe* 3–4, 184, 191, 193, 215
- *Homage* 172, 175, 179, 205, 212
- *In the Heart of the Country* 158, 162, 174, 184
- *Inner Workings* 149
- *Life & Times of Michael K.* 3, 148, 169, 181
- *Scenes from Provincial Life* 145–147, 155
- *Short Works* 177
- *Slow Man* 4, 177–178, 184, 193, 215–218
- *Stranger Shores* 198
- *Summertime* 6, 29, 147
- *The Childhood of Jesus* 174, 178, 184, 209
- *The Lives of Animals* 198
- *The Master of Petersburg* 162, 167, 184, 192
- *The novel today* 165
- *The Schooldays of Jesus* 178, 184, 209
- *Truth in Autobiography* 145
- *Waiting for the Barbarians* 3–4, 22–23, 158–181, 183, 191, 195–196, 209, 211
- *What is Realism?* 198, 203
- *White Writing* 181
- *Youth* 147–148
Cohen, Gary B. 102
Colonialism
- American 173
- British 13, 153
- Dutch 173, 194
- European 43, 206, 212
- French 85, 138, 165
- hard 1, 101, 153, 180
- soft 1, 101, 180
Colony
- animal 206
- British 179
- cultural 32
- economic 32
- European 33, 206
- French 85, 138, 165
- German 120
- inner 20, 110
- penal 85, 120–121, 137–138
- political 33, 85, 120, 179, 206
Community
- anachronous 29–30
- anchored 38
- of belonging 34–35
- bond 31
- Christian 36
- consensual 24
- dissensual 24
- ethical 222–224
- imagined 31
- imperial 84, 110
- literary 223, 235
- national 34–35
- 'New International' 40, 222
- organic 38
- provincial 33–34, 179
- sacrificial 136
- scattered 199
- vs. society 20, 34
- to-come 55, 57, 218
- transborder 5–6, 14, 33–35, 179, 185
- unmoored 22, 141
- uprooted 22
Conen, Naomi 74
Congo/an 161–162, 165
Conrad, Joseph 5, 23, 161, 173, 175, 178–180, 194
Conti, Christopher 2, 93, 96, 98, 138, 149, 184–185, 196
Cormack, Alistair 226
Cornwall, Mark 33
Creature 3
- aboriginal 206
- debased 158, 190
- degenerate 36, 120, 122, 140, 158–159, 180–181, 206
- discarded 193
- dumb beings 210
- inanimate 190
- infinitesimal 149, 169, 204
- insignificant 158
- negligible 190
- non-humans 6, 34
- spectral humans 6, 34, 126
- subaltern 37, 52, 118
- subhuman or animal 4, 6, 19–21, 37, 115, 126–129
- would-be humans 6, 34
Croatia/n 31–32, 177, 217
Currie, Mark 201

Czech/oslovakia 5, 6, 30–31, 83, 129–130, 151–153, 159, 182

Danta, Chris 193, 207
Defoe, Daniel 5, 175, 179, 194, 198, 215
Deleuze, Gilles 17–18, 56–57, 66, 76–83, 88–90, 96, 128
De Man, Paul 10
Derrida, Jacques 38, 40–41, 48, 60, 67, 89, 132, 148, 154, 164, 217, 221–224, 227, 232–235
Désoeuvrement
– unworking (Blanchot) 17, 61–62, 81–82
Deterritorialization (Deleuze/Guattari) 23, 98, 161, 198–218
– actual 17, 22, 32, 57, 66, 76
– virtual 17, 22, 32, 57, 66, 71, 73, 76, 80
Dialogism
– Bakhtin's 213
– in Coetzee 167, 174, 213–214
– in McEwan 230–231, 234–235
Dickens, Charles 124
Diepeveen, Leonard 177
Disjunctive conjunction
– art and life 228–229
– attachment and detachment 5, 7, 197, 212
– author and character 197
– center and periphery 146–147, 212
– community and society 34
– contagious entanglement 118–120
– dis/identification 7, 22, 99, 146, 196
– fathers and sons 135–138, 141–142
– females and males 213
– fiction and faction 10
– fiction and philosophy 63, 213
– humans and animals 213
– humans and gods 213
– imagination and reason 213
– inferior and superior 118–120, 128, 141
– internal exterior 128
– irreconcilable interdependence 10, 99
– majors and minors 79, 217
– of "original sins" 91–99, 134–142
– past and present 16, 60, 90, 212
– powerless and powerful 3, 40, 61, 65, 67, 119, 136–140, 189
– predecessor and successor 62

– religion and art 213
– subhuman and superhuman 195–198, 148–149, 157
– the juridical and the literary 213
– toxic infiltration 5, 141
Dispossession 3
– of belonging 38, 57, 149
– dispossessed dispossessor 22, 65, 148, 151–156
– enforced "animal" 40
– free "human" 40
– by humans 148
– of humans 148
– of identity qualities or attributes 55, 149
– multiple 21, 129–130, 152
– source of pride 44–46, 55, 67
Dodd, William J. 2, 138
Dostoevsky, Fyodor 2, 5, 93, 97, 138, 149, 165, 167–168, 174–175, 179, 194
Du Bois, William E. B. 123, 150
During, Simon 173
Durrant, Sam 167
Dutch 154, 173, 194, 217

Écriture
– Barthes/Blanchot (writing) 17, 61–62, 75
Elam, Julie 224, 227, 230–232
Elective affiliation 5, 44
– "affiliative solidarity" 46
– affinities 226
– alliance 14
– "insurgent intersubjectivity" (Bhabha) 44
– kindred souls 8, 176
– kinship 9–10, 15–16
– relatives 167–168, 172–176, 178, 190, 194, 211
Eliot, Thomas S. 233
Elshamy, Nashwa Mohammad 175
Empire
– administration 102, 158
– Austro-Hungarian 6, 11, 14, 19, 66–67, 100, 151–153, 162 (Dual Monarchy 5, 101, 158)
– vs. barbarians 22, 29, 159–167, 169–181
– Belgian 161, 165
– borderland 158, 161
– breakup 152

– British 5, 7, 14, 55, 132, 153, 224
– Byzantine 159
– Carolingian 159
– center 29, 101, 110, 145–147, 160–161
– Chinese 19, 84–85, 100–101, 162, 165
– disintegration 19, 153
– dissolution 35
– Dutch 7, 14, 132, 153
– East-Central European 1, 11, 14, 34
– French 14, 85, 165–166, 180
– frontier 158, 172
– German 11, 14, 44, 46, 55, 85, 150
– Habsburg 19, 32, 34, 67, 102
– Islamic 159
– late/outgoing 32, 121, 153
– modernization 31–33, 101
– vs. nation-state 30
– Ottoman 11, 14, 34
– periphery/province 33, 101, 110, 147, 151, 160
– Portuguese 14
– reform 138
– Roman 159
– Russian 11, 14, 32, 138, 162
– Spanish 14
– transition 101
– unification 19, 101, 162
– West European 1, 14, 138
England/English 35, 46, 177, 194–195
– language 7, 13, 15, 154, 178–179, 190
Enlightenment 11, 36–37, 222
Entrusting
– to attendants 199
– call or dictate of the Muse 202
– deathbed 104
– direct 84, 118, 124, 199
– to a distant addressee 21, 104, 199–202
– indirect 104, 118, 124, 136, 199–200, 202
– intended 199
– via lecture 24, 98–218
– via lesson 24, 98–218
– "secretary of the invisible" 108, 202, 212
– shouting 119–120
– summoning or interpellation 107–108, 123, 200–202, 209–211, 216
– the author by the character 118–119
– unintended 199

– whispering 104, 119, 131
– "you" 110–112, 130–131, 199–201, 203
Erasmus 191
Eshel, Amir 164–165
Esposito, Roberto 34
Ethics 223, 233
– commitment to 25, 227
– vs. politics 17, 21, 25, 52, 64, 67, 132–134, 221–235
– transcendental 71
Europe 9, 155, 170
– Central 1, 5, 41
– Christian 30
– East Central 1, 14–15, 29, 30, 31, 35, 40–41, 66, 101, 158, 217
– external others 29
– geographical E. 39
– hybrid origin 39
– indistinct entity 39, 41
– infinite task 39–40
– internal others 29
– platform of unification 35, 42
– post-imperial 14, 29–42
– postcolonial 36–41, 223
– rescuer of humankind 39
– spiritual 39
– Turkish 30
– West 1, 14–15, 29, 30–31, 35, 41, 66
Evans, R. J. W. 33
Extemporality vs. extratemporality 50, 81, 128–129, 131, 166
Exterritoriality vs. extraterritoriality 3, 50, 81, 128–129, 166

Face 32, 141, 172
– vs. defacement 42, 172
– frightened 113
– grimacing 176
– withdrawing 80, 176
Fanon, Frantz 123, 135, 150
Finney, Brian 227, 232
Floating signifier 165, 172, 175
– apology of 50
– elusive signification 75
– Lévi-Strauss 47
– subhuman 157, 177
– superhuman 157, 177

Foster, Greg 166
Foucault, Michel 16–17, 41, 59–67, 83–84, 102–105, 108, 110, 137, 149–150, 165, 173, 182, 186, 189, 191, 202, 211, 223
Franz Joseph, Emperor 105
France/French 35, 170, 217
– culture 46
– Empire 85, 138, 180
– language 137, 140, 154
– Republic 17
– Revolution 8–9, 44, 59–60
Freud, Sigmund 12, 38, 49, 59, 112, 135–136
Friedman, Lawrence M. 105
Fritzsche, Peter 35, 116, 126, 201

Gasché, Rodolphe 39
German/y 6–8, 15, 30, 35, 55, 85, 129, 155, 177
– baroque 208
– Germandom 11, 150
– Germanization 11
– Jews 11
– identity 46
– language 82, 129–130, 151–153
– nation/alism 11, 150
– Nazi/sm 13, 215
– Romanticism 44, 46, 63, 90, 222
– Weimar 11, 13, 30, 51, 150
Gilroy, Paul 9
Goethe, Johann Wolfgang von 51
Graham, Lucy 174
Gray, Richard T. 127
Greece/Greek 30, 154
Groes, Sebastian 224, 226, 228, 232
Guattari, Félix 17–18, 56–57, 66, 76–77, 79–83, 88–90, 96, 128
Guha, Ranajit 29, 158
Guilt 94, 235
– attracted by 86, 92
– cleansed of 92, 96–98
– reparation for past misdeeds 187, 235
– vs. shame 18, 98, 176, 196–197
– toward animals 207

Haase, Ulrich 223
Habermas, Jürgen 40
Hanson, Stephen E. 35

Hartman, Geoffrey 176, 193
Head, Dominic 176, 231
Hedin, Sven 163, 171
Hegel, Georg Wilhelm Friedrich 90, 100, 148, 157–158, 160
Heidegger, Martin 38–39
Heindl, Robert 120, 138, 171
Herder, Johann Gottfried 39, 46
Highman, Kate 161–164
Hirsch, Marianne 126
History
– vs. cyclical time of nature 59–60, 166
– vs. divine destiny 146–147
– exemption from it through evocation, through exploration, through mimicry 113–118
– vs. historicity or "prose of the world" 148, 157–158
– vs. indistinct province or mythic space 3, 53, 146–148
– as law 157
– vs. now-time or *Jetztzeit* 50, 55, 80
– vs. prehistory 21, 52–53, 57, 80, 112–113, 116–118, 120, 124, 128, 133, 136–137
– waiting room of 29
Hitler, Adolf 51
Hobsbawm, Eric J. 32
Hofmannsthal, Hugo von 3, 5, 12, 25, 37, 127, 151, 178–179, 190, 207–211
Hu, Xiaoran 191
Hungary/Hungarian 30, 32
Hunt, Lynn 59
Husserl, Edmund von 39

Identification
– vs/cum disidentification 7, 22, 99, 146, 196
– heteropathic vs. homeopathic 10
– non-appropriative 126
– of vs. with 181, 193
Il y a (Lévinas) 81, 171
India/n 15, 45, 55
Indistinct
– compensatory 29–36, 55–58
– hybrid 43, 45, 51, 54–55, 158
– in-between 43, 51, 53–55, 158, 234
– indeterminate 54

- indifferent 16–17, 41, 61, 63–67
- *je ne sais quoi* 41, 65
- liminal 43, 51, 55
- mixture 53, 158
- rise of 43
- repenting 36–41
- return of 29–42
- self-interrogating 39
- *Unheimliche* or uncanny 38, 42, 51–52, 59–60, 222

Intertextual
- hall of echoes 173, 229
- hint 233
- space 173–174
- transfers 5, 173–174, 218, 226
- transmission 218
- unavoidable redoubling 5, 140–142, 217–218, 233–235

Italy 31

Jacobs, Johann U. 175, 178, 218
Janouch, Gustave 98, 113
Jesus Christ 25, 136, 156, 191
Jews/Jewish 5, 31, 35, 130, 154, 178
- Algerian 223
- antisemitism 6, 11, 12, 13, 31, 151–152
- assimilation 12
- Austrian 12, 151
- Berlin 11
- conversion 152
- Czech 6, 13, 152
- dispossessed 67, 151
- family 152
- father 151–152
- German 6, 15, 129, 150–151,
- glory 152
- Holocaust 16–17, 60, 132–133
- homeless 45
- internal exteriority 45
- migrant destiny 45
- mixed marriage 152
- mother 151–152
- Ottoman 11
- Prague 13, 82, 129, 151
- pursuit of profit 152
- religion 54
- Russian 11

- two-child system 152
- Ukrainian 12–13
- Vienna 12
- Zionism 11, 45

Johansson, Perry 163
Joseph II, Emperor 32
Judson, Pieter 31–32, 34, 67, 102

Kafka, Franz 1–3, 5–7, 8, 9, 13, 17–19, 25, 51, 54, 71–141, 148, 158, 175, 177–178, 182, 194, 202, 209–211
- *A Country Doctor* 131
- *A Hunger Artist* 131
- *An Imperial Message* 19–20, 104, 107, 110–111, 115, 118, 130–131, 189, 199–201, 204
- *An Old Manuscript* 129, 159–160
- *Aphorisms* 91, 106, 112–114, 134, 137, 149, 189, 202
- *A Report to an Academy* 20, 24, 115, 128–129, 206
- *At the Construction of the Great Wall of China* 19–20, 23, 84, 87, 100–108, 129, 131, 159–160, 162–163, 165, 173
- *Before the Law* 20, 86, 89, 111, 113–115, 118, 129, 131
- *Castle* 97, 129
- *Diaries* 6, 71, 93, 95, 106–107, 114, 117, 122–124, 128, 130–131, 133, 136–137, 145
- *In the Penal Colony* 23, 85, 97, 105, 118, 131, 137, 165, 171, 173, 180
- *Investigations of a Dog* 20, 115–116, 129
- *Josephine the Singer* 100, 129
- *Letter to the Father* 20, 93, 117, 120, 122, 124, 135, 139
- *Letters* 53, 108, 113, 145, 149, 207
- *Letters to Felice* 93, 130, 137, 147, 149
- *Letters to Milena* 122
- *Memoirs of the Kalda Railway* 162, 169
- *Metamorphosis* 96, 129, 135, 169
- *On parables* 74, 104
- *Reflections on sin, suffering, hope, and the true way* 145, 165, 202
- *The Blue Octavo Notebooks* 176
- *The Bridge* 129, 203
- *The Bucket Rider* 129

- *The Burrow* 108, 129, 178–179
- *The Cares of a Family Man* 20, 50, 117, 127
- *The Hunter Gracchus* 96, 135, 168
- *The Judgment* 94, 96, 135
- *The Knock at the Manor Gate* 129
- *The Married Couple* 129
- *The New Advocate* 20, 115
- *The Problem of Our Laws* 19–20, 103, 105, 115, 129
- *The Refusal* 100, 103, 129
- *The Trial* 19–20, 23, 52, 71–99, 105–106, 112–113, 115, 117–118, 124, 168, 182, 185–187, 198

Kannemeyer, John Christoffel 175
Kant, Immanuel 36, 134, 160
Kemp, Peter 232
Keyder, Caglar 34
Koch, Hans-Gerd 185
Koch, Manfred 46
Königgrätz 101
Kojève, Alexandre 63
Kożuchowski, Adam 31
Kraus, Karl 45, 67
Kristeva, Julia 39–40
Kundszus, Winfried 97
Kurtz, Arabella 7, 155–156, 170, 188, 194
Kyrgyz/stan 162, 177

Labarrière, Pierre-Jean 222
Lacan, Jacques 22, 65, 148, 166, 170, 172, 176, 191–192
Lamb, Jonathan 208
Large, William 223
Law
- abuse of 91, 187
- Anglo-American 85
- Austrian 85–87, 105, 130, 153, 186
- vs. contingency 18
- counter 186
- crime 85, 92, 105, 186
- criminal 85, 105, 186–187
- disciplinary 18, 83–84, 87–88, 91–92, 103, 186
- egalitarian 20, 34, 84–86, 103, 117, 186
- German 85

- "imaginary norm" or *fictio legis* 19, 85, 87, 105, 108
- inquisitorial or investigative process 87, 105, 186
- judge 86
- of laws 40
- vs. legal or juridical system 87, 89
- magistrate 87, 105, 186
- martial 85, 167, 184
- operators/executives 86–91, 96, 105–106
- outside of 88–91, 96, 98, 130, 153
- prehistorical 20, 52, 55, 116–117, 124
- reform of 186
- sovereign 18, 83–84, 86
- summary justice 85, 184, 186
- suspension of 16
- targeting evil 85, 186
- targeting wrong 85
- transcendent 36
- trial 88, 92
- tribunal of conscience 93–96, 184–185
- vestibules of 184

Lawrence, David H. 228, 233
Leavis, Frank R. 228–229
Lévinas, Emmanuel 64, 81, 171
Lévi-Strauss, Claude 47, 75
Lewis, Alison 87
Life
- vs. art 2
- bare 18, 21, 47–48, 65
- common tissue of 208
- creaturely 208
- in Agamben 47, 56
- in Benjamin 47, 56
- in Deleuze 56, 77–79
- in Kafka 73, 133
- shared substrate of 208
- substitute 215–218

Liska, Vivian 67, 74
Litowicz, Douglas 83, 129
London 145–146, 155
Loomba, Ania 15, 56
Louvel, Liliane 167
Luhmann, Niklas 88–90
Lynn, David 230

Macedonia/n 32
Mahler, Gustav 45, 67
Mallarmé, Stéphane 61, 63
Mandela, Nelson 162
Marais, Mike 158, 169, 184, 189, 191
Marcus, Laura 226, 228, 230–232
Marx, Karl 180
Matar, Anat 73
McEwan, Ian 13, 21, 25–26, 171, 179
– *Atonement* 25–26, 221–236, 170
– *Black Dogs* 133
– *Saturday* 132, 224, 231
– *The Cement Garden* 224–225
Melville, Herman 56, 63
Micali, Simona 161, 163, 180
Mignolo, Walter 37
Migration or mobility
– beneficial 31
– communicational 9, 31–32, 102
– enforced 14, 31, 67
– free 67
– of imagination 9, 39, 126, 198–218
– individual 217
– institutional 31, 102
– mass 31, 33
– mercantile 9, 32
– monetary 9
– physical 39
– traffic 31–32, 102
Milosz, Czesław 108
Mitchell, Mike 85
Mongol/ian 100, 162–163
Montenegro 32
Montesquieu, Charles-Louis de Secondat 39
Mosca, Valeria 174, 214, 218
Motyl, Alexander 147
Müller-Seidel, Walter 83, 85, 93, 97, 120, 122, 135, 138–139
Muir, Edgar 100, 103, 108, 118, 178
Muir, Willa 100, 103, 108, 118, 178
Mulhall, Stephen 203
Musil, Robert 11, 37–38, 116, 179

Napoleon Bonaparte 46
New Caledonia 165
Ng, Lynda 177–178, 217–218

Nietzsche, Friedrich 9, 33, 37, 134, 149–150
Northover, Richard Alan 174, 213, 216

O'Sullivan, Michael 193

Parable 74, 100–101, 111
– embedded 84, 104
Paris 145
Patočka, Jan 39
Pawel, Ernst 194
Penner, Dick 162
Performance
– in Coetzee 203–204, 206, 209
– executor's and victim's 137–140
– in Kafka 131–143, 204
– subalterns' 138–140
Periphery
– artistic 147
– vs. center 14, 102, 211
– colonial 14–15
– European 14
– German Eastern 11, 158
– godforsaken 13, 145–147, 187, 200–201
– instrument of self-elevation 147, 166
– province 33
– resistance 33
– South African 5
– subhuman 186
Philippou, Eleni 192
Piłsudski, Józef 31
Plato 5, 25, 213–215
Poland/Polish 13, 30–31, 155, 178
Politzer, Heinz 92
Pollak, Oskar 149
Positional outsiders 3, 6–7, 17, 126–142
– enforced subalterns 21, 129, 150, 152, 188
– prehistorical 21, 129
– self-appointed 21, 98, 129
Possibility or potentiality
– evoking 106–108
– exploring 108–109, 116
– vs/cum impossibility 221
– mimicking 117
– pure 47, 56
– reservoir of 45–47
– sense of 116
– unexplored 106, 151

Povinelli, Elisabeth 34, 53, 66
Power
– administration of 5
– aggression 119–120, 139
– anonymous machine 19
– asymmetry or imbalance 8
– "capillary supervision" 7, 19, 24, 83–84, 102, 186–187, 203
– class 4, 182–183
– disciplinary 1, 2, 83, 102, 137–138, 202, 218
– disempowering vs/cum empowering 3, 40, 61, 65, 67, 119, 136–140, 189
– educational 4
– institutional 183–184
– omnipresent and omniscient 202
– operator 202
– opposition 2
– parental 4
– political 181
– racial 181–184
– relations 4, 23, 103, 181–182, 184, 194
– relationship 43, 189, 235
– sexual 182
– sovereign 1, 57–58, 83, 102, 137–138, 203
– technologies of 5
Prague 6, 31, 129–130, 152–153
Press, Gerald A. 213–214
Probyn, Elspeth 57
Promitzer, Christian 158
Proust, Marcel 49
Protection 5, 221–25
– authorial 4, 26, 158, 217
– by children or dependents 184, 189–191, 204, 225
– colonial 4
– vs. exposure 183, 189
– maternal or motherhood 4, 184, 204, 224–225
– paternal or fatherhood 4, 23, 25, 169, 183–184, 187, 189–191, 217, 224–225
– political 12–13, 23, 157
– vs/cum repression 180–183, 188–189
– social 130
– substitute 4
– unprotectedness or defenselessness 25, 130, 153, 169, 189, 221–236

Protestant/ism 11, 154
Puchner, Martin 214

Race 161
– black 163, 181–182, 206
– exotic 181, 183
– white 163, 181, 206
Rancière, Jacques 79, 150
Realism 24, 202–203, 210, 218
Reality 145, 202
– artificial 24–25, 205, 215–217
– consensual 24, 205
– vs. contingency or possibility 18, 71–72, 89–90
– deterritorialized 17–18, 71–74, 162, 166
– dismembered 205
– fake 25, 218
– intertextual 215–216
– literary 215–216
– r. conditions 72, 86, 88, 92
– simulacrum 215–216, 218
– vs. 'real' 22–24, 65, 145, 148, 158–179, 203, 205, 218
– vs. world 71–72, 76, 78, 86, 89–90, 99, 106
Renan, Ernest 35
Revolution
– American 59
– French 8–9, 44, 59–60
– May '68 16, 59–60, 67, 132
– vs. re-evolution 16, 59
Robertson, Richie 93, 97
Robinson, Forrest 98, 146, 173, 196–197
Romania/n 30–32
Rosa, Hartmut 34
Roth, Joseph 12–13, 158–159
Rushdie, Salman 54
Russell, Bertrand 72
Russia/n 11–12, 30, 32, 67, 162–165, 177, 206
Ryan, Michael 59

Said, Edward 180
Samolsky, Russell 161, 165
Schenk, Frithjof Benjamin 33
Schlegel, August Wilhelm 46
Schmitt, Carl 51, 103

Schuman, Rebecca 86
Scott, Joanna 174
Seaboyer, Judith 170, 230
Sedgwick, Kosofsky Eve 167
Self-exemption 180–197
– "I am what I am not" 22, 89–90, 146, 214
– 'negative capability' 8, 25, 209, 212, 213–214, 218
– neither-nor attitude 122, 212, 214
– of the narrator from the law 105
– from the past 36, 59
– from the protagonist 97, 113–114, 124, 129, 131, 136, 146, 229, 232
– self-deterritorialization 74–75
– self-devaluation 88, 123
– self-disentanglement 97, 113–114, 124
– self-displacement 113–114
– self-dispossession 23, 37, 41, 65, 185, 192–193
– self-humiliation 23, 135, 169
– self-othering 136, 148–150, 156
– self-punishment 122–123
– self-sacrifice 21, 135
– self-torment 23, 94, 135, 150
– vs. state of exception 8–9, 19, 48
– "to say no is to say yes" 149, 213
– weak messianism 44, 48, 49, 61, 81–82, 145
Serbia/Serbs 32
Sexuality
– abundant or hypertrophied 22–23, 168–169, 182
– aged 22, 168–169, 183
– erotic appetite 183, 187
– male 22
– passion 187
– possession drive 183
– promiscuity 187
– rape 168
– service to Eros 23, 183–185
– stimulated by racial exotics and age difference 181, 183
– 'ungovernable impulses' 195
– unlimited thirst 183
– womanizing 22, 168, 180, 187

Shame
– being-overwhelmed 22–24, 167–168, 175–176, 185, 195–196
– of belonging 185, 192–196
– vs. guilt 18, 98
– for history 117, 153
Sheehan, Paul 177–178, 217–218
Silverman, Kaja 3, 10, 126, 200
Slander
– of others 90–91, 94–95, 99
– self-blame 89, 96
– self-slander 89–91, 94–97, 99
Slaughter, Joseph R. 85, 105, 189
Slav/ic 11, 30, 39, 101–102, 158
Slovakia/n 31
Society
– 'casings of the bondage to the future' [M. Weber] 88, 161
– compartmentalized 20, 88, 97–98, 110–111, 115–116, 160, 188
– differentiated 88–89, 202
– embattled self-enclosures 20, 98
– encapsulated 88, 98, 111, 160
– individualized 20, 202
– modern 20, 88–89, 97, 110, 202
– "the watchfulness of all over all" 160–161, 182, 188
Socrates 25, 145, 174, 213–214
South Africa/n 1, 5, 6, 7, 13, 15, 132, 145–146, 153–156, 161–165, 168, 175–178, 182, 186, 194, 196, 212, 217
Soviet Union 32
Spanish 35
Stalin, Joseph 215
Starr, Peter 59
State of exception 9, 52, 86, 100–109, 128–129, 166, 192, 221, 234–235
– definition 48, 51, 189
– dominant paradigm 51, 226, 235
– permanent 16, 57
– post-imperial 226
Stern, David G. 72
Stölzl, Christoph 152
Stourzh, Gerald 102
Subversive mimicry (Bhabha) 20–21, 33, 117, 123, 131–132, 139

– inverse ventriloquism [Anderson] 10, 55, 176, 193
– subversion through adoption 34, 97, 131, 141, 150
Sympathetic imagination
– Coetzee 167, 170, 209
– Costello 167, 170, 209, 213
– entering other minds 137–141, 213, 230–231
– Jesus 192
– Kafka 97, 121–125, 137
– Lurie 192
– McEwan 167, 230–231

Tegla, Emanuela 196
Teubner, Günther 87–90
Thum, Gregor 11, 158
Todorova, Maria 35
Torture 140
– apparatus 170
– chamber 165–166, 175
– of others 94
– self-torment 23, 94, 135, 150
Transcendental
– vs. empirical 17, 62
– flawed 17, 62, 64
– vs. immanence 79
Translatio imperii 1, 3, 5–6, 9–10, 110, 130, 148–149, 152, 159, 163–164, 173, 182, 191, 194
Translation
– cultural 5, 15–16, 43, 178
– generator of differences 43
– inter-lingual 15–16, 43, 45, 178
– intra-lingual 45
– of reality into fiction 11
– unprocessed residues 6, 10, 16, 20, 34, 110, 179
Transmission
– chain 91, 200–201
– endless mission 218
– envoy 200
– via lecture 24, 98–218
– via lesson 24, 98–218
– mediator 200
– oral 19, 84, 107, 200
– transmissibility 201, 218

– of truth 200
– whispering 107
– of Will 200
Treaty of Versailles 14, 29, 31
Truth
– adapted 193
– all-embracing 24, 185, 191, 193, 213, 234
– being dazzled by 113, 176
– disfigured by 113, 231
– distorted 111, 146
– elusive 73, 168, 234
– evoking 113
– exclusionary 233–234
– exploring 115–116
– facing 113
– flash or flame or radiance or light 111–112
– forgotten or lost 113, 115
– giving birth to 145, 213
– grimaces of 176
– in confessional discourse 145
– in fiction 228
– the language of (Benjamin) 50
– postponement of 201
– vs. reality 72
– self-enclosed 111
– telling 181, 191, 232
– to-come 185
– vs. transmissibility 111, 201, 218
Truth and Reconciliation Commissions (extraordinary academic committees) 184, 186
Turkey/Turkish 30, 32, 162, 206
Twin Towers (9/11) 212

Ukrain/ian 12–13, 31–32, 158–159
Unhomeliness/homelessness 10, 18, 52, 211
– double 216
– in one's identity 76
– in one's language 25, 208–209
– outside of one's home amidst of it 38, 45, 198
United States– see America/n
Untranslatable 18
– Benjamin's notion 16, 44–48
– between languages 16
– commonality 56
– Jewish 45

- leftover/residue 6, 10, 16, 20, 34, 110
- linked with the state of exception 48
- miming as its medium 48–50
- reservoir of potentiality 45–47
- translation of 10, 15, 42, 49, 58
- within a language 45–47

Valdez Moses, Michael 163, 170, 180
Vermeulen, Pieter 208
Vienna 12–13, 31, 145
Vietnam War 132, 153, 175
Violence 36–37, 132, 207
- exclusionary logic of 194–196
- hunt 168
- introverted 156–157
- male 4, 168, 181–184, 195
- murdering or killing 168
- paternal 135, 139
- raids 182, 189
- rape 168, 182, 189
- retributive 157
- verbal 120, 139
- vicious circle of 36, 194
- war 194
Vlies, Andrew van der 191

Wachtel, Eleanor 174
Walkowitz, Rebecca 10, 177, 179
Wanberg, Kyle 127, 210–212
Watson, Stephen 175
Weber, Max 88, 161
Weber, Samuel 49
Wetzell, Richard F. 105, 187

Wicomb, Zoë 166, 203, 217
Wiedemann, Conrad 46
Wilhelm II, Emperor 11, 105, 158
Wittenberg, Herman 161–164
Wittgenstein, Ludwig 52, 71–73, 76, 86, 106, 226–227
Wolff, Larry 11
Woolf, Virginia 233
World War
- One/First 1, 11, 14–15, 21, 29, 30, 41–42, 51–52, 130, 149–150
- Two/Second 1, 14–15, 41–42, 149, 223

Yugoslavia 30–31

Zagreb 31
Zahra, Tara 34
Zimbler, Jarad 169–170, 203
Ziolkowski, Theodore 83, 85, 87–88, 105, 186
Zone
- cluttered 188
- heterotopia 20, 110, 114
- of indifference 34, 56, 83, 234
- of indiscernability 56, 82
- of indistinction 6, 8–9, 47, 53–54, 61–65, 128
- of neighborhood 56, 78, 82
- pockets of resistance 6
- of solidarity 6
- translation 157–160
- vestibules of law 184

www.ingramcontent.com/pod-product-compliance
Lightning Source LLC
Chambersburg PA
CBHW020225170426
43201CB00007B/321